FEDERAL STRUCTURE

FEDERAL STRUCTURE

(Under The Government Of India Act, 1935)

K. T. SHAH

GYAN

Published by

GYAN

Gyan Publishing House
5, Ansari Road
Daryaganj, New Delhi-110002
Phone: 011-47034999, 9811692060
E-mail: books@gyanbooks.com

Distribution Network
gyanbooks.com
India, USA, Canada, UK, Australia

ISBN: 978-93-7316-029-0 (PB)

First Published, 1937

2nd Impression 2025

Printed at: Gyan Press, Delhi.

FEDERAL STRUCTURE
Author: K. T. SHAH

FEDERAL STRUCTURE

FEDERAL STRUCTURE

(Under the Government of India Act, 1935)

By

K. T. SHAH

TO

G.E.M.

(*En Souvenir. 10-10-31*)

LIST OF CONTENTS

THE NATIONAL PUBLICATIONS SOCIETY OF INDIA.

This Society has been formed to undertake and carry out the publications of books, etc., describing, explaining, or criticising institutions and organisations of public administration in India, as also those affecting the collective life and consciousness of the people of India.

These books, etc., are to be so selected and written up, under the directions of the Society's Board of Editors, as to indicate wherein changes should be made, so as to promote most effectively the freedom and collective well-being of the Indian people. In their general plan and substance, these publications should provide for a reconstruction of the Social System on the basis of complete Socialisation of the means of Production, Distribution and Exchange of material commodities and services needed for the maintenance and advance of the community.

Each Book or Monograph will, whether written by one of the Editors or by a selected writer, be edited by the Society's Board of Editors, who will contribute two Chapters to each such volume: one, by way of introduction, explaining the place of the institution or organisation studied in other countries; and the other, at the end of the work, giving constructive suggestions for the reform of the Institution in question so as to make it more in accordance with the main objective of the Society, viz., to bring about a planned reconstruction of the Social System so as to socialise all means of production, distribution, and exchange, of all material commodities and services.

The Board consists of Pandit Jawaharlal Nehru. Acharya Narendra Dev, and K. T. Shah. They will arrange for the writing of such books and other publications of the Society, as also for their translation into the principal Indian languages, translation being an essential item in the Society's programme.

The Society consists of Members, who may be either Foundation Members (for life) named in the schedule, or other Life Members, who accept the aims and objects as well as the Rules and Regulations of the Society, and are elected as such by the Managing Committee. The Life Member's subscription is Rs. 250, and that of the Foundation Members Rs. 100, for life. In addition, the Society may have associates, sympathisers, or regular customers for its publications, in accordance with the resolutions of the Society passed in that behalf. Copies of the Aims and Rules of the Society as also the list of subjects, the Society intends to have written upon, can be had from the Honorary Secretary, Sjt. R. Saran, 2-A, Metcalfe House Road, Delhi.

PREFACE

The author owes an apology to the reading public for the inordinate delay in the appearance of the present volume. It had been planned for publication early in last April, soon after the publication of the first edition of the "Provincial Autonomy." Circumstances, however, over which he had no control prevented the realisation of this purpose; and all that the author can now do is to tender an earnest apology for the delay that has taken place.

Whether the time that has intervened since the appearance of the first edition of the "Provincial Autonomy" has been utilised in this work to any advantage is for the discerning reader to judge. Many of the issues discussed in these pages have not advanced a step towards their final solution, since the actual advent of autonomy in the Provinces. Many more are being created by the inherent divergence of viewpoint and ideals between those who have fashioned this Constitution, and those who have to work it. The present writer cannot but leave those various issues at the stage at which they are. Those who realise to the full the intrinsic injustice and unworkability of this Constitution have declared their resolve to "work" it so as the soonest to show up its inherent impossibility. Whether they succeed in this aim or not depends upon the soundness of the tactics employed. Their success or failure would not question the absolute unsuitability of the instrument of government as provided for in this Act.

Under these circumstances, the attempt at a detailed, critical examination of the basic idea as well as the operative portions of this new Constitution,—particularly in its Federal portion—may be open to misconstruction. The dissection of the Constitutional provisions contained in the following pages has only one justification: It shows why and how, in detail as well as in principle, the projected Federation must be unacceptable to the Indian people. It is designed to discover the pitfalls, which British Imperialism has laid so skilfully in the path of our constitutional evolution; so that, knowing them, and understanding their true nature and significance, we may avoid them in any corresponding instrument of our own devising.

As promised in the first volume of this Series, the present volume embodies two chapters contributed by the Editors of the Series,—one by way of Introduction, explaining the basic conditions for a Federation, and showing the extent to which they exist in India to-day; and the other by way of conclusion, outlining the directions in which radical recasting of the entire system of governance must take place, if it is at all to meet the requirements of India. The work is, of course, not intended, primarily, for constitutional lawyers, nor legal practitioners. It is addressed rather to that much wider class of our fellow citizens, whose consciousness of political wrongs is growing, whose longing for social justice is no less keen, and whose desire to be enlightened on the ways and means of effecting radical reconstruction requires to be met before we can hope for any substantial impulse from our own people for a change. Perhaps this standpoint adopted in preparing this work would explain, even if it does not excuse, the defects of prolixity, repetition, or undue polemics, which a critical reader might discover in the work. The author's defence against such a charge can only be that, given his objective, repetition, prolixity and even polemics are, in the nature of the task, inevitable.

Constitutional forms and mechanisms are, essentially, not of an abiding nature. With the constantly changing circumstances of a dynamic organism, they needs must change, if they are to continue to be suitable to the new conditions and requirements. Criticism, therefore, advanced against given forms; or particular alternatives suggested for specifically defective forms or devices, must not be understood to imply the writer's conviction that the remedies suggested are to be of everlasting use. It has been the author's aim to make the criticism in the following pages suggestive rather than dogmatic; to point the way to a new system, rather than to provide the goal to be attained. That is because he holds that constitutions are instruments rather than objectives. They are valuable, not in themselves, but in so far as they aid in achieving the important aim of social justice and human happiness. Experience shows that many of the existing forms have signally failed to accomplish these aims. Hence, even in the concluding Chapter, the Editors have contented themselves, rather with indicating the broad lines of change, than with any specific alternative offered as the *sine qua non* for remodelling the frame-work of our constitution. What is needed is to inform our mechanism of Government with a new vision, to inspire it with a new motive, to arm it with a new purpose. Any alternative constitution, which we fashion ourselves, must assure us on these points.

The rest would be a matter of detail, which may be changed or reconditioned at any time we find it necessary to do so.

The writer has tried to profit in this volume by the many friendly hints and criticisms advanced against the first volume on Provincial Autonomy whose second edition was out a month ago. But, even so, he is aware that there may remain many points in the following pages, which expose them to just criticism. For these, the writer alone is responsible, and trusts to an indulgent public to overlook these blemishes in his work.

25th September, 1937. K. T. S.

CHAPTER I

FEDERAL STRUCTURE IN INDIA

INTRODUCTORY

Ingredients of a Federation

A Federation is usually a voluntary association of autonomous States to form a closer union among themselves in order more effectively or expeditiously to attain a common objective. The union involves a considerable surrender of the previously existing independent sovereignty of the combining States. The resultant entity from their combination is more powerful than any one, and often all, of the combining States.

Sovereignty in a Federation

The new creation is not a fully sovereign State by itself. In so far as international relations or recognition is concerned, it is the only sovereign representative of the combination. But in domestic matters, and by the implication of the constitutional law of such creations, the sovereignty is divided. Certain specified functions of the State are assigned exclusively to the Federal or the united State; and certain other functions are similarly reserved to the uniting States. Even in the central, national, or Federal Government, the functions of government are clearly demarcated between the Legislature, the Executive, and the Judiciary. Each authority—the State or the Federation—is sovereign within its own allotted or agreed sphere of action, and has no right to interfere in the sphere assigned exclusively to the other. In the undefinable sphere of no-man's land—the so-called residuary powers, or inevitably overlapping functions—the practice is by no means uniform. In some federations, *e.g.*, Canada, it is the Union Government which is vested with all the balance of undistributed powers;* while in others, *e.g.*, Australia or the United States of America, the corresponding powers are given to the constituent States of the Federation.† The same holds good also for the several representatives of sovereignty—the Legislature, the Executive, and the judiciary—each all-powerful in its own peculiar domain; but utterly excluded from the corresponding domain of its sister authorities.

Written, Rigid Constitution

A definite, written, rigid instrument of Government, the Constitution, is another distinctive feature of Federations. It is open to interpretation as well as amendement by the authority appointed for the purpose; and, pending such amendment, or interpretation,—which in effect sometimes even amends the Constitution, that document is the sole authority for defining the nature of the various governmental bodies, their powers, or functions. This written Constitution embodies the will of the people, the ultimate, *de jure* as well as *de facto* sovereign in all Federations; and it is more potent than either the Federal or the Constituent State authority.‡

*The Legislature of the Dominion of Canada is not only vested with all residuary powers; it is empowered to disallow any provincial legislation which it deems to be injurious to the welfare of the country as a whole.

†cp. Amendment X of the U.S.A. Constitution.

‡cp. MacIver, **The Modern State**: "The written Constitution is the expression of a will more fundamental than either the Federal State, or the constituent State can exercise."

Divided Allegiance

The union among the several units composing the Federation is, as already observed, a voluntary association and is essentially a union of equals. It must, therefore, function on a basis of equal participation in the rights and benefits accruing from the Federation. Every Federation must, accordingly, have not only divided sovereignty; its citizens must owe a divided, or rather, a dual allegiance; one to the State of their birth or domicile forming part of the Federation; the other to the Federation itself. This often causes complication, and sometimes a conflict, to which we shall refer later on a little more fully.

Constitution Democratic

Federations must, likewise, be democratic, in the sense of having responsible, constitutional governments, exercising delegated authority, in accordance with the written instrument of government. A Federation is essentially a union of equals, and must, therefore, needs be democratic. Empires, like the Roman, or the British for a long time before 1900, are thus marked out from Federations, for want of an equal participation of all the members of the Empire in the concerns of the Empire. So also are all component parts of a united kingdom—two or more States under one Crown, such as the Kingdoms of England and Scotland from 1603 to 1707; amalgamated in 1707, with Ireland added in 1801.

Federations Distinguished from Feudal Combines

Feudal or semi-feudal combines under a common suzerain are also not the same thing as modern Federations, since the latter are essentially democratic, and must have responsible Governments; while the former are as essentially autocratic; the latter have divided sovereignty amongst the constituent States and the Federation, as well as a divided or double allegiance from its citizens, while the former claims to be based on unified sovereignty and common allegiance.

Distinguished from Leagues

On the other hand, a voluntary union for a given purpose, and for the time being only, *e.g.*, the alliance of the Greek States under the Achaean League, or the unity of command in the European War between British, French and American Armies, is also not the same thing as a Federation, the essence of which is a permanent association for common purposes. Because of this characteristic, Federations generally dislike any tendency in their member States to disruption, or separation of one component part from the rest, however considerable the powers of local autonomy left to the individual States under the ordinary constitution, may be.* The sentiment of State or local patriotism, however powerful at the start, insensibly undergoes a change, as the common sentiment for the nation collectively gathers strength; and becomes daily more serviceable and vocal in all material concerns of the people affected. If the local allegiance is allowed scope, it is in the purely domestic sphere of each component unit of a Federation. Even there, the growing interdependence of modern industrialised communities upon one another tends to undermine the State patriotism as against the national; and so weakens

*"Federalism, like democracy itself, is a matter of degree, but the general tendency is towards a stronger unity." MacIver, The Modern State, p. 363.

the authority, within its own proper constitutional sphere, of the State, or the component unit of the Federation.

Pre-requisites of a Federation

The essential pre-requisites, then, of a sound and lasting federal organisation are:—

Geographic Contiguity

(i) An obvious geographic contiguity, and a certain community of material interests, which can be served better in union than by keeping apart of states often at variance with one another. Apart from the exceptional case of the British Commonwealth of Nations, which it would do considerable violence to the accepted terminology of Political Science to describe as a Federation, there is no instance on record of a Federation among units geographically separated from one another. The federating units may occupy a territory as vast as that of the United States of America, or the Union of Socialist, Soviet Republics; or they may be confined in a space so limited as that of the Cantons of Switzerland, forming the most ancient as well as the smallest example of a democratic Federation in the world. Mere distance is no bar, especially in modern times. But, though distant from one another, the federating parts must nevertheless be contiguous to one another, so as to form a single whole as a unit in space.

Cultural Community

(ii) Community of cultural heritage, or race consciousness, or other such political cement, also goes a long way in stimulating, emphasizing, and eventually realising the desire for union. In all the classic examples of Federations in the world, from the loose association of the Greek States to the latest instance of the Russian Union of Socialist Soviet Republics, stretching over 8½ million square miles of territory, this community of heritage and sentiment, of initial impulse and continued urge under modern conditions, is noticeable in all cases of successful Federations. True, in a case like that of the U.S.S.R., there are, within the Union, a number of cultural or racial minorities, differing widely *inter se* in historical tradition and cultural background. But despite this difference or divergence, there is a stronger cement holding them together, in the consciousness of a common economic purpose more effectively than under separate Statehood for each of these racial or cultural minorities. United in a vast, powerful, Federation, whose aggregate resources are, at a pinch, available for the benefit of every member of that community of peoples, each combining unit finds itself much better off, more able to achieve successfully the objective of a radical reconstruction of society, than each existing as an independent State by itself would be able to realise. The terms and conditions of the Union, loose enough to allow the fullest possible scope for the realisation of the individuality of each racial and cultural minority in the U.S.S.R. are also such, that there is no obvious purpose to be served by disintegration. Hence we find economic interest transcending the more intangible factor of racial or cultural distinctness, in order to form and maintain a Federal Structure, under conditions like those prevailing in Russia.

Common Danger

(ii) The presence of a common danger, such as that which drove the British Colonies in North America, when freed from the British domination, to form a union among themselves, has often accounted for the desire among States to federate, which would otherwise have remained apart, and even antagonistic. The political danger which forms the original motive force may disappear in course of time; but the Federation once formed, will not be discarded simply because the original impulse has been exhausted. New advantages discovered from the continued association will almost always prove strong enough to restrain disruptive tendencies, if any; and so such considerations have often no more than historical importance in the life of an accomplished Federation.

Common Characteristics of Federations

Given these pre-requisites for a Federation, the resultant State has certain common characteristics or features, which, in its normal life, distinguish it from the other communities organised as States.

As already noticed, (a) Federations invariably connote a **divided Sovereignty**, divided between the component or constituent parts of the Federation, and the Federation itself. As a corollary to that, the citizens owe a two-fold allegiance, which, however, insensibly transforms itself into an overwhelming sentiment of loyalty to the Union, often in opposition to the claims of local patriotism. The advantages of the Federal System are too material, too direct, to be dropped, once they have been tasted. And though the larger size of the Federal State may make it difficult, if not impossible, to exercise real self-government on a national scale, even that may be regarded as an immaterial sacrifice in virtue of the direct material benefits resulting from a Federation. Each component part will, of course, continue to be democratically governed in itself; and all will be equal *inter se* in the Federation. But in the latter the principle of democracy would be realised rather by delegation than by actual exercise. As the concerns reserved for federal action are not of immediate concern to the individual citizen, the latter does not perceive the sacrifice of his democratic privileges involved in the creation of the Federation. The advantages of the Federation are direct, and immediate; its disadvantages or burdens indirect and imperceptible.

(b) The Union thus formed, loose as it may seem to be, must remain an *enduring association*, a perpetual bond between the communities federating, which the Federation collectively would, if need be, maintain by force of arms in the last instance. It is not merely the hyphen that joins, the buckle that links, two distinct entities. It is the cement which makes one out of many distinct parts. Of course, the Union cannot subsist on the oppression or suppression of minorities within the Federation; and hence certain rights are usually reserved, or guarantees given, for the continued individuality and equal opportunity for self-expression to the peoples of the uniting States, and to the racial or cultural minorities which may be scattered all over the union. The actual form of each Federation is essentially influenced and largely determined by such factors within it; but the overriding feature is observable in all modern Federations, that, once formed, they seem to be setting their face sternly against any centrifugal tendency noticeable within the Union.

(c) For these features of modern Federations to work in harmony together, all such organisations provide, not only a rigid, written constitution, but also postulate the ultimate and absolute sovereignty in the people of the Federation collectively. Popular sovereignty in Federations is a living reality. It is the sole guarantee of the equal rights of all component parts of the Federation, and the final power to amend the Constitution if and when needed. The exercise of this sovereignty usually takes the form of the will of the majority, and majorities to be effective must be moderate; to be acceptable, must be reasonable; to be obeyed, must be considerate. The only limits that popular sovereignty is subjected to by the Constitution, itself an expression of the sovereign will, may be found in the rights of equal representation, as distinguished from *pro rata* representation, granted in the Upper Chambers to the member States;

association of that body in certain functions of sovereignty; or provisions by which a given majority, or a prescribed procedure, is needed to carry out structural emendations or constitutional amendments.

Conditions in India

In India, the factors making for a Federation, are not all present in an equal degree. The component parts of a Federation of India are not all, *inter se*, of equal status; they have not the same system, principles, or ideals of government; nor have they all the same urge to unification. The British Provinces are, in their present form, all the creations of the Central Government, or of the British Parliament acting as the absolute and final sovereign authority for this country. The motive force in setting up each Province was administrative convenience, rather than any recognition of the intrinsic unity of the entity created. Their equal status, *inter se*, is a creation of the Act of 1935, and their constitutional autonomy derives from the same source. The economic strength of each province, again, is markedly different from its neighbour's; and so the objective sub-consciously sought in federating is necessarily not identical. There is, thus no definite principle of intrinsic unity, of political or economic homogeneity, among the Provinces internally, which could make of each of them a distinct and organic whole. There can, therefore, be no question of a voluntary association of these units to form a Federation of British India, since they are already integral parts of that entity, and have no rights either to separate from, or to come into closer union with, the national State. They have, in themselves individually, no trace or attribute of sovereignty, and so can make no pretence at sharing sovereignty, or sacrificing any part of it. Federation is imposed upon them by an act of their present sovereign authority the British Parliament, which neither consults the people of the Provinces, nor would abide by their decision in such matters if incompatible with British Imperialist interests and requirements. If Provinces are re-formed, if old associates of the Empire are cut away and disjointed from it, or new ones created within the Empire, that is all the doing of the same absolute sovereign authority.* Neither real democracy nor working

---

*Says Section 2 of the Government of India Act:—

(1) All rights, authority and jurisdiction heretofore belonging to His Majesty the King, Emperor of India, which appertain or are incidental to the government of the territories in India for the time being vested in him, and all rights, authority and jurisdiction exercisable by him in or in relation to any other territories in India, are exercisable by His Majesty, except in so far as may be otherwise provided by or under this Act, or as may be otherwise directed by His Majesty.

Provided that any powers connected with the exercise of the functions of the Crown in its relations with Indian States shall in India, if not exercised by His Majesty be exercised only by, or by persons acting under the authority of, His Majesty's representative for the exercise of those functions of the Crown.

(2) The said rights, authority and jurisdiction shall include any rights, authority or jurisdiction heretofore exercisable in or in relation to any territories in India by the Secretary of State, the Secretary of State in Council, the Governor-General, the Governor-General-in-Council, any Governor or any Local Government, whether by delegation from His Majesty or otherwise.

This declaratory provision makes a unilateral assertion of the rights, authority and jurisdiction exercised by or appertaining to the British King, for which it would be difficult to find satisfactory juridical authority. Even if it be conceded in regard to the British Provinces, as sanctifying the right of conquest and annexation, it is difficult to justify similarly its effect in ascribing practically identical powers and authority in regard to the territories and government of the Indian States whether federating or not. The right of the British Parliament to regulate, from time to time, the governance of British India has been exercised too often to justify its being questioned at this date. But the essence of Federation is undeniably the voluntary association of equals, to promote some common purpose, or realise some common interest. The Government of India Act, 1919, (9 & 10, Geo. V. c. 105) had, in its preamble, promised the progressive realisation of responsible government in this country,—presumably only for British India. That Act is now repealed, except, curiously enough, for its preamble, and subsection (1) of section 47.

The present Act does not substitute any other preamble; and as the Act of 1935 applies or is intended to apply, to the British Indian

(*Continued on page 11*)

autonomy, on the basis of a responsible government, has obtained until now, in any of the Provinces. The political consciousness of their peoples, however aroused and in whatever degree, is utterly dumb or non-existent, in so far as the accomplishment of the Federation is concerned. Neither the governments, nor the peoples of the Provinces, are consulted, before any change of boundaries, powers or functions, status or purpose, is resolved upon and carried out by the supreme authority, which has constituted itself the absolute trustee of India's destiny. Hence the basic ingredient of a free consent to be united, or federated, by equal and autonomous units, who have some common interest to promote by such closer union, or some common purpose to serve, is lacking in India.

This does not mean that we have no common purpose to serve, no common interest to realise, if all the Provinces could be united in a closer organism of

(Continued from page 10)

Provinces, as well to such Indian States as accede to the Federation, it is open to question how far that Preamble can apply to and explain the purpose of the new Constitution. The Act of 1935 is described, in its title, as "An Act to make further provision for the government of India," and Section 1 simply lays down:—

"1.—This Act may be citied as the Government of India Act, 1935."

Without any Preamble, or any more enlightening description, it is impossible to appreciate the purpose and objective of this Act, the more so as it is intended essentially, fundamentally, for a different structure from all its predecessors regulating the Government of India. A declaration of Lord Irwin as the Governor-General of India (October 31, 1929) solemnly affirmed that Dominion Status is implicit in the constitutional evolution of India; but that declaration, however authoritative of British policy at the time it was made, forms no part of the present Act; while its express provisions make a marked differentiation between the Constitution of British Dominions, and that applied to India under this enactment.

Even the principle of Responsibility, introduced in the Central Government of India for the first time was distinctly conditional upon the States joining the new system upto a required minimum.

equal and autonomous units.* India has been hitherto exploited in the British capitalist interests, who have only recently admitted a small section of the Indian people as their junior and sleeping partners. Our trade and industry, our domestic and foreign policy, our national impulse and international contribution, are all suppressed, or perverted into channels ministering to the growth and nourishment and fulfilment of British Imperialism. If we would reverse this exhausting process of a century and more, and redress the social injustice of an archaic system, undoing the might of the vested interests now being rapidly allied with foreign imperialism, we must have a Federal system, in which each component unit of the nation would function as an integral, but at the same time a distinct, autonomous, part of the whole, and wherein all would collaborate for a common regeneration of the country and its people.

Given this community of purpose and interest, India cannot be said to be lacking in the essential pre-requisite of a successful Federation; given likewise the history we have passed through and the traditions we have evolved, the terms and conditions on which an effective Federation could be formed out of the Indian Provinces merit serious discussion.

Reconstitution of Provinces

In another volume on the new Indian Constitution† it has been pointed out that the existing Indian

*cp. the Report of the Statutory Commission, Vol. II, ch. 3, also para. 120 of the Montagu-Chelmsford Report, which says: "Granted the announcement of August 20th (1917) we cannot at the present time envisage its complete fulfilment in any form other than that of a congeries of self-governing Indian Provinces, associated for certain purposes under a responsible Government of India; with possibly what are now the Native States of India finally embodied in the same whole, in some relation which we will not now attempt to define.

†cp. Provincial Autonomy, Ch. 2.

Provinces cannot claim to be integral local units, with a distinct homogeneity of their own, which could justly make of them independent States. But within many of the present units called Governors' Provinces, there are distinct cultural entities, or sub-provinces, which could well constitute a people, each by itself, and make a State. The tendency in some distinct homogeneous Provinces, or historical communities, to emphasise local patriotism, or sectional loyalty, may perhaps be deemed to militate against the development of national solidarity. In so far as national solidarity is indispensable at the present juncture for the effective development of India's inherent natural resources, the central national authority would have to be vested with powers, which would easily ensure such development being carried on unimpeded by parochial loyalty or communal sentiment. When, however, due safeguards have been provided for this end, wide scope could still be left for effective local autonomy to the constituent units of a Federation of India, which seems to be the most feasible form of political organisation and constitutional machinery for the governance of this country.

Communal Cleavage

There is, also, another hindrance in the way of a proper formation and satisfactory working of a Federal State in India, *viz.* the presence of the communal sentiment. But the communal antagonism between the two chief communities of India, is superficial, confined only to the upper strata. So long as the end of political agitation in India was merely a sharing of the spoils of Government, his rivalry in the two communities had its own explanation. But as the purpose of India's demand for political independence is being better appreciated by the mass of the people; as the leaders and spokesmen of India's political aspiration begin more and more to give concrete form to this urge for self-expression of a whole people; as the necessity of political power to effect social justice and economic amelioration all round is being understood, the artificial divisions emphasised by the communalists will weaken, and in course of time be obliterated.

In so far as these communal lines of division at all conceal real cultural differences, which are incompatible with a uniform mould, the Federal form will be the most serviceable to afford the utmost scope for such genuine differences between the communities without injuring their common purpose and unity. It is of the essence of modern Federalism that regional minorities which represent also cultural minorities must be duly protected and encouraged, in order to make the resultant life of the entire people as rich and varied as possible, and enable it to contribute in full measure to the sum total of human advancement.

There is still a strong sentiment of local loyalty in India, but that feeling of provincial patriotism does not in the least override the feeling of national unity. Even where the provincial sentiment becomes identified with the communal cleavage,—*e.g.*, in Sind, the advantages of remaining united in a single India are too palpable, and too obvious for this sentiment to constitute a menace to the national integrity of this country. Thus even in the border provinces there is no marked sentiment in favour of separatism, and it is well recognised that this is not a practical proposition. They all look to India as a whole and appreciate the advantages of a federal combination with the rest of India.

Indian States

The Indian States constitute a more difficult problem. Under their present form of government, and with their existing political structure and social organisation, they would be completely out of place in any form of democratic constitutional reconstruction in India. They would neither fit in with democracy, nor with the ideals of social justice and economic regeneration. A chapter in this volume has been devoted to a careful consideration of the judicial, political and economic aspect of the Indian States being incorporated in an All-India Federal system. It is clear that the admission of the States, with their present archaeic form of government, would constitute an obvious anomaly in a democratic Federation of India. The people of the States have not been allowed to have their say in the matter, and the original motive force for including the States in an Indian Federation is the desire of British imperialist policy to exploit and dominate over India the more effectively through the autocratic and feudal elements in the States. And yet an All-India Federation cannot leave out the States. Their geographical position is such as to make this exclusion highly undesirable, for they are dotted about all over the country, and are often islands surrounded by provincial territories. Politically and economically, this exclusion is still less to be thought of, and no homogeneous India can be built up in this way. Nor can the people of the rest of India tolerate willingly the separation of their countrymen in the States from them, and the continuation for the latter of an out-of-date feudal regime which prevents all growth.

This then is the essence of the problem: we cannot leave out the States from an All-India Federation, and we cannot have them as they are without making the Federation a farce, and doing grave injury not only to the people of the States but also to the people of the rest of India.

The Rulers of the States have emphasized that they will only join the Federation with their autocratic powers left intact and fully acknowledged; they are to be local sovereigns in fact; their treaties are to be considered inviolate and unchangeable. And at the same time they will have the power to interfere in all India matters, and thus India as a whole will be subjected to some extent to this autocratic and feudal control. That is a position which the people of India, including the people of the States themselves, have rejected completely and with unanimity, and which they cannot willingly tolerate. That means that the ideal of a democratic India must be given up, and no constitutional process is left open to the people to get rid of autocracy and feudalism.

If the British Indian Provinces do not have the democratic basis, which we consider the pre-requisite of a proper Federation to-day, the Indian States are entirely lacking in this. These States claim now an independent existence and sovereignty in regard to their internal affairs, which is far greater than the Provinces are supposed to possess. Yet in actual practice the largest and most powerful of them is less influential than even the smaller Provinces. The Treaties on which they lay so much stress, it should be remembered, were between the British Power and the Rulers whom they choose to recognise. Even these

Treaties have been transformed in course of time by a continuous process of interpretation and erosion, beyond recognition. They have been insisted upon only when they served the interests of the dominant partner; when they came into conflict with that interest, they were ignored or interpreted so as to suit the Paramount Power. In a dispute between the two, the Paramount Power is both a party to the dispute and the final judge. No appeal or alternative tribunal is possible. Thus the Treaties have not succeeded in safeguarding the rights of the States or their Rulers. Owing to the ever growing pressure of Indian Nationalism, the British Government has sought to rally the States to its side, and has therefore, in recent years, referred to the sanctity of these Treaties and sought to make of them an excuse for the denial of democracy. But the Treaties will not be allowed to come, at any time, in the way of British interests and policy; they will only be used as a barrier to the establishment of democracy and unity in India. If the British Government so desires, a Ruler will have to join the Federation; he cannot keep out of it for long by virtue of his Treaty rights.

It must be borne in mind that most of these Treaties represent an arrangement arrived at a century or more ago. Since then enormous changes have taken place in the world, and even in India, where the outer shell persists, while the inner content of it has changed utterly. The Treaties thus are wholly unreal, and they have persisted so long simply because the British Government so desired. There is no strength or sanction behind them except that of the power of the British

Government. If that support is removed from them, they collapse and fade away. The people of the States object to them as well as to the autocratic and feudal order which they have preserved. They demand to-day, with an ever increasing persistence, a democratic and responsible form of government. They look to their neighbours in British India, with whom their contacts are of the closest kind, and desire to link their political and economic future with them. There is no trace of a separatist sentiment among the people of the States.

The idea that British India and the Indian States should be kept distinct from each other and politically apart is absurd, and entirely out of keeping with present-day forces and developments. No State is by itself so large and compact, and at the same time geographically so situated, as to make isolation and a separate existence desirable. The autocracy that prevails in the States and the archaic social system are so utterly out of tune with facts and modern tendencies that they cannot survive for long.

There has been recently a tendency on the part of some of the Rulers of the States to hold back from the Federation, but this must not be mistaken for an urge to remain apart. It does not represent a real desire to keep separate from the rest of India, for such separation is hardly a possibility to-day. It represents at the most a desire to keep as far as possible from the growing democracy and nationalism of the Indian people. But the real explanation of the bargaining that has been going on between the Rulers of the States and the British Government is the wish of the former to exploit the opportunity offered to them, by the provisions of the new Constitution, to obtain the best terms they can for acceding to the Federation. It is to the interest of the British Government to meet them as far as they can, without neutralising the fundamental idea underlying their scheme of Federation. In that scheme the Rulers have an important part to play, for they are meant to be one of the main props of British Rule in India. Thus the bargaining between the Rulers and the British Government is at the expense of Indian solidarity and India's national and economic emancipation.

Differences Between States and Provinces

A. The differences, then, between the Indian States and the Provinces, joining in a Federation of all India, are threefold: (a) While the States can claim a vestige of independent sovereignty, at least for their local concerns, the Provinces are, in all instances, the creations of a central authority, and exercise only delegated authority. (b) The States had, in some cases, an existence prior to that of the British Government of India itself; not one of the Provinces can claim this distinction. In combining these two mutually distinct elements into a Federation of all-India, the technical procedure followed is, accordingly, radically different. (c) While the Provinces are combined into a Federation by a superimposed fiat of the British Parliament, the States are, in theory at least, free to choose to join or not to join the Federation; and if they do so choose, they have, nominally at least, the right to make special terms, reservations, or conditions.

B. Forms of Government. The States are almost entirely based on the absolute autocracy of the Ruler, while in the Provinces, there is visible, in however slight a form, a germ of real democracy. Some of the States have, in recent years, introduced partly elective assemblies and councils, but these legislatures have hardly any democratic element or power, and their executive is solely responsible to the Ruler. The British Government have no legal right to dictate to the Rulers of Indian States the choice of their Ministers; but, in practice, not the most powerful State, nor the most determined Ruler, can have a Minister unacceptable to the Paramount Power. There is, therefore, no possibility in the States, under present conditions, for a government responsible to the people. The political leaders of British India, busy with their own problems, have been unable to organise the people of the States and to develop their political consciousness, which has grown so rapidly in recent years in the rest of India. It has, indeed, been the express policy of the Government of India to keep the concerns of the Indian States and Princes rigorously outside the field of British Indian politics. If they have agreed to the Federation of the States and the Provinces, and conceded the principle of responsible government in the Federation so formed, it is because they expect the Indian State Rulers to provide just that element of conservatism, or reaction, which is essential for the continued domination of India by the British, and her exploitation by British Imperialism. The proposed Federation thus represents the continuation of that basic policy which has governed England's relations with India in the past.

C. Economic Position. The third main difference lies in the economic contrast between the States and the Provinces. While the former are still mostly semi-feudal organisations, the latter are already aggressive individualists, and ambitious capitalist entities. The emanence, in them, of a still more progressive tendency towards a greater social justice, and a better chance for individual self-expression, is a question of time, indeed these tendencies are already visible. But the people of the States are very backward in this respect as in others, and in a federal union they might act as a drag on the others, thus impeding the economic evolution of the rest of India.

Objective of Indian Federation

With these differences between the component units of the proposed Federation of India, various questions inevitably arise: How far closer association of these mutually incompatible units of a Federation of India is likely to be beneficial to the combining units themselves, and to the nation collectively? The answer to this question largely depends, of course, upon what we consider their respective benefit to consist in; what is our aim and ideal in desiring or accomplishing such a combination. If the ideal in view is the combination of all parts of the country in a more or less homogeneous, national, unified organisation, motived by a common impulse of securing the emancipation of the country from alien control and domination, in order that the people of this land should be able of their own accord to devise ways and means of affording social justice and perfect civic equality; if we desire, by this device, to secure rapid industrialisation of the country, developing all its known and yet unknown resources; if we aim at a free India taking her due place in the roll of the independent sovereign communities of the world, and co-operating with them for social betterment and the advancement of human civilization, then we cannot have this through a sham federation, which brings neither real unity nor homogeneity, and stops our progress to political and social freedom. We cannot have a house divided against itself, or a system in which neither the form nor the essence of government are identical in all units. The States as well as the Provinces must have the same form and ideals of political organisation and activity. Feudal, reactionary interests and the vested interests that exploit, will have to be abolished in the States, so as to bring them in line with the rest of India. Federalism can only work satisfactorily on this basis with a uniform structure on a common objective. Any other form of federation is likely to be a device to perpetuate existing divisions and differences, and to protect vested interests and privileged groups.

If we have this objective in view, there can be no doubt that a federation based on it would result in benefit to all the component units as well as to the community collectively. Without it India would be divided and weak and unable to achieve anything worth while. Federation is thus indispensible for us, but even so we cannot pay too high a price for it. If the price demanded is too high, as in the proposed Federation, then it is better and safer to do without it, till a more favourable opportunity presents itself.

Federation and Social Re-construction

The question of Federation can also be considered from the point of view of social re-construction. How far is the Federation calculated to help us to achieve social re-construction with a view to nationalising all forms of natural wealth and the sources of new wealth? Such an ideal presupposes the elimination of vested interests and privileged classes. But the Federation, as now conceived, is fundamentally incompatible with and opposed to such an ideal of Social Re-construction; it has been planned to resist all social change and to perpetuate the existing order. It must fail, therefore, to solve the vast social problems that face us to-day.

India as a Federation

Let us consider the position of India as a Federation in contrast with the other important Federal States in the world. The following are some statistics regarding the principal Federations of the world.

Some comparative Statistics of the Leading Federations

Name	Area in Sq. Mls.	Population in Millions	Revenue in Millions of local currency.	Expenditure	Debt
Canada ..	3729665	10.377	$ 67.513	72.360	682.494
Union of South Africa	472347	8,483	39.524	28.222	272.184
Australian Commonwealth	2974581	6,677	73.942*	70.118	1222,559
India ..	1808679	352,838	89.784	89,708	909,315
U. S. A. ..	3685382	122,775	£ 3991.905	3398.402	*27053.085
Switzerland ..	15940	4,066	Fr. 422.400	430.700	5215.273
U.S.S.R. ..	8241921	165.778	Rbl. 6590.5	65400.5	10088.9

There are many who consider the British Commonwealth of Self-governing Nations as also a case of a Federation. In reality, however, it cannot justly be described even as a Confederation; much less can it be called a Federation. The component parts of the Empire are practically independant nations, separated from one another by long distances, and holding objectives, pursuing policies, confronting problems,

*These details are taken from the Statesman's Yearbook for 1935. The U.S.A. figures for Revenue and Expenditure relate only to the ordinary revenue and expenditure. The so-called Emergency Expenditure, which was more than and equal amount, is extra. In each case the figures are the latest available for the year for which the Statesman's Yearbook could supply them. India's figures for area and population include those of Burma. Germany under the Nazis is no longer a Federal State, and so we have left it out of account altogether.

essentially different one from another. This vast mass embraces an area of 13.355 million square miles, or a fourth of the land surface of the earth; and 495.764 million souls, or more than a fourth of the world population. There is, moreover, little or no direct contact between the nominal Sovereign of the Commonwealth and the individual citizen in each component part. The citizen in each unit owes an allegiance to his own local sovereign entity; and hardly any to the common Sovereign.

In point of area, India is fifth in the list, but in point of population, she is the first, being twice as populous as the next most populous Federation,—the U.S.S.R. The latter, however, is more than four and a half times as large in area. In point of national wealth, as measured by the income and expenditure, India is third on the list. In point of individual wealth, she is probably the last on the list,—having a per capita income of probably less than one-fiftieth of the corresponding figure in the United States, or the U.S.S.R. India's chance to develop herself, and exploit the yet unexplored resources of the country to their maximum scientific capacity, lies, undoubtedly, in a regime of unification, Federation. In a system of disjointed and disintegrating units, and territories without any enthnic or geographic bond between them, that is impossible. The separation of Burma from the mainland of India has substantially reduced the area, and affected the population figure; but that would not affect her material position in the scale of comparison.

But India differs markedly from the other Federations of the world, in not only having two distinct types in the proposed Federation, but also in the absence of any final, sovereign authority within her own united borders. The domination of an alien power makes the case of India unique in our political science. The question whether the centre should preponderate over the units, or *vice versa,* is relatively of minor importance so long as sovereignty does not rest in India. Because of the primary importance of the issue of national independence, all other issues and conflicts of interests—between the units and the Federation, between the States and the Provinces, between even different classes—become secondary.

India has also, like Russia, the problem of Cultural Minorities within her federal boundaries. It is worthy of note that this problem has grown more acute with the growth of nationalism, which is a unifying force. But as national unity and strength have grown, attempts to weaken this nationalism by encouraging disruptive tendencies have also grown. British Imperialism, in resisting nationalism, is evidently interested in playing off one group against another and thus hampering the growth of unity. These minorities are not comparable to the European or Soviet minorities, which are racially and culturally distinct from each other. In India the term minority is applied to religious groups, and the racial and cultural background of these groups is almost the same as that of the majority group. Such differences as are noticeable are largely superficial. The problem of minorities therefore in India is far easier of solution than elsewhere where deep-seated racial and cultural animosities are roused. The growth of nationalism will soften the religious divisions, but even more so the spread of social ideas and the consideration of economic issues are diverting the attention of the people to more fundamental matters which affect their daily lives. Thus a new alignment is growing up.

India, in spite of her vast size and variety and diversity, is bound together by a basic unity. This unity is not merely one of geography, but far more of a common cultural background and common traditions. Even when politically cut up into several parts during her long history, this common cultural bond persisted. With political unity and a common purpose, the bond that unites becomes exceedingly strong and almost unbreakable.

Federalism, Nationalism and Democracy

There are two sets of forces, in the political organisation of modern States, which are often considered to be mutually incompatible. Federalism is considered, on the one hand, to be inconsistent with Nationalism; and, on the other, with Democracy. So far as the conflict between Federalism and Nationalism is concerned, it might result only in a given Federation so transcending local State sentiment as to antagonise the latter, and so imply a conflict of Nationalism with Federalism. In so far, however, as the Federation itself is an expression of national integrity: in so far as it embodies the larger unity of homogeneous peoples separated *inter se* by the accidents of history, there can be no incompatibility between the Federation and the local loyalty of its constituent units. All successful Federations in history are of this type; and India is no exception to that claim. The feeling of national unity is there; and the hindrances to its full flowering are largely the creation of outside authority and extraneous circumstances, which must pass away.

As for the other conflict, between Federalism and Democracy, a real self-government of the people as a whole is impossible the moment a political unit attains a size greater than that of a single town. Even in the City States of ancient Greece, it may be doubted if the entire people ever joined in their own government. Vast numbers of slaves and strangers were excluded from the franchise, even though the latter were essentially of the same race. In the classic Village Community of Ancient India, which had persisted down to very recent times, Democracy was both real and an everyday affair. But we are not living in an age when the village could well be upheld as an ideal political unit. Democracy, therefore, in the sense of actual participation of every citizen in the public affairs of the community, is impossible, except on the basis of delegated authority, and vicarious responsibility. By the device of representative popular institutions, to which the executive authority could be made responsible, it is possible nowadays to realise a working Democracy on a scale as large as that of a large Indian Province. By careful demarcation of authority, powers and functions, between the several sections of a hierarchy of self-governing institutions—the Village and the Town Council; the District Council, the Provincial and the Federal Legislature—we can arrange so that in all matters that concern a citizen's life and being immediately, there will be the fullest scope for real self-Government. As those affairs become more and more of remote concern to the citizen personally, there may be representative institutions, each unit wherein may represent an ever increasing mass of humanity, and holding sway over a corresponding field of functions, in which democratic government is realised, only on the basis of the executive government being no more than a mere mandatory of—and therefore responsible to,—the legislative organ, which represents the will of the mass of the citizens.

In Federations, this device is carried a stage further. The actual right of the people to real self-government can only be exercised, either in framing or formulating the fundamental constitution for the Federation; or by such devices as Referendum or Initiative on given questions of legislative or executive policy. Beyond this, there is nothing but representative,—or delegated,—Self-government. In so far as the actual functions of Government commonly entrusted to the Federal authority are concerned, however imposing they may appear in their collective aspect, they are of remote concern to the individual citizen in his daily life. In so far as the ultimate authority of the citizen in his aggregate is reserved, in the supreme sovereignty vested in the mass of the people, the evolution of the Federal organisation is in no way inconsistent with the Democratic principle.

In India, as in other countries similarly situated, for a vast mass of the people, and over such a large area, the only method of realising Democracy, and at the same time maintaining governmental efficiency and national unity, lies in the Federal principle; and as such there is no reason to dread from this device any loss of real self-government.

Jawaharlal Nehru.
Narendra Dev.
K. T. Shah.

CHAPTER II

NATURE AND SCOPE OF THE INDIAN FEDERATION

No Preamble

The Government of India Act, 1935, contains no Preamble.* It is therefore, difficult to judge from the terms of the Act, the exact nature and scope of the Constitution established thereunder. Section 478 of the Government of India Act, 1935, repeals the Government of India Act, 1919; but expressly provides that "nothing in this Section shall affect the Preamble to the Government of India Act, 1919."† The Preamble lays down:—

> "Whereas it is the declared policy of Parliament to provide for the increasing Association of Indians in every branch of Indian Administration and for

*The following observations of Prof. A. B. Keith are significant:—
Speaking of the Government of India Bill, 1935, (now Act) he says:—
"A rather bitter controversy was waged over the question........ to include in the Bill a definite reference to Dominion Status as the goal of Indian Government. The Government adopted a curious attitude. It definitely accepted the pledge contained in the preamble of the Act of 1919 of the gradual development of self-governing institutions with a view to the progressive realisation of responsible government in British India as an integral part of the Empire, and the interpretation put thereon by the Governor-General in 1929 with the authority of the government of the day: "The natural issue of India's progress as there contemplated is the attainment of Dominion Status." But it refused to put anything of this kind in a preamble, and instead insisted on preserving the preamble to the Act of 1919, when repealing that measure under the new Act. The preservation of the smile of the Cheshire cat after its disappearance was justly adduced by the critics as the best parallel to this legislative monstrosity, and the omission of any reference to Dominion Status, following on the complete silence of the Joint Committee, inevitably caused a painful feeling in India, and annoyance to those quarters of the ministry who realised that its action was certain to be interpreted in India as in some way seeking to evade frank acceptance of Dominion Status as the final goal." **A Constitutional History of India**, by A. B. Keith, p. 316.

†Section 478. Proviso (a): Sechedule 16.

the gradual development of self-governing institutions with a view to the progressive realisation of Responsible Government in British India, as an integral part of the Empire; and

Whereas progress in giving effect to this policy can only be achieved **by successive stages,** and it is expedient that substantial steps in this direction now be taken; and

Whereas **the time and manner of each advance can be determined only by Parliament upon whom responsibility lies for the welfare and advancement of the Indian people**; and

Whereas the action of Parliament in such matters must be guided by co-operation received from those on whom new opportunities of service will be conferred, and by the extent to which it is found that confidence can be reposed in their sense of responsibilty; and

Whereas concurrently with the gradual development of self-governing institutions in the Provinces of India, **it is expedient** to give to those provincial matters **the largest measure of independence of the Government of India which is compatible with the** due discharge by the latter of its own responsibilities.

Ultimate Object of Constitutional Evolution

This five-point Preamble is not repealed, and may be taken still to be in force, representing, as the Joint Select Committee of Parliament on the Government of India Bill of 1935 declare, "the ultimate aims of British rule in India."*

But it is difficult to assess its exact legal or constitutional significance at the present day. For even assuming a Preamble to be as good law as the operative portion thereof† even when the rest of the enact-

*Cp. Para. 12, Op. Cit.

†"It must be held a mistake to refrain from including the words (Dominion Status) in the Preamble. Inserted there they would, as Sir T. Inskip insisted have just the same weight as a formal declaration in Parliament of the Governmental intention. Neither Preamble nor Declaration can bind a succeeding Government, and it was inevitable that omission from the preamble would be resented in India." (Keith, Op. Cit. p. 472).

ment in question is repealed, and the Preamble remaining is incorporated in another Act, the conditions under which this particular definition of British policy, *vis-a-vis* the political aspirations of the people of India, was formulated have expressly altered. For whereas the Preamble to the Act of 1919 applied clearly to *British India*, the present Act contemplates and provides for a Federation of all-India, less Burma; *i.e.* the Indian States are now contemplated to be as much part of a Federation of India as the British Indian Provinces,—apart from Burma and Aden, which are separated from the Government of India. Then, again, the Preamble speaks of an "Empire" in its very first paragraph,—a term, which, even if constitutionally a correct description of the conglomerate of the United Kingdom, the British Dominions, Colonies and Dependencies beyond the seas in 1919, is, since the creation of the Irish Free State, and the passage of the Statute of Westminster*, no longer appropriate to describe the British Commonwealth of free, equal, self-governing communities scattered all over the globe. Even if the term Empire could be construed to designate only the Empire of India, that term is nowhere spoken of in the Act of 1935, and much less defined.† His Majesty the King

---

*22, Geo. V, c. 4. "They (Great Britain and the Dominions) are autonomous communities within the British Empire, equal in status, in no way subordinate one to another in any aspect of their domestic or internal affairs, though united by a common allegiance to the Crown, and freely associated as members of the British Commonwealth of Nations" (cmd. 2768, p. 14 commonly called the Balfour Declaration).

†cp. Section 311; also Section 2 of this Act. The latter does speak of the "Emperor of India" but not of the "Empire."

There does not seem to be any official definition of the British Empire. Says the **Encyclopaedia Britannica** (Ed. XIV, Vol. 8, p. 410), after defining the term Empire as "a term used to denote a state of large size, and also (as a rule) of composite character, often, but not necessarily, ruled by an Emperor,—a State which may be a Federation, like the German

(*Continued on page 32*)

of the United Kingdom, etc., is, indeed spoken of, in Section 2 of the Act of 1935, as "Emperor of India";* but there is throughout the Act no definition of the term Empire. It stands to reason, therefore, that, with the advent of the Federation, there could be no Empire of India, even if there was one before that enactment was passed. The title is thus a sobriquet without any political, or constitutional significance. The Preamble to the Act of 1919, which is still unrepealed, is thus without much significance in law, even if it holds good and may be taken to form part of the Act of 1935.†

Dominion Status vs. Complete Independence

It is, accordingly, impossible to judge of the nature and purpose of the new Constitution as embodied in the Act of 1935, so far as a Preamble can be any guide to such a discovery. Assuming, however, for

(Continued from page 31)

Empire from 1870 to 1918, or a unitary State, like the Russian Empire before its collapse, or even, like the British Empire, a loose commonwealth of free States united to a number of subordinate dependencies." (Ibid. p. 402):—

"There is one Empire which remains to be mentioned—an Empire, which unlike the other Empires of which we have spoken, is entirely independent of the tradition and memory of Rome. This is the British Empire (q.v.) or, as it is coming more and more to be called, the British Commonwealth. It is an Empire so much sui generis—a Federation of National States at once so independent and so interconnected, that it is altogether a matter for separate consideration. This much, however, may be said of its nature. The British Empire is, in a sense, an aspiration rather than a reality; a thought, rather than a fact: a common culture, not a common government: but, just for that reason, it is like the old Empire of which we have spoken: and though it is neither Roman, nor Holy, yet it has, like its prototype, one law, if not the Law of Rome: at any rate the Common Law of England—one faith, if not in matters of religion, at any rate in the field of political and social ideals."

The above is from the pen of Prof. Ernest Barker; and though more eloquent than accurate, it shows the impossibility of endowing with a definite juridical, constitutional, connotation a term which has no bearing in reality.

*Cp. ante pp. 10 and 11

†Cp. the Debates in the House of Commons in March, 1935; also Keith, Op. cit. pp. 466 et seq.

the sake of argument, that the Preamble to the Act of 1919 is still part of the Indian Constitution, as enacted by the Act of 1935, the conditions expressly laid down in that Preamble no longer hold valid as they may have been at the time they were laid down. The ultimate goal of constitutional evolution in India is stated to be "the progressive realisation of Responsible Government **in British India**" on the clear understanding that that entity remains "an integral part of the Empire." Even if one eschews the tempting subtlety that an "Empire" and "Responsible Government" are two mutual contradictions, there is no doubt that, under the radically altered conditions of the Commonwealth of free, self-governing communities under the Union Jack, the term Empire is now of no validity outside India. The Indian people, in their turn, refuse to be dominated by the capitalist Imperialism of Great Britain.

Moreover, the two specific manifestations of the realisation of this goal, *viz*:—

(a) increasing association of Indians in every branch of Indian Administration; and

(b) the gradual development of self-governing institutions.

as understood by British statesmen in 1919 or 1937, will now be utterly inadequate to satisfy the political consciousness of the Indian people. Though the pledge for a Dominion Status was repeated,* in the course of the parliamentary discussions on the Government of India Bill, 1935; and though the Instructions to the Governor-General specifically contain a clause enjoining upon that officer to—

> "so exercise the Trust reposed in him that partnership between India and the United Kingdom with-

*See ante, footnote 1, p. 29-30.

> in our Empire may be furthered, **to the end that India may attain its due place** among our Dominions"*

it may safely be assumed that even the so-called "Dominion Status" will not prove adequate for the new political consciousness of India. The capture of all posts and machinery of administration is regarded as the *sine qua non* of any semblance even of self-government. The essence of Dominion Status is the complete control of the domestic affairs of the country as also of inter-Dominions, and of the foreign policy of such a unit in the Commonwealth, exclusively by the people of that unit. So long as that substance of power is not available to the people of India, no constitution, however mighty the shadow, will satisfy the Indian people. It is unnecessary to add that, if self-governing institutions are to be introduced in India, capped with a Responsible Ministry, they must be brought in as fully and immediately as possible, so as to abridge the period of transition, and avoid or minimise the undesirable effects of too rapid a political growth.

Parliamentary Trusteeship

The idea of gradual constitutional evolution from stage to stage is thus easily discounted. The basic principle of British Trusteeship, as embodied in the clause making Parliament the sole judge of the time and manner in which each successive stage of constitutional advance should be effected, is fundamentally at variance with Nationalist opinion of every shade in this country. Parliamentary Trusteeship has never been exercised for the benefit of the

---

*Article XVI of the Instruct

Indian people, when the demands of that Trust went counter to the national interests of Britain. From the day of Warren Hastings to the last Great War, and the enforcement of the Ottawa system of Imperial Preference, India's interests have always been sacrificed in the interests of British Imperialism; and the latest Constitution bears ample testimony to the continued presence of this element in British dealings with India in unabated strength.

Disappointed in the trust placed in the honesty of British politicians, and wiser by the repeated experience of broken pledges, the Indian Nationalist of to-day sees no point in that demand for "co-operation", which is mentioned in the Preamble to the act of 1919, as the condition precedent for the grant of successive stages of India's political advancement by the British Parliament. For, to co-operate is to court disappointment, humiliation, and an enforced association in the ruthless exploitation of this country. Not to "co-operate," in the sense in which the established authorities understand that term, would at least serve to put the Indian on his mettle; and force him to devise other ways of arriving at his goal, which seems impossible to attain by the road of "co-operation." This last condition in the Preamble is, accordingly, equally unfulfillable and so, the vision of India's march on the road to constitutional progress embodied in that document has failed utterly to materialise.

No Fundamental Rights of Citizenship

Lacking in a Preamble, the Act of 1935 is also silent as to those distinguishing features of a truly liberal constitution, which relate to certain guaranteed Fundamental Rights of citizenship. We may speak of these rights collectively as the civil and economic liberties of the people. Such rights are not, it is true, specifically mentioned in any constitutional document relating to the governance of Britain herself. But civil and economic liberties in Britain have been part and parcel of the Common Law of the land; and have grown with the growth of political consciousness and popular power. There was, besides, no need in Britain or the Dominions to fight against an alien power to win the basic political rights of the people, as we have to in this country. In such matters, moreover, as the fact of popular Sovereignty, which constitutions like that of the U.S.A. specifically enunciate, Britain has ample Parliamentary precedents, even if the legal fiction still prevails making the King Sovereign of the United Kingdom. We in India have no such precedents to fall back upon. If the sovereign power is really to be transferred to the people of the country, the fact of the transfer must be unambiguously stated and recognised. Other countries, again, have discarded the British precedent of remaining silent, in their fundamental constitutions, as to the nature and extent of the Fundamental Rights of Citizenship. There is, ample precedent, therefore, to urge that a constitution which does not state the goal clearly, and which offers no substitute in the nature of Fundamental Rights, sufficiently liberally conceived to be really a compensation, cannot prove satisfying to a people so painfully conscious of their political subservience as those of India.

Purpose of Present Constitution

How, then, is one to ascertain the purpose and nature of this system of governance for a whole Continent? Is it to be taken merely as a piece of lifeless mechanism, designed to provide simply for immediate requirements, and incapable of adjusting itself to changing conditions and the varying needs of a living community? Judged from the actual terms of the Act; and read in the light of the attempt to associate the Indian States, or rather their Rulers, in a closer bond called the Federation of India, it is impossible to see in this document any sign of a real emancipation of the Indian people from the controlling might of the British power; any indication of a transfer of effective power, for the leaders of the Indian people to put their ideals of social organisation and political machinery to test. Hedged round with innumerable conditions and reservations; rich in countless safeguards for the vested interests of the alien exploiter of every shade, and his local coadjutor of every class; breathing at every pore unmitigated distrust of the leaders of the Indian people,—there can be no hope, under this Constitution, for any real self-government in India. It belies the pledges, weak and inadequate as they were, given in 1919*; and places a positive barrier in the way of constitutional advance by peaceful means, if the interpretation by the Governors, in the six Provinces where the Congress had obtained a majority of seats in the local Assemblies, of the nature and purpose of their "discretionary powers," is any guide to the possibilities of this Act under unsympathetic interpreters.

The Act, viewed collectively, does not make any real advance on the road to a true Responsible Govern-

*Says Prof. A. B. Keith (Op. cit., p. 468):—"It must be admitted that it did not lie with the government which secured the admission of India to the League of Nations to deny that the goal of India was Dominion Status."

ment in India. In the Central Government of the country, a number of the most important Departments of the State are summarily and completely excluded from the purview of any Ministerial Responsibility.* The Governor-General is, in these excluded or Reserved Departments, the absolute master of the situation; and is vested with powers and authority to find means for their administration as to him seems best. In other Departments, again, where Ministerial aid and advice are not so specifically excluded, the Governor-General has innumerable powers of "discretion," in the exercise of which, also, he need not even consult his constitutional advisers, the Ministers. In still others, he is authorised "to exercise his individual judgment," whereby, even if he seeks the advice of his Ministers, he is not bound to follow that advice in every instance. We shall review these various categories of extraordinary powers given to the Governor-General in some detail in a later chapter of this volume. Suffice it to add here that, taken together, these various powers of the Governor-General serve to make of that officer as complete an autocrat as any King by Divine Right ever wanted to be, or as any Dictator by popular mandate of modern times can afford to be.

Federation and National Unity

Even the plea in favour of this Constitution of unifying India by associating the Rulers of the Indian States in a common scheme of National Government is little better than a pretence. The combination of the British Indian Provinces with the Indian Princes, the Rulers of the Indian States, in a Federation of India, is a **union of two mutually in-**

*cp. Section 11 of the Government of India Act, 1935.

compatible categories, which can never march harmoniously together, unless one of them changes completely its nature and ideals, the purpose of its being and the goal of its activities. To all those who desire the maintenance of the Indian Princes in all their ancient privileges, their archaic forms of government, their obsolete methods and ideals, side by side with the progressive, democratising, socially more liberalising Provinces, the union can have only one objective: the curbing, with the aid of the former, of the more progressive tendencies of the latter.* Since the British Imperial Government and the Indian Public Services,—not to mention all the might of the vested interests of British and Indian Landlordism and Capitalism,—are openly ranged on the side of the former, there can be no question as to which of these two categories is likely to suffer most by this forced association in an utterly misconceived purpose.

Given the presence of the Indian States in the new polity of India as an unconcealed drag upon the progressive tendencies of the Indian people as a whole, the question is almost unnecessary to ask: How far complete national independence, could be achieved for the whole of India under the new Constitution. The Princes, though torn among themselves with personal jealousies and conflict of material interests, may be depended upon never to support the slightest hint of National Independence for India. They have been trained to look upon the

*"For the Federal Scheme it is difficult to feel any satisfaction. The units of which it is composed are too disparate to be joined suitably together, and it is too obvious that on the British side, the scheme is favoured in order to provide an element of pure conservatism in order to combat any dangerous element of democracy contributed by British India." Keith, Op. cit. p. 474.

British garrison in this country as the best guarantee of their own existence, insured against local disorder, immune from any challenge to their absolutist authority, and safe against any outside aggression, so long as they are content to remain in their century old sloth, vice, decrepitude, extravagance, and semi-servitude. Their class interests coincide with and cement this force of their environment and education. They would, therefore, oppose as emphatically any movement from below towards a fuller and a freer national life for the people of India, as they would fight against any manifestation of ambition by one of their own confréres. In each case they would rely upon the British bayonet to protect and preserve them. A Nizam may have his own grudge against the British on account of Berar; or a Kashmir on account of Gilgit, or family intrigues, or personal indignities. Of these the Princes, if only they had courage to speak, could retail far more sensational examples than any commoner in India when pitted against British greed or insolence. But these individual affronts or injustices are seldom vocal and never effective. The British can, therefore, afford to despise these *soi disant* descendants of the Sun and the Moon, of the Great Mughal and the mighty Mahratha, who cannot raise a finger without the connivance of the Resident, who may not receive a brother Prince without the gracious if silent consent of the Political Department; who certainly must not appoint a Minister without the full permission of the Viceroy. To such people, the only thing that can matter is the cut of a coat or the whirl of a skirt. History to them is a bore, when not a personal reproach; politics, a synonym for intrigue; sociology, a subject for ribald jests. With them in his camp, there can be no thought of a national resurrection, which the ardent Nationalist seeks, first of all in an emancipation from British domination, or complete independence.

Even Dominion Status, in its respectable sense, has little chance of realisation, so long as the British elements in the Public Services; British Capital in our Industry and Commerce; and the British Army in our midst, hold a stranglehold on our energies and resources. The new Constitution amply, carefully, categorically provides for them. At the very first test of the reality and the genuineness of the new "Reponsible Government," said to be introduced in the Provinces under the Act of 1935, the Governors refused to promise non-exercise of their own discretionary powers,—not obligatory duties imposed upon them,—even if the Ministers from the Congress Party promised to act within the Constitution, or in regard to their constitutional activities only. And the Governor-General of the Federation is only an *edition de luxe* of the Provincial Governor. Notwithstanding all the safeguards and the reserve powers, or special responsibilities and obligatory functions imposed upon the Governor as the watch-dog of British Imperialism in India, this very modest demand of the Congress Ministers-to-be was rejected without ceremony, proving thereby that real progress toward real self-government, even on this limited scale, was unthinkable to the mandatories of British Imperialism in India. How, then, can one think of the possibility of attaining to Dominion Status under this engine of Imperialist exploitation?

Components of the Indian Federation

The Federation of India is to be composed, as already remarked, of the British Provinces, and such Indian States as execute the required Instruments of Accession,* provided that they do not fall below a prescribed proportion in size or importance.† Part II of the Government of India Act, 1935, is entitled **"The Federation of India"**; and its very first Chapter is styled: **"Establishment of Federation and Accession of Indian States."** There are only two Sections in this Chapter; but they are about as fateful and mischievous; as liable to difference of opinion, in construction and interpretation, as any that might be found throughout the British Statute Book. So far as the British Provinces are concerned, there is no option left to them to join or keep out of the Federation. Except Burma, which has been separated before the Federation of India comes into being. Federation for the Provinces is an act of imposition from above, *i.e.*, by the British Parliament.‡ The unquestionable implication of that Act so far as the Provinces are concerned, is that they cannot sever their connection from the Federation, once they have been "united" into it,—unless, indeed, the same sovereign power which thus

*Cp. Section 6 of the Act.

†Cp. Section 5 of the Act.

‡It is interesting to note that there is no provision in the Act of 1919,—except as regards the Indian States or the so-called excluded areas,—for old associates like Burma, or new partners like Afghanistan or Ceylon, to be incorporated in the Federation of India.

united them decides to sever their connection.* The entity called the Federation of India is thus a creation of the British Parliament. It will come into being, provided the condition imposed is fulfilled, by a Proclamation of the King-Emperor. There is, it may be noted, no time limit imposed, within which the condition laid down is to be fulfilled if the Federation is at all to come into being; though, it is curious to observe, that the States acceding, or any of them, may, under provision (*b*) of Section 6 (1), stipulate a time limit for the coming into birth of the Federation, which, if not fulfilled, would absolve the State so stipulating from acceding at all to the Federation.

*Section 5 provides:—

"5.—(1) It shall be lawful for His Majesty, if an address in that behalf has been presented to him by each *House* of Parliament and if the condition hereinafter mentioned is satisfied, to declare by Proclamation that as from the day therein appointed there shall be united in a Federation under the Crown, by the name of the Federation of India—(a) the Provinces hereinafter called the Governors' Provinces; and (b) the Indian States which have acceded or may thereafter accede to the Federation; and in the Federation so established there shall be included the Provinces hereinafter called the Chief Commissioners' Provinces."

(2) The condition referred to is that States—

(a) the Rulers whereof will, in accordance with the provisions contained in Part II of the First Schedule to this Act, be entitled to choose not less than fifty-two members of the Council of State; and

(b) the aggregate population wherof, as ascertained in accordance with the said provisions, amounts to at least one-half of the total population of the States as so ascertained have acceded to the Federation.

It is obvious that the States,—even those of them that decide to accede to the Federation,—are not members of the Federation, until and unless they execute each an Instrument of accession, (Section 6) and that while executing such an Instrument, they may make any reservation or condition they deem proper to safeguard their treaty and other rights. There is no such option allowed to the Provinces. But there can and will be no Federation until a proclamation is issued by the King; and the latter will not issue such a proclamation unless and until the condition mentioned in Section 5 is fulfilled. No such condition applies in the case of Provinces.

Governors' Provinces and Chief Commissioners' Provinces

There is, again, a marked difference of treatment between the several regions making up British India under the Act of 1935. While those areas, which are described by this Act as the Governors' Provinces, are *united* in a Federation *ipso facto*, the areas called the Chief Commissioners' Provinces are *included* in the Federation if and when born under this Section. The States, on the other hand, *accede* to it.* Why this difference in treatment between the several parts of even British India? True, the Governors' Provinces would be *autonomous* units sometime *before* the Federation comes into being. But their autonomy has no bearing upon their being in the Federation. That is an act of the sovereign authority of the British Parliament, in which these newly created "states"—if we may use the term in respect of the British Indian Governors' Provinces,—have no voice. The same is the case, so far as federating is concerned, for the so-called Chief Commissioners' Provinces. Why then, this difference in treatment in the terms of the Act? The Provinces are all exposed to the same risk of changes of boundaries and jurisdiction,† so that variation in size or population or wealth cannot be regarded as distinguishing features for the differentiation between these two classes of Provinces. With the experience of the partition and re-partition of Bengal; of the creation of such new provinces as the North-West Frontier Province, Sind, Orissa, and elevation, perhaps, hereafter, of Coorg or British Baluchistan into Governors'

*Cp. Sections 311 (3).

†Cp. Section 290 of the Act.

Provinces, we cannot altogether overlook the difference in wording regarding the union or inclusion of certain areas in the Federation of India. It has a significance which cannot be fully grasped to-day; but to ignore or overlook this difference in wording would be short-sighted.

The ingredients of the Federation,—the component parts,—are not stated specifically,—except in so far as the above provision can be held to make such a statement. The Federation, if and when formed, will comprise:

(a) all the British areas, whether Governors' Provinces or Chief Commissioners';

(b) excluded and partially excluded areas;

(c) Tribal regions and backward tracts; and

(d) such of the States as agree to accede.

This will obviously be a conglomerate, the several component parts whereof would be as different *inter se* as chalk from cheese. While the States will come into the Federation by an act of the Ruler in each case, the Governors' and Chief Commissioners' Provinces are united or included in the Federation by Act of Parliament. While the States are independent units, possessing or pretending to a degree of local sovereignty, which not the most considerable Province can lay claim to, some of the Provinces are autonomous units, and others mere appanages of the Government of India. The power, authority and function of each of these categories, combined in the Federation of India, differ, *inter se*, very minutely; and in several important respects, as will be seen more fully below.

But they all go to show that the Federation of India, created under the Act of 1935, is a peculiar entity without precedent or parallel; and that, therefore, it must be judged in every respect on its own merits or performances.

Sovereign Authority in the Indian Federation

Thus brought into being by a variety of acts and deeds, the Indian Federation is a State whose Sovereign authority, in the theory of the Act of 1935, is expressly located outside India. Section 2 of the Act is very explicit on this point; and is notably different from all the enactments hitherto passed by the British Parliament concerning the governance of India. The Proclamation of British Sovereignty has nowhere been so explicit and unabashed as in this enactment.* Neither in the Act of 1858, which abolished the East India Company and vested the Government of India directly in the British Crown; nor in all the subsequent Acts relating to the governance of India, down to 1919, is there any such statement of the complete Sovereignty of the British Sovereign over all India as in this Act. The irony of it is that this Act is supposed to advance India substantially on the road to self-Government. if not to that of Dominion Status, or National Independence. We shall consider in the next Chapter the bearing of these provisions on the Indian States, and their claim to local sovereignty, of however limited a degree. Here it is necessary to point out that, short of the sanctification of the right of conquest or arbitrary annexation or brute force, there is no authority, historical or juridical, for such a bald

* For text of Section 2, see foot-note, ante p. 10-11.

enunciation of complete British Sovereignty all over India, as is done in this Act.

It may, also, be pointed out, in passing, that "the rights, authority and jurisdiction" vested in the King-Emperor by this Act are, so to speak, a gift of Parliament to the King. They are certainly not in the nature of Common Law or Prerogative features of British Sovereignty. Otherwise there would be no need to specify them so explicitly. When the British Parliament abolished the East India Company, and vested the Government of India in the British Crown, it was alleged that the Company had been governing those regions "in trust" for Her Majesty; and that, the beneficiary of the Trust having resolved to end the Trust, the real Ruler stood forth directly in *propria persona* to claim her rights, authority, and jurisdiction. But neither in the Act of 1858, nor in the Queen's Proclamation, nor in any subsequent Act or Proclamation, has there been anything to indicate that the British Sovereign claimed absolute Sovereignty in and over all India.

The grant by Parliament to the British Sovereign of all those "rights, authority and jurisdiction," which had hitherto been exercised by the Secretary of State by himself or in Council, by the Governor-General by himself or in Council, by a Governor or a Local Government, is, likewise, inconsistent with the doctrine of Parliamentary Trusteeship over India, which was specifically mentioned in the Preamble to the Act of 1919, unless one assumes that there is really no transfer of power, since the British King is only a dummy, and would always act as the mouthpiece of the

Parliament. The transfer, however, if it was to be made, should have been made to the people of India, on whose behalf Parliament had constituted itself a Trustee, even though it is not clear against whom or for what purpose the Trust was constituted. Again, even the British Parliament has never enunciated the doctrine of Trusteeship for the Indian States, which are now proposed to be made part of a common polity for the whole of India. The Prerogative or Paramountcy rights of the Suzerain, as successor of the Mughal Emperors, are not touched by this Act. But even so, the Act cannot escape the charge of anomaly. By the theory of this Trust, by the fundamental principles of all Trusts, the Trust is valid only upto the day the legal incapacity or disability of the beneficiary of the Trust is ended, or upto the time limit of the Trust fixed in advance. Politically speaking, India is admitted to have come of age. Witness her independent membership of the League of Nations. She is thus no longer in need of a Trustee who has appointed himself to the charge. Parliament seems itself to have recognised this fact of the political majority of the Indian Nation, in so far as the provisions of the Act of 1935, conferring Provincial Autonomy, may be regarded as real and not a sham. Even in the Central National Government of India, with the advent of the Federation, there will have to be Responsible Government,—in however circumscribed a field. If these indices be taken to mean the political majority of the Indian Nation, the Trust, where it did apply, must be assumed to be automatically ended; and the Trustee *functus officio*. The transfer of power must, therefore, be to the people of India; and the

Sovereignty over and in India must be admitted and recognised in the people of India. The Act of 1935, however, clearly does not contemplate, any such transfer even as an ultimate eventuality, or a remote contingency.

As another index of the recognition of the political majority of the Indian people, Parliament has, within limits, allowed the people's representatives of India to propose certain amendments in the Constitution,—however restricted the scope of these amendments; while certain other Amendments may be made by Parliament, under Section 6, Schedule II of the Act, without affecting the fact of the Federation. Structural and fundamental changes in the Constitution imposed upon India by Parliament cannot, of course, be made by the people's representatives of India, however completely they command the confidence of their constituents, and however fully the latter desire those changes. Nevertheless, the very basis of Responsible Government would be negatived, if the people were denied all right or title to affect their own system of Government. After all, the Australian and the Canadian Federal Constitutions are really the creations of these peoples themselves,—though, in form, they have been enacted by the British Parliament as desired by the Australian and the Canadian peoples. If Parliament persists in denying such a right to the Indian people, it would not only evince a complete distrust of the Indian people; but will, in addition, transform itself, from a self-made Trustee of the Indian peoples, to a Trustee and Guardian of the British interests in India. Every tyro knows this is the stark fact of the real politics in India; but, in words at least and formally, it is still not explicitly admitted by the powers that be. Their own acts, however, would, as outlined above, vindicate this charge far more thoroughly than any condemnation of the present Constitution by its critics.

Scope and Extent of the Federation

The Federation conceived in the Act of 1935 would embrace, as already stated, British India less Burma; and such Indian States as accede to the Federation. In the system thus made up there is no room for separatism; so that the separate statehood, or political individuality, of all federating units will be merged and lost in the larger entity,—except in so far as the Constitution itself permits or recognises in a limited degree the local individuality of the federating or combining units. The separation of Burma was effected, not in any desire to vindicate the right of the Burmese to self-determinism; but to keep Burma reserved for the undiluted might of British Imperialism to exploit. No unit in the Federation of India will, presumably, be allowed to secede or withdraw from the Federation, once it has entered it, whether the original entrance was by Act of Parliament, or by a separate Instrument of Accession under the Act.* Local sentiment, if ever and anywhere it becomes strong enough to demand separate self-expression, will not be permitted to seek such mark of a distinct individuality, unless it suits British Imperialism to accord it such separate recognition and right to self-expression. It has happened in Sind, Orissa, and the Frontier Province, in that these are made into separate Provinces. It has happened in

*See next Chapter.

Burma, in that that Province is completely separated from India. It might happen in Bengal,—if by encouraging such separatism, the ends of British Imperialism in India could be more effectually served. But, unless such separatism is calculated to serve the objects of British Imperialism, there will be no countenance shown to separatism, whether to a British Province, or to an Indian State so long as Britain remains master in India. And the same logic applies to the entire country, which will not be permitted in peace to break away from the Empire, so long as Britain can raise a soldier, or fire a shot, in holding this country down in absolute subjection to her sway.

If the units of the Federation would not be allowed to part company, there is equally little chance of the adjoining tracts to combine with the Federation,—however much such combining might help the combining units to develop themselves more fully and more rapidly. Burma will not be allowed to rejoin; Ceylon will not be admitted; Nepal or Afghanistan would not even be thought of. There are political as well as strategical reasons for the separation of Aden from India; and, apart from the Indian capital invested in that region, no Indian would, perhaps, desire to continue this liability. But the same cannot be said of Ceylon, Nepal, Burma, or even of Afghanistan. These regions have more affinities with the main Continent of India and may be able more fully to realise their own national advantage, than is healthy for the British Rulers to recognise to-day. With their local autonomy guaranteed,—let us say, as that of the associated Republics in the U.S.S.R., these regions might find it much more useful to combine in the Indian Federation of their own accord than to keep apart,—ever a prey to British exploitation, ever in dread of British intrigue. But the Constitution, as contained in the Act of 1935, has no device by which such adjoining units might be assimilated in the Federation of India,—unless we press into service Section 290 of the Act, or use the analogy of the States' Instruments of Accession to facilitate this measure.

CHAPTER III

ACCESSION OF THE INDIAN STATES

As already stated, we have to consider, in this Chapter the accession,—as it is called in the Act,—of the Indian States to the Federation of India. The States, it must be repeated, are not, nor become, parts of the Federation,—constituent, or component,—merely by authority of the Act of Parliament. They elect to become such parts by an act of their Rulers', individually in each case, and subject to such terms and conditions, as, conformable to the general scheme of the new regime outlined in the Act of 1935, are laid down in the Instrument of Accession, and accepted by the King-Emperor.

Place of States in Federation

The place and rôle of the States in the scheme of the Federation of India is, however, not wholly determined by the Act; or even by the Instrument of Accession; or by the two combined. A considerable field of public or constitutional dealings or activities relating to the States is still covered by their Treaties, Engagements, etc., which are not all necessarily abrogated, superseded, or rendered null and void, because of any state acceding to the Federation. What are known as the incidents of Paramountcy,—the rights and obligations, the powers and authority, the jurisdiction and control, appertaining to or derived from Suzerainty,—will continue to be exercised outside the terms and conditions of the Federal Constitution, not only with regard to those States which, if any, do not accede to the Federation; but even as regards those States which join and form part of the Federal system.

Even within the Federal system, the question is by no means absolutely free from doubt as to the restrictions and obligations imposed upon the States forming part of the Federation,—even though voluntarily, so far, at least, as the Ruler is concerned. Much less is the nature of the bond created by acceding to the Federation free from doubt; *i.e.*, whether, or not, the association thus formed, is revocable, dissoluble, terminable at will, or under operation of the law, by any one party, or by both acting together.

Some of these questions are impossible to answer at the present moment. We must have experience of the working of the new system; we must have the actual terms of the accession settled, at least as regards the first accessors to the new regime; we must even await the authoritative interpretation of certain clauses of the new Constitution by the appropriate Tribunals, before we can pronounce a dogmatic opinion on the bearings and consequences of the new scheme. No precedent derived from any existing Federal system,—within or outside the British Commonwealth of Nations,—will avail in this extraordinarily peculiar system created by the Act of 1935, and the Instrument of Accession executed thereunder.

For our present purpose, however, it will suffice to describe:—

(i) the scheme of Federation as outlined in the Act; its nature, purpose, and binding force;

(ii) the Instruments whereby the actual federating would take place; functions assigned to the Federation;

(iii) the terms and conditions of those Instruments, and the extent to which limitations or reservations would be suffered to be included;

(iv) the reservations, or safeguards, for the States, their peoples; and for British India, and its people, on account of the Federation having come into being;

(v) the reaction of this union, or association, upon the future constitutional development and political progress of India.

I—SCHEME OF FEDERATION

Formation of the Federation

The Federation of India, as we know, is to be formed, under Section 5 of the Act of 1935,* and the *modus operandi* for forming the Federation is prescribed by Section 6.

Several features of this unique provision have already been noted and commented upon; but for the clearness of argument in the present Chapter, it is necessary to repeat some of those comments.

Initial Distinction between States and Provinces

(1) It will be noticed, in the first place, that the Federation is not formed merely because of the passing of an Act of Parliament. It will depend, for its being brought into being, upon the concurrence of a number of factors, not all of them being under one and the same control. The Provinces are "united" or "included"

*Cp. ante p. 43.

in the Federation *ipso facto* the Act; but the States join, accede to, or become united with, the rest of India in a Federation, only after the Rulers have executed an Instrument of Accession.

Its Consequences

This difference in *modus accendi* has important consequences on the status and function of the States in the Federation.

(a) While the Provinces are there ready and waiting for the Federation to be born; and, when born, automatically part and parcel of the new organism, the States join deliberately by a specific act of the Ruler in each case.* The Provinces, accordingly, cannot claim, in law at least, to be equal partners *inter se*, or with the States. Though the Instrument of Accession of a State is neither a deed of partnership, nor an act of association, the States can claim each to be a partner with British India as a whole—not with individual Provinces—as also *inter se*, in the Federation. Sections 138-140 clearly imply the benefits as well as the burdens of this partnership.†

(b) While the States are free to join, or not to join the Federation, the Provinces have no such freedom of choice.‡ They are for ever united in a Federation of India, or included in it, by an act of Parliament which they have no right to amend or alter. The States, too, are *not* free to leave the Federation once

*Cp. Section 311 (3).

†Cp. Chapter on Federal Finance.

‡Cp. Section 5.

they have joined it; but they have a limited right to vary their Instrument of Accession once they have executed it.

(c) The form of Provincial Government is prescribed by this Act. But, notwithstanding their being united in a Federation with autonomous units having popular Legislatures and Responsible Government, the States' form of government is left absolutely unaffected by their accession to the Federation, however, incompatible the basis and methods of their government may be with that of the Federation, or of other members in the Federation.* Even the seats assigned to them in the Federal Legislature may be filled by their Rulers as they like, irrespective of the laws in that behalf governing the rest of the Federated units. They are, moreover, free to make any changes in their internal constitution, which the Provinces are not.

(d) The functions assigned to the Provinces are fixed by the Act; those assumed by the States, as units in the Federation, are determined by their Instrument of Accession; and are subject to such conditions or reservation as may be laid down in that document.

The nature and condition of this Instrument of Accession will be discussed more fully hereafter in a later section of this Chapter. Here we must note the important consequences to the future of the Federation, due to the difference in the original position in the Federation of the States and the Provinces, though all of them cannot be accurately envisaged to-day. It may be that the supposed deliberate act of the Rulers, in joining the Federation, may be a farce. It will be so in most cases, inasmuch as many of the Indian States Rulers are notoriously under the domination of the British Government. By character or attainments, many of them are not in a position to demur to the advice of their mentors from the Indian Foreign and Political Department, even if they had an inclination against federating. It must be admitted, also, that the decisive considerations, which would, generally speaking, influence the Indian State Rulers in making this fateful choice, are not likely to be such as would command public sympathy and popular support in this age. Unless, therefore, they could, in any particular case, convince the British Indian Foreign and Political Department, that a concession to sentiment or tradition, or a confirmation of a vested interest, is necessary in the larger interests of British Imperialism in India, they will plead to deaf ears, should they incline against federating, or demand impossible terms. They would be told, and not without some show of reason, that even their interests, as States or as Rulers, would be better safeguarded by acceding to the Federation. And, of course, in so far as the mere act of acceding would make them the avowed or implied allies of British Imperialism in India, they may count upon the solid support of the British bayonets in all their well-known tendencies to be extravagant and oppressive, reactionary and parasitical.

But, when every allowance is made for these well-known factors, the formal act would be a deliberate choice by each Ruler himself. That alone is enough to mark out the States, so far as their entrance into the Federation is concerned, from the British Provinces of every class. Neither the peoples, nor the governments, of those areas, would have any choice in the matter. They are part and parcel of the Federation from the moment Part III of the new Act was put into operation. Even if the Federation itself should not come into being, the new Constitution, in so far as it is applicable to the Provinces as autonomous units (within limits), of a future Federation, will continue until modified by the same authority that enacted it.*

Lawful—not obligatory—to Proclaim the Federation

(2) The Act makes it "lawful" for the King to proclaim a Federation of India as from a given date. It does not make it *obligatory* for the King to do so, even if the condition laid down is fulfilled. This is inherent in the peculiar circumstances under which the scheme was conceived, and has come to be executed. It was unknown, at the time the Act was passed, whether or not the States would join; and if they did, how many of them, and under what conditions. It is made a condition precedent to the establishment of the Federation that States aggregating one-half the total population in those areas,—or the Rulers whereof are entitled to choose not less than 52 members of the Council of State,—should have executed their Instruments of Accession, accepted by the King-Emperor, and acceded to the Federation, before the King can issue the Proclamation required in Section 5 to establish the Federation.†

---

*cp. Part XIII of the Act of 1935, Sections 312-319.

†See Appendix I to this chapter. Broadly speaking, this distribution of seats does not reveal any general principle governing the allotment in each case. Sometimes, it seems to be population, sometimes geographic position, (e.g., Kalat), sometimes Treaty importance of the State concerned; but nowhere a uniform principle.

It is evident from this distribution of seats that the most important of the States can prevent the Federation becoming an accomplished fact,

(*Conitnued on page 60*)

No Time Limit

(3) The States need not all join at once, or within a given time,—at least, so far as the express terms of the Act are concerned. No time limit is, in fact, laid down in the Section, or anywhere else in the Act, within which the Federation must be proclaimed, *i.e.*, within which the statutory condition must be fulfilled. Nor is any alternative provided in case the condition is not fulfilled, and the Federation does not come into being. A Federation of all British Indian Provinces,—including

(*Continued from page 59*)

if they all choose to keep apart. Less than twenty States, with an aggregate population between them of 50,377,402, command 41 seats in the Council of State as shown in the subjoined Table. 13 States, with a population of a million or more each, command only 33 seats in the Council between them, though their aggregate population is over 46 3|4 million out of a total States' population of just under 79 millions, as given in this Schedule. Four States with population each from 3|4th of a million to nearly a million command 8 more seats between them; but even so, the required total of 52 seats out of an aggregate of 104 seat in the Council is not made up, though, between them, they have a population aggregating over 5|8ths of the total States population.

State	Seats	Population
Hyderabad ..	5	14,436,148
Mysore ..	3	6,557,302
Travancore ..	2	5,095,973
Kashmir ..	3	3,646,243
Gwalior ..	3	3,523,070
Jaipur ..	2	2,631,775
Baroda ..	3	2,443,007
Jodhpur ..	2	2,125,982
Patiala ..	2	1,625,520
Rewa ..	2	1,587,445
Udaipur ..	2	1,566,910
Indore ..	2	1,325,089
Cochin ..	2	1,205,016
Total .. 13		46,769,480
Bhawalpur ..		984,612
Kolhapur ..		957,137
Bikaner ..		936,218
Bhopal ..		729,955
Total		3.607,922
Grand Total ..	41	50,377,402

It is, however, unlikely that the important States would all apprehend the consequences of Federating in such a prejudicial light as to

(*Continued on page 61*)

the Chief Commissioners' provinces, and the areas wholly or partially excluded from the scheme of provincial autonomy laid out in other parts of this Act,—is clearly not contemplated by the Act, even during the period,—whatever that may be,—required by the necessary number of States to make up their mind for joining the Federation. That is why Part XIII of the Act continues, *mutatis mutandis*, the existing Constitutional arrangement for British India as a whole during the period of transition. A confederation of States among themselves, prior to joining the Federation, is, of course, utterly outside,—if not even incompatible with,—the scheme and purpose of this Act.

It is, indeed, reasonable to assume that the States would not be allowed an unlimited period to make up their minds: to join, or not to join, the Federation. But whatever time limit is imposed by the authorities in India or in London will be only an executive firman; and not under a provision of the Act. The situation is, accordingly, extremely intriguing, in this regard,

(*Continued from page 60*)

refuse to Federate, even on the lines provided for in this Act, and the Instrument of Accession to be executed thereunder. Defection of a single State like Hyderabad from such a non-federating group,—assuming, for the sake of argument, that there is such a group,—would sabotage the entire plan of anti-federationists; as also a similar action on the part of the leading South Indian States; or the important Central Indian and Rajputana States. To any one, familiar with the actual position of the Rulers of Indian States **vis-a-vis** the Political Department of the Government of India, it cannot but seem utterly unlikely that the required number of them can resist the influence of the British Government of India, if once the latter have made up their mind that the States shall join the Federation in the required proportion at least. The smaller States have, indeed, neither the magnitude of interests to protect which would justify them in offering a stiff resistance; nor weight enough of their own to succeed in doing so, if they should be advised to demur to Federating. And, in general, the States afford too good a foil to their own pretensions of Liberal Government; are likely to serve as too efficient checks or brakes upon the popular elements coming from the British Indian Provinces; and are expected to prove too rich preserves, for the British Imperialists not to strain every nerve to bribe, induce or stampede the necessary number of States to accede to the Federation,—on the former's own terms.

especially if the States do not accept the Federation; or if the requisite number of them do not do so, within a reasonable time; or if they insist upon impossible or unreasonable conditions.

Provision on the Transition Period

(4) Part XIII of the Act of 1935, Sections 312-319, both inclusive, contains what are described as transitional provisions, intended, not for the emergency mentioned above, but for the period* which must necessarily elapse between the coming into operation of the portions of the Act relating to Provincial Autonomy, and the establishment of the Federation, under Section 5. These 8 sections keep in tact, *mutatis mutandis*, the constitution under the Act of 1919, in so far as the Central authority is concerned. We shall notice these provisions more fully in their appropriate place, later on in this volume; but here it is important to point out: (i) that, by Section 313 (3):—

> "References to the provisions of this Act for the time being in force to the Governor-General and the Federal Government shall, except as respects matters with respect to which the Governor-General is required by the said provisions to act in his discretion, be construed as references to the Governor-General in Council, and any reference to the Federation, except where the reference is to the establishment of the Federation, shall be construed as a reference to British India, the Governor-General-in-Council, or the Governor-General, as the circumstances and the context may require."

Dualism in Governmental Machinery during the Transition

(5) With very little modification in essential particulars, the authority and powers of the Indian Le-

*Section 312:—"The Provisions of this Part of this Act shall apply with respect to the period elapsing between the commencement of Part III of this Act and the establishment of the Federation."

gislature, as established by the Act of 1919; of the Governor-General-in-Council, and of the Governor-General, of the Secretary of State,—in Council, or by himself,—have been maintained for use during the transitional period, which may extend to any length. If, by this kind of dualism in constitutional machinery, —the one designed for an essentially unitary State, the other for a Federal system,—there grows up lack of harmony in the administrative mechanism, the Act does very little to smooth away that very possible contingency. The provisions applicable in the transitional period are intended only to mark time; they are not designed specifically to promote one type of constitution for the whole of India, or the other. If Federation does not eventuate for any reason the present form of the Government of India will presumably continue indefinitely. If Federation is rendered abortive because of the unworkability of the system of Provincial Autonomy over the larger part of British India; or because the Constitution in the Provinces has to be suspended even before the Federation is brought into being, the situation then created is provided for even less satisfactorily than the former contingency.

The States are acceding to a Federation, which, consists, on the one hand, of a number of autonomous units; and on the other of themselves. They are not federating with the whole of British India, no matter under what form of government the territories spoken of in Section 2 of the Act may be for the time being.*

*The language of Section 5 read together with Part III of the Act, is not very helpful on this point. The States can perfectly reasonably refuse to execute their Instruments of Accession, so long as any of the Governors' Provinces is without the Constitution laid down for it in this Act. It is doubtful, if, having executed an Instrument which is accepted by the King-EEmperor, they can resile from the Association thus formed.

If, however, the autonomous units are without any autonomy; if the Constitution assuring them a degree of autonomy, however illusory, is abrogated or suspended, would the States have any right to urge that they cannot be called upon to join such a system? Would they be entitled to urge that the first requisite of a Federation, as contemplated in the Act of 1935, is lacking, under the contingency mentioned above? As one reads Sections 5 and 6, and the Instrument of Accession to be executed thereunder, one finds it difficult to hold that the States have any say in the matter. They are entitled to consider their own position; and free to execute the Instrument of Accession, with such conditions or reservations as they deem to be necessary for safeguarding their own interests. But they are not entitled, under the provisions of the Act, to scrutinise the constitution of their fellow members in the future Federation of all India. Hence, the States, by executing the Instruments of Accession in a hurry,—and before any experience has been gained of the actual working of Autonomy and Responsible Government in the Provinces,—may be committing themselves to a position, from which there would be no easy withdrawal once the commitment has been made. However much British Imperialism may, for its own reasons, be anxious to secure the necessary accession of the States, need the latter allow themselves to be hurried into such a union, even while the fate of the Constitution in some of the most important of their future associates in the Federation hangs perilously in the balance?

Proclamation not without Address from Parliament

(6) The Royal Proclamation establishing the Federation may, it must further be observed, be issued

only upon an address to that effect from either House of the British Parliament. The intervention of Parliament may prove to be a mere formality; or it may be fraught with serious complications, either because of the difficulties discovered in the actual working of autonomous government in the Provinces; or because of vicissitudes of Party politics in Britain herself. India is conventionally regarded as being outside Party politics in Britain. That may not be quite a very accurate description of the state of affairs; but it is certainly true that among British politicians such an abysmal ignorance prevails regarding the Indian problem, that, one might well say, there are no Parties regarding India. A few vocal elements alone form the British public opinion regarding India, and the average politician simply joins in the refrain. Unforeseen development in the European situation may quite possibly affect the balance of Parties in the British Parliament; and, in that event, the advent of Federation, as planned in the Act of 1935, may be seriously affected.

Union Federation—an indissoluble Union

(7) It has been already pointed out that the word " united " used in Section 5 (1) has a significance, which is apt to be underestimated by those whose interest it may be to regard the union thus created as a loose bond to be adjusted or abandoned at will. The union formed, or created, by or under this section is organic, permanent, and indissoluble. If the parties to the Union wished to dissolve it; and even though the expression " Indissoluble Union " is not used anywhere in this Act, as it has been used in the Preamble to the

Commonwealth of Australia Act,* they have no power to do so. So far as the British Indian Provinces are concerned, the question can, of course, never arise, since they have been "united in a Federation under the Crown" by this Act, and without any exercise of volition in the matter by themselves. In the case of the Federating States, there is seemingly a deliberate choice on their part. But once they have chosen solemnly to be "united" in the Federation of India; and their choice has been accepted and acted upon by the King-Emperor, there is no possibility even for the States to dissolve the Union, or withdraw from it. In other words there is no right of secession even for the States, as the Act stands to-day. All the provisions regarding unforeseen emergencies or deadlocks, which might lead to the suspension of the entire Constitution in British India, would not afford ground to the Federated units to terminate their union, once it has been duly effected.† In the absence of an express right of secession reserved to any of the component units of the Federation, the Union will be considered and interpreted by the appropriate tribunals or authorities as **permanent, organic, indissoluble.** The rejection by Parliament of the petition of Western Australia for withdrawing from the Commonwealth of Australia but too clearly shows this.‡ Even the British Commonwealth of Nations, which is not united *inter se* by the same close, formal, constitutional

*Says, Sir T. B. Sapru:—

"I am definitely of the opinion that the Accession of the Indian States to the Federation is to be perpetual so long as the Federation created by the Act is in existence..........Shortly put, under the Act, the Indian States do not appear to me to possess the right of secession." Opinion, para. 8.

†cp. Section 45 particularly, and the remarks below on Section 6.

‡The Joint Parliamentary Committee, which examined the Petition not only rejected it, but even expressed the opinion that the established Constitutional conventions of the Empire put it "outside the competence" of Parliament to give effect to such a Petition. Cp. Report, J.P.C., p. x.

bonds, as the component parts of the Federations within the Empire have been held to be,—is held to be a sufficiently close Union to preclude any single, autonomous member of it from severing the ties of the Empire by unilateral action. Says Prof. A. B. Keith, after citing the Preamble to the Statute of Westminster regarding the unity of the Crown in all parts of the British Commonwealth of Nations:

> "The declaration solemnly asserts that any change in the succession must be made by common action, and it is inevitable that the conclusion should thence be derived that the union of the parts of the Commonwealth is one which cannot be dissolved by unilateral action. This was the sense given to the proposed clause when it was accepted by the Conference of 1929 by General Smuts, who naturally insisted that the intention of the Preamble was to negative the idea of the right of any part of the Commonwealth to sever itself from the rest, save as the result of common assent.*

True, both in the Union of South Africa and in the Irish Free State, this interpretation of the situation created by the Statute of Westminster has been questioned; and the Imperial Conference of 1930 took note of the assertion regarding a right of unilateral secession, urged by General Smuts. But it has done no more; and the law stands as it was passed in 1931. Under that law, and under the respective Constitutions of the several Dominions, eminent jurists have held, that it would be competent for the King to disallow an Act of secession passed by a Dominion Legislature, as being *ultra vires*.† If the admittedly autonomous and even

*cp. Keith, Constitutional Law of the British Dominions, p. 59.

†cp., Keith, Op. cit., p. 69. The same authority observes, indeed "what is obvious and is never denied is that, if any Dominion should really decide to sever itself from the Empire, it would not be held proper by the other parts of the Empire to seek to prevent it from doing so by the application of armed force." (p. 60).

"Sovereign" Dominions cannot, off their own bat, sever the ties of the Empire; if even where the States composing a Dominion Federation had full autonomy before the Federation came into being have not been permitted to dissolve the Federation by unilaterial action of their own, it is clear beyond dispute that the Union created by the Act of 1935 is impossible to rupture or terminate by any Act of a Federated State. The opinion of Mr. J. H. Morgan, K.C., constitutional adviser to the Chamber of Princes, may accordingly be accepted without hesitation that:

> "The Union provided for by the Act is, in the absence of any right of secession, an organic union and indissoluble."*

This aspect of the question has been considered at such length at this stage, partly as a sort of caviat against those who, for their own ends, would misrepresent the nature of the bond to be created by this Federation; and partly also as a warning to the Princes, who expect to find in the Federation a strengthening of their own autocratic position by the elimination of control from the Indian Political Department, and a prospect of access of real power and influence in the Government of India as a whole by their assured share in the Federal Legislature, and perhaps in the Federal Executive too.

Re-action upon States Sovereignty

(8) As an inevitable consequence of this indissoluble and permanent union, the sovereignty of the States, or their local autonomy, must be taken to be considerably diminished, and radically altered. Of this, perhaps, it would be more convenient to speak when

*cp. Opinion, para. 8, dated 17th February, 1937.

considering the *modus operandi* for the accession of the States. Here it may be added, that since no "purpose" has been,—or could have been,—laid down for effecting this Union, it may be presumed that the intention of the Legislature was to make a United State of India, under a single, homogeneous Government, though subject to the autonomous position of the component units, as defined by the same Act. Since there is no Preamble to the Act, its intention may, no doubt, be difficult to read in the terms of the Act. But the terms of the Act themselves indicate clearly that *unifying spirit*, which, once given effect to, will not be restrained, however much the Federating States might find themselves denied their local sovereignty or autonomy under the irresistible operation of constitutional conventions, and the unavoidable canons of judicial interpretation in such cases.

II Instruments of Accession to the Federation

Let us, next, consider the nature and purport of Instruments of Accession to the Federation. The governing Section of the Act is 6, the text of which is appended below. Before we proceed to consider the legal forms laid down in this connection, it would be worth while remarking, that it was on the phraseology of this Section that the greatest difference of opinion occurred between the sponsors of the Federation in the British Government, and the spokesmen of the Indian States. The clause, as originally framed, made the Federal system provided for in this Act applicable, by a declaration of the Ruler, to his State as well as to his subjects. But to this wording the leading Princes raised almost irresistible objection, with the result that, the term "subjects" was dropped from the

Section in its final form.* The diminution, however, of the Ruler's sovereignty, implied in the act of acceding to the Federation, was in no way avoided by this verbal alteration. Because there is no right of sµces-sion, once the federating has been accomplished; and because the executive as well as the Legislative authority entrusted, under the Act, to the Federal organs are, in all material respects, Sovereign and overriding, those required to advise the Princes in regard to this problem of federating, have opined: " That Sovereignty" (*i.e.*, the local Sovereignty of the Federating States) "is very considerably 'impaired', and wholly, transformed."†

*British Indian opinion seems to have been strangely silent on this Section.

†cp. J. H. Morgan, K.C., **Op. Cit.** para. 6 **et seq.** See also Prof. A. B. Keith: "A Constitutional History of India 1600-1935, p. 311:

> "The position of the States raised serious objections on the part of the Princes, who were most anxious to maintain that their acceptance of Federation must not be treated as if they were subject to the Legislative Authority of Parliament. The sixth clause of the Bill as introduced provided that a Ruler must accept the Act as applicable to himself and his subjects, specifying in his Instrument of Accession the subjects on which the Federation was to have power to legislate for the State, and specifying any condition to which his accession was to be subject. The Princes seem to have desired to establish the point that the Act should be in force in each State solely by Authority of the Instrument of Accession. Obviously, if there were any substance in the view of the princes, it was impossible to give effect to it, and the position was dealt with merely by verbal changes, and the clause as altered provides that a Ruler "accedes to the Federation as established by this Act" instead of accepting the Act. It may be doubted if the position of the Princes is in any way improved by the change of phrase.............. Government declined to accept the suggestion that in the case of suspension (of the Constitution under Section 45) any State should have the right to secede from the Federation, and it equally declined to undertake to define and limit the paramount powers as an inducement to the States to accept Federation." (**Op. Cit.**, p. 311-12.)

On the other hand, Sir T. B. Sapru, in his Opinion already quoted says:—

> "I do not think that the Sovereignty of the States is at all affected by this Act, except so far as the States voluntarily concede certain powers or functions under Section 6. On the contrary it seems to me that the Draft Instrument of Accession reinforces sovereignty in the most explicit manner. I would particularly refer to Clauses 6 and 7 of the Draft Instrument of Accession." (Opinion, para. 16, p. 10.)

In this section of this Chapter, we shall notice:—

(a) the terms of Section 6, analysing them and examining them more particularly with reference to accession of the States, and the formation of a Federation;

(b) the conditions and reservations possible to introduce in the Instrument of Accession, bearing in mind the nature and purpose of the Instrument; scrutiny of the Draft Instrument, and review of the comments and alternative draft suggested by the States.

(c) summing up the net result achieved by the execution of the Instrument of Accession, and its acceptance by the Crown.

6.—(1) A State shall be deemed to have acceded to the Federation if His Majesty has signified his acceptance of an Instrument of Accession executed by the Ruler thereof, whereby the Ruler for himself, his heirs and successors—

(a) declares that he accedes to the Federation as established under this Act, with the intent that His Majesty the King, the Governor-General of India, the Federal Legislature, the Federal Court and any other Federal authority established for the purposes of the Federation shall, by virtue of his Instrument of Accession, but subject always to the terms thereof, and for the purposes only of the Federation, exercise in relation to his State such functions as may be vested in them by or under this Act; and

(b) assumes the obligation of ensuring that due effect is given within his State to the provisions of this Act so far as they are applicable therein by virtue of his Instrument of Accession:

Provided that an Instrument of Accession may be executed conditionally on the establishment of the Federation on or before a specified date, and in that case the State shall not be deemed to have acceded to the Federation if the Federation is not established until after that date.

(2) An Instrument of Accession shall specify the matters which the Ruler accepts as matters with respect to which the Federal Legislature may make laws for his State,

and the limitations, if any, to which the power of the Federal Legislature to make laws for his State, and the exercise of the executive authority of the Federation in his State, are respectively to be subject.

(3) A Ruler may by a supplementary Instrument executed by him and accepted by His Majesty, vary the Instrument of Accession of his State by extending the functions which by virtue of that Instrument are exercisable by His Majesty or by any Federal authority in relation to his State.

(4) Nothing in this section shall be construed as requiring His Majesty to accept an Instrument of Accession or supplementary Instrument unless he considers it proper so to do, or as empowering His Majesty to accept any such Instrument if it appears to him that the terms thereof are inconsistent with the scheme of Federation embodied in this Act:

Provided that after the establishment of the Federation, if any Instrument has in fact been accepted by His Majesty, the validity of that Instrument or of any of its provisions shall not be called in question and the provisions of this Act shall, in relation to the State, have effect subject to the provisions of the Instrument.

(5) It shall be a term of every Instrument of Accession that the provisions of this Act mentioned in the second schedule thereto may, without affecting the accession of the State, be amended by or by authority of Parliament, but no such amendment shall, unless it is accepted by the Ruler in a supplementary Instrument, be construed as extending the functions which by virtue of the Instrument are exercisable by His Majesty or any Federal authority in relation to the State.

(6) An Instrument of Accession or supplementary Instrument shall not be valid unless it is executed by the Ruler himself, but, subject as aforesaid, references in this Act to the Ruler of a State include references to any persons for the time being exercising the powers of the Ruler of the State whether by reason of the Ruler's minority or for any other reason.

(7) After the establishment of the Federation, the request of a Ruler that his State may be admitted to the Federation shall be transmitted to His Majesty through the Governor-General, and after the expiration of twenty years from the establishment of the Federation, the Governor-General shall not transmit to His Majesty any such request until there has been presented to him by each

Chamber of the Federal Legislature, for submission to His Majesty, an address praying that His Majesty may be pleased to admit the State into the Federation.

(8) In this Act a State which has acceded to the Federation is referred to as a Federated State, and the Instrument by virtue of which a State has so acceded, construed together with any supplementary Instrument executed under this section, is referred to as the Instrument of Accession of that State.

(9) As soon as may be after any Instrument of Accession or supplementary Instrument has been accepted by His Majesty under this section, copies of the Instrument and of His Majesty's acceptance thereof shall be laid before Parliament, and all courts shall take judicial notice of every such Instrument of Accession.

It may be remarked, at the very outset, that the actual process of federating, under this Act, is complicated to a degree. (a) There is, in the first place, the Act itself, Section 6, which is the *fons and origo* of the whole process. It does not make a Federation; but provides the indispensable machinery for establishing a Federation. (b) Next, there is the Instrument of Accession for each State* which is the indispensable mechanism or device, whereby any State desiring to join the Federation can do so. (c) The Instrument, when duly executed by the required minimum number of States, —and immense time has already been devoted to negotiations for bringing about an agreement regarding the form and contents of the Instrument, its nature and purpose, the reservations and conditions possible to

*Though several States are to be combined, for purposes of representation in the Federal Legislature, under Part II of Schedule I to this Act, the Instrument of Accession shall have to be executed and accepted by and for each State severally, no matter what its size, population, wealth or history. It is also not at all clear that, under the Federation, the States are to be considered, in this respect, individually, or as groups, or as all States collectively. The presumption is in favour of individual treatment, uniformity of treatment being rather the exception, or the accident, than the rule or deliberate design.

introduce therein,—has to be accepted by His Majesty. His Majesty is in no way bound to accept any and every Instrument; and he has no power to accept any Instrument which is not compatible with the general scheme of the Act. No express conditions are laid down, fulfilling which the States desiring to accede may reasonably expect His Majesty to accept the Instrument. A Ruler who has executed his Instrument of Accession will not be allowed to resile from the terms and conditions therein contained, much less to avoid federating altogether, even though incalculable time may elapse between his executing the Instrument, and the King-Emperor signifying his acceptance of the same. The latter is free in every instance to accept or not to accept; nor is he bound to give any reason for his action. The States seeking to accede are, indeed, allowed, by a proviso under Section 6 (1) (b), to name a day, within which, if the Federation occurs, they would be held to their bond; but beyond which they may be released from their offer to join the Federation. This is a conditional offer; and if the condition is not satisfied, the offer will naturally lapse. It is, however, utterly insufficient to provide for the kind of contingency considered above.

(d) Even after the King-Emperor has signified his acceptance,—and it is not clear whether each Instrument will be severally accepted, or all of a pattern accepted *en bloc*,—the process is not ended. There remain still the two Houses of Parliament, who must each present an Address to His Majesty, praying that a Federation of All-India be established, and a Proclamation issued for that purpose, establishing the

Federation of India as from a given date. And Parliament may have its own reason to delay or suspend the advent of the Federation.

Instrument of Accession

Who can execute? Let us now scrutinise, a little more carefully, the actual terms of Section 6. Unlike British Indian Provinces, no State can be regarded as being included in or forming part of the proposed Federation of India, unless and until the Ruler thereof executes an Instrument of Accession.

The Ruler does this "for himself, his heirs and successors;" but there is no mention, throughout the Act of the people of these States. So far as the Act goes, it might seem as though 40 per cent of the area of India is occupied,—inhabited,—by only 700 odd persons, as against some 80 million souls recorded by Schedule I to this Act. as constituting the population in the States.

The Rulers are " united " in the Federation,—if and when one comes into being,— for themselves, their heirs and successors; but the Provinces of British India are united or included, neither as governments, nor as people, but simply as so many units. Should strong centrifugal tendencies develop in the Provinces, and the principle of self-determinism is given its maximum scope; or, should the people in the Provinces perceive the real disadvantage of becoming united with such essential incompatibles as the Rulers of the Indian States, the situation will have its own elements of danger that the framers of this Constitution do not seem to have at all perceived.

The Instrument must, to be valid, be executed by the Ruler, *de jure* as well as *de facto*. A minor Ruler, or President of a Regency Council, or Council of Administration during the minority, incapacity, or absence of a given Ruler, will not be entitled to execute such an Instrument, or any supplement to the same. Clause (6) of this Section expressly excludes all substitutes for *de facto* and *de jure* Ruler from executing an Instrument, of accession* or any variant thereof. This recognises the sole right of the Ruler to make binding and perpetual engagements for his State, to dispose of his State as though it was his private estate. We can appreciate the motive which prompted the British Parliament to accord such a supreme authority to the Ruler personally regarding his State and the people therein. This very Act appears to be aware of a necessary distinction between the Ruler's public capacity as Ruler, and his individual personality.† But yet, in this matter of supreme importance, not only is no distinction made between the public and private personality of the Ruler; but the Ruler for the time being in charge of a State,—provided he is of full legal capacity, and personally entitled to be and is the Ruler of the State,—can sign away all the authority and possibilities of the State, for himself, his heirs and successors, and for all time to come. If ever an important Indian State develops real self-governing institutions, the responsible Government in that State must bear this obligation without any right to scrutinise. This is an aspect of the matter which those responsible for this clause do

*Contrast this with Section 311 which defines "Ruler" as follows:— "Ruler in relation to a State means the Prince, Chief or other person recognised by His Majesty as the Ruler of the State."

†See Section 155. See also the Sea Customs Act, Section 23: or the Income-tax Act, Section 60.

not seem to have taken adequately into account. Not only are the people of the State not at all mentioned; there is no reference whatsoever to the Constitutional Government in a State. The Act, therefore, seems to contemplate an indefinite continuance of purely personal rule in these regions. If any Ruler is enlightened enough to set up, of his own authority, a regular Constitutional Government "for himself, his heirs and successors" for all time to come under this Act, the Federal Government, or the Governor-General need not recognise such a Government in any State at all; and the latter might insist upon all dealings being carried on with the Ruler personally, so far as federating is concerned.

III. Ingredients of the Instrument

When a Ruler executes his Instrument of Accession to a (prospective) Federation, he declares:

(1) That he accedes to the Federation as established under this Act. Should the form and nature of the Federal system, or structure,—as established by this Act,—be materially changed, even by an amending Act of Parliament, would the States acceding to the Federation as established under this Act, be automatically released from their bond, and their Federation dissolved? Will a new Instrument of Accession, under the altered system be necessary? These questions cannot be asked without considering fully the bearings of Sections 308 and 45 of this Act; and even then, the answer may not be satisfying in all particulars.

Clause (5) of Section 6 permits Parliament to make amendments in certain portions of this Act, indicated in Schedule II, which, if and when made, would not entitle the Federated States to claim that their accession is affected thereby. Such a stipulation would be definitely included in every Instrument. But even if the accession is affected, the Federation does not become necessarily dissoluble thereby.

Section 45 relates to the suspension of the whole system of Government under the Act of 1935, "if at any time the Governor-General is satisfied that a situation has arisen in which the government of the Federation cannot be carried on in accordance with the provisions of this Act." Clause (4) of that Section says:—

> "If at any time the government of the Federation has for a continuous period of three years been carried on under and by virtue of a Proclamation issued under this section, then, at the expiration of that period, the Proclamation shall cease to have effect and the government of the Federation shall be carried on in accordance with the other provisions of this Act, subject to any amendment thereof which Parliament may deem it necessary to make, but nothing in this sub-section shall be construed as extending the power of Parliament to make amendments in this Act without affecting the accession of a State.

Let us understand the full significance of this extraordinary provision.

(a) During the three years that the government of the Federation may be carried on under a Proclamation issued by the Governor-General, without even the forms of constitutional or responsible government being necessary to maintain, the States would have no right to demur to the altered conditions of the Federation. They joined a system, in which their fellow-members of the Federation, *viz.*, at least the so-called Governors' Provinces, were autonomous internally, and equal *inter se*. Should the **autonomy of these Provinces be destroyed, as is not** impossible to conceive,—even apart from Section 93 permitting the suspension of the Constitution in a Province by a Governor's Proclamation,*—the States are not entitled, *ipso facto* this state of affairs, to demand a termination of their association in the Federation with such deformed units as fellow members. But even if the entire Federal system of constitutional government is abolished, or suspended, for a period of three years, the Federated States cannot object.

(b) It has been seriously suggested, by at least one learned Constitutional lawyer, that, by means of "secret" instructions to the Governor-General, the period of Proclamation rule can be extended indefinitely, by withdrawing an existing Proclamation just before 3 years expired, and issuing a new one to last for another 3 years minus a day. In that way the government of the Federation can be carried on indefinitely without any Constitution, without any amendment by Parliament, and at the same time without any right or opportunity to the States to terminate their association in a system which is so completely defunct.†

(c) Even if we do not take such an uncharitable view of British maxims of Empire Government, the fact remains that the section offers no

*cp., Schedule II to this Act, wherein practically all the important elements of Constitutional Government are allowed to be amended by Parliament "without affecting the Accession of a State."

†cp., Para 61 of the Opinion of J. H. Morgan, K.C.:—

"If Section 45 did give a right of secession at the end of the three years' period of the contemplated dictatorship, the Secretary of State for India would be able to defeat the apprehended secession of the States by instructing the Governor-General to withdraw the Proclamation of Emergency just before the termination of the statutory period of three years, and then, after the lapse of one of two months, issuing a new Proclamation. In this way, the whole of India, including the Federated States, might, subject to the necessary resolutions being passed by Parliament, be subject indefinitely to the dictatorial power of the Governor-General."

safeguard to the States feeling aggrieved at the suspension of the Constitution throughout the Federation, and termination of Responsible Government at the centre.* The representatives of the Princes at the Round Table Conference had pinned their faith entirely to the existence of a Responsible Government at the centre in India, without which they saw no advantage in federating. But the Act establishes no necessary connection between the continuance of the Federation and the maintenance of Responsible Government. This Section 45 (4) as well as Section 6 (5) only speak of *affecting* the accession of the States. But *affecting* does not mean "terminating", especially as, in the terms of the Act, the accession of any State to the Federation is not in any way conditional upon the maintenance of responsible government in the Federation. The Princes may be supposed to be indifferent to the forms of constitutional government in modern democracies. But, in this case, their own strong safeguard, especially against a dictatorial authority in the Governor-General, is to be found in a responsible and constitutional government being maintained at the centre. If they are denied that safeguard, the States intending to federate may well ponder if Federation under such circumstances would be worth their while.

(d) Observe, also, that Section 45 (4) expressly bars *any extension* of Parliament's authority to make amendments in the constitution of India; it says nothing about changes made in virtue of the existing authority of Parliament to do so under Section 6 (5) Schedule II. Section 2 of this Act, and the practice

*So far as the Provinces are concerned, there is, of course, [illegible] a shadow of the right to reconsider their union in a Federation with some units where the Constitution is suspended, and others who have no Constitution at all.

governing this whole legislation, affords a margin of power and authority to Parliament to legislate **for any part of India, as well as for the whole of India,** which under circumstances like those contemplated in Section 45 or in Section 6, may prove, on the British side, more than ample for any emergency, and, on the side of the Indian States, more than proportionately embarrassing.

(e) The fact, again, that by explicit, statutory declaration under Section 6 (1) (a), the States " accede to the Federation as established under this Act," will not permit them to plead that the operation of a Proclamation Regime, under Section 45, for 3 years has changed the Federation as established by this Act, since Section 45 is also part of the same Act. The States must be presumed when they execute the Instrument of Accession to know its meaning and understand its implications.

Purpose of Federating

(ii) The intent or purpose of this accession is that the various Federal authorities, enumerated in clause (a) of sub-section (1) should exercise in relation to the State such functions as may be vested in them by or under this Act. The authority, it is true, is to be exercised only in virtue of the Instrument of Accession, subject to the terms and conditions laid down in the Instrument, and for the purpose only of the Federation. But all those reservations and limitations do not abate by an iota the plenary powers conferred upon the Federal authorities in virtue of this clause. There are many sections of this Act, especially those in connection with Federal finance and Federal judiciary,—not to mention currency, transport, communications or defence,—which give Federal Legislature plenary powers to legislate for the entire Federation. The effects of these upon the local autonomy or sovereignty of the State, and upon the authority of its Ruler within the State, cannot be fully foreseen to-day, but is impossible to be exaggerated in its prejudicial character. Even Section 8 (2) does not avail the States, once they have federated, to restrict or avoid the exercise of Federal authority even within their own territories. For that Section merely says:—

> "8 (2)—The executive authority of the Ruler of a Federated State shall, notwithstanding anything in this section, continue to be exercisable in that State with respect to matters with respect to which the Federal Legislature has power to make laws for that State except in so far as the executive authority of the Federation becomes exercisable in the State to the exclusion of the executive authority of the Ruler by virtue of a Federal law."

The right of the Federal Government to exercise Federal executive authority in order to give effect to Federal law, even in Federated States, is bound to be so universal and all-embracing, that the State seeking protection for its Ruler's authority within the State, in virtue of this provision, is bound to be severely disappointed and speedily disillusioned. The analogy of decided cases from Australia as well as from Canada makes it amply clear that the powers of the Federal Legislature, within the field assigned to it, will be deemed to be absolute; and the necessity to exercise Federal executive authority to give effect to the Federal laws will be merely corollary.*

The exercise of Federal executive authority outside the State limits, but so as vitally to affect the authority of the Ruler within the State, cannot of course be precluded by the Instrument of Accession.

(3) The States executing the Instrument of Accession must assume the full obligation to ensure that due effect shall be given within the State to this Act, so far as it applies there. The application of this Act may be regulated by the Instrument of Accession, in some specific manner. But, read in the light of

*cp., the judgment of the Privy Council in In re-Air Navigation Act (1936) as also The State of New South Wales vs. the Commonwealth and others.

Section 122 (1), this provision becomes useless, at least in so far as it may be intended or relied upon to safeguard the executive authority of the Ruler of a State within his State. Says Section 122 (1):—

> **"The executive authority of every Province and Federated State shall be so exercised as to secure respect for the laws of the Federal Legislature which apply in that Province or State."**

" Hence, even if a given Federal law, applicable to a Federated State, should prove incompatible with the local law on the same subject " within the State, the Federal law will prevail.*

Reservations in the Instrument of Accession

(4) Sub-section (2) of Section 6 allows the Ruler of a State intending to federate to " specify matters which the Ruler accepts as matters with respect to which the Federal Legislature may make laws for his State." We shall review, briefly, the subjects on which the Instrument may possibly make such specification, with special reference to the reaction of such specification upon the Treaty rights and other position of the State concerned. Here let it be added that, besides specifying these matters, the Instrument may introduce limitations on the Legislative authority of the Federal Legislature, as applied to the State; and also as regards the exercise of the executive authority. How far these limitations or reservations, sought by the Ruler while executing the Instrument of Accession, will be accepted by the British Government of India; how far, if accepted, they would hold valid in law when cases concerning those come up for judgment before the appropriate tribunal; and how far, even if they hold valid, they would serve the turn of the Rulers insisting upon such safeguards, are questions impossible to answer satisfactorily at present.

Variation of Instrument

(5) The Ruler is entitled to make a supplementary Instrument varying the terms and conditions of the

---

*cp., Section 107 (3).

original one. But the variation can only be one-sided, *i.e.*, it can only *extend*, not *restrict*, "the functions which by virtue of that Instrument are exercisable by His Majesty or any Federal authority in relation to his State." This emphasises, were further proof necessary, the utterly one-sided character of the arrangement contemplated under this Act.*

The bond created can only be drawn closer, never relaxed. And once the functions of any Federal authority are extended by a supplementary Instrument, because of a special emergency like the minority or incapacity of a Ruler, the extension cannot be negatived or neutralised when that emergency has passed. The Federation is thus no help to a State in temporary difficulties; but always an incubus on every State that has federated, if it desires to maintain in tact its Ruler's authority or local autonomy. In this respect the States are at a marked disadvantage compared to the Provinces in the Federation; for the list of Provincial subjects is fixed by the Act, and not capable of extension in favour of the Federation as is the case with the States.

Free Hand to the King-Emperor

(6) The King is not bound to accept any Instrument. The Section clearly lays down:—

> "Nothing in this section shall be construed as requiring His Majesty to accept any Instrument of Accession or supplementary Instrument, unless he considers it proper so to do, or as empowering His Majesty to accept any such Instrument if it appears to him that the terms thereof are inconsistent with the scheme of Federation embodied in this Act."†

While the King is not *obliged* to accept every Instrument, he is not *entitled* to accept an Instrument which does not conform to the general lines of the Federation laid down in this Act. This means that the

*cp., Section 6 (3).

†Section 6 (4).

Instruments will all have to conform to a common mould to a large degree. The States have, among themselves, a variety of Treaty rights and other engagements *vis-a-vis* the Central Indian Government. It is but natural that if and when they decide to federate, they might desire each to safeguard and preserve as many of these rights as possible. But the authors of this Act,—of this whole scheme,—have made no secret of their desire that there must be some uniformity, otherwise Federation would be useless to establish, and impossible to work if established. Says the Report of the Joint Select Committee of Parliament, who considered this measure in its Bill form:—

> "It would, we think, be very desirable that the Instrument of Accession should **in all cases be in the same form,** though we recognise that the list of subjects accepted by the Ruler as Federal may not be identical in the case of every State".

After giving some highly sophisticated reasons for this view, the Committee add:—

> **"We do not need to say that the accession of all States to the Federation will be welcome; but there can be no obligation on the Crown to accept an accession, where the exceptions or reservations sought to be made by Ruler are such as to make the accession illusory or merely colourable."***

Nothing can be a clearer notice to the States than this that, whatever the past relations between any State and the Government of India, in future they must all conform to a common pattern. And in so far as the special rights, privileges or immunities enjoyed by any State under treaty, convention, usage or precedent, are incompatible with the Federal system, there is no legal means provided for safeguarding and preserving the same under the Federation, especially so far as the Instrument is concerned.

*Page 156. Op. Cit.

In this desire for uniformity of the Instruments, the more far-sighted of the Princes and their advisers perceive a negation of their individuality as integral political units. This has induced them to suggest conditions and reservations, stipulations and limitations,—legal as well as fiscal, legislative as well as executive,—that are responsible for protracting the negotiations with the Princes to such a length.* These demands have, hitherto, been made for the Princes as a class, since only such collective demands, or class requirements, stand the slightest chance of being at all considered or accepted. That, however, does not mean that individual States have not, each, their own special interests or position to safeguard; or even that, within the Princes as a class, there are not groups who have their interests differing from those of other groups in material particulars.† When each particular State considers its own separate Instrument, many more difficulties would emerge than seem evident for the

*The following extracts from a newspaper report illustrate the apprehensions voiced in the text:—

"The 'Statesman' understands that the Chamber of Princes has put up four new stipulations for incorporation in the Instrument of Accession.

These stipulations are: that Federation shall not have the right to introduce or enforce conscription or any other form of compulsory military service in the States.

The present position as regards taking of censuses in the States shall be maintained and administration relating thereto shall be carried out by States as heretofore.

If the States should so desire, it should be provided that no railway be constructed within their territory except with their consent.

The fourth stipulation is regarding the judicial and fiscal rights of States, which are anxious that these rights should not be adversely affected."

†Thus the interest of the so-called Maritime States naturally differ essentially from those of the Inland States in the matter of Customs Revenue; or of the Salt and Opium producing States from those producing minerals like iron. States are still woefully backward, industrially; but, inter se, there are considerable differences in the level of economic development attained by each State, and, still more, in the possibilities for intensive development in each considerable State. These last are likely to be in the gravest conflict with the Federal Government.

moment, while the draft is still being considered by the Princes collectively as an Order. Of course, it is possible, the supreme domination of the Government of India and their Political Department may cajole, corrupt, or coerce the majority of the Princes into an irretrievable acceptance of the conditions offered them; and so the real, inherent difficulties of a Federal Government in India would not be apparent until after the Federation has been formed.

States and Constitution Amendment

(7) We have already referred to the provision of this section,—as also of Section 45 (4) connected herewith—whereby Parliament is entitled (and authorised) to make amendments in parts of this Act specified in Schedule II "without affecting the accession of the States."* On the whole, it may be said that the portions in which Parliament has thus reserved its authority expressly to make amendments in the present Constitution are of exclusively British Indian importance. But, inasmuch as, under a Federal system, the Federated States and the British Provinces will have to live in a common mould, changes made in the structure and function of the latter cannot but have their profound reactions upon the former. As it is, the fact that all the Provinces united in the Federation will have some sort of responsible, popular government, while their colleagues from the Federated States will be under undisguised autocracy, is bound to have its repercussion, causing grave friction or misunderstanding between the two sets of the Federal units almost from the outset. But even if we overlook this inherent incompatibility, we cannot ignore altogether the reaction upon the States particularly of constitutional changes of a radical nature in the British portion of the Federation. The fact that, under Section 6 (5) and Section 45 (4) those changes in the governmental machinery of the Federation, or its important parts,

* See Appendix II to this Chapter.

will not affect the accession of the States, will render the amending authortiy free from any restraint in proposing and effecting amendments within the permitted field.

On the other hand, if that authority constitutes itself the guardian and protector of the States, and, as such, declines to entertain proposals for amendment which the rest of the country might be agreed upon, it would imperil the very foundations of the system on which this Constitution rests. The States cannot be allowed, merely because they are part of the Federation, to impose a veto on such constitutional progress.

Nor do we suggest that the peoples in the Indian States have no right to political progress, constitutional government, or popular institutions, simply because the British Imperial Government have chosen, in this Act, to recognise only some 700 odd Rulers as the spokesmen of 80 millions of peoples in the Indian States. India, if she is to work out her destiny, must be re-united in a homogeneous system of government, acceptable to the largest majority of her people. If that ideal is to be achieved consistently with democratic forms, some sort of Federal arrangement is inevitable. But that does not mean that the system as envisaged in the Act of 1935 meets with our approval.

Accession after Proclamation of Federation

(8) Clause (7) of this section provides that, even *after* the Federation has been established, States can accede who have not acceded from the beginning. But the period for such subsequent accession is limited to 20 years. During this period of 20 years after the establishment of the Federation, any State wishing to join can request the Governor-General to be admitted to the Federation; and this request shall be transmitted by that officer to His Majesty, whose acceptance (or otherwise) will

then follow the usual course. After that period has elapsed, no such request for admittance to the Federation is to be transmitted by the Governor-General unless an address is presented, for submission to the King-Emperor, by each House of the Federal Legislature, praying that the request may be granted by His Majesty. Those who do not elect to join the new system in the first flush have thus 20 years to wait and watch the fruits. It is unlikely that the delay would cost the hesitant anything materially; and it is possible that the delay may actually result in some material benefit, if only in a negative shape,—especially if, by developments in British India alone, the new Constitution is rendered abortive.

Instrument and Courts

(9) The Instrument, once duly executed and accepted, must be taken cognisance of by the Courts concerned. This means that the terms and conditions of the State's union will be interpreted by the Federal Court; and, when pronounced upon by that body, will be enforced by the Federal executive. There will be no room for negotiation, influence, or intrigue between the Indian Political Department and the State concerned, as has been the case so far. For the larger, wealthier or more influential States, this may not prove quite a blessing, even apart from the implication of this practice that the States would be placed, in this respect, in the position of ordinary citizens of British India. But the right to have disputes between the Government of India and a given State tried by a judicial tribunal, in stead of having one of the parties in the dispute acting also as judge in the dispute, will be welcomed by the large mass of the smaller states. Treaties, except in so far as expressly or by implication modified by the Instrument, will of course, not be affected by this procedure.

The Instrument—not a Treaty

Having considered the salient characteristics of the Instrument of Accession, let us now attempt to answer the question: What is the Instrument itself, legally considered? Is it a **Treaty** between equal and Sovereign States? Clearly, no. The Indian States have no Sovereignty in the international sense. The Dominion of Canada has more international existence than the State of Hyderabad; for while the former can receive and send out diplomatic agents, apart from those of the British Government, and negotiate and conclude Treaties, the latter cannot. India is no doubt a member, in her own right, of the League of Nations; and the Covenant has been signed on her behalf by the representatives of the Indian Princes as well as peoples. The Princes and peoples of India have, since 1917, been represented separately at the British Imperial Conferences. But these do not confer the status of a Sovereign State upon India collectively,—much less upon the Princes of India, still less upon individual Indian States, however considerable in themselves. The Instrument of Accession to the Federation of India under the British Crown is thus no better than a petition for a privilege, an aspiration for an advantage, which the Sovereign overlord of all these States, the British King, may be graciously pleased to grant or refuse.*

The Instrument of Accession not being a Treaty is, in one aspect of that document, to the advantage of the States. A Treaty between Sovereign States is outside the jurisdiction of local Courts of either party to be interpreted, though legislation enacted in accord-

*Cp. **Inter alia**, the Opinion of Mr. J. H. Morgan, Section V; preface to the Hyderabad Memorandum (Confidential).

ance with the Treaty will be so interpreted and enforced. If this Instrument were regarded as a Treaty, the States would have no means to seek an impartial and authoritative interpretation of its terms by the proper Tribunals. They would have to rely for such interpretation on the goodwill of the British Imperial Government, as they have done in the past. Experience, however, of such interpretation by the Political Department,—which is, more frequently than not, itself a party to a dispute involving the interpretation of a Treaty,—is by no means so happy for the States that they could safely rely on the impartial and just interpretation of the rights and obligations incurred by either party under such documents.

Nor a Contract

If the Instrument is not a Treaty, as understood in International Law, it is not exactly a **contract** as between private citizens, or a deed. For its validity, as distinguished from the interpretation of its contents, cannot be questioned by any Tribunal. It is, therefore, something a little inferior to a Treaty which could be registered at Geneva, or enforced at the Hague; and something a little superior to a mere contract or deed between private citizens. **It is a legal document whose nature and contents are defined by an Act of Parliament.** The Courts will give effect to this document in the same way that they give effect to a Statute. Hence every reservation, or stipulation, which any State feels necessary to make in order to safeguard its position, will have to be inserted in the Instrument. It may even be found advisable to make a supplementary agreement, annex it to the Instrument proper as a Schedule, and incorporate it thereby with the main document, so as to secure for this supplementary agreement the same force and effect as for the original document.*

Contents of the Instrument

The Instrument must deal only with the "matters with respect to which the Federal Legislature may make laws" for the State.† Not all the matters which concern or interest an Indian State, in its relation with the Government of India; or even which interest or concern a Ruler personally, are included in the long and somewhat haphazard list of Federal Subjects for legislation, which alone can be the subject matter of the Instrument, its reservations and stipulations, conditions and limitations. Where, then, and how, could be secured those other advantages and privileges of the Rulers, their immunities, and special Treaty or other rights of the States, which are no less important to the States than the subjects listed in Schedule VII as exclusive ground for Federal legislation? How, also, is to be regulated, *vis-a-vis* the States, that field of discretionary authority vested in the Governor-General under this Constitution, which he exercises apart from the need to enforce the laws made by the Federal Legislature or any existing Indian law? What would happen to those matters of personal privilege or prestige,—the right to certain salutes, the provision for Minority Government in the States, the education of Minor Rulers, the position of members of their family, like the Heir Apparent, and the like,—to which Indian Princes attach not the least important? They are, it is true, utterly outside the scope of the Federa-

*For example see Section 125.

†Cp. Section 6 (2).

tion; and will continue to be governed by those prerogatives of Paramountcy, which have never been codified, and seldom enforced consistently. The States who accede to the Federation cannot but find that even these rights and privileges of theirs are insensibly,—but unquestionably,—affected by the mere fact of the Federation. The Instrument of Accession cannot quite aid them in safeguarding this portion of their rights and privileges; but a Supplementary Agreement,—especially with the Federal Government, and made under authority of an Act of Parliament, might be found advisable to afford as much security in this regard as the Princes can reasonably demand, and the Federal Authorities as reasonably offer,—apart, of course, from the vital consideration how far the new India of democratic consciousness and socialistic aspiration would continue to respect such rights.

IV. Form of the Instrument, and Alternative Suggested

In Appendix III to this Chapter is given the Draft Instrument of Accession issued by the Government of India, and the alternative proposed by the Indian States. It would add unduly to the size of this Chapter, were we to scrutinise each clause of the Draft Instrument, or its alternative. We shall, therefore, in this section, content ourselves with a brief review of the most important points at issue. This treatment is the more advisable, since the final form of the Instrument to be executed by each acceding Ruler has yet to be settled.

The (Draft) Instrument mentions the "purpose" of the Federation as "co-operating in the furtherance of the interests and welfare of India," which is to be achieved "by uniting in a Federation under the

Crown." The States have demurred to the inclusion of a "purpose" in a statutory document, expressed apprehension at the possible reaction of being united in a Federation upon their individuality, and suggested total deletion of a "purpose" or its modification so as to import as little of ethical, idealistic, considerations in such a legal document as possible.

They would have, likewise, a clear enunciation of the extent of powers or jurisdiction accorded by this Instrument to the Federal Authorities, and of the field left free for the Paramount authority to deal with matters not falling within the Federal field.*

They would guard clearly against sections of the Act, which, by implication, may confer legislative powers upon the Federal Legislature, thereby affect the States both legislatively and in executive matters, and so constitute a serious indirect invasion of their local sovereignty, or the authority of the Ruler. They would, therefore, by positive affirmation declare the continuance of the Ruler's Sovereignty in and over the State; and, except as provided for in the Instrument, they would reserve the unabated exercise of those rights, powers, and authority.

---

*Section 285 says:—

> "Subject in the case of a Federated State to the provisions of the Instrument of Accession of that State, nothing in this Act affects the rights and obligations of the Crown in relation to any Indian State."

This, however, is silent as to the **rights of the Ruler** under existing Treaties, etc.; nor can the mention of "obligations of the Crown" be interpreted to include all those rights of the Rulers, not mentioned expressly in this Section. These rights, again, may be affected inevitably by the mere fact of the Federation; and the States are naturally anxious to safeguard those rights even against the silent action of constitutional conventions growing in a Federation which has a written and therefore rigid Constitution. Section 2, also, refers to the exercise of the powers in connection with the functions of the Crown in relation to the Indian States; and so the Princes are anxious to see clearly stated and provided for that the relations of the Ruler and the Crown are separate and distinct from their relations with the Federation, and without interference by the Federal Authorities.

The distinction between Federal powers and Paramount powers, especially as exercised by the Governor-General and the Viceroy, in the dual personality of that combined office, is particularly important to the States; and as such they stress, in the wording of the Instrument, everything that tends to maintain and emphasise that distinction. With that object in view, they desire particularly to convert the Resident in the States to be purely and simply an agent of the Viceroy, as representing the Crown in its relations with the States, and dispense with the present Political Agent, as representing the Federal Government in the States altogether.

On the same reasoning, the States desire to exclude, from the jurisdiction of the Federal Court, the right to interpret Treaties. They naturally desire to preserve their Treaty rights, even in matters affected by the Federation, inside as well as outside the State, the former by appropriate limitations in the items accepted for Federation, the latter by a specific Schedule attached to the Instrument setting out the Treaty rights which need not be touched by the Court.

Conditions & Reservations in the Instrument

As for the terms and conditions, stipulations, limitations, or reservations, subject to which the Instrument is to be executed, they relate to those subjects on which the Federal Legislature may make laws for the whole Federation, including the Federated States. If the Instrument of Accession specifies any of them as being matters on which the State in question federates, and so allows the Federal Legislature to legislate for it, it may also contain the modifications or reservations and limitations by and on behalf of the

States. Generally speaking, the States, besides being anxious to reserve their local Sovereignty, and such of the Treaty rights as are likely to be adversely affected by federating,—*e.g.*, in regard to Customs, or Currency, wherever that right is still maintained,—design their limitations to see that, neither in Legislation nor in the Executive government following such legislation, the internal administration of the States is affected to the prejudice of their local autonomy. The individual items would vary with the different States, as much because of the variety of Treaty rights, as because of the difference in geographic situation and economic development or possibilities between different States.

A common mould is, however, not impossible to evolve out of this variety, especially as the British Government have accepted the principle of compensation to the States for the loss of privileges, immunities, or rights.* The distinction sought to be maintained by the States throughout this section of the Federal scheme, between what they called 'Policy and legislation' on the one hand, and 'Administration' on the other, on subjects like railways or transport facilities, is however, in the nature of things, impossible to maintain always and rigorously in units welded into a common State, however loosely knit together the several joints of that organism may be. As things stand at present, the negotiations for working out a generally acceptable Instrument of Accession, together with the various Schedules of Reservations or conditions attached, seem to cause the greatest headache to the Indian Political Department and the Ministers of the Indian States.

*Cp. Sections 147 and 149 of the Act. For General Reservations, cp., the Report of the Constitutional Committee, Chamber of Princes, p. 40.

As for individual items for federating, the main differences seem to centre round: (a) financial items, like the Customs and Excise revenue, Income-tax surcharge, or Corporation Tax; (b) administrative items, like the Railways, Water-supply, Broadcasting, acquisition of land for federal purposes, etc.; (c) purely legislative matters of general policy.

On the financial side, the differences concern the fitness of making the States federating bear any portion of the obligations of the Government of India, incurred prior to the Federation, such as the Public Debt, the Pensions charge, and the Defence expenditure. If these have to be shared without question, the additional resources will also have to be provided; and, in so far as the proposed scheme of Federation takes away the sources of revenue hitherto enjoyed by the States,—*e.g.* Customs or Excise revenues,—the latter naturally demur to the suggestion. The compensation proposed to be offered under Sections 147 and 149 might not be found adequate, even if objection on ground of principle is obviated. Even the distribution of surplus proceeds of certain taxes may not do justice to the States. As this part is considered more fully in the Chapter on Federal Finance, it is unnecessary to dwell further upon it here.

Matters of administrative complication are too many to be considered in detail. They vary with the different treaties or conventions applying to the several States. The common solution of separating matters of policy from matters of administration,—of legislation from executive action,— does not seem adequate to the case, even if the solution suggested is considered just. The alternative proposals put forward by the States do not advance any radical solution of the problem, which is inherent in the nature of federations.

On matters of general policy, to be embodied in legislation, the objections raised by the States to particular items are not very considerable at this stage; but it is not unlikely that they may arise soon after the Federation may be in working order.

It is still premature to sum up the net effect of these proposals and counterproposals for federating. The first flush of the Princes' enthusiasm, which was witnessed at the opening of the First Round Table Conference, had cooled off even in the very next year. As years have passed, the grim realities are becoming more and more apparent as to the liabilities to be shouldered, and the benefits to be derived, by joining the Federation. The attempts to obtain amendments of the Act so as to maintain in tact the States' Local Sovereignty, such as it still remains, have failed. The second line of attack,—that regarding the actual Instrument of Accession and the reservations to be introduced therein,—is now in process. But, even there, the Princes are discovering everyday more and more fully the inherent weakness of their own position. Lacking in any popular support in their own territories; and torn among themselves by conflict of interest as well as clash of personality,* the Princes are unable to present throughout that united front which is indispensable if they are to obtain the least of their

*The last election to the Chancellorship of the Chamber was about as sorry an exhibition of pettiness, corruption, and intrigue among this exalted order of India's anachronisms as could be found in any popular assembly of ill-educated, but interested partisans.

demands. The essentially insupportable nature of their demands,—even where they are agreed among themselves,— in that they are entirely for the narrow, self-seeking, personal advantage of the Ruling House, rather than for the people of the State, and much less for the peoples of all the States put together collectively, has yet to be perceived. If the British Government of to-day have resisted those demands, it is not out of any regard to the long-term interests of the peoples of the Indian States, or of British India; but simply out of consideration for the interests of that microscopic class of foreign exploiters and vested interests, which are represented by the present British Government of India. When the peoples of India, in Federal organisations assembled, come into direct contact with the scheme of Federation and the Princes' Representatives or demands, the real weakness of the position would become more evident.

V. Reaction of this upon the people of India

In the preceding sections of this chapter, indications have already been given of the inevitable apprehension, which any careful student of this Constitution is bound to feel after an intensive study. The roots are rotten, the entire structure jerry-mandered, the outside dressing, varnishing, painting, mean and flimsy and revolting to a degree. No healthy growth can be expected from such roots; no reasonably happy life possible in such a structure. Throughout the protracted years that went to the gestation of this Instrument of British Imperialism, at no stage was the consent or approval of the Indian people ever sought, whether in

British India, or in the Indian States,* to strengthen the foundations, and make the countless checks and balances of this Constitution at all understood by the people, and so workable. The people in the States have been wholly ignored; and those in British India practically so, at least so far as the Federal machinery is concerned. The Constitution, in every section, not only breathes a mortal distrust of the Indian people, their leaders or ideals; but also seeks to perpetuate itself by emphasising the division in the local ranks, the seeming conflict of material interests, the incipient antagonism of economic classes. By exploiting our unfortunate internal differences, grossly exaggerated for their own purpose, British Imperialists seek allies to-day in those classes and strata of Indian Society, which themselves need local, popular support for their continued existence. While in this Constitution every conceivable safeguard has been devised and applied to protect and maintain the British Imperialist elements; the Capitalist exploiters in alliance with those elements; the Princes and parasites on Land, in Industry, or the Public Services, not a thought seems devoted to the rights of the Indian People, their hopes of political emancipation, or economic regeneration. No reservation is made in *their* interest, no safeguard provided to protect them against princely oppression or capitalist exploitation. Their very poverty, ignorance, and lack of organisation are turned into weapons for use against them, their liberty, and aspirations.

*The Round Table Conferences, and Parliamentary Committees cannot really speak for the people of India, since the nominees to each of these innumerable bodies were mere dummies for the British Imperialist. Even the Gandhi-Irwin Pact, which provides for a Federation, with Responsible Government at the Centre, and temporary safeguards in the interests of India, has been belied in the ultimate fruit now proffered us for consumption.

In every instance, then, the prospect presented by this Constitution is gloomy and forbidding. Its express terms are like a hedge of spears presented in every direction to any one who would storm the serried ranks of Imperialist forces guarding vested interests and privileged classes. Its unexpected possibilities and implications are like submarine mines, which would blow up any who dares venture into such carefully guarded preserves. For such a citadel, force,—the naked sword,—can be the only sanction. Moral sanction for the maintenance of this engine of Imperialist greed is absolutely unavailing. The cement of community of class interest is unlikely to hold together for long a fundamentally uncongenial organism. Neither communal nor economic differences between the Indian people are insurmountable, especially when it comes to an opposition to the British. For these, in their day of power, which is not done yet, have never concealed their greed, curbed their arrogance, or checked their antagonism to every class of Indians. India enlightened; India economically emancipated; India free and conscious of her rich heritage and mindful of her high destiny, would not be content to remain for ever the handmaid of British Imperialism; and so the wardens of that World Force are ever seeking to snub her, suppress her, deny her, frustrate her.

The idea of a Federation has its own recommendation to the Imperialist Britisher. Federation being with the Princes only; and the Princes of India being regarded as the main props of British Imperialism, and the arch-enemies,—for their own reasons,—of democratic progress, every safeguard and entrenchment offered to this class is so much bulwark for the British domination of India. It is a curious fact of recent Indian history, that a number of important States are without their legitimate Rulers, or are under the direct administration of British officers as Prime Ministers. Alwar, Bharatpur, Kashmir may have their own circumstances to account for their present plight under British domination. Udaipur, Hyderabad, Nabha, Bhawalpur, Khairpur, are directly or indirectly so overwhelmed with British Imperialist influence, that it is impossible to conceive the present generation of representatives from these States to have any opinion, except the one in favour with these who pull the strings of some of these gorgeous puppets.

On the other hand, the more far-sighted of the British Rulers of India having realised that sooner or later they would have to abandon their monopoly of place and power in the British Provinces, they are carving out, so to speak, a second line of retreat for themselves. Positions of immense pecuniary benefit, with little or no responsibility, are being daily found in ever increasing numbers in the Indian States, whose Rulers, by their fads, their vices, or their weaknesses, are only too prone to admit such people in their entourage. The Rulers, on their side, have found, in the advent of the Federation, a chance to shake off the strangling hold of the Indian Political Department; and so they welcomed, at first, the proposal for a transfer of responsibility from White hall to Delhi or Simla. A closer scrutiny of the actual proposals for the Federation they had plumped for must have revealed this queer creation of British ingenuity to be not all that the Rulers had desired; and so they are now seeking to alter at leisure what they had asked for in haste. The people in these States, as already remarked, are not regarded in any way as a party to the deal, though it is they who would have to bear the burdens of the Federation in a larger measure than seems realised to-day. But political consciousness is growing even in the States population; and a talent for intrigue has never altogether disappeared from these regions. The people in the Indian States are concerned, however, for the moment, with obtaining a recognition for their own civic rights, which is denied them under the Act of 1935. The real benefits of the Federation to the States or otherwise, is a matter of secondary importance for them. The British Indian people,—and, much less, the British Parliament.—do not seem to have realised the political rights of the people in the Indian States. Hence a new source of division has come into being, with possibilities of infinite damage to the idea of national solidarity, which, it is to be hoped, such an organisation as the Indian National Congress will attend to before it is too late.

Finally, the people in British India seem to be anything but infatuated with the notion of an Indian Federation, particularly of this brand presented to them. They are, however, occupied too closely, for the moment, with the immediate problem of making Provincial Autonomy, such as it is under the Act of 1935, real and living to be able to attend to the wider problem of the political unity of British India and the States. To the British Imperial Government this is all to the good. So long as Indians continue to be divided *inter se*; so long as they are unable to appreciate fully the mysteries of the new Constitution, and its innumerable devices to keep India under a perpetual mortgage to the British, there is no need to show undue haste in solving any particular difficulty. Nor are they too anxious to demonstrate the implications of the Federation, as they have devised it, lest the Indian people of all classes and ranks should combine completely and irretrievably to repudiate it. It is possible that fate awaits the Federation. But, if so, there will be no transfer of even a nominal Responsibility at the Central Government of India; and, until the Indian people have convinced the British Imperialists that India can no longer remain in tutelage, she must continue to be the Cinderella of the British Commonwealth of autonomous Nations.

APPENDIX I

Table of Seats

The Council of State and the Federal Assembly.
Representatives of Indian States.

1. States and Groups of States.	2. Number of seats in Council of State	3. States and Groups of States.	4. Number of seats in the Federal Assembly.	5. Population.
		Division I.		
Hyderabad	5	Hyderabad ...	16	14,436,148
		Division II.		
Mysore	3	Mysore	7	6,557,302
		Division III.		
Kashmir	3	Kashmir ...	4	3,646,243
		Division IV.		
Gwalior	3	Gwalior	4	3,523,070
		Division V.		
Baroda	3	Baroda	3	2,443,007
		Division VI.		
Kalat	2	Kalat	1	342,101
		Division VII.		
Sikkim	1	Sikkim	—	109,808
		Division VIII.		
1. Rampur	1	1. Rampur ...	1	465,225
2. Benares	1	2. Beneras ...	1	391,272

1. States and Groups of States	2. Number of seats in Council of State	3. States and Groups of States.	4. Number of seats in the Federal Assembly	5. Population.
		DIVISION IX.		
1. Travancore ...	2	1. Travancore ...	5	5,095,973
2. Cochin	2	2. Cochin ...	1	1,205,016
3. Pudukkottai ... }	} 1	3. Pudukkottai. }	} 1	400,694
Banganapalle ... }		Banganapalle }		39,218
Sandur ... ... }		Sandur ... }		13,583
		DIVISION X.		
1. Udaipur ...	2	1. Udaipur ...	2	1,566,910
2. Jaipur	2	2. Jaipur ...	3	2,631,775
3. Jodhpur ...	2	3. Jodhpur ...	2	2,125,982
4. Bikaner ...	2	4. Bikaner ...	1	936,218
5. Alwar	1	5. Alwar ...	1	749,751
6. Kotah	1	6. Kotah ...	1	685,804
7. Bharatpur ...	1	7. Bharatpur ...	1	486,954
8. Tonk	1	8. Tonk ...	1	317,360
9. Dholpur ...	1	9. Dholpur ... }	} 1	254,986
10. Karauli ...	1	Karauli ... }		140,525
11. Bundi	1	10. Bundi ... }	} 1	216,722
12. Sirohi	1	Sirohi ... }		216,528
13. Dungarpur ...	1	11. Dungarpur ... }	} 1	227,544
14. Banswara ...	1	Banswara ... }		260,670
15. Partabgarh ... }	} 1	12. Partabgarh ... }	} 1	76,539
Jhalawar- ... }		Jhalawar- ... }		107,890
Shahpura ... }		Shahpura ... }		54,233
16. Jaisalmer ... }	} 1	13. Jaisalmer ... }	} 1	76,255
Kishengarh ... }		Kishengarh }		85,744
		DIVISION XI.		
1. Indore	2	1. Indore ...	2	1,325,089
2. Bhopal	2	2. Bhopal ...	1	729,955
3. Rewa	2	3. Rewa ...	2	1,587,445
4. Datia	1	4. Datia ... }	} 1	158,834
5. Orchha	1	Orchha ... }		314,661
6. Dhar	1	5. Dhar ... }	} 1	243,430
7. Dewas (Senior)... }	} 1	Dewas (Senr) }		83,321
Dewas (Junior) }		Dewas (Jr.) }		70,513

1 States and Groups of States.	2. Number of seats in Council of State	3. States and Groups of States.	4. Number of seats in the Federal Assembly	5 Population.
		Division XI—*cont.*		
8. Jaora	1	6. Jaora ...	1	100,166
Ratlam ...		Ratlam ...		107,321
9. Panna		7. Panna ...		212,130
Samthar ...	1	Samthar ...	1	33,307
Ajaigarh ...		Ajaigarh ...		85,895
10. Bijawar ...		8. Bijawar ...		115,852
Charkhari ...	1	Charkhari ...	1	120,351
Chhatarpur ...		Chhatarpur		161,267
11. Baoni		9. Baoni ...		19,132
Nagod		Nagod ...		74,589
Maihar	1	Maihar ...	1	68,991
Baraundha ...		Baraundha ...		16,071
12. Barwani ...	1	10. Barwani ...	1	141,110
Ali Rajpur ...		Ali Rajpur ...		101,963
Shahpura ...		Shahpura ...		54,233
13. Jhabua		11. Jhabua ...		145,522
Sailana	1	Sailana ...	1	35,223
Sitamau ...		Sitamau ...		28,422
14. Rajgarh ...		12. Rajgarh ...		134,891
Narsingarh ...	1	Narsingarh ...	1	113,873
Khilchipur ...		Khilchipur ...		45,583
		Division XII.		
1. Cutch	1	1. Cutch ...	1	514,307
2. Idar	1	2. Idar	1	262,660
3. Nawanagar ...	1	3. Nawanagar ...	1	409,192
4. Bhavnagar ...	1	4. Bhavnagar ...	1	500,274
5. Junagadh ...	1	5. Junagadh ...	1	545,152
6. Rajpipla ...	1	6. Rajpipla ...	1	206,114
Palanpur ...		Palanpur ...		264,179
7. Dhrangadhra ...		7. Dhrangadhra		88,961
Gondal	1	Gondal ...	1	205,846
8. Porbandar ...		8. Porbandar ...		115,673
Morvi	1	Morvi ...	1	113,023
9. Radhanpur ...		9. Radhanpur		70,530
Wankaner ...	1	Wankaner ...	1	44,259
Palitana ...		Palitana ...		62,150

1. States and Groups of States.	2. Number of seats in Council of State.	3. States and Groups of States	4. Number of seats in the Federal Assembly.	5. Population.
		DIVISION XII—*cont.*		
10. Cambay ...		10. Cambay ...		87,761
Dharampur ...	1	Dharampur	1	112,031
Balasinor ...		Balasinor ...		52,525
11. Baria		11. Baria ...		139,429
Chhota Udepur ...	1	Chhota Udepur ...	1	144,640
Sant		Sant ...		83,531
Lunawada ...		Lunawada ...		95,162
12. Bansda		12. Bansda ...		48,839
Sachin	1	Sachin ...		22,107
Jawhar		Jawhar ...		57,261
Danta		Danta ...	1	26,196
13. Dhrol		Dhrol ...		27,639
Limbdi	1	Limbdi ...		40,088
Wadhwan ...		Wadhwan ...		42,602
Rajkot		Rajkot ...		75,540
		DIVISION XIII.		
1. Kolhapur ...	2	1. Kolhapur ...	1	957,137
2. Sangli	1	2. Sangli ...	1	258,442
Savantvadi ...		Savantvadi ...		230,589
3. Janjira ...		3. Janjira ...		110,379
Mudhol ...	1	Mudhol ...	1	62,832
Bhor		Bhor ...		141,546
4. Jamkhandi ...		4. Jamkhandi ...		114,270
Miraj (Senior) ...		Miraj (Sr.) ...		93,938
Miraj (Junior) ...		Miraj (Jr.) ...		40,684
Kurundwad (Senior)	1	Kurundwad... (Senior)	1	44,204
Kurundwad ... (Junior)		Kurundwad... (Junior)		39,583
5. Akalkot... ...		5. Akalkot ...		92,605
Phaltan... ...		Phaltan ...		58,761
Jath	1	Jath ...	1	91,099
Aundh		Aundh ...		76,507
Ramdurg ...		Ramdurg ...		35,454

1. States and Groups of States.	2. Number of seats in Council of State	3. States and Groups of States.	4. Number of Seats in the Federal Assembly.	5. Population.
		Division XIV.		
1. Patiala	2	1. Patiala ...	2	1,625,520
2. Bahawalpur ...	2	2. Bhawalpur ...	1	984,612
3. Khairpur ...	1	3. Khairpur ...	1	227,183
4. Kapurthala ...	1	4. Kapurthala	1	316,757
5. Jind	1	5. Jind	1	324,676
6. Nabha	1	6. Nabha ...	1	287,573
		7. Tehri-Garhwal	1	349,574
7. Mandi		8. Mandi ...		207,465
Bilaspur ...	1	Bilaspur ...	1	100,994
Suket		Suket ...		58,408
8. Tehri-Garhwal				
Sirmur	1	9. Sirmur ...	1	148,568
Chamba ...		Chamba ...		146,870
9. Faridkot ...		10. Faridkot ...		164,364
Malerkotla ...	1	Malerkotla	1	83,072
Loharu		Loharu ...		23,338
		Division XV.		
1. Cooch Behar ...	1	1. Cooch Behar	1	590,886
2. Tripura ...	1	2. Tripura ...	1	382,450
Manipur ...		3. Manipur ...	1	445,606
		Division XVI.		
1. Mayurbhanj ...	1	1. Mayurbhanj	1	889,603
Sonepur ...		2. Sonepur ...	1	237,920
2. Patna	1	3. Patna ...	1	566,924
Kalahandi ...		4. Kalahandi ...	1	513,716
3. Keonjhar ...		5. Keonjhar ...	1	460,609
Dhenkanal ...		6. Gangpur ...	1	356,674
Nayagarh ...	1	7. Bastar ...	1	524,721
Talcher ...		8. Surguja ...	1	501,939
Nilgiri				

1. States and Groups of States.	2. Number of seats in Council of State.	3. States and Groups of States.	4. Number of seats in the Federal Assembly.	5. Population.
		Division XVI—*cont.*		
4. Gangpur ...		9. Dhenkanal ...		284,326
Bamra		Nayagarh ...		142,406
Seraikela ...	1	Seraikela ...		143,525
Baud		Baud ...		135,248
Bonai		Talcher ...		69,702
5. Bastar		Bonai ...		80,186
Surguja ...		Nilgiri ...		68,594
Raigarh... ...	1	Bamra ...		151,047
Nandgaon ...				
		10. Raigarh ...		277,569
6. Khairagarh ...		Khairagarh		157,400
Jashpur... ...		Jashpur ...		193,698
Kanker ...	1	Kanker ...		136,101
Korea		Sarangarh ...		128,967
Sarangarh ...		Korea ...		90,886
		Nandgaon ...		182,380
		Division XVII.		
States not mentioned in any of the preceding Divisions, but described in paragraph 12 of this Part of this Schedule.	2	States not mentioned in any of the preceding Divisions, but described in paragraph 12 of this Part of this Schedule.		3,032,197

Total population of the States in this Table: 78,981,912

APPENDIX II

SECOND SCHEDULE

Provisions of this Act which may be Amended Without Affecting the Accession of a State

Part I, in so far it relates to the Commander-in-Chief.

Part II, chapter II, save with respect to the exercise by the Governor-General on behalf of His Majesty of the executive authority of the Federation, and the definition of the functions of the Governor-General; the executive authority of the Federation; the functions of the council of ministers, and the choosing and summoning of ministers and their tenure of office; the power of the Governor-General to decide whether he is entitled to act in his discretion or exercise his individual judgment; the functions of the Governor-General with respect to external affairs and defence; the special responsibilities of the Governor-General relating to the peace or tranquillity of India, or any part thereof, the financial stability and credit of the Federal Government, the rights of Indian States and the rights and dignity of their Rulers, and the discharge of his functions by or under the Act in his discretion or in the exercise of his individual judgment; His Majesty's Instrument of Instructions to the Governor-General; the superintendence of the Secretary of State; and the making of rules by the Governor-General in his discretion for the transaction of, and the securing of transmission to him of information with respect to, the business of the Federal Government.

Part II, chapter III, save with respect to the number of the representatives of British India and of the Indian States in the Council of State and the Federal Assembly and the manner in which the representatives of the Indian States are to be chosen; the disqualifications for membership of a Chamber of the Federal Legislature in relation to the representatives of the States; the procedure for the introduction and passing of Bills; joint sittings of the two Chambers; the assent to Bills, or the withholding assent from Bills, by the Governor-General; the reservation of Bills for the signification of His Majesty's pleasure; the annual financial statement; the charging on the revenues of the Federation of the salaries, allowances and pensions payable to or in respect of judges of the Federal Court, of expenditure for the purpose of the discharge by the Governor-General of his functions with respect to external affairs, defence, and the administration of any territory in the direction and control of which he is required to act in his discretion and of the sums payable to His Majesty in respect of the expenses incurred in discharging the functions of the Crown in its relations with Indian States; the procedure with respect to estimates and demands for grants; supplementary financial statements; the making of rules by the Governor-General for regulating the procedure of, and the conduct of business in, the Legislature in relation to matters where he acts in his discretion or exercises his individual judgment, and for prohibiting the discussion of, or the asking of questions on, any matter connected with or the personal conduct of the Ruler or ruling family of any Indian State; the making of rules by the Governor-General as to the procedure with respect to joint sittings of, and communications between, the two chambers and the protection of judges of the Federal Court and State High Courts from discussion in the Legislature of their conduct.

Part II, chapter IV, save with respect to the power of the Governor-General to promulgate ordinances in his discretion or in the exercise of his individual judgment, or to enact Governor-General's Acts.

Part III, chapter I. The whole chapter.

Part III, chapter II, save with respect to the special responsibilities of the Governor relating to the rights of Indian States and the rights and dignity of the Rulers thereof and to the execution of orders or directions of the Governor-General, and the superintendence of the Governor-General in relation to those responsibilities.

Part III, chapter III, save with respect to the making of rules by the Governor for prohibiting the discussion of, or the asking of questions on, any matter connected with or the personal conduct of the Ruler or ruling family of any Indian State, and the protection of judges of the Federal Court and State High Courts from discussion in the Legislature of their conduct.

Part III, chapter IV. The whole chapter.

Part III, chapter V. The whole chapter.

Part III, chapter VI. The whole chapter.

Part IV, The whole Part.

Part V, chapter I, save with respect to the power of the Federal Legislature to make laws for a State; the power of the Governor-General to empower either the Federal Legislature or Provincial Legislature to enact a law with respect to any matter not enumerated in any of the Lists in the Seventh Schedule to this Act; any power of a State to repeal a Federal law, and the effect of inconsistencies between a Federal law and a State law.

Part V, chapter II, save with respect to the previous sanction of the Governor-General to the introduction or moving of any Bill or amendment affecting matters as respects which the Governor-General is required to act in his discretion; the power of Parliament to legislate for British India or any part thereof, or the restrictions on the power of the Federal Legislature and of Provincial Legislatures to make laws on certain matters.

Part V, chapter III. The whole chapter.

Part VI, save in so far as the provisions of that Part relate to Indian States, or empower the Governor-General to issue orders to the Governor of a Province for preventing any grave menace to the peace or tranquillity of India or any part thereof.

Part VII, chapter I, in so far as it relates to Burma.

Part VII, chapter II, save with respect to loans and guarantees to Federated States and the appointment, removal and conditions of service of the Auditor-General.

Part VII, chapter III, save in so far as it affects suits against the Federation by a Federated State.

Part VIII, save with respect to the constitution and functions of the Federal Railway Authority; the conduct of business between the Authority and the Federal Government, and the Railway Tribunal and any matter with respect to which it has jurisdiction.

Part IX, chapter I, in so far as it relates to appeals to the Federal Court from High Courts in British India; the power of the Federal Legislature to confer further powers upon the Federal Court for the purpose of enabling it more effectively to exercise the powers conferred upon it by this Act.

Part IX, chapter II. The whole chapter.

Part X, save with respect to the eligibilty of Rulers and subjects of Federated States for civil Federal office.

Part XI. The whole Part.

Part XII, save with respect to the saving for rights and obligations of the Crown in its relations with Indian States; the use of His Majesty's forces in connection with the discharge of the functions of the Crown in its said relations; the limitation in relation to Federated States of His Majesty's power to adapt and modify existing Indian laws; His Majesty's powers and jurisdiction in Federated States, and resolutions of the Federal Legislature or any Provincial Legislature recommending amendments of this Act or Orders in Council made thereunder; and save also the provisions relating to the interpretation of this Act so far as they apply to provisions of this Act which may not be amended without affecting the accession of a State.

Part XIII. The whole Part.

Part XIV. The whole Part.

First Schedule. The whole Schedule, except Part II thereof.

Third Schedule. The whole Schedule.

Fourth Schedule, save with respect to the oath or affirmation to be taken or made by the Ruler or subject of an Indian State.

Fifth Schedule. The whole Schedule.

Sixth Schedule. The whole Schedule.

Seventh Schedule. Any entry in the Legislative Lists in so far as the matters to which it relates have not been accepted by the State in question as matters with respect to which the Federal Legislature may make laws for that State.

Eighth Schedule. The whole Schedule.

Ninth Schedule. The whole Schedule.

Tenth Schedule. The whole Schedule.

Eleventh Schedule. The whole Schedule.

Twelfth Schedule. The whole Schedule.

Thirteenth Schedule. The whole Schedule.

Fourteenth Schedule. The whole Schedule.

Fifteenth Schedule. The whole Schedule.

Sixteenth Schedule. The whole Schedule.

APPENDIX III

DRAFT INSTRUMENT OF ACCESSION RECEIVED FROM THE GOVERNMENT OF INDIA

Instrument of Accession of ....

(*insert full name and title*)

Whereas proposals for the establishment of a Federation of India comprising such Indian States as may accede thereto and the Provinces of British India constituted as autonomous Provinces have been discussed between representatives of His Majesty's Government, of the Parliament of the United Kingdom, of British India and of the Rulers of the Indian States.

And whereas those proposals contemplated that the Federation of India should be constituted by an Act of the Parliament of the United Kingdom and by the accession of Indian States.

And whereas provision for the constitution of a Federation of India has now been made in the Government of India Act, 1935, but it is by that Act provided that the Federation shall not be established until such date as His Majesty may by Proclamation declare and such declaration cannot be made until the requisite number of Indian States have acceded to the Federation.

And whereas the said Act cannot apply to any of my territories save by virtue of my consent and concurrence signified by my accession to the Federation.

Now therefore

I ....

(*insert full name and title*)

Ruler of .... (*insert name of State.*)

In the exercise of my sovereignty in and over my said State.

For the purpose of co-operating in furtherance of the the interests and welfare of India by uniting in a Federation under the Crown by the name of the Federation of India with the Provinces called Governors' Provinces and with the Provinces called Chief Commissioners' Provinces and with the Rulers of other Indian States.

Do hereby execute this my **Instrument of Accession** and

1. (1) I hereby declare that subject to His Majesty's acceptance of this Instrument, I accede to the Federation

of India as established under the Government of India Act, 1935 (hereinafter referred to as "The Act") with the intent that His Majesty the King, the Governor-General of India, the Federal Legislature, the Federal Court and any other Federal authority established for the purposes of the Federation shall, by virtue of this my Instrument of Accession, but subject always to the terms thereof, and for the purposes only of the Federation, exercise in relation to the State of .... (hereinafter referred to as "this State") such functions as may be vested in them by or under the Act.

2. I hereby assume the obligation of ensuring that due effect is given to the provisions of the Act within this State so far as they are applicable therein by virtue of this my Instrument of Accession.

3. All functions exercisable by any Federal authority in relation to this State by virtue of Clause 1 of this Instrument shall be exercised exclusively by a Federal authority except as, in so far as the same are exercisable by the Ruler of this State the same may be exercised by him.

4. I accept the matters specified in the First Schedule hereto as the matters with respect to which the Federal Legislature may make laws for this State, and in this Instrument and in the said First Schedule I specify the limitations to which the power of the Federal Legislature to make laws for this State, and the exercise of the executive authority of the Federation in this State, are respectively to be subject.

The Federal Legislature shall not have power to make laws for this State save with respect to the matters so specified and subject to the said limitations.

Where under the First Schedule hereto, the power of the Federal Legislature to make laws for this State is subject to a limitation the exercise of the executive authority of the Federation in this State shall be limited to the same extent, it being the intent that the said executive authority shall not be exercisable in this State with respect to any matter specified in the said First Schedule otherwise than within the limits within which the Federal Legislature may make laws for this State or otherwise than in accordance with and subject to the limitations specified in the said First Schedule.

5. All duties, taxes and excises levied by the Federation pursuant to any law applicable in this State shall be uniform throughout the Federation.

Nothing, however, in this clause shall prohibit the Federation from imposing such taxes or taking such measures with respect thereto as the Federation may determine with respect to a State which imposes duties, taxes or excises affecting commerce between the units of the Federation.

A. Whereas I am desirous that functions in relation to the administration in this State of laws of the Federal Legislature which apply therein shall be exercised by the Ruler of this State and his officers and the terms of an agreement in that behalf have been mutually agreed between me and the Governor-General of India and are set out in the Schedule hereto:

Now therefore I hereby declare that I accede to the Federation with the assurance that the said agreement will be executed and the said agreement when executed shall be deemed to form part of this Instrument and shall be construed and have effect accordingly.

B. The provisions contained in Part VI of the Act with respect to intereference with Water Supplies, being Sections 130 to 133 thereof inclusive, are not to apply in relation to this State.

4. The particulars to enable due effect to be given to the provisions of Sections 147 and 149 of the Act are set forth in the Second Schedule hereto.

5. Reference in this Instrument to laws of the Federal Legislature include references to Ordinances promulgated. Acts enacted and laws made by the Governor-General of India under Sections 42 to 45 of the Act inclusive.

6. Nothing in this Instrument affects the continuance of my sovereignty in and over this State or, save provided by this Instrument or by any law of the Federal Legislature made in accordance with the terms thereof, the exercise of any of my powers, authority and rights in and over this State.

7. Nothing in this Instrument shall, be construed as authorising Parliament to legislate for or exercise jurisdiction over this State or its Ruler in any respect.

Provided that the accession of this State to the Federation shall not be affected by any amendment of the provisions of the Majesty or any Federal authority in relation to, this State and nothing in this Instrument shall be construed as authorising Parliament to legislate for or exercise jurisdiction over this State or its Ruler in any respect.

16. The Schedules hereto annexed shall form an integral part of this Instrument.

17. The Instrument shall be binding on me as from the date on which His Majesty signifies his acceptance thereof, provided that if the Federation of India is not

established before the ....day of ....
Nineteen hundred ...., this Instrument shall, on that day, become null and void for all purposes whatsoever.

18. I hereby declare that I execute this Instrument for myself, my heirs and successors, and that accordingly any reference in this Instrument to me or to the Ruler of this State is to be construed as including a reference to my heirs and successors.

This Instrument of Accession (then follows the attestation to be drawn with all due formality appropriate to the declaration of a Ruler).

List of Safeguards which were proposed on behalf of the Chamber of Princes for incorporation in the Government of India Act

(A) ESSENTIAL SAFEGUARDS

1. The sovereignty and autonomy of the States shall be fully respected and guaranteed and there shall be no intereference direct or indirect with the internal affairs of the States.

2. No unfriendly act shall be permitted by one Federating unit against the other.

3. No direct tax or levy of any kind including income tax and corporation tax shall be imposed in the State by the Federal Government.

Federal sources of Revenue shall be strictly confined to those mutually agreed upon and no addition to this list will be permissible without the free consent of each State.

4. Federation shall be confined to subjects mutually agreed upon and no addition to these will be permissible without the free consent of each Federating State.

All residuary powers shall remain with the States.

5. No change in the constitution shall be permissible without the free consent of the parties concerned except in regard to minor details which may be agreed upon in less rigid manner to facilitate the day to day working of the constitution.

6. The Viceroy will have the power to disallow any Bill or veto any Act which may adversely affect the rights recognised by treaty or otherwise of any State or States. The Viceroy will also have power to disallow or arrest any executive Act of the Federation which may have similar tendencies.

7. The powers of the two Houses shall be co-ordinate and equal except that money bills may be introduced in the lower House.

8. The decisions of any matter referred to a joint session shall be by two-third majority of the two Houses sitting in a joint session.

9. The States must have at least 40% representation in the Upper House and 33-1|3 per cent. in the Lower House. The system and method by which their representatives will be chosen must be purely a State concern and no interference of any kind by Federation shall be permitted.

10. The States will enter Federation by means of Treaties made with the Crown for the purposes of Federation.

11. The position of States and British India as partners in Federation shall be that of equal partners; there shall be no question of any partner being directly or indirectly subordinate to the other.

12. There shall be a separate Instrument of Instructions to the Viceroy—as distinct from the Governor-General—and it shall be laid down in it that the Viceroy as the Representative of the King Emperor shall be responsible to ensure respect for the rights of the States as guaranteed to them by their Treaties, engagements and sanads which have been declared as "inviolate and inviolable" and are unalterable without the free consent of the contracting parties.

13. That India shall remain an integral part of the Empire.

14. Federal Court shall derive its authority from the Crown as well as from the Rulers of each Federating State.

15. The jurisdiction of the Federal Court over the Courts of the Indian States shall extend only to questions arising out of the Constitution, in issue before the State Courts. The procedure adopted by the State Courts operating as Federal Courts should be as follows:

The State Courts should refer for opinion to the Federal Court and the State Courts shall give their decisions on the points referred in accordance with the opinion of the Federal Court.

16. An appeal shall lie to the Privy Council in England from the decisions of the Federal Court on matters connected with the Constitution where Constituent Units are involved provided that a suitable formula can be devised which will preserve the sovereignty of the Federating States.

17. The fundamental rights shall find no place in the Federal Constitution and shall not be treated as a Federal

subject. They may subject to His Majesty's pleasure find expression in the King Emperor's proclamation as applying only to His British Indian Dominion.

(B) SAFEGUARDS OPEN TO NEGOTIATION

1. Through some suitable method of augmentation or otherwise it should be secured that the comparative influence of the States in the control of Federal matters is not prejudiced, if only a majority and not the entire body of States join Federation.

2. In the event of a Federating State refusing or otherwise failing to discharge its Federal obligations the enforcement upon that State of compliance with the terms of its Instrument of Accession shall be the function of the Viceroy. In the case of the States which have collectively joined the Federation, the good Offices of the Confederation, will be utilised in the first instance.

3. Provision will be made empowering the Governor-General in his discretion in any case in which he considers that a bill introduced or proposed for introduction or any clause thereof or any amendment to a Bill moved or proposed would affect the discharge of his "Special Responsibility" for safeguarding the rights of the States guaranteed to them by treaties or otherwise to direct that the bill, clause or amendment shall not be further proceeded with.

4. In matters not specifically delegated to the Federal Government the servants of the Federal Government in the execution of their duties within the territories of a State shall be subject to the internal sovereignty and laws of the State concerned.

5. The power to make legislation in Federal matters will be:

(a) Exclusive, being vested in the Government and being confined only to matters where the States units had not retained the work of administration.

(b) Concurrent, remaining with the Federal Government as well as with the legislature of the States units. In matters where the Federal Legislature has made no law the States may make their own legislation, but where the Federal Government has already passed any law the States may also pass laws adapted to their own local conditions provided there is no conflict;

Federal laws will prevail over State laws where there is a conflict.

In all remaining matters the States have the residuary power of legislation.

GENERAL LIMITATIONS

(a) The Federal Legislature shall not levy or impose any tax or duty in or upon this State or provide for the payment of any contribution by this State which discriminates against this State.

(b) No land or other property shall be acquired in this State on behalf of His Majesty for any Federal purposes, or on behalf of the Federal Railway Authority or any other authority of the Federation except with the consent of the Ruler of this State and upon such terms as may be mutually agreed upon.

(c) The Federal agents, officers and representatives, while engaged in the exercise of their functions in this State shall be subject to, and observe the laws and regulations of this State, not inconsistent with the due exercise of their Federal functions.

(d) The Legislative power of the Federal Legislation to make laws in and for this State shall not, except in item 44, 45, 46, 47 imply the power to impose any duty or tax.

CHAPTER IV

THE GOVERNOR-GENERAL

The Governor-General is appointed, under Section 3 of the Act of 1935, by a *Commission* under the Royal Warrant. Says the Section:—

> 3 (1) The Governor-General of India is appointed by His Majesty by a Commission under the Royal Sign Manual and has—
>
> (a) all such powers and duties as are conferred or imposed on him by or under this Act; and
>
> (b) such other powers of His Majesty, not being powers connected with the exercise of the functions of the Crown in its relations with Indian States, as His Majesty may be pleased to assign to him.
>
> (2) His Majesty's representative for the exercise of the functions of the Crown in its relations with Indian States is appointed by His Majesty in like manner and has such powers and duties in connection with the exercise of those functions (not being powers or duties conferred or imposed by or under this Act on the Governor-General) as His Majesty may be pleased to assign to him.
>
> (3) It shall be lawful for His Majesty to appoint one person to fill both the said offices.

The distinction in the appointment by a *Warrant* under the Royal Sign Manual, and by a *Commission* under the same, is a nicety of the mysteries of the British Constitution with which we need not trouble ourselves. It may be pointed out, however, that whereas the Governors and the Governor-General are, for instance, appointed by Commission under the Royal Sign Manual,* the Commander-in-Chief is appointed

*cp. Sections 3 and 48: by Section 34 of the Government of India Act, 1919, the appointment used to be by warrant under the R.S.M.

by a mere *Warrant* under the Royal Sign Manual.* The office is constituted by Letters Patent† and the appointment by Commission under Royal Sign Manual, it may be added, is accompanied by special Instructions, which are issued under the Royal Prerogative, though the issue of these Instructions, in the case of the Governor-General and the Provincial Governors, is provided for by specific Sections of this Act.‡

History of the Office of the Governor-General

We need not dwell at length upon the evolution of the office of the Governor-General, and of his powers. Every school-boy knows of the charter to the East India Company, and its 3 Presidencies; of the Regulating Act, and the appointment of Warren Hastings as the first Governor-General of Bengal having a sort of supremacy over the Presidency Governors of Madras and Bombay. These last were co-equal and independent authorities before the passing of the Regulating Act; and even after that enactment, as well as after Pitt's India Act, 1783, they continued to enjoy an independence of, and claimed an equality with, the Governor-General of Bengal, which often caused grave complications and endless troubles. Similarly, the Governor-General was given a Council, which, under the Regulating Act, had an equality of power and status that Pitt's India Act considerably modified. After the appointment of Lord Cornwallis, the Governor-General was secured an ascendency over his

*cp. Sections 4, 200; etc.

†For the Letter Patent constituting the office of the Governor-General. cp. the Gazette of India Extraordinary, April, 1937.

‡cp. Sections 13 and 53. These documents, however, cannot be enforced in a Court of Law.

colleagues in the Council, which has continued till this day.*

The Governor-General of Bengal was converted, after over 50 years from Pitt's India Act, into the Governor-General of India (1834), though continuing at the same time to be Governor of Bengal. The Province of Bengal was separated from the immediate charge of the Governor-General in 1853. When the Government of India was transferred from the East India Company (abolished) to the British Crown direct, the Governor-General also became the Viceroy. The distinction between the Governor-General as the chief civil executive officer; and the Viceroy, as the representative of the Crown, particularly in the exercise of certain Royal Prerogatives (*e.g.*, pardoning criminals or the conferment of titles), and in conducting the relations with the Indian States, was not always maintained in daily parlance. It is needless now to dwell upon the relations between the Governor-General and the Secretary of State. The latter was unquestionably the superior officer, being responsible directly to Parliament. The Governor-General was by law enjoined to obey him in all matters relating to the Government of India which the Secretary of State was empowered to supervise direct and control.

Under the Act of 1935, the two offices of the Governor-General and the Viceroy are, by express provisions, made distinct. Even now, it is lawful, however, for His Majesty to appoint one and the same individual to hold both the offices and to authorise him to exercise their combined functions. The distinction in the dual capacity is necessitated, more than

*cp. Section 41 of the Government of India Act, 1919, and Section 9 of the Act of 1935.

ever before, by the proposal to establish a Federation of India, in which Indian States may be united with the British Provinces. But even after the Federation comes into being, the use of Royal Prerogative and Paramount authority in relations with the Indian States will not be discontinued. Hence the need by law to emphasise the distinction between the two offices.

The two sets of duties are so closely connected, and have such an intimate bearing, one upon the other, that the combination of the two offices in one and the same individual seems unavoidable, at least for years to come. It is true the establishment of the Federation will make the distinction of something more than merely ceremonial or academic importance. But, even under the Federal system, the two sets of duties would interact and mutually influence, if not condition, one another.

It must be noted that the salary is provided for, in the Act (Schedule III) for only one office, *i.e.*, for the Governor-General. Hence, if and when the two offices are placed in two different hands, fresh and additional provision will have to be made, not only by way of salary to the Representative of the Crown, or the Viceroy proper, dealing with the Indian States so far as the exercise of Paramountcy functions is concerned; but also to enable that officer to maintain his position and dignity, and to discharge his duties with convenience.*

*cp. Section 145, under which sums required by His Majesty's representatives for the conduct of his relations with Indian States have to be paid to that officer, and charged upon the revenues of the Federation under Section 33 (3) (f). It may be doubted, however, whether this will be sufficient authority by executive action, or even by an Act of the Federal Legislature, to fix a salary for the Representative of the Crown. The safer course would be a new, special Act of Parliament for this purpose.

Appointment of Governor-General

The Governor-General of India is appointed on the advice of the British Prime Minister (not on that of the Secretary of State for India), and will, presumably continue to be so appointed even when he becomes the executive head of the Federation of India. This practice is in marked contrast with that in the leading Dominions, where now the Governor-General is appointed, and is removable, on the advice of the Dominion Prime Minister. The formal appointment is by the King, under Letters Patent; but the King acts exclusively on the advice of His Dominion Ministers concerned; and the British (Imperial) Ministers may have no knowledge of the act.* Indian Ministers are not only not consulted; but there seems to be no provision for their being consulted hereafter, when the Federation comes into being, simply because the Statute of Westminster does not apply to this country; and because it is not a Dominion of the same status and function as Canada or Australia, let alone the Union of South Africa or the Irish Free State. Besides the internal conditions of this country, and particularly the peculiar situation caused by the presence of so many Indian States,† reasons of Imperial policy will prevent Britain for a long time to come from acquiescing in the appointment of the Governor-General of the Federation of India being advised by the Indian Ministers. It must be admitted, however, that there is nothing in the Constitution to prohibit Indian Federal

*cp. A. B. Keith, Constitutional Law of the British Dominions, p. 16-18.

†Native Tribes are to be found in Australia, Africa, as well as New Zealand; and these may seem to suggest a parallel with the protected Indian Princes. But India is not a Dominion, and so such analogies from acknowledged Dominions will not be allowed to apply to the Indian parallel.

Ministers from offering such an advice when the occasion arises.

Qualifications

The British Prime Minister, when advising the appointment of a Governor-General of India, has no definite rules to guide him. Usually, it is frankly a conferment of a party favour, even though the convention is loudly proclaimed by the British statesmen that Indian affairs are outside Party politics in Britain. The men who have been chosen to fill the post, ever since the Government of India passed directly to the British Crown, have been distinguished public men, or high placed servants of the British Empire, sometimes drawn from the ranks of similar satraps in the Dominions, sometimes from the leading lights of British Diplomacy; sometimes from merely successful, promising, or inconvenient politicians at home. But none of these three categories guarantee the possession of any special qualification for the supreme executive office in India; and it is not utterly unjust to add that any special knowledge or experience of India might even be considered a disqualification in an aspirant for this post.* Even experi-

*Says the Historian of Lord Curzon:—

"Reduced to a simple formula, their contention is that the less a Viceroy elect knows about India, the better Ruler he would make, provided he has an open mind and a balanced sense of judgment. The proposition hardly bears a serious examination, but it is typical of a certain school of British thought. No one maintains that a man would be a better admiral, or a better general, or a better surgeon if he was entirely without learning or special knowledge: but the task of steering the Government of India through the vast and complex issues which constantly beset it is supposed by these publicists to be best accomplished by an unprepared man with a cross-bench mind. India cannot be properly governed upon such theories in these stormy days. It is a mistake to think of the Viceroy as a judicial referee, surrounded by men necessarily more competent than himself. A good Viceroy will initiate as well as adjudge."

This was written about 30 years ago; but the British policy regarding the choice of a Viceroy for India remains in the same undefined, muddling stage in which it has always been. In the atmosphere in which they live, and under the conditions in which they work, every Viceroy flatters himself to be a success, and no Viceroy is ever more than a puppet of the Home Government.

ence as Secretary of State for India might be regarded as a disqualification; while having been a member of the Civil Service of the Crown in India is distinctly not welcome, since the one solitary experiment of Sir John Lawrence in the early years of the direct government under the Crown.*

This is, indeed, not wholly objectionable. Officers of that exalted station are best without the preconceived prejudices, or prepossessions, which previous experience due to service in the country might imply. On the other hand, if and when Federation with its concomitant of responsible government comes into being, the qualities required in this officer would rather be those of a politician accustomed to work representative institutions, and to deal with Ministers responsible to the Legislature, than of an experienced official well versed in the details of administrative routine, or a trained diplomat, or even a departmental expert. So far as knowledge and experience of the administrative problems and routine is concerned, such officers always command the services of experts in each line; and provided they have the normal intelligence of an adult, they need not fear for the usual success in their office merely because of lack of personal knowledge.

On the other hand, so long as the Indian Ministers are not entitled to offer advice to the King in the choice of this officer; or so long as Indians themselves are not appointed to this post, the chances of the appointment being made rather on Party grounds than on any other are too many to be neglected. Even if the British

*The case of Lord Willingdon, Governor-General between 1931-36, stands on a different footing. He had previously served as Governor in two of the leading Provinces; but there he had been appointed as a promising British politician; while to the Governor-Generalship he was appointed after serving a term as the corresponding officer in the Dominion of Canada.

advisers of the King make their choice from among Britishers who have made a success as Dominion satraps, there is no guarantee that the same individual, who proved a success, let us say, in Africa, would prove equally a success as the Governor-General of India. If the choice is made as Party favour in the British political world, the danger may be still greater, especially if an unwritten convention requires,—as it does to-day,—that the individual chosen as the Governor-General of India should be a scion of the British titled aristocracy. The social status of the Governor-General is considered to be more important in India than in any other Dominion, even though Society in India is yet not so thoroughly westernised as to appreciate fully such snobbishness. The daughter of a Railway contractor,or of a Chicago meat-packer, would in India command the same respect as Vicereine as the daughter of a hundred earls; and an ex-stock broker would carry the same weight as Viceroy as a Landsdown or a Curzon. Nevertheless, the exigencies of dealing with Indian Princes on a footing of social equality has led to this unwritten law of choice, that the Viceroy and Governor-General should be selected from the highest social circles in Britain.

In those classes, however, sympathy for popular institutions,—and particularly for the nationalist aspirations of what have hitherto been regarded as backward peoples,—is conspicuous by its rarity, if not by its complete absence. Men like Curzon or Linlithgow may be peers of the Indian Princes by right of birth; but there is no guarantee that all individuals drawn from the British aristocracy would be similarly endowed intellectually, and so make something more than mere rubberstamps for the Secretaries to affix to official documents, figure-heads to decorate official Parties, or mouthpieces of the British Imperial Government.

In the volume dealing with Provincial Autonomy, we have already discussed the suggestion,—now, happily, not very commonly heard,—of choosing the Provincial Governor from the British Royal Family. The dangers and drawbacks of a Royal Governor-General are even greater than those of a Royal Governor. Even if the post of the Governor-General is separated from that of the Viceroy, the appointment of the latter from the British Royal Family will have the same objection, notwithstanding the precedent of the Duke of Connaught in Canada, or of the Earl of Athlone in Africa.

Personality of the Governor-General

The personality of a Governor-General, is not a matter of utter indifference to the weal or woe of India. So long as India does not enjoy a full and complete system of self-Government,—within or outside the British Empire,—the personal equation will have the utmost bearing upon the commonweal in this country. Even under the Federal system proposed in the Act of 1935, the Governor-General will continue to have immense powers of direct administration in several departments; and of exclusive discretion in those departments of the State also, which are by law apparently made over to the charge of Responsible Ministers. Given these powers; given the peculiar circumstances of India, with its Minorities, its Princes and guaranteed classes of exploiters; given the relative lack of experience in the Responsible Ministers drawn from the leaders of the Indian people, and the known antagonism of the severely entrenched Public Services to India's popular ideals and the Nationalist urge; given finally, the needs and requirements of a foreign garrison in India, the personality, the sympathy or idiosyncracies of the Governor-General are bound to have an immense importance on the day-to-day administration of the country, and the general well-being of its people. Indians must, therefore, not be considered to be exigent, or needlessly suspicious of the methods and motives of British Government in India, if they demand that the choice of the supreme executive officer should hereafter be made on the advice of the Indian Ministers; and that, as far as possible, it must be confined to Indians born and bred, Princes or commoners, preferably latter.

Governor-General as Supreme Executive

In the Dominions, the Governor-General, as representative of the King, is also the Commnader-in-Chief of the Defence forces.* In India, though the Governor-General is the Chief Executive head of the governmental machinery, who controls also the Department of Defence, the Commander-in-Chief is a distinct entity, provided for as such by the Constitution.

> "4—There shall be a Commander-in-Chief of His Majesty's Forces in India appointed by Warrant under the Royal Sign Manual."

The Office being thus distinctly established, it is not provided, as is provided by Section (3) for the Viceroyalty, that it shall be open to the King to combine the two offices into one and the same person.

Cost of the Governor-General to India

We have reproduced in the volume on Provincial Autonomy, Schedule III to the Act of 1935, which

*"Constitutionally, of course, the Crown is the head of the various forces throughout the Empire, but the practice or law is to grant to the Governor-General the title of Commander-in-Chief" Keith, Constitutional Law of the British Dominions, p. 414.

prescribes the salaries payable to the Governor-General, and lays down the general principles of other allowances. The Order in Council referred to in that Schedule has yet to be issued with regard to the Governor-General of the Federation of India. The aggregate cost of this exalted office to India is budgeted, in the Budget for 1937-38, at Rs. 15,54,000 distributed as follows:—

	Rs.
Salary	2,50,800
Sumptuary Allowance of the G.-G. ..	40,000
Expenditure from Contract Allowance ..	1,44,300
State Conveyance & Motor cars ..	43,000
Private Secretary & Department ..	2,63,800
Military Secretary & Department ..	3,22,400
Tour Expenses,—Special Trains etc. ..	4,70,700
Total ..	15,54,000

This, however, does not include the charges for the Band and Bodyguard, included in the Military Budget, and costing, in the Budget for 1937-38, an aggregate sum of Rs. 1,84,600. Nor does it provide for the cost of maintaining Viceregal residences, Leave allowance to the Governor-General,—which is now regularly taken once in the period of office; or Outfit and Equipment Allowance when first appointed of £5,000. If these were added, the annual average cost of the Governor-General, his office and its maintenance would be over Rs. 17,62,000. Compared to the pay and allowance granted to the other Chief Executives in the British Empire, or in other countries, like France or the U.S.A.,—and viewed particularly in correlation with the ability of the Indian people who have to bear such burdens,—this seems too excessive to be in any way defensible.

CHAPTER V

THE FEDERAL EXECUTIVE

The Federal Executive is composed of:

(i) the Governor-General;

(ii) the Council of Federal Ministers; and,

(iii) if we include the Departmental heads, the administrative services. In this last category we might comprise all the Superior Services; but, as these have very little scope to determine the policy of Government; and as they are mainly Ministerial officers, it might not be strictly correct to include these in a description of the Indian Federal Executive. Similarly, it would be equally open to objection to include the special Counsellors to the Governor-General in the Reserved or Excluded Departments, since they have no executive responsibility placed upon them by the Constitution.

The Executive Government of a country must needs include Civil as well as Military branches. Though the Governor-General is in charge of the Department of Defence, it is nevertheless not so clearly brought within the constitutional ambit as to justify the belief that a description of the executive functions would necessarily include and exhaust and military side of the Indian Administration. A separate Chapter will, accordingly, be devoted to the consideration of the constitutional aspect of our national defence; including the consideration of the position of the various Arms of Defence, of the Commander-in-Chief, and of the Defence Services and problems in general.

The executive administration has also its financial aspect. There are sections in the Government of India Act, 1935, which closely regulate some portion of that administration. But though the Department of Finance is not excluded wholly from the constitutional activities of the Federal executive, the Governor-General is saddled with a Special Responsibility in this behalf; and has, besides, a special Adviser in this department, which necessitate a separate treatment of **Federal Finance** in its financial as well as constitutional aspect. The addition, moreover, of such special machinery as that provided by the Reserve Bank, has a considerable constitutional significance. Though we cannot include a detailed study of the Reserve Bank in this volume, even in so far as its constitutional or political importance is concerned, reference must nevertheless be made to it in the Chapter on Federal Finance, if only to make the study of the financial constitution of India more comprehensive.

The study of the Executive would thus include a consideration of:

(i) the Governor-General;
(ii) Federal Ministry;
(iii) Federal Services;
(iv) Federal Finances; and
(v) Federal Defence.

Governor-General as head of the Executive

(i) Let us begin with the Governor-General.

The powers of the Governor-General are generally described in Section 7 of the Act, which reads:—

Functions of Governor-General

7.—(1) Subject to the provisions of this Act, the executive authority of the Federation shall be exercised on behalf of His Majesty by the Governor-General, either directly or through officers subordinate to him, but nothing in this

section shall prevent the Federal Legislature from conferring functions upon subordinate authorities, or be deemed to transfer to the Governor-General any functions conferred by any existing Indian Law on any court, judge or officer, or on any local or other authority.

(2) References in this Act to the functions of the Governor-General shall be construed as references to his powers and duties in the exercise of the executive authority of the Federation and to any other powers and duties conferred or imposed on him as Governor-General by or under this Act, other than powers exercisable by him by reason that they have been assigned to him by His Majesty under Part I of this Act.

(3) The provisions of the Third Schedule to this Act shall have effect with respect to the salary and allowances of the Governor-General and the provision to be made for enabling him to discharge conveniently and with dignity the duties of his office.

Under Section 3 (1) (b), the Governor-General has such other powers of His Majesty as may be assigned specifically to him,—other than powers of the Sovereign in his relations with the Indian States. These last also are, as it happens, entrusted to the present Governor-General, as representative of the Crown; but may, in future, as already remarked, be kept separate and entrusted to another officer. Section 3 (1) (a) gives him all the powers which are conferred upon him by or under this Act. Hence he has (i) the powers conferred by or under this Act; (ii) special powers of His Majesty, specifically conferred by His Majesty; (iii) powers of His Majesty conferred upon him as representative of the Crown.

The extent of the Federal Executive authority is defined by Section 8, which says:—

8.—(1) Subject to the provisions of this Act, the executive authority of the Federation extends—

(a) to the matters with respect to which the Federal Legislature has power to make laws;

(b) to the raising in British India on behalf of His Majesty of naval, military and air forces and to the governance of His Majesty's forces borne on the Indian establishment;

(c) to the exercise of such rights, authority and jurisdiction as are exercisable by His Majesty by treaty, grant, usage, sufferance, or otherwise in and in relation to the tribal areas:

Provided that—

(i) the said authority does not, save as expressly provided in this Act, extend in any province to matters with respect to which the Provincial Legislature has powers to make laws;

(ii) the said authority does not, save as expressly provided in this Act, extend in any Federated State save to matters with respect to which the Federal Legislature has power to make laws for that State, and the exercise thereof in each State shall be subject to such limitations, if any, as may be specified in the Instrument of Accession of the State;

(iii) the said authority does not extend to the enlistment or enrolment in any forces raised in India of any person unless he is either a subject of His Majesty or a native of India or of territories adjacent to India; and

(iv) commissions in any such force shall be granted by His Majesty save in so far as he may be pleased to delegate that power by virtue of the provisions of Part I of this Act or otherwise.

(2) The executive authority of the Ruler of a Federated States shall, notwithstanding anything in this section, continue to be exercisable in that State with respect to matters with respect to which the Federal Legislature has power to make laws for that State except in so far as the executive authority of the Federation becomes exercisable in the State to the exclusion of the executive authority of the Ruler by virtue of a Federal law.

Nature and Extent of Federal Executive Authority

The Executive authority of the Federation relates, generally speaking, to Federal affairs; and is exercisable subject to the provisions of this Act. Under this

Act, the Federal Executive authority does not extend:

(a) to the Provinces with respect to those matters on which the Provincial Legislature is entitled to make laws,—*i.e.*, under Schedule VII, List II;

(b) to the Federated States, except as to matters with respect to which the Federal Legislature has power to make laws, under Schedule VII, List I,—and, then, too, subject to such limitations as may be laid down in that behalf in the Instrument of Accession of each State;

(c) to the enlistment or enrolment of non-Indians in the defence forces of India.

The authority of the Ruler of a Federated State, in his State, is attempted to be specifically safe-guarded by sub-section (2); but it must be admitted the safeguard is a very slender and illusory one.

The Governor-General: Fivefold Powers

Analysed into their proper categories, the several powers and functions of the Governor-General fall into 5 classes:—

(i) Powers and Functions in regard to the Reserved Department;

(ii) Powers and Functions exercised **in his discretion;**

(iii) Powers and Functions exercised **in his individual judgment;**

(iv) Powers and Functions exercised on the advice of his Council of Ministers;

(v) Extraordinary Powers, (a) of Legislation; (b) of supervision over Provincial Governments; (c) and in relation to the States, Federated or non-Federated.

These, it will be noted, do not include the Powers and Functions exercised by this officer as Representative of the Crown, in the latter's relations with the Indian States and in regard to Paramountcy,—so long as the Governor-General and the Viceroy (representative of the Crown) continue to be one and the same person. They do not include, also, the special Prerogative Powers of the Crown entrusted to him specifically.

Reserved Departments

Under Section 11, there are four main Reserved Departments of the Federal Government, which are taken to be excluded wholly from the scope of the Governor-General's Constitutional Advisers. These Departments are:—

(a) Defence,—the problems and the constitutional aspect of which is considered in another Chapter separately;

(b) Ecclesiastical Affairs;

(c) External Affairs; but not relations with the Dominions;

(d) Excluded Areas.

(b) Ecclesiastical Affairs

(b) Under Section 11 (2), the Governor-General is empowered to appoint at most 3 Counsellors to advise him in the administration of these Departments. Let us begin this portion of our study by taking up first the Department of Ecclesiastical Affairs. These concern-only the Christian Church,—and mainly the Protestant Church of England, maintained in India at the expense of the Indian tax-payer to afford spiritual ministrations to the Christian Public Servants of the Crown in India. A few stipends are also allowed to Chaplains of the Christian Catholic Church, and to the Ministers of the Church of Scotland, under the terms of Section 269. In the main, however, this Department provides the spiritual ministration for only a microscopic minority of the people in India. By Section 33 (3) (e), the expenditure on this Department is not to exceed Rs. 42 lakhs a year, exclusive of pensions.

Provisions as to Chaplains

269.—(1) There may, as heretofore, be an establishment of chaplains to minister in India to be appointed by the Secretary of State and the provisions of chapter II of this Part of this Act shall, with any necessary modifications, apply in relation to that establishment and to persons appointed as chaplains by the Secretary of State or by the Secretary of State in Council, as they apply in relation to the civil services to which appointments are to be made by the Secretary of State and to persons appointed to a civil service under the Crown in India by the Secretary of State or by the Secretary of State in Council, and for the purposes of the provisions of chapter II relating to persons who retired before the commencement of Part III of this Act, the said establishment shall be deemed to be an All-India service.

(2) So long as an establishment of chaplains is maintained in the Province of Bengal, two members of that establishment in the Province must always be ministers of the Church of Scotland and shall be entitled to have out of the revenues of the Federation such salary as is from time to time allotted to the military chaplains in that Province.

This sub-section applies to the Province of Madras and to the Province of Bombay as it applies to the Province of Bengal.

(3) The ministers of the Church of Scotland so appointed chaplains must be ordained and inducted by the Presbytery of Edinburgh according to the forms and solemnities used in the Church of Scotland, and shall be subject to the spiritual and ecclesiastical jurisdiction in all things of the Presbytery of Edinburgh, whose judgments shall be subject to dissent, protest and appeal to the Provincial synod of Lothian and Tweeddale and to the General Assembly of the Church of Scotland.

The justice of this charge being thrown upon the Indian tax-payer has been always open to serious question, especially as, apart from this connection with spiritual affairs, the State in India professes to be wholly a secular organisation. For the vast majority of the children of the soil, and for any religious ministration to them, the Government of India have always professed an attitude of neutrality. This they would not disturb even for the purpose of effecting most overdue social reforms, which are inextricably interconnected with the religious beliefs of the people. The desire to keep this department outside party politics in India is understandable; but the justice of making this expenditure wholly non-votable, or even non-discussable, is impossible to realise. The people directly benefited by such ministrations could, if they really value such services, make their own contributions; and so obtain a solace or an opiate without being an unjustifiable burden upon the Indian people. The parallel alternative of active interest by the State in the local religions of the peoples of the country is not only not advisable under present conditions of India; it is positively dangerous and objectionable. The Communal tangle, bad enough as it is, will become seriously complicated, if the State becomes financially involved in the maintenance of mosques and temples, shrines and durgahs. In their own country, the precedent of the Disestablishment of the Protestant Church in Ireland, long before the Irish demand for national independence had become anything like a reality, is sufficient warrant, even if there were not unanswerable arguments in the intrinsic weakness of the Ecclesiastical Department maintained by the Indian Government as a charge upon the revenues of India, to demand an immediate disestablishment of this charge. And the proportion of the Irish people following this particular brand of the Christian religion was much larger, in comparison with the population of that country in the aggregate, than is at all the case of the Christian people in proportion to the rest of this country.

(c) External Affairs

The second of the excluded Departments concern the Foreign Affairs of India,—relations with the neighbouring States.

(i) Relations with Britain and the Dominions

Relations with the Dominions are expressly excluded from this term "External Affairs." These relations with the Dominions,—and, presumably, also the relations with the Colonies, like Ceylon,—are to be conducted by the Governor-General in the usual constitutional manner, *i.e.*, on the advice of the Federal Ministers.

The relations with the British Government proper are comprised in neither of these classes. Their conduct is in the hands of a number of authorities, beginning with the Secretary of State for India, the Governor-General and his Council of Ministers, and ending with the High Commissioner for India, who may be trusted to see to it that British interests in India do not suffer in the least because of the growth of Constitutional Government responsible to the people in India. A whole chapter of the Act of 1935 is devoted to prohibiting Indian Legislatures or Indian Governments of any degree from taxing, legislating or treating in any manner invidiously British traders and professional men settled in India;* while another still

*cp., Part V, cp. III, Sections 111-121. See Chapter XIII below.

longer portion of the Act is devoted to devising innumerable safeguards for protecting the interests of British public servants, civil as well as military, stationed in India. There is, therefore, no reason to provide still further in this behalf additional safeguards.

For years to come India's relations with the British Government and with the Dominions must constitute the gravest and most complicated block of her foreign affairs. They would concern not only the constitutional status of India, but also her foreign trade and credit, and even her contacts of all kinds with other European and American peoples. It may, therefore, seem satisfactory to find the conduct of these relations placed within the scope of Ministerial Responsibility, if and when the Federation of India is established. There is, however, no hope of a radical change resulting from this new constitutional arrangement.

Such conventions as are said to have been established already under the Act of 1919,—*e.g.*, the Fiscal Autonomy of India,—that is to say, freedom from British Imperial dictation when the Government of India and the Indian Legislature agree on issues of fiscal policy,—may materially influence the trend of policy hereafter. The possibility, however, of India's prompt and effective retaliation against such of the British Dominions as injuriously affect the status of Indians within their jurisdiction, or their rights to settlement, trade, or acquisition of real or personal property, seems still rather remote, even after the advent of Responsible Ministries at the Centre.

Relations with other countries

The possibility of adding to the economic strength of India by a proper conduct of her External Relations is very remote, however, because of the withdrawal of the rest of the External Affairs from the purview of Ministerial Responsibility. The Governor-General is entitled to appoint special Counsellors to advise him on these subjects; and these will be in no way responsible or subordinate to the people's representatives in the Federal Legislature. Even their salaries and conditions of service are, under Section 11, to be prescribed by His Majesty by an Order-in-Council. Hence, even the Governor-General would not have such control over them as to prevent them from acting as watch-dogs of British vested interests rather than Indian Public Servants, acting primarily and entirely in the interests of those who pay them. The Governor-General, for instance, cannot recommend the removal, much less himself remove any of these Counsellors from his post, even if he found such a Counsellor acting —not in the best interests of India. Needless to add these salaries, etc., are, under Section 33 (3) (c), placed outside the vote of the Legislative Assembly, being charged on the revenues of the Federation. The persons likely to be appointed to these posts, as also to the post of the Financial Adviser to the Governor-General, under Section 15, will be, most probably, non-Indians, with, perhaps, a strong bias against Indian ideals and aspirations, Indian demands and requirements, in such matters. Being appointed by an outside authority and irremovable by any authority in India, no matter how gross may be their dereliction of duty; with the salaries and allowances, determined in the first instance by an outside authority and beyond the vote of the Indian Legislature; with their training and temperament, traditions and environment being unsympathetic, if not antagonistic, to India, it may be easily realised how these functionaries may work against India, and put the clock of her material advance substantially backwards.

Legislature and External Affairs

Item 3 in List I, under Schedule VII, detailing the subjects on which the Federal Legislature would be entitled to make laws, is worded as under:—

"External Affairs; the implementing of treaties and agreements with other countries; extradition, including the surrender of criminals and accused persons to parts of His Majesty's Dominions outside India".

This is,—as indeed all these Lists are,—an extremely clumsily worded item. All that we can glean clearly from it is that while extradition as between Dominions is particularly mentioned, all other aspects of our relations with the British Dominions are not specified at all. Those aspects of the Foreign Relations, which require to be legislated for in order to be given effect to, are, perhaps, included in this item. If not, all "External Affairs" could be necessarily the subject matter of legislation. Treaty-making is, undoubtedly, an executive prerogative; and so, also, the appointment or accrediting of envoys, ambassadors, ministers, or counsels to Foreign Governments. India has, so far, no right to employ her own diplomatic or consular agents,—except, perhaps, the High Commissioner in England and in some of the Dominions, and Trade Commissioners in Britain, Germany, Italy, or Japan. It may be doubted if these officials could be rightly classed as diplomatic or consular agents. Such as they are, they come within the scope of the Executive Government, and as such may be within the power of the Governor-General to appoint and control. Negotiations for treaties of all kinds,—trade treaties, political engagements, financial pacts,—are to be conducted by the Governor-General, in so far as that officer has the right to conduct negotiations and conclude Treaties with India's immediate neighbours, or farther afield in Asia, Africa, Europe, or America.

Needless to add that relations with Indian States, within the Federation or outside, are not included under this term "External Affairs"; but that they will be, in so far as not included in the Federal Government, within the purview of the Representative of the Crown; and, as such, outside the scope of Ministerial Responsibility.

Critique of exclusion of External Affairs

The exclusion from the purview of responsible Ministers of the Federation of all our Foreign Relations weakens enormously the effective authority of those Ministers, and effectually undermines their power to do any real good to the people whom they represent. No other proof is necessary, in the face of this exclusion, that this Constitution is designed to keep India for ever within the leading strings of British Imperialism; that her Foreign Policy,—and, as a strong, indispensable prop of that policy, her provision for national defence,—is kept entirely and exclusively under the control of the supreme agent of that Imperialism, the Governor-General. To any one who understands in the least the most intimate connection between the Foreign Policy of a modern nation and its economic well-being, it is unnecessary to emphasise further evidence of the first charge made above. And to those who realise the close dependence of Britain herself on the foreign trade as a means of maintaining her own prosperity and pre-eminence in the nations of the world; to those who know the part the effective control of India's foreign policy in British hands plays for securing Britain's economic prosperity, this device of excluding the Foreign Affairs as a mark of distrust of Indian Nationalist statesmen, as an engine of rivetting Britain's economic drain from India, and her domination over all material concerns of this country, would require no further proof.

Dyarchy in the Federation

The Governor-General's powers are, under the Act of 1935, more extensive than those of the Provincial Governors. This is so not only because, in the ultimate analysis, he is the final boss of all provincial administrations,—and, for the matter of that, of the government even in the Indian States,—but also because important departments of Government are summarily excluded from the scope of the Federal Government altogether. These exclusions are, under the proposed regime, essentially different from the so-called Reserved Departments in the Provinces in the days of the Dyarchy. For, whereas in the latter, all departmental chiefs—Ministers and Executive Councillors,—worked together in a comman Cabinet in each Province, and so obtained inevitably the benefits of constant exchange of views under the proposed Federation there need be no such exchange of views, between those in charge of the Excluded Departments, and those responsible for the conduct of the administration in the other departments. The Governor-General is, of course, nominally, in sole charge of the excluded Departments. He is to be assisted by special Counsellors, under Section 11 (2) already referred to; and, apart from the Instrument of Instructions specially issued to the Governor-General, there is nothing to show that there will be a constant contact between the Reserved and the Responsible Department.* We shall comment upon the Instructions to the Governor-General in another section of this Chapter; and point out there how far a real unity, or even a co-ordination of national policy in the principal departments of State in India, is likely at all to be evolved.

II—Governor-General's Discretionary Powers

Besides the Departments of Government formally and expressly excluded from the scope of Ministerial responsibility,—and in which he is vested with sole discretion for all executive and administrative purposes,—the Governor-General is endowed, by the Act of 1935, with innumerable powers and functions to be exercised "in his discretion". The term discretion is nowhere defined in this Act. But the contrast it offers to the powers and functions to be exercised, under the same Act, "in his individual judgment", especially as made clear by Section 9 (1) of the Act, shows, that while the purely discretionary powers and functions are those in which the Governor-General need not even consult his Ministers, if he so chooses, in these in which is authorised "to exercise his individual judgment", he must, presumably, consult his Ministers, though he need not necessarily follow their advice; and that, if he does not accept their advice in these matters, his action would not be rendered invalid simply because it is not in accordance with the advice of the Ministers. By section 10 (4):

> "The question whether any and, if so, what advice was tendered by Ministers to the Governor-General shall not be enquired into in any Court".

*Cp. Article VIII of the Instrument of Instructions to the Governor-General.

The result would be that such matters would never be capable of being judicially decided, and the Constitution in this respect being legally interpreted by competent tribunals.* The vagueness, ambiguity, uncertainty, would accordingly remain uncorrected even though occasions should arise for a proper determination of what is meant by exercising powers in the Governor-General's sole discretion; and exercising them in his individual judgment.

It must be noted, however, that neither in the list of Discretionary powers, nor in those permitting the exercise of individual judgment, there is anything which makes it necessarily impossible for the Governor-General to consult his Ministers, even in these fields, and to abide by their advice. In no section of the Act is it anywhere laid down that in any given case, the Governor-General shall **not** ask, or shall not follow, the advice of his Ministers. Conversely, in more than one section giving him sole discretion, it is expressly provided that he must exercise those powers "after consultation" with named authorities, *e.g.*, the Minister, in making rules of business for his government, or the Speaker or the President in the Legislature for making certain rules of procedure. The ordinary, dictionary, meaning of "Discretion" makes it euivalent with the sole right of choice or decision, whether or not to do a thing,—especially if that thing is not expressly prohibited by law. If the Governor-General chooses to exercise his discretion, so as to seek the advice of his responsible Ministers, and even to follow it when given,—even in those matters in

*The law, note, does not say that no Court is competent to entertain such matters, or that no Court has jurisdiction, either originally or in appeal, in such matters; it only says such matters shall not be enquired into in any Court. The difference in wording is significant and suggestive.

which he is not bound to seek such advice, or to adopt it when obtained,—there is nothing in the Act to render such action of his unconstitutional. For instance, the Governor-General is authorised, by Section 9(2) "in his discretion" to preside at meetings of the Council of Ministers. If, however, following the practice of the King in Britain herself, and of the Governors-General in the Dominions, as also out of consideration of the fact that Ministers would never be free in their deliberations if at those deliberations the executive head of the Government is personally present, and comes to know their internal differences, if any, he uses his "discretion" so as ordinarily **not** to be present at such meetings at all, he would not be violating the Constitution in any regard. In fact, he would be following the best precedents already existing, and exalting the spirit of the Act above the mere letter thereof. He might even safeguard his position still further by being present and presiding, at times, when the Council meets for some purely formal function, *e.g.*, the announcement of the demise of a King, so that the right to preside at meetings of the Ministers should not fall completely into disuetude, and so be regarded as unconstitutional by convention.

The following are Sections giving most of the "discretion" to the Governor-General:—

1	(9)	1	General Authority.
2	(9)	2	Presiding at the meetings of the Council of Ministers.
3	(9)	3	Deciding questions in dispute as to whether a particular matter was a matter for the Governor-General's discretion or individual judgment.
4	(10)	10	Chosing, summoning, and dismissal of Ministers.

5	(10)	3	Determination of the Salaries of the Ministers until settled by an Act of the Legislature.
6	(11)	1	(i) Departments of Defence (ii) Ecclesiastical Affairs, (iii) External Affairs and (iv) Tribal Areas.
7	(15)	4	Appointment of Financial adviser, dismissal and determination of salary and allowances, as also the numbers of his staff and their conditions of Service. (Proviso: He must consult the Ministers before making any appointment *after* the first appointment as to the person to be selected).
8	(17)	2	Making of Rules for authentication of the orders and instruments of the Government.
9	(17)	3	Rules for the convenient transaction of the Governmental business and distribution of work amongst Ministers; and
10	(17)	4	Special Rules for keeping Governor-General informed.
11	(19)	2	Summoning of the Chambers, their proroguing and dissolution of Federal Assembly.
12	(20)	1	Addressing Federal Legislature.
13	(20)	2	Sending messages to Federal Legislature regarding pending Bills.
14	(22)	3	Appointment of acting chairman for Council of State in the vacancy of President and Deputy President.
15	(26)	1	(e) The fixing of period for removal of disqualification due to sentence of transportation or imprisonment.
16	(26)	1	(f) Removal of disqualification due to failure to lodge Election expenses return.
17	(31)	1 & 2	Summoning of joint meetings of two Chambers.
18	(32)	1	Disallowance of Bills, assent to Bills, withholding assent, or reserving Bills for His Majesty's consideration.
19	(32)	1	Proviso: Return Bills with a message for reconsideration.

20	(33)	4	Decision on question whether any expenditure is chargeable on the revenues of the Federation or not.
21	(38)	1	Making of Rules of procedure for Federal Assembly and Council of State regarding business which involve Governor-General's discretion or individual judgment; secondly, timely completion of Financial business; thirdly, prohibition of discussion or questions regarding affairs in Indian States, also waiving of such prohibition; fourthly, prohibition of discussion or Questions regarding a Foreign State or Ruler; fifthly, discussion or Questions on matters connected with Tribal or excluded areas; sixthly, discussion or questions regarding Governor-General's discretionary action in relation to Provincial affairs, or discussion or questions regarding personal conduct of any Indian Ruler or member of any Ruling Family,—and consent to waive all these.
22	(38)	2	Making of rules for procedure at Joint sittings.
23	(38)	3	First Rules of Procedure.
24	(40)	2	Prohibition of further proceedings on any Bill or Amendment certified to affect his special Responsibility regarding any menace to peace and tranquillity.
25	(43)		Making of Ordinances under Special Circumstances to enable Governor-General to discharge his discretionary functions, and those involving the exercise of his individual judgment, more satisfactorily.
26	(44)		Enactments of Governor-General's Acts or sending message with draft Bill for the purpose under special circumstances affecting his functions under these two classes.
27	(45)		Issuing of Emergency Proclamation, suspending constitution and assuming specified powers for himself.
28	(54)	1	Control over and issuing directions to Provincial Governors acting in *their* discretion or in their individual judgment.
29	(76)	1	Assenting to Provincial Bills reserved for Governor-General's assent, withholding

			assent, reserving same for His Majesty's pleasure, or directing return of such Bill to the Provincial Chamber with a message to reconsider the Bill or introduce certain amendments therein.
30	(88)	1	(b) Issuing instructions to Provincial Governors for promulgation of Ordinances.
31	(89)	5	Concurrence in issuing of Ordinances on certain subjects involving Governor's discretion or individual judgment; withdrawal of such Ordinances issued without such concurrence.
32	(90)	5	Concurrence in the enactment of the Governor's Acts.
33	(92)	2	Assenting to regulations made by the Governors regarding administration of Excluded or partially excluded areas.
34	(93)	5	Concurrence in the issue of Emergency Proclamations in the Provinces suspending Constitution.
35	(94)	3	Appointment of Chief-Commissioners.
36	(95)	1	Direction and control of the Administration of the British Baluchistan.
37	(95)	2	Directing that Acts of Federal Legislature shall apply to British Baluchistan, and making exceptions or modifications therein.
38	(95)	3	Making of regulations for the peace and good government of British Baluchistan.
39	(96)		Making of regulations for the peace and good government of Andaman and Nicobar.
40	(98)		Provisions as to Police rules regarding crimes of violence intended to overthrow Government.
41	(102)	1	Declaring that an Emergency exists for Federal Legislature to make laws for any province. And giving previous sanction to introduction of such Bills.
42	(104)	1	Empowering either Federal Legislature or any Provincial Legislature to make laws on

			subjects not included in their respective lists; but directing that the executive authority of the Federation or Province need not extend to the administration of such laws.
43	(107)	2	Giving previous sanction to Bills or amendments for making provision repugnant to existing Provincial Law which has received assent of Governor-General or His Majesty after having been reserved.
44	(108)	1	Giving previous sanction to seven classes of Bills in the Federal Legislature.
45	(108)	2	Giving previous sanction to Four Classes of Bills in the Provincial Legislatures.
46	(111)	3	Certifying that suspension of 111—(1) is necessary to prevent grave menace to peace and tranquillity of India or to combat crimes of violence.
47	(119)	1	Granting previous sanction to Bills or Amendments prescribing or permitting any authority to prescribe professional or technical qualifications, or imposing any disability, etc., for practising any profession, etc. (see also 2).
48	(123)		Directing Governors to discharge certain functions as his agents.
49	(125)		Making of agreements with rulers of Federated States for the exercise by the Ruler, etc., of the functions regarding the administration of any Federal Law applying therein.
50	(125)		Inspection, etc., of such administration; and issue of directions to the Ruler in this behalf.
51	(126)	4	Issuing of *Orders* to Governors for carrying out certain *Directions* and also Orders as to the manner in which the Executive authority is to be exercised.
52	(128)	2	Issuing of Directions to the Rulers of Federated States regarding fulfilment of obligations, after considering representations made to the Governor-General.

53	(129)	5	Decision on dispute whether any condition imposed regarding Broadcasting on any Provincial Governor or Ruler is lawfully imposed, or refusal to comply with the same is unreasonable.
54	(131)		Decision on complaints regarding the use of interprovincial or interstate-and-province water supplies.
55	(132)		Decision on complaints regarding Chief Commissioners' Provinces.
56	(132)	2	B. (ii) Modifications of the refund of Income-tax to the Provinces in the second prescribed period.
57	(141)		Previous sanction to Bills or Amendments (i) imposing or varying tax or duty in which provinces are interested; (ii) Varying meaning of "Agricultural income" for purposes of Indian income-tax; (iii) Affecting principles governing the distribution of monies to the provinces or Federated States. (iv) imposing Federal surcharges.
58	(152)		(a) Appointment and removal of Governor and Deputy Governor of Reserve Bank, approval of their salaries and allowances, fixing of their terms of office; (b) Appointment of officiating Governor or Deputy Governor; (c) Supersession of Central Board; (d) Liquidation of the Bank.
59	(153)		Previous sanction to Bill, etc., affecting coinage or currency, and constitution and functions of the Reserve Bank.
60	(163)	4	Decision on dispute regarding the refusal of Federal consent for Provincial borrowing or imposing of any condition.
61	(166)	3	Previous sanction to Bills regarding the duties and powers of the Auditor General regarding Federal or provincial accounts.
62	(170)		Previous sanction to Bills regarding the duties and powers of the Auditor of the Indian Home accounts.
63	(175)	1	Concurrence for the sale of land or building used as official residence.

64	(182)	1	Appointment of 3|7 of the members of the Railway Authority and the President thereof.
65	(182)	2	Previous sanction to Bills affecting appointment, qualifications and conditions of Service of members of Railway Authority.
66	(183)	2	Decision on disputed questions regarding policy.
67	(183)	4	General discretion in regard to the Railway Authority.
68	(187)	1	Determination of the sums equivalent to the amount of monies provided out of the revenue of India for capital purposes regarding Railways in India.
69	(187)	3	Decision on disputes regarding expenses for police on Railway premises between a province or a State, and the Railway Authorities.
70	(189)	1	Determination of the rate of interest on the balances of certain Railway Funds if there is no agreement for the same.
71	(195)	1	Making of rules for requiring Railway Authorities and any Federal State to give notice on any proposal for constructing or altering a Railway or for deposit of plans.
72	(195)	3	Suspension of this section where reasons of Defence require that effect should or should not be given to such a proposal.
73	(196)	1	Appointment of a panel to form a Railway Tribunal and selection of persons to constitute one.
74	(196)	2	Appointment of President of Railway Tribunal from Judges of Federal Tribunal.
75	(196)	6	Approval of rules made by President of Railway Tribunal regarding practice and procedure before Railway Tribunal and charging of fees.
76	(196)	8	Determination of remuneration to members of Railway Tribunal.
77	(199)		Appointment of Directors and Deputy Directors of Indian Railway Companies.

78	(206)	3	Previous sanction to Bill or amendment enlarging Appellate jurisdiction of Federal Court.
79	(213)	1	Referring questions of Law for opinion to the Federal Court.
80	(222)	1 & 3	Appointment of *temporary and additional* Judges of the High Courts, as also of the officiating Chief Justice of a High Court, and revocation of appointment of any temporary or additional Judge.
81	(226)	2	Previous sanction to Bill or amendment in the Federal Legislature for the Grant of jurisdiction in revenue matters.
82	(242)	4	(a) Appointment of persons not attached to a Court to any office connected with a Court after consultation with the Federal Public Services Commission.
83	(244)	4	Informing the Secretary of State regarding the operation of this section, and recommendation for its modification.
84	(251)		Proviso: (a & b) Approval of the numbers, salaries, qualifications of the staff of the Auditor of the Indian Home accounts.
85	(265)	1	Appointment of Chairman and members of the Federal Public Service Commission;
86	(265)		Determination of number, tenure of office and conditions of Service, and provision re: the staff and their conditions of Service.
87	(265)		(c) Previous approval of appointment of members of Federal Public Service Commission to any other post under the Crown.
88	(266)		Making of regulations to make consultation with public Services Commission necessary re: posts in connection with the Federation.
89	(267)		Previous sanction to Bill or amendment regarding enlargement of functions of the Public Service Commission.
90	(270)	1	Consent to civil or criminal proceedings against the Public Servants for Acts done in their official capacity.
91	(271)	1	Previous sanction to Bill or amendment abolishing or restricting protection to cer-

tain public servants under Section 197 of the Indian Code of Criminal Procedure, or Sections 80-82 of the Indian Code of Civil Procedure.

92 (286) 1 Use of His Majesty's forces in connection with the functions of the Crown in relation to Indian States.

93 (299) 3 Previous sanction to Bill or amendment for compulsory acquisition of any land, or any commercial or industrial undertaking, or any land or property of any commercial or industrial company subject to compensation.

(305) Secretarial Staff.

94 (308) Report on proposals for amending certain portions of this Act, and Orders in Council, especially as affecting any minorities.

Critique of these Powers

It is impossible to comment at length upon each of these powers to be exercised by the Governor-General in his sole discretion. Not only can we not foresee to-day the exact reaction in each case of the exercise of any of these powers; we cannot, also, fully appreciate the modes and forms, the occasions and circumstances under which they may come to be exercised, and the consequences to the economic well-being and the political consciousness of the people of India. Past experience is no guide in such matters, simply because the basic idea of the Government India is altered. In place of an essentially non-responsible alien bureaucracy,—controlled, directed and supervised from Whitehall,—there is to be, when the Federation of India is an accomplished fact, a Responsible Ministry for the whole of India in all common concerns, or such as are agreed to be such. But, looking upon the letter of the law of these numerous powers, we cannot help observing that a very substantial portion of the normal powers and duties falling to the share of Responsible Ministers in all parliamentary democracies has been taken away from the Responsible Ministers of the Federation of India; and that what remains will also be materially affected to the prejudice of the Ministers just because of these powers denied to them. The exercise of practically autocratic, exclusive powers by the head of the executive government,—himself a bird of passage,—overriding his Responsible Ministers, and often without any consultation with those Ministers, is bound to have repercussions of which we can predict nothing to-day when all experience of such exercise has yet to be. No analogy from the British or Dominions constitutional law or practice would, also, serve the turn; and so all we can offer by way of comment or criticism would be necessarily in the nature of a general summary of reflections unbacked by substantial documentation.

III—Governor-General's Powers in which he may Exercise his Individual Judgment.

List of the Sections conferring powers on the Governor-General to be exercised in his individual judgment

1	(9)	1	General.
2	(12)	1	Special responsibilities of the Governor-General, *viz.*;
3			(i) Prevention of grave menace to peace and tranquillity of India.
4			(ii) Safeguarding financial stability and credit of Federal Government.
			(iii) Safeguarding legitimate interests of Minorities.
5			(iv) Safeguarding legitimate interests of Public Services.
6			(v) Securing by executive action enforcement of anti-discremination provisions (Ss. 111-121).

			(vi) Preventing discremination against goods imported from United Kingdom or Burma.
			(vii) Protection of the rights of the Indian States and rights and dignity of their Rulers.
			(viii) Securing adequate funds for due discharge of *these*, and of functions to be discharged *in his discretion.*
10	(16)	1 & 3	Appointment, dismissal and remuneration of the Advocate General.
11	(25)	1	Making rules for regulating vacation by a member chosen for both Chambers his seat for one of them.
12	(28)	4	Proviso: Making of regulations for attendance before Committees of Inquiry of persons in Government Service, and safeguarding confidential information.
13	(42)	1	(a) Promulgation of Ordinances under special Emergencies.
14	(119)	3	Disallowance of regulations, etc., regarding technical qualifications.
15	(119)	4	Exercise of executive authority under a Federal law re: the proceeding.
16	(151)		Making of rules for the custody of public money.
17	(152)	2	Nominating and removing Directors of the Reserve Bank.
18	(184)	1	Making of rules for convenient transaction of business between Federal Government and Railway Authorities.
19	(196)	8	Determination of the amount of expenses to be included as administrative expenses of Railway Tribunal to be laid before Federal Legislature.
20	(216)	2	Inclusion of the administration expenses of the Federal Court in estimates of expenditure laid before Federal Legislature.
21	(246)	2	Appointments and postings to Reserved posts in connection with the affairs of the Federation.

22	(247)	2	Making of orders for promotion or granting leave or suspending an officer from office—as regards certain classes of officers.
23	(247)	3	Reduction of remuneration of an officer suspended from Office.
24	(248)	1	Consideration of complaints by Civil officers and their remedy.
25	(248)	2	Order regarding punishment, censure, reduction of emoluments or of pension or deciding adversely any memorial from him.
26	(258)	1	(a) Abolition of any civil post in certain classes or Central and Railway Services;
27	(258)	2	Rules affecting adversely the pay, allowances or pension to officers as above.
28	(262)		Declaration of eligibility of Rulers or subjects of particular Indian States not being Federated States to hold permanent or temporary civil posts under the Crown.
29	(271)	2	Exercise of powers under Section 197 to sanction prosecutions against public servants in connection with the affairs of the Federation.
30	(271)	3	Defraying of costs in the civil suits against such public servants from Federal revenues.
31	(300)	1 & 2	Protection of certain rights, previleges or pensions from land or grant of land revenue.
32	(302)	1	Appointment of High Commissioner for India, his salary, and conditions of service.

Critique of Extraordinary Powers

Taken collectively, substantially the same criticism must be offered against this long list of the Discretionary powers given to the Governor-General,—nearly a hundred items in all,—as has been levelled, in the earlier part of this work on the system of Provincial Autonomy in India, against the corresponding powers of the Provincial Governors. Not only does it remove the most considerable part of governmental routine from the hands of the Responsible, popoular, Ministers; it denies them any initiative in some of the most important aspects of national administration, and takes away all sense of responsibility from them, even in such cases as require the executive head of government to consult his Ministers. Whether we consider the purely administrative routine;—the Rules and Regulations of public service; the promotion and postings of officers in certain specially favoured services; the inclusion of certain items of public expenditure in the list of those charged upon the revenues of the country; or we take into account the innumerable classes of Bills or amendments of existing laws, attempting to do away with certain impossible privileges, requiring previous sanction of the Governor-General *in his discretion* for being introduced or moved in the Federal Legislature; or think of the direct powers of legislation by way of Ordinances, or Governor-General's Acts, or giving and withholding assent to measures passed by the Federal Legislature, or recommending certain classes of Bills,—we find, at each step, a dead wall of distrust against the Indian element said to be introduced by or under this Act in the responsible councils of the Federation of India. The Ministers are liable, at every stage, to be kept out of their legitimate sphere of responsibility in all normal constitutions; to be thwarted and overridden; baffled and frustrated in their attempt to add to the prosperity and self-respect of the people.

The Governor-General is thus not only the supreme executive head of the Indian Government; he is also the dominating chief of the Ministry, and the controlling, directing, almost dictating factor in all aspects of *government,—legislative, executive*, or even judicial.

There are no doubt certain concerns of the supreme Government in India,—*e.g.*, the functions of the Crown in its relations with the Indian States, particularly in regard to the so-called powers of Paramountcy,—which may need a certain exclusiveness, that cannot but impede the growth of collective responsibility for the entire governmental policy of the country. The Governor-General, even more than the Provincial Governors, is the representative of the British Crown in India. If ever he is to evolve into a perfect replica of the model set by the British Sovereign, these special and extraordinary powers of exclusive discretion cannot but go effectively counter to this intended transformation of the autocratic chief of an irresponsible Bureaucracy into the Constitutional head of a Responsible Government.

Special Responsibilities of the Governor-General

Let us here also comment in brief upon the Special Responsibilities placed upon the Governor-General by this Act Section 12, and those other analogous powers and functions which he is charged to exercise in his individual judgment, *i.e.*, without being obliged to follow in every case the advice of his Responsible Ministers. The genesis and essence of the doctrine of Special Responsibility has been already explained; and so we need not cover the same ground over again.* The list given above of these Special Responsibilities, is much wider than those of the Provincial Governors

*cp. "Provincial Autonomy, ch. 3, pp.96, et seq.

though in all other respects the wording of the corresponding sections seems to be identical. The three added items are:—

(i) The safeguarding of the financial stability and credit of the Federal Government; Section 12 (1) (b);

(ii) The prevention of action which would subject goods of United Kingdom or Burmese origin imported into India to discriminatory or penal treatment; Section 12 (1) (f);

(iii) The securing that the due discharge of his functions with respect to matters with respect to which he is by or under this Act required to act in his discretion, or to exercise his individual judgment, is not prejudiced or impeded by any cause of action taken with respect to any other matter; Section 12 (1) (h).

The inclusion of (i) above has been justified on the report of one of the Committees of the Round Table Conference, which held that "a fundamental condition of the success of the new Constitution that no room should be left for doubts as to the ability of India to maintain her financial stability and credit, both at home and abroad"

and that it is therefore necessary

> "to reserve to the Governor-General in regard to budgetary arrangements and borrowing, such essential powers as would enable him to intervene if methods were being pursued which would in his opinion seriously prejudice the credit of India in the money markets of the world".

The Joint Select Committee of Parilament, therefore, recommended:

> "In our opinion, though the expression 'budgetary arrangements and borrowing' indicates generally the

sphere in which it is desirable that the Governor-General should have power, if necessary to act, it would be unwise to attempt to describe this special responsibility in more precise terms than are proposed in the White Paper".*

Financial Responsibility

It is thus a deliberate act to leave this most serious concern of government undefined, so that the field of action reserved to the Governor-General, and that entrusted to the Responsible Ministers of the Federation, is obviously overlapping. The Act adopts the recommendation of the Joint Select Committee of Parliament in authorising the appointment of a Financial Adviser to the Governor-General.† His advice, however, would be available to the Ministers as much as to the Governor-General. But, inasmuch as the Financial Adviser would not be a member of the Ministry, he would be unable to appreciate the motives of National Policy leading a Ministry to propose measures which may not, immediately considered, appear

*op., op. cit. para 174.

†Says Section 15:—

(1) The Governor-General may appoint a person to be his financial adviser.

(2) It shall be the duty of the Governor-General's financial adviser to assist by his advice the Governor-General in the discharge of his special responsibility for safeguarding the financial stability and credit of the Federal Government, and also to give advice to the Federal Government upon any matter relating to finance with respect to which he may be consulted.

(3) The Governor-General's financial adviser shall hold office during the pleasure of the Governor-General, and the salary and allowances of the financial adviser and the numbers of his staff and their conditions of service shall be such as the Governor-General may determine.

(4) The powers of the Governor-General with respect to the appointment and dismissal of a financial adviser and with respect to the determination of his salary and allowances and the numbers of his staff and their conditions of service shall be exercised by him in his discretion:

Provided that if the Governor-General has determined to appoint a financial adviser, he shall, before making any appointment other than the first appointment, consult his ministers as to the person to be selected.

perfectly orthodox to an old-fashioned, conservative Financial Adviser. The latter might even view those measures with an amount of distrust which is really not their due. And because the Governor-General is vested with a Special Responsibility, over the entire field of finance and credit of the Federal Government, he may, on the advice of his Financial Adviser, override his Ministers, and defeat their policy.

This must needs be a matter of grave concern to those who would work the Constitution embodied in the Act of 1935. The fact that the Governor-General is entrusted with the administration, in his sole discretion, of some of the largest spending departments of Government,—whose expenditure results in no material addition to the wealth of the country; the fact, further, that, even apart from these excluded Departments of extravagant cost, the Governor-General is entrusted with innumerable powers of *discretion*, which may not only involve heavy outlay charged upon the revenues of the Federation* but which may interfere substantially with fundamental lines of policy; and, finally, the fact that, by sub-section (1) (h) of this Section 12, the Governor-General is granted plenary powers to interfere with and override any line of policy pursued by his Ministers, if he considers them at all likely to come in the way of the due discharge of all his discretionary functions, and his powers to be exercised in his individual judgment, makes this arrangement fraught with the gravest menace to the growth of true constitutional practice in regard to finance, and even to the prevalence of sound finance, considered in the long run.

*See below, Chapter on the Federal Legislature, and Section 33, for explanation of this phrase: "charged upon the revenues of the Federation."

It would be interesting to add that this particular Special Responsibility is not imposed upon the Provincial Governors. But, in their case, not only is the danger not very considerable of Ministers following lines of policy that are calculated to endanger the financial stability and credit of the country; but even the Governor has ample powers to prevent any such untoward development in his Province. The financial responsibilities of the Federal Government are, however, deemed to be so considerable, that Parliament has thought it proper to make it a Special Responsibility of the Governor-General, and allow him an expert adviser for the purpose.

Special Responsibility for British Trade

The other Special Responsibility of the Governor-General, not paralleled in the list of the corresponding Responsibilities of his Provincial prototype, relates to treatment of British or Burmese goods imported into India. The *raison d'etre* of this particular Responsibility, at least so far as the Burmese goods are concerned, is a little difficult to appreciate. Perhaps it was imagined that the relations between the Federation of India and Burma are likely, in the near future, to be so strained that Responsible Indian Ministers might be inclined to advise retaliatory measures affecting Burman imports into this country. So far as present indications go, this is, however, a very unlikely contingency. But, in regard to British goods imported into India, apart from a whole Chapter of the Constitution devoted to prevent unfair discrimination against British goods imported into India, this Special Responsibility is added to see that, even administratively, there is no unfair, penal, or invidious treatment accorded to British goods imported into India. Except for the all too powerful impulse of British Imperialism,—and the memory of the treatment given to Indian goods, and Indian aspirants for acquiring industrial technique in British establishments,—there is no reason why this Special Responsibility should be so specifically added. India can use no weapon against British competitors, which the Governor-General cannot, in effect, stultify or veto, whether in the legislative or in administrative field.

We have already commented on the third of these additional Special Responsibilities not to be found in the corresponding list of the Governor's Responsibilities; and so need not comment at further length upon it here.

Instrument of Instructions to the Governor-General

Let us, at this stage, consider the Instructions given to the Governor-General for the conduct of the Executive Government of the Federation,—if and when it comes into being; for the interpretation of his Special Responsibilities, and for the exercise of his Discretionary powers and functions. Under Section 13 of the Act of 1935.

13.—(1) The Secretary of State shall lay before Parliament the draft of any Instrument of Instructions (including any Instrument amending or revoking an Instrument previously issued) which it is proposed to recommend His Majesty to issue to the Governor-General, and no further proceedings shall be taken in relation thereto except in pursuance of an address presented to His Majesty by both Houses of Parliament praying that the Instrument may be issued.

(2) The validity of anything done by the Governor-General shall not be called in question on the ground that it was done otherwise than in accordance with any Instrument of Instructions issued to him.

Appendix I to this chapter gives the Draft Instrument of Instructions to the Governor-General to be enforced when the Federation is established.* Though these Instructions will be issued under an express provision of an Act of Parliament, they are unenforceable in any Court of Law. To guard against a possible litigation, the law actually lays down that actions of the Governor-General, even though in violation of his Instructions, cannot be questioned in any Court of law. The only sanction—wholly academic—upon the officer for the due observance of these Instructions is the power of the King-Emperor to recall him from office, or that of Parliament to impeach him,—out of use for over 150 years. These weapons, if they exist in the armoury Imperialist Governance, are rusted, obsolete, and utterly ineffective under modern conditions.

The principal features of the Instructions to the Governor-General of the Federation of India is the clarification of the conduct to be pursued in the appointment of the Council of Ministers, infusion in them of a spirit and tradition of collective responsibility, and the amplification of what is meant and intended by the Special Responsibilities imposed by the Act upon the Governor-General. In so far, however, as the Special Responsibilities come in the way of the full sense of Ministerial Responsibility; or in so far as the rigorous discharge, in the traditional

---

*The Gazette of India Extraordinary, dated April 1, 1937, contains the Letters Patent constituting the office of the Governor-General of India: the Commission under the Royal Sign Manual appointing Lord Linlithgow as the Governor-General and Viceroy, investing him with the power to exercise the Royal Prerogative of Mercy, as also to issue Commissions to officers in the Indian Army, Navy and the Air Force, and to exercise the rights of Paramountcy, as representing the King-Emperor, in relation to the Indian States. It also contains Instructions which are valid during Transition period till the Proclamation of Federation. The Instructions contained in the appendix apply when the Federation comes into being.

channels of these Special Responsibilities of the Governor-General impede the economic development of India, or the fruition of Nationalist ambitions, the Instructions do not remove the Nationalist objections. In fact, they explain the real intention of the framers of the Constitution, and stress in a somewhat reactionary direction what the exigencies of legal draftsmanship have necessarily left vague and undefined in the body of the Act.

The Governor-General of India is instructed, for example to

> "avoid action which would affect the competence of his Government and of the Federal Legislature to develop their own fiscal and economic policy, or would restrict their freedom to negotiate Trade Agreements whether with the United Kingdom or with other countries for securing mutual tariff concessions; and he should intervene in tariff policy or in the negotiations of tariff agreements only if in his opinion the main intention of the policy contemplated is by trade restrictions to injure the interests of the United Kingdom rather than to further the economic interests of India".*

Stated in ordinary language, this should mean that, unless the Governor-General is satisfied that the intention of **a Tariff Policy, or of a proposed Trade Agreement with** a foreign country is to hurt British Trade interests in India, he is to leave absolute freedom of action to his Constitutional Advisers in taking economic and fiscal steps, which are calculated to promote the economic interests of India. But, in practice, this would be extremely difficult always to achieve. Given the atmosphere of distrust and conflict of interest, sharp differences are inevitable between a strong-willed Governor-General, and an equally determined Council of Ministers, as to whether or not a given line of economic policy or trade treaty is primarily in the interests

*Vide Article XIV of the Draft Instructions.

of India, or rather intended to injure the interests of Britain, whether or not Indian interests are promoted thereby. The Ministers might well urge, that if the substantial result of a projected measure or a Treaty is to promote the interests of India, even though, incidentally, the interests of Britain might conceivably be affected thereby, the Governor-General is not entitled to intervene. The Governor-General, on his part, might equally pertinently point out that the original, determining consideration in the minds of his Ministers,—the intention,—of their proposal was rather to injure the interests of Britain,—possibly by that means to attain some other political object,—than really, directly to further the economic interests of India; and, as such, he was bound by his Instructions to intervene. As the Instructions are not open to a judicial interpretation, this debatable land is likely to be productive of constant conflict, irritation, and lack of harmony.

This illustration has been deliberately selected because the department of External Affairs is in the sole charge of the Governor-General, and to be administered under his discretion. Only when Treaties require legislation to implemented that the Federal Ministers would get a *locus standi* to put in a word. Under his specific Instructions, however, the Governor-General is asked, not only to give them freedom to shape the country's economic policy as they think fit and proper. They seem also entitled to conduct the negotiations for trade treaties with the United Kingdom as well as with foreign countries. The conflict is, therefore, much more likely in such a case of overlapping authority and conflict of powers,—especially in view of the known cleavage of economic interests between Britain and India.

Under Articles XVII—XIX relating to Defence,—another reserved or excluded department of State to be administered by the Governor-General in his discretion,—

> "Our Governor-General shall encourage the practice of joint consultation between himself, his Counsellors and his Ministers. And seeing that the Defence of India must to an increasing extent be the concern of the Indian people, it is our will in especial that our Governor-General should have regard to this instruction in his administration of the Department of Defence; and notably that he shall bear in mind desirability of ascertaining the views of his Ministers when he shall have occasion to consider matters relating to the general policy of appointing Indian Officers to Our Indian Forces, or the employment of Our Indian Forces on Service outside India".

If this analogy of joint consultation between Ministers and Counsellors of the Governor-General on questions affecting a Reserved Department is adopted, the Ministers should be able to acquire knowledge and experience relating to this branch of the administration; and even influence the policy concerning that administration. The same may also happen in the Department of External Affairs,—more particularly in regard to the conduct of negotiations for Trade Treaties, even though, under the strict letter of the law, the Council of Federal Ministers would have no right to intrude in such matters. So long, however, as there prevails an atmosphere of mutual distrust; so long as the Governor-General regards himself, not as the constitutional head of a great country, but as primarily the trustee of foreign vested interests, which are presumed to be endangered by every growth of Nationalist sentiment in this country, there can be no hope of such Instructions modifying the rigour of the Constitutional law in the right direction.

The same must be said of the injunction that the Federal Ministry,—and, more particularly, the Federal Finance Minister,—should be consulted before estimates for the Defence Department are settled and laid before the Federal Legislature, as also that the Federal Finance Minister should be kept in close touch of the expenditure on that department. Mere consultation with the Ministry and information to the Finance Minister will not avert the mischief of complete absence of any legal authority to shape the defence policy or regulate such expenditure.

IV. Powers exercised on the Advice of his Ministers

If we deduct the two large classes of powers and functions, which the Governor-General is entitled by law to exercise in his sole discretion, or in his individual judgment, the field of real power and effective authority open to the Council of Ministers is necessarily extremely limited. As we have already seen, Section 7 gives the extent of the executive authority of the Federation vested in the Governor-General. This is much wider than that of his Constitutional Advisers, the extent as well limitations of whose powers and authority are indicated in Section 9.

9.—(1) There shall be a council of Ministers, not exceeding ten in number, to aid and advise the Governor-General in the exercise of his functions, except in so far as he is by or under this Act required to exercise his functions or any of them in his discretion:

Provided that nothing in this sub-section shall be construed as preventing the Governor-General from exercising his individual judgment in any case where by or under this Act he is required so to do.

(2) The Governor-General in his discretion may preside at meetings of the council of Ministers.

(3) If any question arises whether any matter is or is not a matter as respects which the Governor-General is by or under this Act required to act in his discretion or to

exercise his individual judgment, the decision of the Governor-General in his discretion shall be final, and the validity of anything done by the Governor-General shall not be called in question on the ground that he ought or ought not to have acted in his discretion, or ought or ought not to have exercised his individual judgment.

The Ministers have no legal right to be consulted in Departments specifically excluded from the purview of Ministerial Responsibility, nor in such matters as are placed in the sole discretion of the Executive head of the Federal Government. Even in powers and functions of government, in which the Governor-General is enjoined to exercise his individual judgment, that officer is not necessarily bound to follow the advice of his Ministers. The only portion, therefore, in which the executive authority of the Federal Government is exercised by the Governor-General exclusively on the advice of his Ministers is in regard to matters on which the Federal Legislature is competent to legislate, provided that any other section of the Constitution Act does not place a specific limitation upon the Ministers' powers in that behalf.

Even in the field assigned to the Legislature, the Governor-General has a vast margin of extraordinary powers which may cripple the independence of the Legislature considerably.

Governor-General's Powers over the Legislature, and in regard to Legislation

These powers of the Governor-General may be enumerated under the following heads:—

(i) Power to summon the Legislature, and address the two Chambers, and order the attendance of the members for the purpose.

(ii) Power to make Rules of Procedure for regulating the business before either House of the

Legislature; introducing certain reserve powers for forbidding the asking of Questions on certain subjects, or permitting those Questions, as also discussion on the same; authorise certain officers to address the Assembly;

(iii) Power to accord previous sanction to the introduction of any Bill or Amendment in either Chamber of the Legislature, regarding certain subjects affecting his Discretionary powers, or those functions which he is enjoined to exercise in his individual judgment;

(iv) Power to recommend certain classes of Bills to the Legislature;

(v) Power to send Messages suggesting certain changes, or modifications, in a proposed measure which must be considered and adopted by the Legislature;

(vi) Power to order Joint Sittings of the two Chambers of the Legislature on certain occasions, and under certain conditions;

(vii) Power to assent to, withhold assent, or reserve certain Bills, passed by the Legislature for the signification of the King's pleasure,—who may disallow these measures after as much as a year since their enactment;

(viii) Power to pass Ordinances, either on the advice of his Ministers, or in his discretion;

(ix) Power to enact Governor-General's Acts;

(x) Power to suspend the Constitution, and govern under powers assumed to himself under a Proclamation of Emergency.

Summoning, etc. Legislature

(i) Summoning the Legislature to meet, ordering joint sittings, addressing the Chambers, and a margin of reserve powers to make rules regarding certain qualifications, or rather disqualifications of members,* are not unparalleled in the Constitutional usages of the Governor-General's controlling powers over the Legislature. Unless the entire Constitution is suspended under Section 45, the Governor-General must call at least one session every year; and he must not allow twelve months to elapse without calling a meeting. Sections 19 and 20 give powers, which, on their face, are not unparalleled in the Constitutional usages of Britain.

Rule-making Powers

(ii) The power to make Rules of Procedure for either Chamber of the Legislature, and, through that device, to influence materially the course of business in the Legislature, is contained in Section 38.

Procedure generally

38.—(1) Each Chamber of the Federal Legislature may make rules for regulating, subject to the provisions of this Act, their procedure and the conduct of their business:

Provided that as regards each Chamber the Governor-General shall in his discretion, after consultation with the President or the Speaker, as the case may be, make rules—

(a) for regulating the procedure of, and the conduct of business in, the Chamber in relation to any matter which affects the discharge of his functions in so far as he is by or under this Act required to act in his discretion or to exercise his individual judgment;

(b) for securing the timely completion of financial business;

(c) for prohibiting the discussion of, or the asking of questions on, any matter connected with any Indian State, other than a matter with respect to which the Federal Legislature has power to make laws for that State, unless the Governor-

*cp. Section 26 (1) (e) and (f).

General in his discretion is satisfied that the matter affects Federal interests or affects a British subject, and has given his consent to the matter being discussed or the question being asked;

(d) for prohibiting, save with the consent of the Governor-General in his discretion,—

(i) the discussion of, or the asking of questions on, any matter connected with relations between His Majesty or the Governor-General and any foreign State or Prince; or

(ii) the discussion, except in relation to estimates of expenditure, of, or the asking of questions on, any matter connected with the tribal areas, or the administration of any excluded area; or

(iii) the discussion of, or the asking of questions on, any action taken in his discretion by the Governor-General in relation to the affairs of a Province; or

(iv) the discussion of, or the asking of questions on, the personal conduct of the Ruler of any Indian State or of a member of the Ruling family thereof;

and, if and in so far as any rule so made by the Governor-General is inconsistent with any rule made by a Chamber, **the rule made by the Governer-General shall prevail.**

(2) The Governor-General, after consultation with the President of the Council of State and the Speaker of the Legislative Assembly, may make rules as to the procedure with respect to joint sittings of, and communications between, the two Chambers.

The said rules shall make such provision for the purposes specified in the proviso to the preceding sub-section as the Governor-General in his discretion may think fit.

(3) Until rules are made under this section the rules of procedure and standing orders in force immediately before the establishment of the Federation with respect to the Indian Legislature shall have effect in relation to the Federal Legislature subject to such modifications and adaptations as may be made therein by the Governor-General in his discretion.

(4) At a joint sitting of the two Chambers the President of the Council of State, or in his absence such person

as may be determined by rules of procedure made under this section, shall preside.

This power, it is needless to add, is unprecedented in the British model. The rationale of this reservation in the hands of the Governor-General lies in the diplomatic necessity to prevent questions or discussions in the Legislature, which may complicate the relations with the neighbouring powers, or embarrass the dealings of the Crown Representative with the Indian Princes. So far as the former are concerned, since the department of External Affairs is wholly excluded from the scope of the authority of Responsible Ministers of the Federation of India,—except in so far as any Treaty needs legislation in India to be implemented,—there may be a justification for excluding any inconvenient matters being discussed in the Legislature, or Questions asked thereon. Those, however, who can appreciate the utility of such Questions or discussions in the popular Legislature of a country, as aids to negotiations in Trade or other Treaties, will not need much argument to demonstrate the impolicy of keeping out such matters from the scope of the Parliamentary interrogations or discussions. Even if the Indian people, and their chosen representatives, are deemed yet too unfamiliar with the niceties of Foreign Relations,—or too unworthy to be trusted entirely with the care of those relations in so far as they might affect the deeper economic interests of British Imperialism,—the limitation on discussion or interpellation in the Legislature might have been more fittingly, or less offensively, made by Standing Orders of the House itself, vesting such powers of disallowing Questions of a given type in the presiding officer; or even in the

Government as a whole, and not in the Executive head personally, acting throughout **in his discretion.**

The logic and policy of excluding Questions or discussions regarding Indian Princes, or any member of these Ruling Families, are still more difficult to appreciate,—especially after the advent of the Federation of India, in which, sooner or later, all Indian Princes may be expected to join. Unwritten rules of public decorum might, perhaps, dictate the exclusion of legislative interpellations regarding the private lives or personal vagaries of actual Rulers,—though even there, given the average standard of conduct among these relics of ancient India, it is open to question if the interests of India in the long run would benefit by such privilege. The Indian Ruling Princes have no dread nor restraint upon any indulgence in follies or vices, save, perhaps, the frown of the Paramount Power, which may be stimulated by such timely enquiries in the Legislature of the country. If that door is also to be closed, on the pretence of public propriety or political courtesy, the plight of the people in those unfortunate areas will become even more intolerable than it is to-day. And, even if considerations of courtesy or public propriety are allowed to extend a measure of indulgence to the Ruling Princes proper, there is no reason why similar indulgence should be extended to the members of their families. This criticism has always been urged in British India against the doings of particular Princes, even when they could justly claim a privileged position as being not partners in a Commonwealth. Now, however, that the Federation of India is likely to be established, by or under the Act of 1935, what little reason there ever was for such special treatment will cease to be. The power given to the Governor-General cannot, therefore, but appear to be a needless impediment to the full growth of the National Legislature.

Powers of Previous sanction to Legislative Measures

(iii) We have already detailed the various sections and sub-sections of the Act, relating to the discretionary powers of the Governor-General, or those involving the exercise of his individual judgment, under which the previous sanction of the Governor-General is necessary before a Bill or Amendment of certain existing laws could be introduced in the Legislature. Inasmuch as these are almost all Bills or Amendments of the existing laws which affect vested interests of the Public Services and similar bodies fattening at the expense of India, the reservation of this power to the Governor-General, and the possibility thereby of his blocking any improvement in these matters in the interests of India, indicate the true origin and the real purpose of such powers. Determined Ministers, conscious not only of the public behind them in this country, but also of the sterling justice of their cause, might not be deterred, merley because the Governor-General has such powers initially to block any such legislation, from attempting the reforms necessitated by such vested interests. A strong-willed Governor-General, on the other hand might equally conceive it to be his bounden duty, under the law, not to sanction the introduction of such measures which may endanger the special interests he is intended to protect and safeguard. A Constitutional conflict would then become unavoidable. An appeal to the country by a dissolution of the Legislature will not help matters, as the

Governor-General's powers in this behalf are irrespective of popular opinion in this country. He is a champion of British vested interests, not a constitutional head of the executive in India.

Power of Veto over Legislation

It may be added that, under the law, the mere fact that previous sanction has been accorded to a class of measure which requires it, does not preclude the Governor-General from subsequently withholding assent to such measures when the Legislature has duly passed the same. The presence of this double power,—of initial blocking, and of subsequent veto,—is an astute form of Constitutional obstruction from above, a deliberate device of political distrust, and a calculated measure of Imperialist safeguard. For, given this power of initial blockade, intensification of sentiment might be nipped in the blood, especially if,—as is commonly assumed in Imperialist circles,—Indian politicians are still too much lacking in self-confidence to insist on a line of policy which could be thus prevented from materialising *ab initio.* In proportion as Indian politicians learn the full measure of the confidence reposed in them by their constituents; in proportion as they realise the havoc wrought by such vested interests upon the general well-being of their country; and in proportion as they appreciate the tactics necessary to counteract such devices of Imperialist diplomacy, provisions of the Constitution like those instanced above are likely to cause the gravest and the most frequent impasse.

Power to recommend Legislation

(iv) The Governor-General's power to recommend certain classes of Bills to the Legislature, and insist that his recommendations be accepted and adopted by the Legislature, applies principally to Finance Bills says.

37.—(1) A Bill or amendment making provision—

(a) for imposing or increasing any tax; or

(b) for regulating the borrowing of money or the giving of any guarantee by the Federal Government, or for amending the law with respect to any financial obligations undertaken or to be undertaken by the Federal Government; or

(c) for declaring any expenditure to be expenditure, charged on the revenues of the Federation, or for increasing the amount of any such expenditure,

shall not be introduced or moved except on the recommendation of the Governor-General, and a Bill making such provision shall not be introduced in the Council of State.

(2) A Bill or amendment shall not be deemed to make provision for any of the purposes aforesaid by reason only that it provides for the imposition of fines or other pecuniary penalties, or for the demand or payment of fees for licences or fees for services rendered.

(3) A Bill which, if enacted and brought into operation, would involve expenditure from the revenues of the Federation shall not be passed by either Chamber unless the Governor-General has recommended to that Chamber the consideration of the Bill.

Authenticated Schedule of Expenditure

Under Section 34 (4) no demand for a grant for any item of public expenditure can be made in the Legislature "except on the recommendation of the Governor-General."

Under Sections 35 and 36,—the most considerable powers are granted to the Governor-General for overriding the Legislative Assembly in matters of Finance. By the device of an "Authenticated Schedule of authorised Expenditure,"—certified as such by the Governor-General,—any item of expenditure, whether of the class which the Assembly is entitled to vote or not, may be required to be granted by the Assembly upto the amount originally specified in the Financial Statement laid before the Assembly under Section 33. If the Assembly declines to adopt that recommendation of the Governor-General, the amount will nevertheless be granted lawfully, and defrayed as originally provided for in the Financial Statement. Says,

35.—(1) The Governor-General shall authenticate by his signature a schedule specifying—

(a) the grants made by the Chambers under the last preceding section;

(b) the several sums required to meet the expenditure charged on the revenues of the Federation but not exceeding, in the case of any sum, the sum shown in the statement previously laid before the Legislature:

Provided that, if the Chambers have not assented to any demand for a grant or have assented subject to a reduction of the amount specified therein, the Governor-General may, if in his opinion the refusal or reduction would affect the due discharge of any of his special responsibilities, include in the schedule such additional amount, if any, not exceeding the amount of the rejected demand or the reduction, as the case may be, as appears to him necessary in order to enable him to discharge that responsibility.

(2) The schedule so authenticated shall be laid before both Chambers **but shall not be open to discussion or vote therein.**

(3) Subject to the provisions of the next succeeding section, no expenditure from the revenues of the Federation shall be deemed to be duly authorised unless it is specified in the schedule so authenticated.

This applies, it is true, to cases where any of the Governor-General's Special Responsibilities are involved. But reading this provision along with the injunction of Section 12 (1) (b) and Section 12 (1) (h), it is evident that almost any item of Public Expenditure can be so authorised and included in the certified schedule by the Governor-General over the head of, or in spite of, the Legislative Assembly. The corresponding power in the Constitution of 1919 was at least a little more guarded. For, under the terms of Sections 67-A (7) and (8), the Governor-General is obliged formally to declare that the grant withheld or reduced by the Assembly was essential to the discharge of his responsibilities; or that a given expenditure, authorised by him in an emergency was necessary for the safety or tranquillity of British India. No such certificate or declaration is apparently needed under the provision of the Act of 1935 quoted above. Section 36, permits an unlimited amount of Supplementary Expenditure, without even the qualifying condition of a national emergency, or the endangering of the safety and tranquillity of India, added to restrain the Governor-General, or to make him and his Counsellors moderate in regard to the exercise of such extraordinary powers granted to the executive head of the Government in matters financial. With such powers in reserve, held by the practically non-responsible chief executive, it would be no surprise, if the Legislature, and the Ministers responsible to that body, acquire little sense of responsibility in framing their financial policy.

A list of the other Bills which the Governor-General may recommend to the Legislature, and which must be passed in the form recommended, will be found in the lists of his discretionary powers, and of the functions to be exercised in his individual judgment.

Communications with the Legislature

(v) Sending of Messages, addressing the Chambers of the Legislature, ordering,—for that purpose,—the attendance of the members of both Chambers in one of these, and addressing the Chambers on lines of policy, are practices which may seem to be borrowed from the British model. In Britain, however, most of these devices are utilised to emphasise solemn occasions,—such as the accession of a new King, or his or her marriage, or request to make provision for the Royal Family, as each succeeding King takes the place of his predecessor. In this country, on the other hand, messages from the Governor-General have dictatorial air and purport in a number of instances provided for in the Constitution, or under the rules made thereunder.

As for addressing the two Chambers of the Legislature, the practice in England is for the Ministers to prepare the Speech from the Throne at each new sessions of Parliament, which would review the policy of the Cabinet during the period elapsed since the last such occasion, and outline the proposal for legislation the Ministers may have in contemplation. In India, Lord Willingdon, as Governor-General, did try to follow this model. But even in his case, the speech was prepared by his non-responsible, bureaucratic colleagues, which, instead of the usual programme of proposed measures for public welfare in a speech from the Throne in Britain, more often than not breathed fire and sword to those who had the misfortune not to see eye to eye with His Excellency in regard to the repressive policy so characteristic of his regime, and the reaction in all political and economic fields which was the undisguised order of the day in those years. In the years to come, when Federation is an accomplished fact,—if it ever is so,— one cannot say if that practice will be followed literally; whether the speech of the Governor-General to the Legislators will be confined only to those departments of the State on which the Legislature has any control, or whether it would be a review of the policy pursued and measures contemplated. Section 20 of the Act imposes no limit on the discretion of the Governor-General in such matters.

20.—(1) The Governor-General may in his discretion address either Chamber of the Federal Legislature or both Chambers assembled together, and for that purpose require the attendance of members.

(2) The Governor-General may in his discretion send messages to either Chamber of the Federal Legislature whether with respect to a Bill then pending in the Legislature or otherwise, and a Chamber to whom any message is so sent shall with all convenient dispatch consider any matter which they are required by the message to take into consideration.

Even if similar in form to the British practice, this is, in spirit, not at all like its model. The British Parliment has always maintained the tradition of looking to the people's grievances before the proposals of the Executive are attended. " Redress of grievances before the voting of supplies " is a maxim of Constitutional practice, which finds expression even to-day in the formal motion, before the debate on the Speech from the Throne commences, to take into consideration some matter of popular importance. In India, under this section, there may be no such recognition of the redress of popular grievances proceeding the voting of supplies, or consideration of the other proposals placed before the Legislature by the message or the Address of the Governor-General. The Legislature shall take into consideration forthwith any matter which the message of the Governor-General orders them to attend to. This makes the position of the Legislature,—and, consequently, that of the Ministry which holds power simply as the leaders of the Legislature,—distinctly subordinate to that of the Governor-General.

Under Section 40 (2):—

> "If the Governor-General **in his discretion** certifies that the discussion of a Bill introduced or proposed to be introduced in the Federal Legislature, or of any specified clause of a Bill, or of any amendment moved or proposed to be moved to a Bill, would affect the discharge of his Special Responsibility for the prevention of any grave menace to the peace or tranquillity of India or any part thereof, he may **in his discretion** direct that no proceedings, or no further proceedings, shall be taken in relation to the Bill, clause or amendment, and effect shall be given to the direction."

This, along with the provision of Sections 35 and 36, regarding an Authenticated Schedule of Authorised Expenditure, as also regarding Supplementary Estimates of Expenditure, make up the three most important instances in which the Legislature must, without further discussion or vote, give effect to the mandate of the Governor-General.

The Instructions given in regard to the stay of proceedings in the Legislature provide that:—

> "The power vested by the said Act in Our Governor-General to stay proceedings upon a Bill, clause or amendment in the Federal Legislature, in the discharge of his Special Responsibility for the prevention of grave menace to peace and tranquillity shall not be exercised unless, in his judgment, the public discussion of the Bill, clause or amendment would itself endanger peace and tranquillity.*"

*Article XXIX of the Instrument of Instructions.

The Governor-General is not only made the sole judge as to whether or not, in a given situation, there is a serious menace to the peace and tranquillity of India; he is also made the exclusive authority in deciding whether or not a particular measure pending before the Legislature would endanger the Country's peace and tranquillity. No definition, or indication, is given as to what class of measures this provision is intended to apply to. Ordinarily, one might think communal tension is the principal objective of such safeguards. But it is not inconceivable that even industrial disputes, and political sentiment mixed up with proposals for radical, social or economic reforms, might be interpreted by an overcautious Governor-General as likely to contain a menace to the country's peace and tranquillity. But, whether this is intended to guard against communal tension reaching an undesirable height, or economic and political matters coming to a crisis, the point may well be urged: How does the Governor-General judge the situation, and decide correctly that it contains elements of danger against which he has been vested with special powers? After all, he is not in touch with the people, as his Ministers, through their fellow members in the Legislature, and the latter through their constituents, may well claim to be. He is, again, very likely a foreigner, unfamiliar with the local language, unacquainted with local customs and sentiments. Nevertheless the Governor-General,—an utter outsider,—is invested with powers of judging a situation, and guarding against, overriding the Legislature and the Ministry, which, the latter, if they are worth their salt, and at all know their responsibilities, would be far better able to appreciate correctly and remedy effectively!

Messages under Section 44 are frankly extraordinary, and will be touched upon in their proper place.

Summon Joint Sessions

(vi) The power to summon Joint Sittings of the two Chambers of the Federal Legislature is contained in Section 31 which says:—

31.—(1) If after a Bill has been passed by one Chamber and transmitted to the other Chamber—

(a) the Bill is rejected by the other Chamber; or

(b) the Chambers have finally disagreed as to the amendments to be made in the Bill; or

(c) more than six months elapse from the date of the reception of the Bill by the other Chamber without the Bill being presented to the Governor-General for his assent,

the Governor-General may, unless the Bill has lapsed by reason of a dissolution of the Assembly, notify to the Chambers, by message if they are sitting or by public notification if they are not sitting, his intention to summon them to meet in a joint sitting for the purpose of deliberating and voting on the Bill:

Provided that, if it appears to the Governor-General that the Bill relates to finance or to any matter which affects the discharge of his functions in so far as he is by or under this Act required to act in his discretion or to exercise his individual judgment, he may so notify the Chambers notwithstanding that there has been no rejection of or final disagreement as to the Bill and notwithstanding that the said period of six months has not elapsed, if he is satisfied that there is no reasonable prospect of the Bill being presented to him for his assent without undue delay.

In reckoning any such period of six months as is referred to in this sub-section, no account shall be taken of any time during which the Legislature is prorogued or during which both Chambers are adjourned for more than four days.

(2) Where the Governor-General has notified his intention of summoning the Chambers to meet in a joint sitting, neither Chamber shall proceed further with the Bill, but the Governor-General may at any time in the

next session after the expiration of six months from the date of his notification summon the Chambers to meet in a joint sitting for the purpose specified in his notification and, if he does so, the Chambers shall meet accordingly:

Provided that if it appears to the Governor-General that the Bill is such a Bill as is mentioned in the proviso to sub-Section (1) of this Section, he may summon the Chambers to meet in a joint sitting for the purpose aforesaid at any date, whether in the same session or in the next session.

(3) The functions of the Governor-General under the provisos to the two last preceding sub-sections shall be exercised by him **in his discretion.**

(4) If at the joint sitting of the two Chambers the Bill, with such amendments, if any, as are agreed to in joint sitting, is passed by a majority of the total number of members of both Chambers present and voting, it shall be deemed for the purposes of this Act to have been passed by both Chambers: Provided that at a joint sitting—(a) if the Bill, having been passed by one Chamber, has not been passed by the other Chamber with amendments and returned to the Chamber in which it originated, no amendments shall be proposed to the Bill other than such amendments (if any) as are made necessary by the delay in the passage of the Bill; (b) if the Bill has been so passed and returned, only such amendments as aforesaid shall be proposed to the Bill and such other amendments as are relevant to the matters with respect to which the Chambers have not agreed, and the decision of the person presiding as to the amendments which are admissible under this sub-section shall be final.

(5) A joint sitting may be held under this section and a Bill passed thereat notwithstanding that a dissolution of the Assembly has intervened since the Governor-General notified his intention to summon the Chambers to meet therein.

This device of a Joint Sessions of the two Chambers is, without any disguise, a means to make the will of the executive head prevail over that of his Responsible Ministers, and the representatives of the Indian people, without recourse to frankly unconstitutional methods, or extraordinary powers. We shall see, when we consider the composition of the Federal Legislature, what hidden safeguards are provided for the maintenance of the British Imperialist hold over India, in the very composition of the Federal Legislature. While the Assembly,—the so-called Lower House,—is to be elected by indirect election and proportional voting,—so that all the groups and cross divisions in the Local Legislatures might be mirrored in the National Legislative Assembly,—the Upper House, with 250 members, as regards British Indian representatives is elected in a manner which is bound to give the greatest influence to the Governor-General, especially through the hundred odd representatives of the Indian Princes joining the Federation. In a Joint Sitting, the maximum membership would be 635, out of which the States would have at the most 229 members; 6 more could be, at most, nominated by the Governor-General. We may take it that, in any conceivable crisis, these 235 members would stand solid behind the Governor-General. The Representatives of the Indian Provinces, —both in the Assembly and in the Council of State,— will, however, scarcely ever be united to such a degree, in questions of policy that might lead to a crisis and demand a joint sitting, as would override these instruments of the will of the Governor-General. To carry a point against the Governor-General in a joint sitting of the Federal Legislature, his opponents would need an aggregate voting strength of 320. Though the elected Representatives of British India total 400, it may be readily assumed that, in such a crisis as is herein contemplated, they would themselves be divided, so that the 85 votes needed to swamp the opposition to the Governor-General could be easily obtained at a pinch.

Under Section 34 (3) it is compulsory on the Governor-General to summon a joint sitting if the two

Chambers have disagreed as to any demand for a grant of money; and the decision of the majority at such joint sitting shall prevails. This means, that even in financial matters, the Assembly is not final, nor exclusive.

Power of Assent or Veto

(vii) The power of the Governor-General to assent to a Bill passed by the Legislature, or to withhold assent, or to reserve it for the consideration of His Majesty is no dead letter. Says Section 32 of the Act of 1935:—

> 32.—(1) When a Bill has been passed by the Chambers, it shall be presented to the Governor-General, and the Governor-General shall **in his discretion** declare either that he assents in His Majesty's name to the Bill, or that he withholds assent therefrom, or that he reserves the Bill for the signification of His Majesty's pleasure:
>
> Provided that the Governor-General may in his discretion **return** the Bill to the Chambers with a message requesting that they will reconsider the Bill or any specified provisions thereof and, in particular, will consider the desirability of introducing any such amendments as he may recommend in his message, and the Chambers shall reconsider the Bill accordingly.
>
> (2) A Bill reserved for the signification of His Majesty's pleasure shall not become an Act of the Federal Legislature unless and until, within twelve months from the day on which it was presented to the Governor-General, the Governor-General makes known by public notification that His Majesty has assented thereto.
>
> (3) Any Act assented to by the Governor-General may be disallowed by His Majesty within twelve months from the day of the Governor-General's assent, and where any Act is so disallowed the Governor-General shall forthwith make the disallowance known by public notification, and as from the date of the notification the Act shall become void.

Under these provisions, five several kinds of fate may befall measures passed by the Indian Legislature:

(a) A Bill passed by the Legislature may be assented to by the Governor-General; or

(b) assent may be withheld; or

(c) the Bill may be reserved for consideration by the King-Emperor;* or

(d) the Bill may be returned to be reconsidered, with amendments or modifications suggested by the Governor-General, which must be considered by the Legislature; or

(e) the Bill, even after being assented to by the Governor-General, may be disallowed by the King-Emperor, not by any positive act, but by simple silence on a Bill reserved for the significance of His Majesty's pleasure for more than a year.† The

*Says Clause XXVII of the Instructions (draft) to the Governor-General: "Our Governor-General shall not assent in our name to, but shall reserve for the signification of our pleasure, any Bill of any of the classes herein specified, that is to say:—

(a) any Bill the provisions of which would repeal or be repugnant to provisions of any Act of Parliament extending to British India;

(b) any Bill which in his opinion would, if it became law, so derogate from the powers of the High Court of any Province as to endanger the position of which these Courts are by the said Act designed to fill;

(c) any Bill passed by a Provincial Legislature, and reserved for his consideration which would alter the character of the Permanent Settlement;

(d) any Bill, regarding which he feels doubt whether it does, or does not, offend against the purposes of Chapter III, Part V of the said Act.

†Says Prof. A. B. Keith, in his Constitutional Law of the British Dominions:—

"While reservation of Bills (passed by the Dominion Legislatures) was, at the time when the Conference of 1926 met, an essential element of the Dominion Constitutions, the power of disallowance, though provided for in all cases save the most recent Constitution, that of the Irish Free State, had long been a dead letter." (p. 22). The learned writer mentions instances, such as a Bill severing the connection of a Dominion with the British Commonwealth, as one in which disallowance, on the advice of the Imperial British Cabinet, and against the advice of the Dominion Ministry, may properly be ordered by the King. But he also mentions that, in the case of the Australian States, though the power to disallow local Acts of the States has been expressly given to the King, the King has never exercised that power on the advice of the Commonwealth Ministry. Would the same precedent be followed in regard to the Provincial Legislation from India? The power to disallow Indian Acts,—whether Federal or Provincial, will not, it may be apprehended, be a dead-letter,—whether as regards Indian Loans, or for any of the purposes on which the Imperial British interests may be in conflict with the immediate Indian interests.

existing Constitution seems liberal in comparison to the Act of 1935, in this regard. In the former case, a Bill passed by the Indian Legislature and assented to by the Governor-General could be disallowed by a positive act of the King-in-Council, and not by simple silence, as in this instance.*

This five-fold power of the executive chief over the Legislature, in regard to its most important business, will effectually tie the Federal Legislature to the apron strings of the Governor-General. The power of veto, disallowance, compulsory reconsideration, are all either unknown in the Constitutions of other Dominions, or practically dead for want of use.

Ordinances and Governor-General's Acts

(viii & ix) The direct Legislative powers of the Governor-General, **viz.**, passing Ordinances, either on the advice of his Ministers, or in his discretion; and passing the so-called Governor-General's Acts, are provided for in Section 42-44 of the Act. These are extraordinary laws, but have the same validity as any ordinary act of the Indian Legislature, and are subject to the same supervision, or disallowance by the King, as apply to oridnary legislation. The provision to submit certain Ordinances to the Federal Legislature is of only a nominal safeguard of the authority of the Legislature, since the disapproving resolutions of the Legislature, even if passed, will not have retrospective effect; and, for the time that the Ordinance is

*Compare the language of Sections 68 and 69 of the Government of India Act, 1919, and that of Section 32 quoted above, or with that of Sections 76 and 77 as regards Provincial Legislation.

in operation, it will be as good as any law of the land. Even this safeguard does not avail in case of the Ordinances passed under Section 43, which relate to the Governor-General's extraordinary powers: and they do not apply at all to the Governor-General's Acts. For the rest, the actual terms of the three Sections are more eloquent than any comment we can offer.

42.—(1) If at any time when the Federal Legislature is not in session the Governor-General is satisfied that circumstances exist which render it necessary for him to take immediate action, he may promulgate such ordinances as the circumstances appear to him to require:

Provided that the Governor-General—

(a) shall exercise his individual judgment as respects the promulgation of any ordinance under this section if a Bill containing the same provisions would under this Act have required his previous sanction to the introduction thereof into the Legislature; and

(b) shall not, without instructions from His Majesty, promulgate any such ordinance if he would have deemed it necessary to reserve a Bill containing the same provisions for the signification of His Majesty's pleasure thereon.

(2) An ordinance promulgated under this section shall have the same force and effect as an Act of the Federal Legislature assented to by the Governor-General, but every such ordinance—

(a) shall be laid before the Federal Legislature and shall cease to operate at the expiration of six weeks from the re-assembly of the Legislature, or, if before the expiration of that period resolutions disapproving it are passed by both Chambers, upon the passing of the second of those resolutions;

(b) shall be subject to the provisions of this Act relating to the power of His Majesty to disallow Acts as if it were an Act of the Federal Legislature assented to by the Governor-General; and

(c) may be withdrawn at any time by the Governor-General.

(3) If and so far as an ordinance under this section makes any provision which the Federal Legislature would not under this Act be competent to enact, it shall be void.

43.—(1) If at any time the Governor-General is satisfied that circumstances exist which render it necessary for him to take immediate action for the purpose of enabling him satisfactorily to discharge his functions in so far as he is by or under this Act required in the exercise thereof to act in his discretion or to exercise his individual judgment, he may promulgate such ordinances as in his opinion the circumstances of the case require.

(2) An ordinance promulgated under this section, shall continue in operation for such period not exceeding six months as may be specified therein, but may by a subsequent ordinance be extended for a further period not exceeding six months.

(3) An ordinance promulgated under this section shall have the same force and effect as an Act of the Federal Legislature assented to by the Governor-General, but every such ordinance—

(a) shall be subject to the provisions of this Act relating to the power of His Majesty to disallow Acts as if it were an Act of the Federal Legislature assented to by the Governor-General;

(b) may be withdrawn at any time by the Governor-General; and

(c) if it is an ordinance extending a previous ordinance for a further period, shall be communicated forthwith to the Secretary of State and shall be laid by him before each House of Parliament.

(4) If and so far as an ordinance under this section makes any provision which the Federal Legislature would not under this Act be competent to enact, it shall be void.

(5) The functions of the Governor-General under this section shall be exercised by him in his discretion.

44.—(1) If at any time it appears to the Governor-General that for the purpose of enabling him satisfactorily to discharge his functions in so far as he is by or under this Act required in the exercise thereof to act in his discretion or to exercise his individual judgment, it is essential that provision should be made by legislation, he may by message to both Chambers of the Legislature explain the circumstances which in his opinion render legislation essential and either—

(a) enact forthwith, as a Governor-General's Act, a Bill containing such provisions as he considers necessary; or

(b) attach to his message a draft of the Bill which he considers necessary.

(2) When the Governor-General takes such action as is mentioned in paragraph (b) of the preceding sub-section, he may at any time after the expiration of one month, enact, as a Governor-General's Act, the Bill proposed by him to the Chambers either in the form of the draft communicated to them or with such amendments as he deems necessary, but before so doing he shall consider any address which may have been presented to him within the said period by either Chamber with reference to the Bill or to amendments suggested to be made therein.

(3) A Governor-General's Act shall have the same force and effect, and shall be subject to disallowance in the same manner, as an Act of the Federal Legislature assented to by the Governor-General and, if and in so far as a Governor-General's Act makes any provision which the Federal Legislature would not under this Act be competent to enact, it shall be void.

(4) Every Governor-General's Act shall be communicated forthwith to the Secretary of State and shall be laid by him before each House of Parliament.

(5) The functions of the Governor-General under this section shall be exercised by him in his discretion.

Power to suspend the Constitution

(x) But the most considerable power over the Legislature is given to the Governor-General by Section 45. It permits him practically to suspend the entire constitution, if in his opinion an emergency has arisen necessitating such a course. The emergency herein contemplated is a purely political impasse, such as was reached at the time Provincial Autonomy was introduced under this Act,* and not one in which the entire country's security was endangered.

*Contrast, for this purpose, the language of Section 192, and that of Sections 45 or 93.

45.—(1) If at any time the Governor-General is satisfied that a situation has arisen in which the Government of the Federation cannot be carried on in accordance with the provisions of this Act, he may by Proclamation—

(a) declare that his functions shall to such extent as may be specified in the Proclamation be exercised by him in his discretion;

(b) assume to himself, all or any of the powers vested in or exercisable by any Federal body or authority,

and any such Proclamation may contain such incidental and consequential provisions as may appear to him to be necessary or desirable for giving effect to the objects of the Proclamation, including provisions for suspending in whole or in part the operation of any provisions of this Act relating to any Federal body or authority:

Provided that nothing in this sub-section shall authorise the Governor-General to assume to himself any of the powers vested in or exercisable by the Federal Court or to suspend, either in whole or in part, the operation of any provision of this Act relating to the Federal Court.

(2) Any such Proclamation may be revoked or varied by a subsequent Proclamation.

(3) A Proclamation issued under this section—

(a) shall be communicated forthwith to the Secretary of State and shall be laid by him before each House of Parliament;

(b) unless it is a Proclamation revoking a previous Proclamation, shall cease to operate at the expiration of six months:

Provided that, if and so often as a resolution approving the continuance in force of such a Proclamation is passed by both Houses of Parliament, the Proclamation shall, unless revoked, continue in force for a further period of twelve months from the date on which under this subsection it would otherwise have ceased to operate.

(4) If at any time the Government of the Federation has for a continuous period of three years been carried on under and by virtue of a Proclamation issued under this section, then, at the expiration of that period, the Proclamation shall cease to have effect and the Government of the Federation shall be carried on in accordance with the other provisions of this Act, subject to any amendment thereof which Parliament may deem it necessary to make,

but nothing in this sub-section shall be construed as extending the power of Parliament to make amendments in this Act without affecting the accession of a State.

(5) If the Governor-General, by a Proclamation under this section, assumes to himself any power of the Federal Legislature to make laws, any law made by him in the exercise of that power shall, subject to the terms thereof, continue to have effect until two years have elapsed from the date on which the Proclamation ceases to have effect, unless sooner repealed or re-enacted by Act of the appropriate Legislature, and any reference in this Act to Federal Acts, Federal laws, or Acts or laws of the Federal Legislature shall be construed as in including a reference to such a law.

(6) The functions of the Governor-General under this section shall be exercised by him in his discretion.

V-(a) The Governor-General's Powers over the Provincial Governments

The immense field of the Governor-General's discretionary powers and functions, and those to be exercised in his individual judgment, is perhaps, nowhere so vividly illustrated as in his controlling, supervisory, and even directive powers over the Provincial Governors, or Governments, including the Provincial Legislatures. The bare list of the sections under which these powers have been assigned to the Chief Executive Officer in India will serve, without any commentary, to show how effective and universal is the power of the Governor-General over the Provinces, their Governors, Ministries, or Legislatures. The claim, in view of these enormous powers vested in the Governor-General, that Provincial Autonomy is a real fact of the New Indian Constitution, will, after a careful study of all these provisions, vanish into thin air, even if it does not become an insult added to the injury effected by this Constitution as a whole.

Speaking generally, these powers extend;—

(i) to the maintenance of general peace and tranquillity of India or any part thereof, including Provinces and States;

(ii) to superintendence and direction of the Provincial Governor in the latter's powers of a discretionary character, or even those to be exercised in his Individual Judgment;

(iii) to the prior sanction needed for certain classes of Bill or amendments to be introduced in the Provincial Legislature; the recommendation of specific amendments to Bills passed by the Provincial Legislature, if the Bill in question had been reserved for consideration by the Governor-General; or for the significance of His Majesty's pleasure; assenting to Provincial Bills reserved for his consideration,—or withholding assent; or reserving such Bills for the significance of His Majesty's pleasure; extraordinary Legislative Powers of Ordinances and Governor-General's Acts, as well as Emergency Legislation by the Federation;

(iv) Financial powers for the distribution of the net proceed of certain taxes, for the postponement of the period during which the agreed, or sanctioned, share of the Income-tax is to be distributed between Provinces; making of certain grants to the Provinces; and control over Provincial borrowing. This flows from the special responsibility for the maintenance of India's Credit, and the financial stability of the country;

(v) Certain Administrative powers, including the right to issue Orders to the Governors, for carrying out Federal Laws, or the Governor-General's special directions or orders; for the control of Broadcasting; for investigation of disputes as regards water-supplies;

(vi) Judicial,—including appointments of Acting Chief Justice of a Provincial High Court,—and the power of pardoning criminals;

(vii) Powers over the appointment, etc., of the High Commissioner, and the approval of the terms on which he is to do business for the Provincial Governments;

(viii) Miscellaneous.

List of Sections giving Powers to the Governor-General over the Provincial Governors or Governments

Section 7: General powers which may include Provincial Governors and Governments.

Section 12: Two items in the list of the Governor-General's Special Responsibilities,—(i) safeguarding the financial stability and credit of the Federal Government; and (ii) prevention of any grave menace to the peace or tranquillity of any part of India.

Section 33 (3) (g): Any grants for excluded areas in a Province to be charged upon the revenues of the Federation, and as such determined by the Governor-General in his discretion [cp. Section 33 (4)].

Sections 42, 43, 44, 45: Relating to Ordinances passed by the Governor-General, either in his Individual Judgment or in his Discretion, the Governor-General's Acts, and the suspension of the entire Constitution under a Proclamation of Emergency, which may undoubtedly affect the Provinces.

Section 54: General control over the Governor, with the right to issue to the latter particular directions, in regard to all matters in which the Governor is entitled to act in his discretion, or to exercise his individual judgment.

This is the most direct and unequivocal power of control and direction vested in the Governor-General as against the Provincial Governors,—particularly in connection with the latter's extraordinary powers. The Governor-General is himself, for similar purposes, under the control direction and supervision of the Secretary of State for India,—as we shall see in another connection. It may be added that the

Governor-General cannot issue to a Provincial Governor directions under this section which would compel the latter to act contrary to his instructions. Opinion may differ as to what constitutes such an act; and, in the event of such a difference, the opinion of the Governor-General shall, for the time being at any rate, prevail, as the wording of the sub-section (2) clearly shows.

Section 76: Assenting to, or withholding assent from, or reserving a duly passed Provincial Bill for the significance of His Majesty's pleasure; returning such a Bill (by direction to the Governor) to the Provincial Legislature, with a message for its reconsideration and for considering the desirability of introducing such amendments in the Bill as may be specified in the Message. This section applies to only those Bills of the Provincial Legislature which have been reserved for the Governor-General's consideration by the Local Governor.

N.B.—In this connection we may also note other Sections giving to the Governor-General such powers over Provincial Legislation, or Legislature.

Section 88: Right to issue Instructions to the Governor before the latter promulgates Ordinances under this section.

Section 89: Right to have certain Ordinances, promulgated under this section, to be communicated to the Governor-General, and the right to concurrence of the Governor-General, before the Governor exercises his powers under this section.

Section 90: Similar right as to communication and concurrence, as regards Governor's Acts passed under this section.

Section 92: Communication to the Governor-General of regulations made by the Governor in his discretion, for the "Peace and Good Government," of any excluded area in a Province; and assenting to the same, before they could have any effect.

Section 93: Concurrence in the issue of Proclamation by a Provincial Governor in his Province, suspending the Constitution in that Province.

N.B.—Sections 94 and 95 grant considerable powers to the Governor-General over the so-called Chief Commissioners' Provinces. As, however, these entities are directly under the Governor-General, these need not be considered as granting supervisory, directive, or controlling powers over Provincial Governors, or Governments, to the Governor-General.

Section 102: Right of the Federal Legislature to legislate for a Province on any matter in the Provincial List of subjects, if the Governor-General declares a state of national emergency by Proclamation, in stating that the security of the country is threatened by war or internal disturbance.

Section 104: The Governor-General may by his discretion empower the Federal or a Provincial Legislature to legislate on any subject not included in any of the Lists in Schedule VII, and exercise executive authority even in a Province to enforce such a law, unless the Governor-General otherwise directs.

Sections 123-128: Purely administrative matters:—

Under **Section 123**, the Governor-General may direct the Governor of any Province to discharge certain functions, as his Agent, in relation to Tribal areas, Defence, Ecclesiastical Affairs, or External Affairs.

Under **Section 124,** the Governor-General may entrust to a Provincial Government, with the latter's consent, functions regarding matters within the Executive Authority of the Federation.

Under **Section 126,** as head of the Federal Executive, the Governor-General may issue **directions** to any Provincial Government necessary for the proper exercise of the authority of the Federal Executive. Directions may likewise be given to a Province for the enforcement of any Federal law on a subject in Part II of the Concurrent List of subjects in Schedule VII, provided that no Bill or amendment relating to the issue of such directions can be introduced in the Federal Legislature without the previous sanction of the Governor-General in his discretion. The same rule applies to the proper maintenance in a Province of means of communications declared to be of military importance. If any of these directions are not properly attended to in a Province, the Governor-General, in his discretion, may re-issue the same directions as **Orders** to the Provincial Governor concerned, or with any modifications he considers necessary. **Orders** may be issued by the Governor-General at any time as regards the exercise of the executive authority in the Province concerned, to prevent any grave menace to the peace or tranquillity of any part of India,—the issue of **Orders** being always a matter of the Governor-General's discretion.

Under **Section 127,** the Federal Executive may require a Province to acquire land for any purpose on which the Federal Legislature is entitled to make laws, at expense of the Federation.

Section 129: empowers the Governor-General, in his discretion, to decide questions in dispute as to whether any conditions imposed by the Federal Government upon a Province, regarding the construction and use of wireless transmitters, are unreasonable, or whether any refusal by the Federal Government to entrust such functions to a Province is unreasonable. The special responsibility of the Governor-General regarding the prevention of any grave menace to the peace or tranquillity of any part of India, through the transmission by wireless is particularly safeguarded and reserved.

Sections 130-131: entitle the Governor-General in his discretion to receive complaints from Provincial Governments regarding the prejudice to their right to water from a natural source, to have the matter investigated by a Commission, and to issue orders on the report of such a Commission.

Section 132: extends this power to water-supplies for the Chief Commissioner's Provinces.

Section 137: authorises the Federation to levy and collect taxes on succession to non-agricultural property, stamp duties mentioned in the Federal Legislative List, Terminal Taxes on goods and passengers carried by railway or air, and taxes on railway fares and freights, for distribution of the net proceeds among the Provinces according to the principles of distribution laid down in a Federal Act. This is a most insidious right of controlling the Provincial Governments, since its full effects are not visible on the surface. Not only is the Federal right to a surcharge on these source of taxation reserved; the rates of each such tax, and the rules for distributing the proceeds are entirely within the powers of the Federal Government. The Provinces can not only not benefit to the full extent of their taxable capacity in such matters; they will always be liable to an indirect mulcting by the Federal Government by way of a surcharge,—and possibly by way of new taxation on these sources of wealth or taxable capacity. We have included this in the list of powers of the Governor-General, even though, in terms the section gives this power to the Federal Government, because the Governor-General is vested with a Special Responsibility for the maintenance of the financial stability and credit of India as a whole; and, in virtue of this responsibility, he has considerable reserve powers that may very easily affect the use of these sources of revenue for Provinces.

Section 138: Relates to the distribution, by stated periods, of a share of Income-Tax among the Provinces, with discretion to the Governor-General to modify the pace of the period for such distribution. Having already commented at length in another work on this section, it is unnecessary to explain it here further.

Section 140: Gives power to distribute, if an Act of the Federal Legislature so provides, part or whole of the net proceeds of the duty on salt, federal excises, and export duties among Provinces, provided that half or more of the net proceeds of the Jute Export duty must be distributed among the jute-growing Province.

Section 141: Requires previous sanction of the Governor-General to any Bill or amendment imposing any tax or duty in which Provinces are interested, or the principles of distribution of the net proceeds of some taxes or duties in the Provinces, or varying the meaning of Agricultural Income, or the imposition of any Federal Surcharge. Not only is this sanction given **in his discretion**; the Governor-General is forbidden to accord such sanction unless he is satisfied that all practicable economics in Federal expenditure have been effected, and that no other means remains to add to the Federal Revenues.

Section 142 (Not to be included): Imposes on the Federal Government the duty to make certain grants to Provinces,—to be charged on the Federal Revenues, and, as such, non-votable.

Section 150: This is another of the two or three insidious provisions in this Constitution, which, innocent-looking on the surface, in reality undo altogether any hope of real power for the good of the country in the hands of its chosen representatives. In terms, the section seems to prohibit the imposition of any burden on Federal, or Provincial, revenues "except for the purposes of India or any part of India." This exception is of the utmost significance, especially if one studies sub-section (2) of the same section, which permits "the Federation or a Province (to) make **grants for any purpose, notwithstanding that the purpose is not one with respect to which the Federal or the Provincial Legislature, as the case may be, may make laws**". Having studied the immense field for the Governor-General's discretionary powers and over-riding authority, this tremendous scope assigned to possible grants from Federal or Provincial funds, for **any** purpose, whether within or outside the scope of the Provincial or Federal Legislatures, necessarily must frighten any one anxious for the full growth of constitutional responsibilities among the Rulers of India.

Section 163: Vests the right to decide disputes between the Federal and the Provincial Governments regarding the conditions to be imposed by the former on the latter's borrowing, or guaranteeing Loans, in the Governor-General, acting in his discretion.

Section 175: Requires the concurrence, given in his discretion, of the Governor-General for the sale or modification of the use of any building used as a Government House, or official residence in the Provinces. This means that any hope of retrenchment to be effected in the Household Allowance charges of the Provincial Governors, due to palatial buildings having to be maintained as official residences, is entirely at the mercy of the Governor-General.

Section 222: Gives power to make the temporary or acting appointment to the Chief Justiceship of a Provincial High Court, or Additional Judges in such courts to the Governor-General **in his discretion.**

Section 226: Requires the previous sanction of the Governor-General to the introduction of any Bill or Amendment in the Federal Legislature which would grant any original jurisdiction to a Provincial High Court in Revenue matters.

Section 295: Grants the Governor-General the power to pardon criminals, conditionally or freely, and the power to suspend, remit, or commute a death sentence,—the power to be exercised **in his discretion.**

Section 302: The High Commissioner for India may do business for a Provincial Government in London, on terms to be aproved by the Governor-General.

Section 313: Even during the transition period between the coming into operation of Provincial Autonomy and the establishment of the Federation, the Governor-General is entitled to use his discretionary authority as regards granting previous sanction to certain classes of Bills in Provincial Legislatures, as also regarding Broadcasting and the Civil Services recruited by the Secretary of State serving in a Province.

The Governor-General and the Federated States

The powers of the Governor-General in connection with the Indian States have been glanced at in a previous Chapter, while dealing with the accession of the States to the Federation of India, and their place in the new Constitutional Government. So far as the powers specially given to the Governor-General by the terms of his Commission, or as representative of the Crown in its dealings with the Indian States are concerned, the Constitution is not directly concerned. Except for the sections, 128-135, dealing with administrative details for the enforcement of Federal Laws in the Federated States; Broadcasting; disputes as regards water-supplies; and except for sections in the Financial Chapter of the Constitution, whereby the net proceeds of certain taxes and duties are made distributable among the States in whom these duties are levied and collected by the Federation, compensation to the States concerned, under Section 147 and 149 for the loss of certain rights, privileges or immunities, as incidental to the accession to the Federation,—there are no great matters in which the Governor-General's directive, supervisory or controlling authority, the Chief Executive of the Federation of India, differs materially from that in the Provinces. His special responsibility in connection with the prevention of any grave menace to the peace and tranquillity of India, or any part of that country, applies as much to the Federated States as to the Provinces,—not to mention the non-Federated

States if any. And though his special responsibility to maintain and protect the rights and dignity of an Indian Prince, or the members of a Ruling Family, seem to be peculiar to the States only; this is no great departure from the existing practice in that behalf. On the whole, the States who join the Federation will be little better than Provinces, or Provincial Governors, *vis-a-vis* the Governor-General, even as regards the internal administration of their own territories. And they might be much worse off, perhaps, than the Provinces, in so far as the latter can, at pinch, urge the name and will of their people, should they desire a line of policy or executive action other than that recommended or enforced by the Governor-General. The States can never allege this excuse to shield themselves in any conflict with the Federal Executive or the Governor-General.

Constitutional Powers of the Governor-General

The powers of the Governor-General, as the chief Executive Officer of the Federation of India, considered in the last two or three sections are what might be called his extraordinary powers given by the Constitution to that officer. The normal Constitutional powers,—*i.e.*, those which he is to exercise on the advice of his Ministers,—would, by elimination, shrink almost into nothing. We shall, however, consider these in detail in the next Chapter dealing with the Council of Ministers.

Reaction of the Powers of the Governor-General

Let us here sum up the reaction of these vast and all but innumerable powers vested in the Governor-General, under one pretext or another, upon (a) his

Council of Ministers; (b) the Provincial Governments; and (c) the Federated States. Because of the immense margin of **discretionary** powers left to the Governor-General,—in which, if he so chooses, he need not consult his Ministers at all,—comparatively very little is left to those Ministers to exercise their discretion in, and to show their concern for the welfare of the people they represent in some concrete form. At every step they take to promote that well-being in some definite shape, the Governor-General is in a position to block them, to circumvent them, to frustrate them. Whether in actual practice he would do so or not is besides the point here discussed. The fact remains that he is armed with constitutional powers, which enable him, if he is so minded, to render his Ministers utterly futile, and the promises of the Federal Legislators to their constituents were mind.

As though the Discretionary Powers of the Governor-General were not enough, he is given other powers, **to be exercised in his Individual Judgment.** In these, even though he may consult his Ministers, he is not bound always to follow their advice. This is adding insult to injury, so far as the Ministers are concerned. The Governor-General is in a position, not only to prevent them from taking any credit to themselves, in such matters, for any concrete service to the public; he can simply ignore them by not following the line they recommend. The Ministers, in the face of such powers in the hands of the Governor-General, will never realise their own responsibility, nor learn to act as responsible rulers of a great country, for the simple reason that they have no assurance that even in the sphere of activity left to them by the Constitution,—a most narrow and limited sphere, in all conscience,—they would be free to develop national policies as they think proper.

So far as the Provinces are concerned, the full bloom of Provincial Autonomy is considerably tarnished by the possession of extraordinary powers by the Provincial Executive chief,—the Governor. As though that was not enough, the Governor-General is entrusted with certain overriding, directive, controlling powers, in every field of Provincial Government, which cannot but materially reduce the real field for Self-Government by the people in the Provinces. Provincial Autonomy, under the Constitution of 1935, is not a mere name; it is much less, and much worse. It is the shadow of a ghost, which needs must frighten to their death those unfamiliar with such unholy, unhappy spirits. It is a cloak for the refusal on the part of British Imperialism to part with any substance of power to the people of India in the management of their own concerns. It is an apology for a flagrant deception.

In the Federated States,—if and when Federation is an accomplished fact,—the reaction of such powers in the hands of the Governor-General would be, still more undesirable. The Indian States are still living in the Middle Ages, so far as any conception of popular responsibility in the Government of country is concerned. The admission of these anachronisms into a progressive, democratic Federation might, at first sight, seem to beckon them towards a more enlightened and responsible administration. The possession, however, of these immense discretionary and extraordinary powers by the Governor-General is calculated to prevent the consummation of the vision of a fully united, homogeneous India, governed on truly democratic lines, with a full sense of popular responsibility among all those set in authority in that country. The Princes can always look to the Governor-General for the full protection of all their obsolete rights and unmeaning dignities; they can even obtain compensation, at the expense of India as a whole, for some of their rights, immunities or privileges, so long as the same do not offend the needs and requirements of British Imperialism in India. Their persons and families might be assured the exceptional position they have occupied so far, in regard to any just criticism of their actions or antics in the public. But did any of them but dream to defeat the aims of British Imperialism, neither their birth nor their services would protect them against any penalty, imposition, or sacrifice.

APPENDIX I

Instrument of Instructions to the Governor-General

Whereas by Letters Patent bearing even date We have made effectual and permanent provision for the Office of Governor-General of India:

And whereas by those Letters Patent and by the Act of Parliament passed on and entitled the Government of India Act, 1935 (hereinafter called "the said Act"), certain powers, functions and authority for the Government of India and of Our Federation of India are declared to be vested in the Governor-General as Our Representative:

And whereas, without prejudice to the provision in the said Act that in certain regards therein specified the Governor-General shall act according to instructions received from time to time from Our Secretary of State, and to the duty of Our Governor-General to give effect to any instructions so received. We are minded to make general provision regarding the manner in which Our said Governor-General shall execute all things which, according to the said Act and said Letters Patent, belong to his Office and to the trust which we have reposed in him:

And whereas by the said Act it is provided that the draft of any such Instructions to be issued to Our Governor-General shall be laid by Our Secretary of State before both Houses of Parliament:

And whereas both Houses of Parliament, having considered the draft laid before them accordingly, have presented to Us an Address praying that Instructions may be issued to Our Governor-General in the form which hereinafter follows:

Now therefore We do by these Our Instructions under Our Sign Manual and Signet declare Our pleasure to be as follows:—

A.—Introductory

1. Under these Our Instructions, unless the context otherwise require, the term "Governor-General" shall include every person for the time being administering the Office of Governor-General according to the provisions of Our Letter Patent constituting the said Office.

II. Our Governor-General for the time being shall, with all due solemnity, cause Our Commission under Our Sign Manual, appointing him, to be read and published in the presence of the Chief Justice of India for the time being, or, in his absence, other Judge of the Federal Court.

III. Our said Governor-General shall take the oath of allegiance and the oath for the due execution of the Office of Our Governor-General of India, and for the due and impartial administration of justice, in the form hereto appended, which oaths the Chief Justice of India for the time being, or in his absence any Judge of Federal Court, shall, and is hereby required to, tender and administer unto him.

IV. And we do authorise and require Our Governor-General, by himself or by any other person to be authorised by him in that behalf, to administer to every person appointed by him to hold office as a member of the Council of Ministers the oaths of office and of secrecy hereto appended.

V. And we do further direct that every person who under these Instructions shall be required to take an oath may make an affirmation in place of an oath if he has any objection to making an oath.

VI. And whereas great prejudice may happen to Our service and to the security of India by the absence of Our Governor-General, he shall not quit India during his term of office without having first obtained leave from Us under Our Sign Manual or through one of Our Principal Secretaries of State.

B.—In Regard to the Executive Authority of the Federation

VII. Our Governor-General shall do all that in him lies to maintain standards of good administration; to encourage religious toleration, co-operation and goodwill among all classes and creeds; and to promote all measures making for moral, social and economic welfare.

VIII. In making appointments to his Council of Ministers Our Governor-General shall use his best endeavours to select his Ministers in the following manner, that is to say, in consultation with the person who, in his judgment, is most likely to command a stable majority in the Legislature, to appoint those persons (including so far as practicable representatives of the Federated States and members of important minority communities) who will best be in a position collectively to command the confidence of the Legislature. But, in so acting, he shall bear constantly in mind the need for fostering a sense of joint responsibility among his Ministers.

IX. In all matters within the scope of the executive authority of the Federation, save in respect of those functions which he is required by the said Act to exercise in his discretion, Our Governor-General shall in the exercise of the powers conferred upon him be guided by the advice of his Ministers, unless in his opinion so to be guided would be inconsistent with the fulfilment of any of the special responsibilities which are by the said Act committed to him, or with the proper discharge of any of the functions which he is otherwise by the said Act required to exercise on his individual judgment; in any of which cases Our Governor-General shall, notwithstanding his Ministers' advice, act in exercise of the powers by the said Act conferred upon him in such manner as to his individual judgment seems requisite for the due discharge of the responsibilities and functions aforesaid. But he shall be studious so to exercise his powers as not to enable his Ministers to rely upon his special responsibilities in order to relieve themselves of responsibilities which are properly their own.

X. It is Our will and pleasure that in the discharge of his special responsibility for safeguarding the financial stability and credit of the Federation Our Governor-General shall in particular make it his duty to see that a budgetary or borrowing policy is not pursued which would, in his judgment, seriously prejudice the credit of India in the money markets of the world, or affect the capacity of the Federation duly to discharge its financial obligations.

XI. Our Governor-General shall interpret his special responsibility for the safeguarding of the legitimate interests of minorities as requiring him to secure, in general, that those racial or religious communities for the members of which special representation is accorded in the Federal Legislature, and those classes who, whether on account of the smallness of their number of their lack of educational or material advantages or from any other cause, cannot as yet fully rely for their welfare on joint political action in the Federal Legislature, shall not suffer, or have reasonable cause to fear, neglect or oppression. But he shall not regard as entitled to his protection any body of persons by reason only that they share a view on a particular question which has not found favour with the majority.

Further, Our Governor-General shall interpret the said special responsibility as requiring him to secure a due proportion of appointments in Our Services to the several communities, and he shall be guided in this regard by the accepted policy prevailing before the issue of these Our Instructions, unless he is fully satisfied that modification of that policy is essential in the interests of the communities affected or of the welfare of the public.

XII. In the discharge of his special responsibility for the securing to members of the public services of any rights provided for them by or under the said Act and the safeguarding of their legitimate interests Our Governor-General shall be careful to safeguard the members of Our Services not only in any rights provided for them by or under the said Act or any other law for the time being in force, but also against any action which, in his judgment, would be inequitable.

XIII. The special responsibility of Our Governor-General for securing in the sphere of executive action any of the purposes which the provisions of Chapter III of Part V of the said Act are designed to secure in relation to legislation shall be construed by him as requiring him to differ from his Ministers if in his individual judgment their advice would have effects of the kind which it is the purpose of the said Chapter to prevent, even though the advice so tendered to him is not in conflict with any specific provision of the said Act.

XIV. In the discharge of his special responsibility for the prevention of measures which would subject goods of United Kingdom origin imported into India to discriminatory or penal treatment. Our Governor-General shall avoid action which would affect the competence of his Government and of the Federal Legislature to develop their own fiscal and economic policy, or would restrict their freedom to negotiate trade agreements whether with the United Kingdom or with other countries for the securing of mutual tariff concessions; and he should intervene in tariff policy or in the negotiation of tariff agreements only if in his opinion the main intention of the policy contemplated is by trade restrictions to injure the interests of the United Kingdom rather than to further the economic interests of India. And we require and charge him to regard the discriminatory or penal treatment covered by this special responsibility as including both direct discrimination (whether by means of differential tariff rates or by means of differential restrictions on imports) and indirect discrimination by means of differential treatment of various types of products: and Our Governor-General's special responsibility extends to preventing the imposition of prohibitory tariffs or restrictions, if he is satisfied that such measures are proposed with the aforesaid intention. It also extends, subject to the aforesaid intention, to measures which, though not discriminatory or penal in form would be so in fact.

At the same time in interpreting the special responsibility to which this paragraph relates, our Governor-General shall bear always in mind the partnership between India and the United Kingdom within Our Empire, which has so long subsisted, and the mutual obligations which arise therefrom.

XV. Our Governor-General shall construe his special responsibility for the protection of the rights of any Indian State as requiring him to see that no action shall be taken by his Ministers, and no Bill of the Federal Legislature shall become law, which would imperil the economic life of any State, or affect prejudicially any right of any State heretofore or hereafter recognised,* whether derived from treaty, grant, usage, sufferance or otherwise, not being a right appertaining to a matter in respect to which, in virtue of the Ruler's Instrument of Accession, the Federal Legislature may make laws for his State and his subjects.

XVI. In the framing of rules for the regulation of the business of the Federal Government Our Governor-General shall ensure that amongst other provisions for the effective discharge of that business, due provision is made that the Minister in charge of the Finance Department shall be consulted upon any proposal by any other Minister which affects the finances of the Federation: and further that no re-appropriation within a Grant shall be made by any Minister otherwise than after consultation with the Finance Minister; and that in any case in which the Finance Minister does not concur in any such proposal, the matter shall be brought for decision before the Council of Ministers.

XVII. Although it is provided in the said Act that the Governor-General shall exercise his functions in part in his discretion and in part with the aid and advice of Ministers, nevertheless it is Our will and pleasure that Our Governor-General shall encourage the practice of joint consultation between himself, his Counsellors and his Ministers. And seeing that the Defence of India must to an increasing extent be the concern of the Indian people it is Our will in especial that Our Governor-General should have regard to this instruction in his administration of the Department of Defence; and notably that he shall bear in mind desirability of ascertaining the views of his Ministers when he shall have occasion to consider matters relating to the general policy of appointing Indian Officers to Our Indian Forces, or the employment of Our Indian Forces on Service outside India.

XVIII. Further it is Our will and pleasure that in the administration of the Department of Defence Our Governor-General shall obtain the views of Our Commander-in-Chief in any matter which will affect the discharge of latter's duties and shall transmit his opinion to Our Secretary of State whenever the Commander-in-Chief may so request

*The procedure for the determination of the right in case of a dispute rests with the Crown's representative for the conduct of relations with the States.

on any occasion when Our Governor-General communicates with Our Secretary of State upon them.

XIX. And We desire that, although the financial control of Defence administration must be exercised by the Governor-General at his discretion, nevertheless the Federal Department of Finance shall be kept in close touch with this control by such arrangement as may prove feasible, and that the Federal Ministry and, in particular, the Finance Minister shall be brought into consultation before estimates of proposed expenditure for the service of Defence are settled and laid before the Federal Legislature.

C.—In Regard to Relations between the Federation, Provinces and Federated States

XX. Whereas it is expedient, for the common good of Provinces and Federated States alike, that the authority of the Federal Government and Legislature in those matters which are by law assigned to them should prevail:

And whereas at the same time it is the purpose of the said Act that on the one hand the Governments and Legislatures of the Provinces should be free in their own sphere to pursue their own policies, and on the other hand that the sovereignty of the Federated States should remain unaffected save in so far as the Rulers thereof have otherwise agreed by their Instruments of Accession:

And whereas in the interest of the harmonious cooperation of the several members of the body politic the said Act has empowered Our Governor-General to exercise at his discretion certain powers affecting the relations between the Federation and Provinces and States:

It is Our will and pleasure that Our Governor-General, in the exercise of these powers, should give unbiased consideration as well to the views of the Governments of Provinces and Federated States as to those of his own Ministers, whenever those views are in conflict and, in particular, when it falls to him to exercise his power to issue orders to the Governor of a Province, or directions to the Ruler of Federated State, for the purpose of securing that the executive authority of the Federation is not impeded or prejudiced, or his power to determine whether provincial law or federal law shall regulate a matter in the sphere in which both Legislatures have power to make laws.

XXI. It is Our desire that Our Governor-General shall by all reasonable means encourage consultation with a view to common action between the Federation, Provinces and Federated States. It is further Our will and pleasure that Our Governor-General shall endeavour to secure the co-operation of the Governments of Provinces and Federated States in the maintenance of such federal agencies and institutions for research as may serve to assist the conduct by Provincial Governments and Federated States of their own affairs.

XXII. In particular We require our Governor-General to ascertain by the method which appear to him best suited to the circumstances of each case the views of Provinces and of Federated States upon any legislative proposals which it is proposed to introduce in the Federal Legislature for the imposition of taxes in which Provinces or Federated States are interested.

XXIII. Before granting his previous sanction to the introduction of a Bill into the Federal Legislature imposing a Federal surcharge on taxes on income, Our Governor-General shall satisfy himself that the results of all practicable economics and of all practicable measures for increasing the yield accruing to the Federation from other sources of taxation within the powers of the Federal Legislature would be inadequate to balance Federal receipts and expenditure on revenue account; and among the aforesaid measures shall be included the exercise of any powers vested in him in relation to the amount of the sum retained by the Federation out of money, assigned to the Provinces from taxes on income.

XXIV. Our Governor-General, in determining whether the Federation would or would not be justified in refusing to make a loan to a Province, or to give a guarantee in respect of a loan to be raised by a Province, or in imposing any conditions in relation to such loan or guarantee, shall be guided by the general policy of the Federation for the time being as to the extent to which it is desirable that borrowings on behalf of the Provinces should be undertaken by the Federation; but such general policy shall not in any event be deemed to prevail against the grant by the Federation of a loan to a Province or a guarantee in respect of a loan to be raised by that Province, if in the opinion of Our Governor-General a temporary financial emergency of a grave character has arisen in a Province, in which refusal by the Federation of such a grant or guarantee would leave the Province with no satisfactory means of meeting such temporary emergency.

XXV. Before granting his previous sanction to the introduction into the Federal Legislature of any Bill or amendment wherein it is proposed to authorise the Federal Government to give directions to a Province as to the carrying into execution in that Province of any Act of the Federal Legislature relating to a matter specified in Part II of the Concurrent Legislative List appended to the said Act, it is Our will and pleasure that Our Governor-General should take care to see that the Governments of the Provinces which would be affected by any such measure have been duly consulted upon the proposal, and upon, any other proposals which may be contained in any such measure for the imposition of expenditure upon the revenues of the Provinces.

XXVI. In considering whether he shall give his assent to any Provincial law relating to a matter enumerated in the Concurrent Legislative List, which has been reserved for his consideration on the ground that it contains provisions repugnant to the provisions of a Federal law, Our Governor-General, while giving full consideration to the proposals of the Provincial Legislature, shall have due regard to the importance of preserving substantially the broad principles of those codes of law through which uniformity of legislation has hitherto been secured.

D.—Matters Affecting the Legislature

XXVII. Our Governor-General shall not assent in Our name to, but shall reserve for the significance of Our pleasure, any Bill of any of the classes herein specified, that is to say:—

(a) any Bill the provisions of which would repeal or be repugnant to provisions of any Act of Parliament extending to British India;

(b) any Bill which in his opinion would, if it became law, so derogate from the powers of the High Court of any Province as to endanger the position which these Courts are by the said Act designed to fill;

(c) any Bill passed by a Provincial Legislature and reserved for his consideration which would alter the character of the Permanent Settlement;

(d) any Bill regarding which he feels doubt whether it does, or does not, offend against the purposes of Chapter III, Part V of the said Act.

XXVIII. It is further Our will and pleasure that if an Agreement is made with His Exalted Highness the Nizam of Hyderabad as contemplated in Part III of the said Act, Our Governor-General in notifying his assent in Our name to any Act of the Legislature of the Central Provinces and Berar which has been reserved for his consideration, shall declare that his assent to the Act in its application to Berar has been given on Our behalf and in virtue of the provisions of Part III of the said Act in pursuance of the Agreement between Us and His Exalted Highness the Nizam.

XXIX. It is Our will that the power vested by the said Act in Our Governor-General to stay proceedings upon a Bill, clause or amendment in the Federal Legislature in the discharge of his special responsibility for the prevention of grave menace to peace and tranquillity shall not be exercised unless, in his judgment, the public discussion of the Bill, clause or amendment would itself endanger peace and tranquillity.

XXX. It is Our will and pleasure that in choosing the representatives of British India for seats in the Council of State which are to be filled by Our Governor-General by nominations made in his discretion he shall so far as may be redress inequalities of representation which may have resulted from election. He shall in particular bear in mind the necessity of securing representation for Scheduled Castes and women; and in any nominations made for the purpose of redressing inequalities in relation to minority communities (not being communities to whom seats are specifically allotted in the Table in the first Part of the first Schedule to the said Act) he shall so far as seems to him just be guided by the proportion of seats allotted to such minority communities among British India representatives of the Federal Assembly.

E.—General

XXXI. And finally it is Our will and pleasure that our Governor-General should so exercise the trust which we have reposed in him that partnership between India and the United Kingdom within our Empire may be furthered, to the end that India may attain its due place among Our Dominions.

CHAPTER VI

THE COUNCIL OF FEDERAL MINISTERS

Powers of the Council of Ministers

With such ordinary and constitutional, as well as extraordinary and superconstitutional, executive powers and functions entrusted to the Chief Executive Officer of the Federation of India, it would need no special comment to show that the Council of Ministers will have very little real power in shaping the policy of the country, in embodying that policy in the shape of laws, or in administering these laws seeking to give effect to the basic conception or decisions of policy.

The Council of Federal Ministers seems, in the basic conception of the Act of 1935, neither the supreme executive body, nor even the principal administering authority, in the land. While the executive government is entrusted, as we have seen, very largely to the Governor-General, the actual administration of the laws and policies of government are in the hands of the permanent officials, the superior Civil Services, who are utterly outside the control or influence of Ministers.

Excluded Departments

Of the various Departments of the Federal Government, 3 of the most considerable, the most expensive, and the most directly influential in affecting the well-being of the country, are summarily excluded from the purview of the Council of Ministers.* The Governor-General administers those Departments "in his discretion." This means that, in conducting their affairs, he need not necessarily make any reference to or have consultation with his Ministers. If, indeed, he is so minded, there is nothing in the Constitution to prevent his consulting with his Council of Ministers, even in regard to these excluded Departments; and to follow their advice in important questions of policy. His Instrument of Instructions from the King-Emperor specifically enjoins upon him to hold and promote joint deliberations between the Counsellors of the Governor-General for the Excluded Departments, the Financial Adviser, and the Council of Ministers.† But the Instructions of the King-Emperor do not constitute a document capable of legal enforcement; and the exercise of the Governor-General's "discretion" does not seem likely, in the existing atmosphere at any rate, to incline towards showing greater and greater confidence in the Constitutional Advisers, especially if they be derived from a Party whose declared goal of Indian aspirations is so wholly unwelcome to British Imperialists. We are, therefore, left with no option but to conclude that, in the administration of the excluded Departments, the Federal Ministers will have no direct say, and very little indirect influence. The latter, it need hardly be added, is entirely dependent on the goodwill of the Governor-General.

Other Departments

As for the non-excluded Departments, the nominal scope of influence assigned to the Ministers may seem

* cp. Section 11.

†cp. Article VIII of the Instrument ante p. 213 also p. 228.

considerable. But when we consider the vast discretionary powers of the Governor-General; when we recall his right to exercise individual judgment in certain matters, *i.e.*, in which, though the Ministers are entitled to tender advice, the Governor-General is not bound to follow it; when we think of the innumerable privileges assured to the Services, the special safeguards and reserve authority in the hands of the Governor-General in matters financial; when we ponder over the infinite possibilities of the so-called "Special Responsibilities" of the Governor-General, on the pretext of carrying out which, he may circumvent, frustrate, or neutralise altogether the policies of his Ministers; and when, finally, we recollect the fact that, in all the non-reserved Departments, the actual government is more a concern of the Provinces, than of the Federal Government,—we cannot but conclude that the position assigned under the new Constitution to the Council of Federal Ministers is ornamental, without being useful; onerous, without ever being helpful to the people they are supposed to represent; responsibility without power, position without authority, name without any real influence.

This general summary of the actual position occupied by the Council of Ministers in the governance of the Indian Federation will be more fully understood if we consider the specific provisions of the Constitution regarding their appointment, working, and scope of authority.

Section 9 permits the Governor-General to have a Council of Ministers to aid and advise him in the administration of the Federal Affairs. Says that section:—

9.—(1) There shall be a council of ministers, not exceeding ten in number, to aid and advise the Governor-General in the exercise of his functions, except in so far as he is by or under this Act required to exercise his functions or any of them in his discretion:

Provided that nothing in this sub-section shall be construed as preventing the Governor-General from exercising his individual judgment in any case where by or under this Act he is required so to do.

(2) The Governor-General in his discretion may preside at meetings of the council of ministers.

(3) If any question arises whether any matter is or is not a matter as respects which the Governor-General is by or under this Act required to act in his discretion or to exercise his individual judgment, the decision of the Governor-General in his discretion shall be final, and the validity of anything done by the Governor-General shall not be called in question on the ground that he ought or ought not to have acted in his discretion, or ought or ought not to have exercised his individual judgment.

Number and Status of Ministers

This section contrasts with the corresponding section 50, relating to the Council of Ministers in the autonomous Provinces, in only one respect. The upper limit of Federal Ministers is fixed by this provision at 10; and there is no provision about Assistant or Junior Ministers, Under Secretaries, or by whatever other name these second rank Ministers might be designated. In the Provinces, there is no such limit fixed by law. Though, even in their case, there is no express provision for the appointment of Junior Ministers, the absence of any legally prescribed maximum, as also of any gradation among the Ministers, might well be argued into the conclusion that, in this respect at any rate. the system of Responsible Government is to work differently in the Federation from that in the Provinces. In the Federation, according to the Instructions to the Governor-General, many more interests will need to be provided for than in the Provincial Council of Ministers. For whereas in the Provinces only important minorities are required to be represented in the Ministry, in the Federation the Federated States also will claim representation. That would be an incongruous element, but in all probability it would have to be included.

The limit fixed by law is thus likely to prove embarrassing to the person entrusted with the task of forming the Federal Ministry from time to time. On the other hand, compared to the present size of the Government of India,—six Councillors, in addition to the Governor-General himself, and the Commander-in-Chief,—the limit of 10 Cabinet Ministers in the future Council of Federal Ministers, cannot be regarded as too low. There will, in addition, be the Counsellors of the Governor-General in the excluded Departments, as also the Financial Adviser; and, very likely, the Advocate-General, present at certain meetings of the Council. It would make a Cabinet of 15 including the Governor-General, his Counsellors and Adviser; and that is not too small a Cabinet for this country.

The Secretaries to the Government of India of today, who have certain definite functions in regard to the Council, are to have, apart from Section 17, no place in the Council of Ministers. The limit fixed by the Constitution may also be defended on the ground of economy in the overhead costs of Government, though the salaries and allowances of the Counsellors and Financial Adviser,—not to mention the Advocate-

General,—do not suggest any excessive regard for economy of this description. The popular Ministers may quite possibly so fix the scale of Ministerial salaries and allowances, that this argument in defence of the statutory limit on the size of the Cabinet has very little significance.

Parliamentary Secretaries

Apart from the constitutional merits, political propriety, or economic advisability, of such a limit on the number of the Ministers, it may yet be pointed out that the presence of Junior Ministers, Parliamentary or Under Secretaries has proved, in Britain herself, of immense value, not only to the Cabinet Ministers themselves, but also to the governance of the country as a whole. The possibility of such appointments is not to be regarded merely as opportunity to exercise a certain amount of patronage at the expense of the country. These appointments help to train promising young politicians, not only in the ways of democratic government, but also in the routine of administration. The division of work between Ministers and their Parliamentary assistants may be regulated by personal convenience, or specific Cabinet regulation. Whatever it is, in practice, the Junior Minister takes over the more routine work of answering minor Questions, or attending to less important details of administration, not involving grave questions of policy. The Cabinet Minister proper is thus freed to attend to the larger issues of national policy as affecting his own particular Department. All sides of the public administration and democratic tradition are thus properly, efficiently, and simultaneously attended to.

In India, however, it is no unjust reflection to say that the leading politicians in every Party are lacking in personal experience of modern administrative requirements for the conduct of a great department of State. They are, at the same time, not over familiar with the intricacies of international relations, and their reaction upon the well-being of the people they might be called on to govern. These would be more important in the Federal Government than in the Provincial. If any set of aspiring politicians ever needed skilled assistance in their parliamentary work, the conduct of departmental routine, and attending to national policy, it is the modern Indian political leader. There are available, no doubt, Civilian Secretaries in every department of government. But the belief is very general in the Indian political world that these officials are much too reactionary, by training and tradition; much too unsympathetic towards popular aspirations—and their exponents the political leaders,—by their very experience and expert knowledge, to make really acceptable and helpful aids, even if we do not question their sincerity in doing the best for the political chiefs of their department. Unable to rely completely on this available assistance, and incapacitated from seeking more suitable aid from the more ambitious talent in their own ranks, this provision of the Constitution, if interpreted as a bar upon the appointment of Parliamentary Secretaries, is bound to prove a serious impediment in the success of popular Ministries in the Federal Government.

Constitution and Collective Responsibility

There is, secondly, no express provision in the Constitution itself, for inculcating a sense of Collective

Responsibility among the Federal Ministers. Collective Responsibility is the essence of tiue Democracy *on the modern, nationwide scale. It is generated and* maintained by identity of political principle and outlook between representatives of the same people. In so far, however, as the Indian Federal Ministry is fundamentally incapable of developing that sense, all indirect, extra-constitutional forces to implant a sense of Collective Responsibility would be of no avail. The Governor-General is, it is true, enjoined by his Instructions to select his Ministers

> "in consultation with the person, who, in his judgment, is most likely to command a stable majority in the Legislature, to appoint those persons (including so far as practicable representatives of Federated States and members of important minority communities) who will best be in a position collectively to command the confidence of the Legislature. But, in so doing, he shall bear constantly in mind the need for fostering a sense of joint responsibility among his Ministers".*

The same desire to promote a spirit of Collective Responsibility is emphasised in the next Article, which contains a general rule about the discharge of the so-called Special Responsibilities of the Governor-General. But, given the fundamental condition of the composition of this Ministry,—*i.e.*, its selection by the Governor-General from the Majority Party, representatives of the Federated States, and of important Minorities,—it is unlikely that these mutually unsympathetic and incompatible elements should really feel or cultivate Joint Responsibility, at least in regard to fundamental national policy. The representatives of the Federated States are, in particular, unlikely to be of homogeneous political views with any Party of

*Article VIII of the Draft Instructions.

the chosen representatives of the Indian people. Political Parties are yet not born in the States. Their representatives will, in all probability, be, therefore, merely nominees of the Rulers personally. And these Rulers may not deem it in the best interests of themselves, or their States, or even the future of the Federation itself, that their nominees should be involved in political partisanship as it is developing in British India. The States' representatives forming part of the British Indian Political Parties has possibilities for the privileges of the Rulers, and the place of the States in the Indian Polity, which no Ruler of to-day would contemplate without trepidation.* The British Indian representatives of the people in the Federal Legislature would find the difference in the origin—one elected, the other nominated,—too great to permit of identity in policy or outlook. Hence any sense of Collective Responsibility, as between members of the same Cabinet drawn from British India and from the Federated States, would be all but unlikely. The latter would be responsible to their Rulers, who, in turn, would be implicitly answerable for the conduct of their nominees to the Imperial Government. They would, accordingly, not be liable to go out of the Cabinet,—particularly. out of the Assembly,—for the same reasons as may lead representatives of British India to resign from the Cabinet, and seek re-election on the dissolution of the Assembly, in vindication of their point of view. This fundamental difference would make it impossible for Collective Responsibility ever to be generated amongst these mutually incompatible elements.

*The Maharaja of Dharampur, an ex-Chancellor of the Chamber of Princes, had hinted in 1936 that the States' Representatives should line up with the other vested interests in India when the Federation was accomplished; but the Maharaja of Patiala, strangely enough, disowned that notion even before he was elected Chancellor in succession to Dharampur.

Incompatible Elements in the Cabinet

The Instructions to the Governor-General, enjoin upon him to hold joint consultations between his Counsellors for the administration of the excluded Departments, the Financial Adviser, and the Council of Ministers, in order to enable each side of the Federal Government to see the other's viewpoint. But the very necessity to issue this Instruction shows that, basically, these elements of the Federal Government are mutually incongruous. The Responsible (Prime) Minister might be excused if he suspects, in this compulsory practice of joint deliberations between two distinct (even if unnatural) divisions of the Government, a snare for the popular element. The requirements of the great spending department of Defence, or considerations of Foreign Policy still tied to the apron-strings of British Imperialism, are bound to be represented, at such joint meetings, as paramount and irreducible; so that all economies and all concessions must be made at popular expense. This apprehension may, perhaps, not materialise in every instance; but there is ample ground for it in the past experience of our own administration hitherto.

Presidency of Governor-General

The presence of the Governor-General as Presiding officer at Cabinet meetings is equally open to question, from the standpoint of developing collective responsibility among the Federal Ministers, and the growth of true Constitutionalism in this new system of government. It must be noted at the outset that the presence of the Governor-General at Cabinet meetings is not compulsory upon that officer, either by the letter of the law, or under his Instructions. The practice in Britain and the Dominions is for the head of the Government to be absent from such meetings,—except on ceremonial occasions, perhaps, of no importance. This is but right and proper, since the presence of the King or the Governor-General might quite conceivably influence the individual Ministers to deviate from the settled policy to seek favour in the eyes of the head of the country. In India this danger is more to be apprehended than in Britain or any of the Dominions, since the composition of the Ministry is itself a hindrance and a bar to the growth of Collective Responsibility among the Ministers. The Governor-General not being compulsorily required by the express terms of the Act to be present at Cabinet meetings and to preside, it is not inconsistent with the letter of the law, nor incompatible with the traditions of British Constitutionalism, that the Governor-General of the Federation of India should, of his own accord, abandon the practice of being present at Cabinet mettings. This would leave his Ministers free to develop their own sense of Collective Responsibility, to settle their own internal differences, if any, and so to reach a goal, which the traditions of government in India so far might render unachievable, if merely the letter of the law were to be stressed in such matters.

Ministers "Aid and Advice"

We have already discussed at some length the difference between the powers and functions which the Governor-General is to exercise "in his discretion"; those in which he is to exercise his " individual judgment"; and those which he is to exercise on the advice of his Ministers. The Council of Ministers is appointed expressly **"to aid and advice"** the Governor-General in the performance of his executive functions. **They have, therefore, no place in the actual administration, strictly speaking, of the country they represent.**

Room for Appeal to the Country?

The Governor-General, likewise, does not become a truly constitutional head of the Government, in view of the extraordinary powers entrusted to him to control, check, and even frustrate his Ministers. Even the latters' remedy of an appeal to the country, and the vindication of their viewpoint by a verdict of the electorate, is not easy to apply, nor within their sole power to apply. For the law empowers the Governor-General, *in his discretion*, to summon the Councillors to their deliberations, to dissolve the Assembly, etc. Says Section 10:—

10.—(1) The Governor-General's ministers shall be chosen and summoned by him, shall be sworn as members of the council, and **shall hold office during his pleasure.**

(2) A minister who for any period of six consecutive months is not a member of either Chamber of the Federal Legislature shall at the expiration of that period cease to be a minister.

(3) The salaries of ministers shall be such as the Federal Legislature may from time to time by Act determine and, until the Federal Legislature so determine, shall be determined by the Governor-General:

Provided that the salary of a minister shall not be varied during his term of office.

(4) The question whether any and, if so, what advice was tendered by ministers to the Governor-General shall not be inquired into in any court.

(5) The functions of the Governor-General with respect to the choosing and summoning and the dismissal of ministers, and with respect to the determination of their salaries, shall be exercised by him in his discretion.

Under these provisions, the Governor-General has sole authority and absolute discretion to summon his

Ministers to office or to select them, in the first place, for appointment; to dismiss them, or dispense with their services; and to determine their salaries pending such determination by Act of the Federal Legislature. This clear dependence of the Ministers upon the Governor-General for being selected and removed from office,—not to mention the remuneration for work done as Minister,—must needs breed a desire to please this mighty officer, whose favour may be so materially advantageous, such a powerful aid in fulfilling ambitions. The Governor-General may not *intend* to be hostile to his Ministers developing the tradition of Joint Responsibility. But the position given him under the Constitution; his native sympathies, so long as he is a Britisher; and the powers and functions he is required to exercise, make it inevitable that his presence at Cabinet meetings, if continued as under the present regime of non-responsible Executive, would prove fundamentally inimical to the growth of Ministerial Responsibility, and true constitutional practice.

Contact with Individual Minister

Even if the Governor-General could be persuaded to absent himself from Cabinet meetings, the danger to the growth of Collective Responsibility is not ended. The provision in Section 10, which precludes any Court from enquiring into what advice was given to the Governor-General by any particular Minister, also makes it evident that the Act does not necessarily contemplate a system of Joint Responsibility. Given the exigencies of Federal Government, it may even encourage the practice of individual consultations between particular Ministers and the Governor-General on given questions of public administration. This, if it evolves at all, would be fatal to any dream of true Constitutionalism ever developing in this country. Ministers cannot be barred access to the head of the Government; but it would be highly inadvisable for any one, anxious to implant proper constitutional usages and conventions in India, to practise what the law permits in this instance. Individual Ministers, even if they have full and free access to the head of the Government, must not, under a convention, speak to him on any matter of Cabinet policy, or internal differences in the Cabinet. Nor should the Governor-General encourage individual complaints against particular Ministers. To the head of the Government, the Ministry must speak in a united voice,—the voice of the people,—on all questions of Government policy. And this united voice must be settled at their Cabinet meetings, from which the Governor-General ought, by his own choice, and by accepted convention, to be excluded. Such an arrangement can be easily made, as the presence of the Governor General is not obligatory by express provision of the Act. It is a matter in his sole discretion; and he may act in it as it seems proper to him. If, in a misconceived sense of his duty, he insists upon being present, the Ministers can render such Cabinet meetings an empty form, by just declaring through the Prime Minister, the decided policy of the Cabinet. Once a right precedent is set, or convention established, no successor in that exalted office would dare to contravene it; and then the proper growth of Constitutional conventions may be assured.

Cabinet Components

Though, under Section 10, the Council of Ministers is to be made up of such persons as the Governor-

General appoints to the office of a Minister of the Federation, the Cabinet will not consist only of the Ministers specifically so appointed. It might be noted, in the first place, that there is no mention of a Prime Minister in the express terms of the Act. The Instructions to the Governor-General seem to contemplate the institution of a Prime Minister when the Federation comes into being. As the Act stands to-day, however, the Governor-General may be his own Prime Minister: and, in any event, overshadow that entity, when and if it is at last evolved. The Cabinet will have in it, besides the Governor-General, (who may be present in the Federal Cabinet without being of it), the Counsellors to the Governor-General in the excluded Departments, and the Financial Adviser. We have already seen what the position of these Counsellors is likely to be under the new regime. The Financial Adviser holds, under Section 15, a somewhat unparalleled place, just as the Finance Department itself is given a particular prominence, because of the Special Responsibility of the Governor-General in that behalf.

Financial Adviser

Says Section 15:—

15.—(1) The Governor-General may appoint a person to be his financial adviser.

(2) It shall be the duty of the Governor-General's financial adviser to assist by his advice the Governor-General in the discharge of his special responsibility for safeguarding the financial stability and credit of the Federal Government, and also to give advice to the Federal Government upon any matter relating to finance with respect to which he may be consulted.

(3) The Governor-General's financial adviser shall hold office during the pleasure of the Governor-General, and the salary and allowances of the financial adviser

and the numbers of his staff and their conditions of service shall be such as the Governor-General may determine.

(4) **The powers of the Governor-General** with respect to the appointment and dismissal of a financial adviser, and with respect to the determination of his salary and allowances and the numbers of his staff and their conditions of service, **shall be exercised by him in his discretion:**

Provided that, if the Governor-General has determined to appoint a financial adviser, he shall, before making any appointment other than the first appointment, consult his ministers as to the person to be selected.

As the Financial Adviser is, under this section, to give advice on matters financial, not only to the Governor-General, but also to his Ministers if and when consulted by the latter, he has an importance in the Cabinet, which cannot be claimed by his confréres the Counsellors. Though primarily an adviser of the Governor-General, his duties will be much more numerous in advising the Ministers. His contact with the latter, therefore, is likely to be much more close. He is not responsible to the Legislature in the sense that his Ministerial colleagues are; and he would, of course, have no vote in the Cabinet, any more than the Counsellors. But his voice in support of or in opposition to any given line of policy, on grounds of financial practicability or otherwise, would have a weight which no other Counsellor's voice can have.

Advocate-General

Compared to the Advocate-General, appointed by the Governor-General in the exercise of his individual judgment, the Financial Adviser is not a Government Adviser in the sense that the Advocate-General would be. The latter is appointed expressly

> "to give advice to the Federal Government upon such legal matters, and to perform such other duties of a legal character, as may be referred or assigned to him by the Governor-General";

while the Financial Adviser is primarily an adviser to the Governor-General appointed particularly to aid that officer in the discharge of his Special Responsibility in regard to finance. The Advocate-General is, accordingly, given a specific right of audience in all Courts in British India, and even in Courts of the Federated States where federal interests are concerned.* The Financial Adviser, however, has no such statutory privilege of audience, even at Cabinet meetings. The Financial Adviser, again, is appointed, his remuneration and staff fixed, by the Governor-General acting in his discretion. They only limitation on that discretion is the obligation to consult his Ministers, before making any appointment to the Financial Advisorship other than the first appointment, as to the person to be appointed. The value of this privilege is less than nominal, since the first appointment is to be made without any such reference to the Ministry at all. As the terms and conditions of the appointment are in the sole discretion of the Governor-General, he may and probably will make the first appointment at least for 5 years; and possibly on a still longer lease of office provided the person appointed shows the ordinary efficiency in his job—by no means an exacting demand when no executive functions or responsibility are attached to the post. Even for subsequent appointments, the consultation with the Ministers may be of no practical value, since the final authority rests with the Governor-General in every instance. The Advocate-General, on the other hand, is appointed, his remuneration fixed, by the Governor-General exercising his individual judgment. We may

*cp. Section 16 (2).

add that while the appointment of a Financial Adviser is optional, that of the Advocate-General is compulsory.

While there is a statutory right, in regard to the Financial Adviser's selection after the first, for the Ministers to be consulted, the appointment of the Advocate-General of the Federation is to be made in the exercise of the Governor-General's individual judgment. Ministers must be consulted as a matter of right; and, unless the Governor-General can show any very specific reason connected with his Special Responsibilities, he will have to follow the advice of his Ministers.

As the Advocate-General,—a Government Adviser, —will not probably be appointed for any specific term, —such as the Financial Adviser of the Governor-General may be,—the removal of a person already appointed by the Governor-General without consulting or accepting the advice of his Ministers, may be more easy than in the case of the Financial Adviser; and the same principle would apply on change of Ministers in the ordinary course of Constitutional vicissitudes. On the whole, Ministers may come, in practice, to have greater authority or influence over the Advocate-General; though they may find the advice and co-operation of the Financial Expert advising the Governor-General more important for the proper framing and carrying out of their own policies. That officer being beyond any control of the Cabinet is thus to the disadvantage of the Cabinet, and eloquent of the distrust and suspicion with which Indian politicians becoming Ministers of the Crown are to be treated with, at least in the initial years of the new Constitution.

Cabinet Procedure

The Ministers' rules of business, the distribution of *portfolios*, the process of deliberation among themselves, are also to be determined by the Governor-General acting in his discretion. Under Section 17:—

17.—(1) All executive action of the Federal Government shall be expressed to be taken in the name of the Governor-General.

(2) Orders and other instruments made and executed in the name of the Governor-General shall be authenticated in such manner as may be specified in rules to be made by the Governor-General, and the validity of an order or instrument which is so authenticated shall not be called in question on the ground that it is not an order or instrument made or executed by the Governor-General.

(3) The Governor-General shall make rules for the more convenient transaction of the business of the Federal Government, and for the allocation among ministers of the said business in so far as it is not business with respect to which the Governor-General is by or under this Act required to act in his discretion.

(4) The rules shall include provisions requiring ministers and secretaries to Government to transmit to the Governor-General all such information with respect to the business of the Federal Government as may be specified in the rules, or as the Governor-General may otherwise require to be so transmitted, and in particular requiring a minister to bring to the notice of the Governor-General, and the appropriate secretary to bring to the notice of the minister concerned and of the Governor-General, any matter under consideration by him which involves, or appears to him likely to involve, any special responsibility of the Governor-General.

(5) In the discharge of his functions under sub-sections (2), (3) and (4) of this section the Governor-General shall act in his discretion after consultation with his ministers.

Governor-General and Routine Business of Government

Here is another proof of the enormous *de facto* power vested in the Governor-General, even in the routine administration of the country. There is nothing in the Act to indicate that the Governor-General is to be the nominal head of a Constitutional Government, and everything to show that he is to be the effective and absolute chief of the whole Governmental machinery. Since the rules of business are to be made by the Governor-General *in his discretion*, in selecting individual Ministers for the particular work each is entrusted with, the Governor-General may arrogate to himself powers which would render the Chief Minister, if any is recognised as such, a cipher. Parliamentary Responsible Ministers are appointed to their *portfolios*, not on any ground of specialist qualification for a given Department, but for such reasons as the internal requirements of a Cabinet may warrant. Every English Cabinet is eloquent of this inherent right of such Ministries to shuffle posts among themselves from time to time; and the power given to the Governor-General, in his discretion may quite possibly be utilised in a manner incompatible with this right of the Ministry.

Again, what matters in the daily routine are to be placed before the Governor-General, and what need not be so submitted, is, also, a question in which the Ministers will have very little say, since the Governor-General will alone, *in his discretion*, prescribe Rules under which his Ministers have to do the business of Government. In matters which involve his Special Responsibility,—or even those which are judged by the Secretary concerned as likely to involve a Special Responsibility,—the law requires the Governor-General to be fully informed, and his attention to be drawn to the point at which, or the manner and the degree in which, his Special Responsibility might be involved in a given question. On these, of course, even if the Rules of business made in his discretion by the

Governor-General do permit individual Ministers to have some voice, and the Ministry collectively to have a say, the last word rests with the Governor-General; and he can override the collective wisdom of all his Ministers. It is difficult to conceive instances in which the reservation of such power may be considered necessary, since Ministers under a democratic regime cannot afford to displease any considerable interest, especially when such interests are so carefully protected by the Constitution. The only explanation lies in the inveterate and unshakable distrust and suspicion of the Indian politician in the mind of British Imperialists. or vested interests for whose protection and safeguard the entire Constitutional machinery seems to be motived.

Special Importance of the Finance Minister

The Instrument of Instructions, it may be added, requires the Governor-General to see that the Finance Minister particularly is kept fully informed of all requirements or proposals of other Departments. Sound finance is, in all democracies, the keystone of the arch of good government. In India, given the variety of vested interests, the excluded spending Departments of State, the innumerable items charged upon the revenues of the Federation, and the incessantly conflicting demands of the Federation, the States and the Provinces, Finance would be more important than anywhere else. But the importance must be felt and recognised by every responsible Minister, and not by only one of them, if a proper sense of Collective Responsibility is to be felt by them.

Dual Responsibility of Ministers

The stress we have levied upon some of these features is the more necessary, and justifiable, because the Ministers will have a dual,—and often mutually conflicting,—rôle to perform. The Constitution makes them, in terms, simply the "**aids and advisers**" of the Governor-General, who towers like a colossus over all his Ministers, dwarfs them into nothingness, and dominates all authority in the land. On the other hand, the same Constitution is supposed to make the Ministers representatives of the people, and spokesmen of their will. The basis of all Constitutional Government of the British pattern lies in the tacit acceptance of the ultimate Sovereignty of the people; that is to say, in every case of a conflict, popular verdict must in the end prevail. But, in the case of the Indian Federal Ministers, this position seems to be made almost wholly incompatible with the powers and functions entrusted to the Governor-General, who is entitled to initiate matters of policy as much as to carry out decisions in the form of laws or executive orders of Government. He is entitled to exclude his Ministers altogether from the Administration of certain specified Departments, even though the fundamental policy in relation to those departments, as well as their actual administration, may materially affect the other departments of the State, and the general well-being of the people. Thus for example, the Department of Defence is excluded from Ministerial authority altogether; and yet, not only will that Department be responsible for over 60 per cent. of the Federal Expenditure; it is concerned with much that might materially assist the industrial development of the country. Industries of vital importance to the country are not concerned merely with the production of guns and shells, gas and *cannon and bullets*. These, perhaps, are only the final, visible end of a system of economy, in which every conceivable industry becomes established in the land, thanks to a system of judicious patronage, protection, and encouragement from such spending departments of the State as that of Defence. Properly handled, there is no modern industry of any importance, which the Defence Department in India could not encourage in the country itself,—and that without needless burdens on the consumer. The Governor-General, however, administering this Department in his sole discretion, may, and probably will, continue the vicious policy of keeping India wholly dependent for the essential requirements of modern defence upon supplies from "Home." The Ministers would have no *locus standi* to offer their views, to urge their opinion that active effort should be made to make India self-sufficient in such matters.

The only matters in which India and Indians are supposed at all to be interested, as the Instructions to the Governor-General seem to suggest, is the amount of money spent, and the number of Indians employed in the grade of Commissioned Officers in their own Defence forces. Even here, there is no special obligation laid upon the Governor-General, by the Constitution or by his Instructions, to see that Indianisation of the Indian Defence forces is accomplished in a given period, or that all possible economies and retrenchment are effected in this wasteful and unproductive item of expenditure. If the Ministers on such matters offer an opinion, the Governor-General is not bound to accept it: and if he considers it at all, it does not in the least follow that he would see it from the standpoint of Indians. If questions relating to the Department of Defence,—and all that it could possibly be made to serve in regard to the industrialisation of the country,—are ever brought before the Federal Council of Ministers, they would rather be by way of mere information to the latter than with any real desire to seek their advice, to understand their point of view on those subjects, and to enlist their real co-operation. Under those conditions, no self-respecting Indian Minister, particularly one of Nationalist sympathies, would be able to avoid a feeling of futility, a sense of frustration for himself and his country, which cannot but undermine his work and authority in other Departments.

Federal Ministers drawn from Indian States

In considering this aspect of the position of the Federal Ministers, we have hitherto overlooked the position of those Ministers, who, if any, are representatives of some Federated States. Being merely nominees of their own Rulers, they have not the ultimate sanction of the British Indian Ministers, who can, in the last analysis, speak of the authority of their Constituents,—the people of those regions. The Minister representing a State will have the most unenviable situation, since he may not be permitted even to resign with his colleagues,—or might be asked to return with other colleagues to office from which, only the day before, he resigned collectively with the Ministry because of a difference of views on some fundamental question of national policy. The Governor-General's Instructions enjoin upon him to include, as far as possible, some Minister from this section of the Federal Legislature; but, if any are so included without forming part of the British Indian Political Parties, the position of such Ministers in the Cabinet and in the country would be most unenviable.

Ministers' Oaths of Office

We have commented, in another volume, upon the Oaths of Office the Ministers will have to take. These will emphasise the divided and conflicting allegiance these individuals will have to shoulder, without any compensating advantage of aid or encouragement from either side to which they swear or bear allegiance.*

Ministerial Salaries

As for the salaries and allowances to the Ministers, they are to be fixed in the first instance, by the Governor-General in his discretion, and subsequently by Act of the Federal Legislature. Indian political opinion has long since recognised that the scale of official emoluments in this country is out of all proportion to the work done, the responsibility shouldered, or even the ability of the paymaster to bear these burdens. Nevertheless, official outlook in this matter remains wholly unchanged, as we can see from the scale of salaries accorded to the Provincial Ministers in some of the Provinces. Even the popular Legislature in these Provinces seem to have taken their cue from the decree of the Governor, as wholly erroneous notions unfortunately do prevail about the cost of dignity, and the compensation for sacrifice (?) made by leading politicians in accepting Ministerial office. It may be added,

* The device, adopted at the National Convention in Delhi, in March 1937, of requiring every elected Provincial Legislator, to take an oath of allegiance to the people of India, is well worth a repetition in the case of Federal Legislators when elected.

that, even when the Federal Legislature comes to fix, by Act, the scale of salaries and allowances to be given to Federal Ministers, if they are fixed at a figure which the Governor-General considers too low for efficiency, integrity or reasonable compensation to the Ministers: or if he considers such salaries to throw into undesirable relief the extravagant burden borne by the Counsellors', or the Financial Adviser's salaries, he may use all his power, even that of vetoing such legislation, and influence with nominees from the Indian States to make a radical modification of those scales.

Prospects of Cabinet-making in the Federation

The Federal Assembly being indirectly elected for the greater part,—with, at most, one-third of its personnel consisting of nominees of Indian Rulers,—the chances of forming Cabinets by the Indian Political Parties, or any of them, are difficult to estimate at this date. Much of the doubt, apprehension, or misgivings, expressed in the preceding pages regarding the actual rôle of the Federal Ministry is, of course, tacitly conditioned by the assumption that popular, Nationalist, Congress Party representatives will command a majority in the Federal Assembly, or be at least, the most numerous, the best disciplined, and the best organised Party in that body; and that they may not be viewed with the same confidence by the powers that be as Ministers drawn from Moderate Parties. The following statistics and observations based upon them, may be taken rather as a rough index of what may happen, than a prophesy of what will.

The seats in the Federal Assembly allotted to British India number 250, distributed as follows among the several Provinces:—

Province		General Seats	Muhammadan Seats		Women's Seats	Other *
Madras	...	19 (4)	8		2	8
Bombay	...	18 (2)	6		2	9
Bengal	...	10 (3)	17		1	9
United Prov.	...	19 (3)	12		1	5
Punjab	...	6 (1)	14	6 Sikhs	1	3
Bihar	...	16 (2)	9		1	4
C. P. & Berar	...	9 (2)	3		1	2
Assam		4 (1)	3		—	3
N. W. F. Prov.	...	1	4		—	—
Orissa	...	4 (1)	1		—	-
Sind	...	1	3		---	1
Delhi	...	1	1		—	—
Br. Baluchistan	...		1		—	---
Ajmer-Merwara	...	1	-		—	
Coorg	...	1	—		..	—
Non-Provincial Seats	...	—	-		—	4
Total	...	105	82	6	9	48

Not more than 190 seats seem to be open to election by the device of Proportional Representation, under a system of a Single Transferable Vote. Elections to the other Constituencies will be under a special procedure; and, except labour, totalling 10, we may take it, the Representatives of these interests will be on anti-Nationalist sympathies in general. Not all women, also, may be regarded as likely to be of Nationalist or Congress persuasion, not more than 5 from that group being likely to be of that Party. Of 82 Mussulman members from the various Provinces and 6 Sikhs, according to the strength of these Communities, and their

* Others include Europeans, Anglo Indians, Indian Christians Commerce and Industry, Labour, Landholders etc.

Party affiliations in the various Provinces, it is unlikely that more than a dozen members from these two combined could be elected on the Nationalist or Congress Ticket to the Federal Assembly. Of the 105 General Seats, 19 are Scheduled Caste seats, of which, on a fair proportion, not more than a dozen may be expected to be of Congress fold. Of the remaining 86, the Congress Party would do very well if it could capture 80, all Provinces put together, while of the others, including Commerce and Industry seats, it would be very fortunate if it secures on its own ticket 10 seats in all. The maximum strength thus computed will be:

General Seats	80
Scheduled Castes	12
Sikhs and Muslims	12
Labour	10
Women	5
Other Constituencies	10
Total ..	129
or, in round terms ..	130

Granted all other allies from other constituencies, the Congress strength in the Federal Assembly will not exceed 140, so long as elections are through the Provincial Assemblies, whose complexion, or Party division, was determined at the last General Elections to the Provincial Legislatures.

In a total House of 375, including 125 (maximum) representatives from the Indian States, a single Party of 140 or even 150 will not be in a majority, unless it can combine with the Muslims, or other such considerable blocks. To combine with representatives (?) from the Indian States is all but unthinkable for the Congress Party. Other elements, like Europeans, Anglo-Indians or Indian Christians, Landlord or Commerce Representatives, are utterly unlikely to share Congress political ideals, at least in the first years of the new regime. Nevertheless, it would be the largest single Party, best disciplined and organised, with an immense popular following in the country at large. The Governor-General cannot ignore it in forming the Federal Ministry; but he can rely on all his extraordinary powers under the Constitution, and still more considerable indirect influence, to render the Congress Ministry, if formed, impeded effectually at every step in every effort to carry out even a part of the Congress programme as ratified by the Electorate.

Summing up the entire position, it seems extremely doubtful if, under these conditions, the popular Ministers of the Federation of India will have any real opportunity to inaugurate constructive schemes of economic betterment, or social reconstruction. As would, perhaps, be better appreciated after a study of the financial side of the Administration, the necessary funds are either unavailable because ear-marked already for non-productive expenditure and lavish scale of overhead charges; or difficult to find in the absence of new taxation, proposals for which the Governor-General may not always view with favour. Additional burdens, moreover, are specially difficult in a Federation to impose; and particularly unwelcome in popular governments, no matter how urgently additional funds may be needed, and how remuneratively they may be employed.

If the financial curb upon Ministerial enthusiasm for the economic betterment of the masses does not prove quite effective, there are the enormous powers of the Governor-General, as protector and champion of foreign vested interests and Imperialist exploitation, which are bound to be employed to impede or frustrate too enthusiastic Ministers. There are, again, specific provisions of the Constitution, such as those against any discrimination against British vested interests;* or in protection and guarantees to the Public Services, or even in grants to Indian States under Sections 147-149, which must needs prevent the Ministers from embarking upon ambitious schemes of national reconstruction and economic re-habilitation, which the stress and strain of modern economic nationalism require in every country. Finally, the Ministers' own internal difficulties,—the want of solidarity among them because of their incongruous composition, or because of lack of sufficient appreciation of their economic policies in the masses of their countrymen,—may prevent their achieving anything by way of constructive benefits to the people, and so making **Swaraj**, or popular Government, a real, visible, tangible advantage.†

*cp. Sections 111-121.

†Soon after the Congress Working Committee had authorised acceptance of Ministerial Responsibility in the Provinces where the Congress was in a majority, the President of the Congress issued a statement (July, 20th 1937) warning the people against the facile feeling that Congress Ministries would mean Congress raj, much less swaraj. Such a caution would, if anything, be more necessary as regards the Federation even if the first Federal Ministry is of Congress complexion.

CHAPTER VII

FEDERAL SERVICES

The actual work of Federal Administration is carried out by well organised, carefully protected, and meticulously safeguarded Public Services. These are not exclusive to any particular Department, except in regard to the Department of Defence; but specialised qualifications and experience are necessarily becoming more and more important in the recruitment, promotion, or postings in the various Departments.

The most difficult single problem of the Indian Constitution, and the one which also affects most immediately the economic side of our national development, is that in regard to the place and function of the Public Services. We shall consider in this Chapter those branches of the Public Service, and add that portion of the general reflections on the matter, which were either omitted from the volume on Provincial Autonomy, or insufficiently discussed there.

The bulk of the Public Services,—including the Indian Civil Service proper, the Police, Judicial, Engineering, Educational and Medical, work in the Provinces. We have already considered, in the volume on Provincial Autonomy, most of the problems connected with their recruitment, discipline, promotion, protection, and emoluments. In this section, therefore, of our study of the Constitution, we need say no more than that what applies in the case of Services operating in the Provinces applies with still greater force as regards the Federation, if and when that entity is established.

We shall, accordingly, confine ourselves, in this Chapter to considering the Federal Services proper, which include:

(1) Secretariat and Counsellors;

(2) the Defence Services;

(3) the Political Services, in the Indian States, and other officers in connection with the External Relations of the Federation of India;

(4) Ecclesiastical Department, and Miscellaneous Federal Services.

(5) the High Commissioner, and the Department under him;

(6) the Audit and Accounts Services;

(7) the Railway Services; Reserve Bank Service; Posts and Telegraphs;

(8) the Customs, Income Tax, Salt and other Services under the Finance Department of the Federal Government;

(9) Inspecting and co-ordinating Staff;

(10) the Federal Judicial Service;

The basic principles of recruitment, payment, promotion, discipline are, as already observed, exactly similar; and so we need devote no space to discussing these; or considering the problems connected therewith. The same question of overweighted superior ranks and overpaid service; of lack of Indianisation; of secured independence from Indian Ministerial authority, militating against good discipline and proper subordination of efficiency in the country's service; of guaranteed communal proportions; of progressive discontinuance of the principle of recruitment by open competitive examination in favour of direct or indirect patronage,—not to mention the possibility of imperceptible corruption due to the progress of the popular elements,—confront the student of the Indian Constitution in the case of the Federal Government as in those of the Provincial Governments; and the means open to deal with them are in no way better. The Governor-General is even more the Patron Saint and the Sovereign Grand Master of the Services,—federally considered,—than the Governor in the Provinces. His powers of appointment, fixing of the terms and conditions of service; scales of pay and allowances, pensions and other privileged forms of exploitation; protection by way of appeal and in matters of discipline; are even more considerable than those of the Governor. On the other hand, the opposition that the representatives of the Indian people in the Federal Cabinet can put up is, if any thing, weaker than in the Provinces from the corresponding quarter.

(1) Secretarial Staff for the Governor-General

Let us consider first the services required for the manning of the Reserved or Excluded Departments under the Governor-General, and those officers needed by him to aid him in the proper discharge of the powers and functions to be exercised in his discretion. The most important of the latter is the Private Secretary to the Governor-General, and the staff needed for that department or office. Under Section 305:—

305.—(1) The Governor-General and every Governor shall have his own secretarial staff to be appointed by him in his discretion.

(2) The salaries and allowances of persons so appointed and the office accommodation and other facilities to be provided for them shall be such as the Governor-

General or, as the case may be, the Governor, may in his discretion determine, and the said salaries and allowances and the expenses incurred in providing the said accommodation and facilities shall be charged on the revenues of the Federation or, as the case may be, the Province.

As the Joint Parliamentary Select Committee, which considered this Constitution in its Bill form, remarks:—

> "The Governor-General will require an adequate staff with an officer of high standing at its head. Whether one of the Counsellors will fill this position it is unnecessary for us to consider, for the question is administrative rather than constitutional; but it is of exceptional importance that the Governor-General should be well served, and we do not doubt that this matter has engaged and will continue to engage the earnest attention of His Majesty's Government".*

In the paragraph of this Report just immediately preceding, the Committee have given consideration to the Indian apprehension that the Counsellors of the Governor-General, placed in charge of his special responsibilities or extraordinary powers, might develop into "super-ministers." While negativing that fear, the Committee cannot conceal the fact that, if the various powers of discretion, and for overriding the Ministry in given cases, entrusted to the Governor-General, are to be properly carried out, he would need highly skilled and experienced aid in the discharge of those Special Responsibilities, and the exercise of those extraordinary powers. The Provincial Governors, with corresponding similar powers and functions, have appointed in this place officers of the rank of a Collector-Magistrate, Civilian of some twenty years' experience in Indian administration. Private Secretaries to the Governor-General have, even under the existing Constitution, been very high officers, who, on completion of their term of office, have frequently been

*cp. Para. 189, Op. Cit.

promoted to be Governors of Provinces. Under the new Constitution, the responsibilities and duties of this office will be particularly onerous. It is, therefore, no surprise, that provision is made for such appointments by the Governor-General in his discretion.

The only comment one might permit oneself to offer is that, so long as the Governor-General is himself an alien officer appointed on alien advice, there is every likelihood that he would select for his Private Secretary a person, who, by race and training, would have greater affinity with British vested interests of all sorts in India than with the leaders of the people. As, more-ever, this appointment will be made by the Governor-General **in his discretion,** the Indian Ministers of the Governor-General will have no necessary say as a matter of right in the choice of the individual or his emoluments of office. There is thus every reason to fear that, in so far as the well-being of the country is closely mixed up with the proper, sympathetic, and discriminating exercise of the extraordinary powers of the Governor-General, the individual appointed, and the terms and conditions of his appointment will militate against adequate attention and sympathy being shown to India's expectations. The Governor-General is usually a high-born gentleman, not particularly distinguished for his capacity for hard work, and much less for intellectual acumen or political discernment. Such personages inevitably become dignified mouthpieces of their competent secretaries. But even when they are not mere automata speaking out the lines put into their mouths by their secretaries, the powers given to the Governor-General under the new Constitution are such and so vast, that his private secretary will necessarily exercise immense, even if invisible, power for the success or failure of the Responsible Ministers, and so for the success or failure of the entire Constitution. It is but natural, then, that Indians should feel particularly concerned in the choice of the individual to fill this place, his outlook and sympathies.

The Counsellors of the Governor-General

The staff needed for the other Reserved or excluded Departments, placed in charge of the Governor-General in his sole discretion, would be headed by the respective Counsellors in each such Department,—except possibly the Department of Ecclesiastical Affairs. Before discussing the Constitutional position of these Counsellors,—half-Ministers, half-secretaries, wholly ambiguous and amphibious creatures,—of the Governor-General, let us note that, under the provisions of Section 244 (2), the Secretary of State is entitled to make appointments, until Parliament otherwise determines, to any service or services which, after the coming into operation of the system of Provincial Autonomy, may be established to secure the recruitment of suitable persons to fill civil posts in connection with the discharge of the Governor-General's discretionary functions. The strength of these services, the conditions regarding pay, leave, pensions, etc., are to be determined by the Secretary of State.* In so far as the persons in such posts are serving in connection with the affairs of the Federation, their salaries, leave allowances and pensions, must be charged upon the revenues of the Federation,—*i.e.*, be not votable by the Federal

*cp., Section 244 (3) and Section 247.

Legislature.* These will be the most costly services under the new regime; and they will have every right of complaint to the Secretary of State, and compensation for any real or fancied ill-treatment. No change can be made in their mode of recruitment, scale of pay and allowances, pensions or Provident Fund contributions, by any authority in India, even though they may be concerned with the most vital affairs of India.

The Governor-General is obliged, under Section 244 (4), to keep the Secretary of State informed as to the working of these special services created under Section 244 (2). As emblem of the continuing Parliamentary Authority in this regard, the Secretary of State must submit every year a statement to Parliament giving the number of appointments made to these services in that period, and of the vacancies therein.† In all this, there is no word or hint of concern for the Indian people, or their ability to support such burdens,—or enjoy such luxuries. The only consolation, if consolation it can be called, is to be derived from the somewhat belated and halting provision in 244 (4) that:—

> "It shall be the duty of the Governor-General to keep the Secretary of State informed as to the operation of this section, and he may after the expiration of such period as he thinks fit make recommendations for the modification thereof."

This may be interpreted to mean,—though with a certain strain upon the spirit of the entire Constitution,—

*The same rule applies as regards those serving in connection with the affairs of a Province,—the salaries, etc., being charged on the Provincial Revenues.

†This last provision is interesting, in so far as the logic of Section 246 would seem to forbid keeping such vacancies, even in these services, for longer than 3 months, thereby effecting savings in public expenditure in an oblique fashion.

that the Governor-General may conceivably see, in some remote future, (a) the unwisdom, impolicy, or extravagance of having such services at all; or (b) having them manned by people appointed by an alien authority, like the Secretary of State, presumably unfamiliar with the requirements of Indian administration or local conditions; or (c) having them in such extraordinarily privileged position. If he so realises, he may recommend modification of this section in the direction he may deem proper and necessary for the efficient conduct of the administration. But even then, he acts on his own authority, without necessarily any reference to or consultation with his Ministers; for the second paragraph of the sub-section expressly provides:

> "In discharging his functions under this sub-section, the Governor-General shall act in his discretion".

There is, therefore, no reasonable hope of relief being obtainable by the Indian exchequer or the Indian people from these innumerable old men of the mountains fastened upon our shoulders.*

The Counsellors themselves are appointed under Section 11. These appointments are not to exceed 3 in number; and their salaries and conditions of service are to be such as His Majesty may prescribe by Order in Council. What exactly will be the rôle of these hybrid relics of a vanishing system of Dyarchy, it is, at the moment, impossible to say. In all probability they would be midway between the Departmental

*Exactly what will be the strength of the Services created under this Section 244 (2), it is impossible to say to-day, even in the roughest estimate. A reference to the Governor-General's discretionary powers (See ante p. 147 is no guide, since he need not have special organised services in respect of all those functions. Much less is it possible to estimate to-day the cost of those services. All that one can now prophesy is that the strength may be quite considerable and the cost very high.

Secretaries and the Executive Councillors of to-day, appointed for definite terms, on fairly high salaries, but without any direct responsibility either to the Federal Legislature, or even to Parliament. The power of the Governor-General under Section 17 to make rules for the distribution of business, and the conduct of the work of government among his Ministers and Counsellors may relieve, or remedy to some extent, the inherent difficulties of this situation. Says the Report of the Joint Select Committee of Parliament, who considered this Constitution in its Bill form:—

> "The Federal Government will be a dyarchical, and not a unitary government, the Governor-General's Ministers having the constitutional right to tender advice to him on only a part of the affairs of the Federation, while the administration of the other part remains the exclusive responsibility of the Governor-General himself. In these circumstances, it is clear that the Governor-General's Counsellors, who will be responsible to the Governor-General alone and will share none of the responsibility of the Federal Ministers to the Federal Legislature, cannot be members of the Council of Ministers".

Without being of the Ministry, or sharing their responsibility to the Legislature, these Counsellors will nevertheless share in all the deliberations of national policy. The Instructions to the Governor-General require that constant consultation, and interchange of ideas, should take place between these two halves of the Federal Government. The justification alleged for the practice is, not only the advisability of acquainting the Responsible, popular Ministers with the working and requirements of the non-responsible half of the Government, but also thereby to train and prepare the former for shouldering the full responsibility for all Departments of Government in the fullness of time, when it pleases the British Imperial Government to make that concession. It may also happen, however, that, from this very practice, the non-responsible Counsellors may come to know of the policies and intentions of the Responsible Ministers for the Departments for which the latter are responsible at their very inception. If the Counsellors are unsympathetic, or unduly alarmist regarding the reaction of such Ministerial proposals upon the departments for which they are responsible to the Governor-General alone, it would be in their power to prejudice the Governor-General from the start against these proposals of his Ministers, even before they reach the stage of being formulated in legislative or other measures. The Governor-General can always plead his Special Responsibility for the maintenance of financial stability and credit of India,—or, failing that, for the prevention of any grave menace to the peace and tranquillity of India or any part thereof,—to veto such proposals from even being formulated, to frustrate them when formulated, or prevent their being properly carried out when enacted or resolved upon by the Legislature and the Ministry.

These Counsellors are thus undesirable from every point of view. They are likely to be a fifth wheel of the coach, and a costly luxury, for the simple reason that their pay, etc., being outside the control of the Legislature, the authority fixing that may,—and, probably, will,—have no regard to the ability of the Indian people to bear such burdens. Their salaries and allowances will, we may assume, be fixed at levels not much below that of the present Executive Councillors. Certainly, we may take the salaries, etc., of the present Secretaries to the Government of India to be the lower limit of these emoluments. Even at that level, they are bound to be a most costly and unwanted addition to the Federal Budgets. They might be appointed for a term of 5 years, and will very likely be all special importations for the purpose from abroad. Or they might be promoted from among British officers serving in India in the Civil, Military, and other Departments, provided they are known to be "strong men" who would not succumb to Indian influences, and hold no sympathy for Nationalist heresies. However appointed and recruited, they may be entitled to serve a further term in the same office, or be interchanged as between their different departments. Their responsibility being primarily and exclusively to the Governor-General, unless the latter in any way feels dissatisfied with their work or ways, they may continue to draw these excessive emoluments for an indefinite period in these relatively cushy jobs, with little responsibility, and perhaps less work.

Financial Adviser

The same, almost, might be said of the Financial Adviser to the Governor-General, except that his work would be much more considerable. His services would be available to the other Departments of Government in charge of Responsible Ministers; and the selection of the individual to be appointed to this post will not always be free from Ministerial influence. But the presence of the Financial Adviser to the Governor-General at Cabinet meetings may not be an unmixed good to the Responsible Ministers, since the primary responsibility of this Adviser is towards the Governor-General; and his duties may include the obligation to keep the Governor-General advised as to the Financial reactions of the Ministers' proposals in the Departments for which they are responsible upon Departments which are excluded from their purview; and for which the Governor-General is alone responsible. As, in discharge of his Special Responsibilities, and to meet the expenditure in the Reserved Departments, the Governor-General is entitled to a prior charge upon the Federal revenues, the information and advice of the Financial Adviser may quite possibly act prejudicially to the interests of the other Departments, and of the country generally.

(2) Defence Services

As already mentioned elsewhere, it is proposed to devote an entire chapter to consider the constitutional side of the problem of our National Defence in this volume. We shall, therefore, devote no further space here to such problems as Indianisation, Conscription, Retrenchment and Economy; Recruitment in the Defence Forces; institution within the country of all branches of industry needed for equipping the Defence Forces.

Considering here only the services in that Department, also an exclusive responsibility of the Governor-General, they are governed by a Chapter of the Constitution exclusively devoted to them. The Commander-in-Chief's appointment is specifically provided for in the Constitution;* and all the various branches of the Defence Services are regulated by Sections 232 to 239, both inclusive. As the entire expenditure in connection with the Department of Defence is excluded from the vote of the Federal Legislature, the pay, pen-

*cp. Section 4, and ante Ch. IV. p. 131.

sion, and allowances of the Commander-in-Chief may well be fixed by Order of the King in Council.* Section 237 provides:—

> "Any sums payable out of the revenues of the Federation in respect of pay, allowances, pensions or other sums payable to, or in respect of, persons who are serving or have served, in His Majesty's forces shall be charged on those revenues, but nothing herein contained shall be construed as limiting the interpretation of the general provisions of this Act charging on the said revenue expenditure with respect to defence".

This principle is extended, by the next following section:

> "to persons who, not being members of His Majesty's forces, hold, or have held, posts in India connected with the equipment or administration of those forces or otherwise connected with defence, as they apply in relation to persons who are, or have been, members of those forces".

This means that responsible Indian Ministers shall have not only no say whatsoever in the appointment of the Commander-in-Chief of their Defence Forces, or in the shaping of the general policy for making proper provision for defence according to their means and requirements, but they will have no say whatsoever in making any disbursements which are covered by the sacred name of National Defence,—whether in regard to persons directly engaged in that task, or those who are only remotely connected with some ancillary service in connection with it. And this in addition to the wide latitude afforded by Section 150 relating to expenditure in general, and the "purposes" on which it may be made, which has already been cited and commented upon in the volume on Provincial Autonomy.

*Section 232. The pay, etc., of the Governor-General is fixed by Schedule III to this Act.

The King in Council may, under Section 233, specify the number of appointments in connection with the Defence of India, which may be made either by himself directly, or in any manner that he may prescribe. This is without prejudice to his general Prerogative right of making all appointments in the Indian Defence Forces. This provision is probably included because of the need for coordinating the entire policy of Imperial Defence of Britain and her Dominions, with that of India. There are some appointments even now, such as that of the Chief of the General Staff in India, which are made under unwritten conventions directly from Britain, in accordance with the requirements of British Imperial Defence considerations rather than strictly those of Indian requirement. This entails a close system of co-relation in high command, and interchange of senior officers between the British Army proper and the Army in India, whether its British section or its Indian section. This may be in the best interests of Imperial Defence, Strategy, and High Command in time of war; but it may spell very little advantage for India, even from the standpoint of retaining in the country the experience gained by Military or Air Force Officers at her expense, to form a sort of trained reserve available in times of national emergency.

The differentiation between Commissions in the Army granted to officers by the King directly and those issued by the Governor-General is perpetuated by statutory provision in Section 234. All the ignominy this distinction has come to imply to Indian officers serving in the Defence Forces of their own country is accorded legal, constitutional recognition and authority. It is a little difficult for a layman to understand why this provision was necessary at all, though, in actual words, it seems no more than the possibility of granting Officers' Commissions to ordinary soldiers who had served in the ranks. Whatever that may be, the very existence of this distinction is fatal to a proper appreciation being developed in India of the motives and circumstances of British Imperial statesmanship, which inflicts such gratuitous insult upon an entire people.

Section 235 empowers the Secretary of State, acting with the concurrence of his Advisers,—or what is known under the existing system as the *Secretary of State for India in Council*,—to specify what rules, regulations and orders affecting the conditions of service of all or any of the forces serving in India shall be made only with his previous approval. This, again, seems a roundabout method of asserting the ultimate supremacy of the Secretary of State. Or it camouflages clumsily the patent fact that in the most important and expensive department in its charge, the Federal Government of India would be as much under the leading strings of Whitehall, as the Government of India under the Act of 1919 have been. The power of making such rules, regulations, etc., is given, apparently, in the first instance, to the Indian authorities,—presumably the Governor-General acting in his discretion. But the right is reserved to the Secretary of State for India, acting with the support of a majority of his new Advisers, to lay down what particular rules of service, made by the Indian authority, should have his previous approval. Any amendment in such rules would also be, presumably, similarly treated. This margin of power left to the Secretary of State seems, in our eyes, to have no justification except to see that the Governor-General does not come to be unduly influenced by his Indian Ministers to the slightest prejudice of the British element in the Indian Defence Forces by land, or sea, or air. Whether that may not operate to the grave prejudice of assuring a proper wholesome respect for the Indian authorities in the personnel of the Defence Forces of India is, of course, not a consideration that weighs at all with those who drafted this Constitution.

(3) Department of External Affairs

The Service in the Department of External Affairs, —as it would be styled under the new regime,—has hitherto been mixed up with that of the Political Department, in charge of the Governor-General. Says the Report of the Joint Select Committee of Parliament, considering the Constitution in its Bill form:—

> "Recruitment to the Political Department is indirect, vacancies being filled by transfers from the Indian Army and the Civil Service (mainly the Indian Civil Service) and, to a smaller extent, by the promotion of subordinate political officers. The Governor-General approves transfers from the Indian Civil Service and the Indian Army; transfers from the other All-India services are approved by the Secretary of State on the recommendation of the Governor-General.
>
> The Statutory Commission made no specific recommendations for the future organisation and recruitment of the Political Department, of which at present the Governor-General himself holds the portfolio. Its total strength on 1st October, 1933, was 108 posts. These include, on the External side, the secretariat, district and judicial appointments in the North-West Frontier Province and Baluchistan, as well as the political agencies in tribal territory; political agencies on the Persian Gulf and a proportion of Consular appointments in Persia; the Civil administration of Aden, and such other appointments as those at the legations in Afghanistan and Nepal and the Consulate-General at Kashgar. On the internal side they include the appointments to

political agencies and residencies through which the relations of the Crown with the Indian States are conducted; and the civil administration of the Chief Commissioners' provinces of Coorg and Ajmer-Merwara, and of the assigned tract of Bangalore and other British Cantonment areas in the Indian States."*

Under the new Constitution, the offices of Political Agents and Residents at the Indian States may become unnecessary, at least so far as those States are concerned which have joined the Federation. It is true, even after the accession of the States to the Federation, there will remain a considerable field of their relations with the Crown, for the proper conduct of which some officers may be needed who will be under the Governor-General (or the Representative of the Crown if the office is separated) exclusively. But, as the Joint Select Committee's Report puts it, responsibility for recruitment to these two branches of the Political Department, and the Department for External Affairs proper, will remain with the Secretary of State. There is a feeling among some Indian Rulers that officers conducting their relations with the Crown should be non-Indians; and it is very likely that this Department, as well as the Department of External Affairs proper, may come to be manned almost wholly by non-Indians, except, perhaps, in very subordinate positions.†

Aden having been separated from the Indian Federation, that portion of the patronage must disappear. Appointments to the Chief Commissionerships,

---

*Paras. 301 and 302 of the Report.

†By Section 257, officers of the Political Department proper, i.e., that dealing with the relations of the Crown with the Indian States, are withdrawn from the operation of Part X of the Act of 1935, which relates to Public Services in general. Existing officers are allowed to hold their posts on the same conditions of service, pay, pensions, etc., as before the coming into effect of Part III of the Act dealing with Provincial Autonomy; and no change can be made by any Indian authority in these terms and conditions of service, which would be unfavourable to the officers concerned.

will remain with the Governor-General under the supervision of the Secretary of State. These, it may be added, might quite possibly be separated from the Political Department proper, and be merged in the Civil Service, or appointments to Civil Posts made by the Secretary of State, as the Chief Commissionerships are within the *discretionary* authority of the Governor-General. Appointments in the Tribal areas,—in Baluchistan, as well as in the North-West Frontier,—will likewise remain with the Governor-General; and here, too, the problem of Indianisation may provoke as much criticism among the Indian people as in the other reserved departments.

Diplomatic, Consular and Trade Commissioners' Appointments

External Affairs proper would, thus, be concerned with such Legations and Consulates in Afghanistan, Nepal, Kashgar, and Persia as the Government of India under the new Constitution are allowed to appoint directly. We have, however, no Indian Diplomatic or Consular Service. Such appointments may, therefore, will be made for years to come by an outside authority from among non-Indians, no matter how the interests of India might suffer thereby.

Trade Commissioners,—four in all so far, including one in Japan,—and their staffs, are another branch of this Service, which will also remain exclusively with the Governor-General. Though hitherto recruited from among the Indian Civil Service Officers, these officers might, quite conceivably, be recruited from the special services created under Section 244. The vital interests of India involved in the due observance of such Trade Treaties require that Indians experienced in matters of the country's foreign trade should alone be appointed to such posts. At the present time, it is by no means an unfamiliar criticism of the Indian Trade Commissioners in European countries, like Italy or Germany, that they are unable to safeguard the interests of the Indian merchants trading with those countries, on such occasions, as, for example, the limitation of credit available for Indian imports into Germany, especially in contrast with the corresponding action of the British Government in protecting the similar interests of British merchants. Experienced Indians in such posts might also not, on similar occasions, be able to defeat Britain's one-sided move to the prejudice of Indian merchants. But they might help to make the case much stronger for the full Indian control of those posts, if the interests of India are to receive something better than step-motherly treatment.

(4) Ecclesiastical Department

The Ecclesiastical Department,—another excluded concern of the Governor-General,—is, relatively, unimportant. Its maximum expenditure being practically fixed under Section 33 (3) (e) at 42 lakhs, it is, even from the financial standpoint, not of great importance. Its importance, however, lies in the injustice implied to the Indian people, in that the religion of a microscopic minority,—and, at that, of alien origin,—receives such state recognition and support, while the religions of the children of the soil have no such recognition accorded to it. The concern of the State with any Religion or Religions is open to criticism on general grounds, and for a variety of reasons. For our part, we would not have the State in India to have any concern with any religion. But, if the State must concern itself with Religion even in the way of financial support, the first claim is obviously that of the religion or religions of the people of the soil, and not of an outside minority of such insignificant proportions as the Anglican civilians and soldiers serving in this country. Appointments in this Department will be made by, and be under the control of, the Secretary of State.

(5) High Commissioner for India

In this connection, we might also dispose of the appointment of the Indian High Commissioner in Britain and that of the Agent to the Government of India in the Union of South Africa. The appointment of the High Commissioner will, in the new regime, be made under Section 302, which leaves the appointment, and the salary and conditions of service, to be prescribed by the Governor-General, acting in his Individual Judgment. This means that this appointment is not completely withdrawn from the advice of the Ministers, though the Governor-General is left a margin of authority to override the advice of his Ministers in choosing the individual, or prescribing his remuneration and conditions of service. No mention is made of any Pension attached to this post; and if it is ranked as a political appointment, it is possible distinguished and retired politicians alone would be appointed to the post. The work, however, which the Indian High Commissioner has to do in Britain involves considerable administrative and business experience; and the choice of a retired politician may not always serve the interests at stake most effectively. No mention is made, in this section, of the Staff for the High Commissioner's office, which, it may be presumed, will also be under the control of the Federal Government.

Agent to the Federal Government in South Africa

The same authority will appoint Agent to the Government (Federal) of India in the Union of South Africa, and such other Dominions in which it may be deemed advisable to have special Agents. This is not excluded from the scope of Ministerial Responsibility in the Federation. Even if we may not regard this to be the means for improving India's relations with the Dominions, the Federal Government may, it may well be presumed, be more active and determine in retaliation for any unjust treatment to Indians in the British Dominions, thanks to the advice and information of such Agents.*

(6) Auditor of Indian Home Accounts

Sections 170, 251 and 252 deal with the appointment of an Auditor of Indian Home Accounts, and his Staff. The Auditor of Indian Home Accounts,—*i.e.*, of the Secretary of State whose cost will not be charged on the British Budget,—and of the Indian High Commissioner's Office, will be appointed by the Governor-General *in his discretion.* The number of his staff, their salaries and qualifications will require to be approved by the Governor-General, also *in his discretion.* The Staff will, of course, be appointed by the Auditor himself. It may therefore, be taken for granted that very little Indian element will be found in these appointments.

The same applies to the staff of the office of the High Commissioner. As however the latter Officer may be an Indian, and his appointment not free from

*Provision is made for the Staff of the High Commissioner in Section 251.

political influence and considerations, the exclusion of the Indian element may not be quite so complete as in the case of the Auditor's staff. Those holding the corresponding appointments before the coming into operation of Part III of the Act of 1935 are guaranteed in their office, and conditions of service regarding pay, pension, etc. The expenses of this department of the Auditor of Indian Home Accounts will be **charged on the revenues of the Federation,** and, as such, non-votable by the Federal Legislature; while that in connection with the staff of the High Commissioner's Office will be charged on those revenues to the extent that corresponding expenditure under the existing system was defrayed without being submitted to a vote of the Indian Legislative Assembly.*

(7) Railway Service

By Section 277, Railway Services, Class I and Class II mean the services, which were, immediately before the commencement of Part III of the Act of 1935, so classed in the Classification Rules under Section 96 B of the Government of India Act, 1919. By Section 242, the provisions of the preceding section as regards recruitment and conditions of service would apply, so, however, that, for purposes of initial appointment and prescribing conditions of service, the Railway Authority is substituted for the Governor-General. This is intended to keep the Railway Staff and Superior Services outside political influence and wire-pulling supposed to operate in Government Departments. The

*cp., Detailed Estimates for 1937-38, pp. 177-8. In the Government of India Budget for 1937-38, this expenditure was divided into: Voted Rs. 993,000; non-voted Rs. 332,000 inclusive of the Education Department under the High Commissioner.

same privileges regarding guaranteed pay, pensions, leave and other allowances, rights of complaint, etc., and compensation, are assured to these Railway Servants as to the other civil servants of the State in India under the terms of Section 241.*

A special feature of the Railway Service is the disproportionate number of appointments in it going to the Anglo-Indian community. Under the provisions of Section 242 (3) this position is specially safeguarded, so that

> "the specific class, character, and numerical percentages of the posts hitherto held by members of that community and the remuneration attaching to such posts"

are guaranteed to them. The Railway Authority is further bound

> "to give effect to any instructions which may be issued by the Governor-General for the purpose of securing, so far as practicable to each community in India a fair representation in the Railway services of the Federation".

As the care of the legitimate interests of Minorities is among the Special Responsibilities of the Governor-General, the extremely small Minority community of Anglo-Indians are guaranteed this profitable privilege as long as this Constitution lasts. With this guaranteed charge acting as a first mortgage on the resources of the Indian Railways,—already in a woefully deficit condition,—it is impossible to expect that any real economy could be made for the general benefit of the Federal Finances.

*Cp. Section 186 which makes the Pay and Pensions and Provident Fund Contributions of such servants be charged on the Railway Fund before other demands can be made against that Fund.

(8) Customs, Posts & Telegraphs, and Court Officials

The same rules of recruitment and conditions of service will apply to those serving under the Federal Government in the Indian Customs Service, the Posts and Telegraphs Department, and the Officials of the Federal Court. The privileged position of the Anglo-Indian community is noted and guaranteed in these Departments also in identical terms. This means considerable patronage at the disposal of the Governor-General, who may exercise it in consultation with the Federal Public Services Commission, or under rules made or suggested by that body; or on the advice of his Ministers. But in no case is he bound to follow that advice if it clashes in his opinion with any of his Special Responsibilities.

Audit Service

Under Section 166, an Auditor-General for India is to be appointed by the King-Emperor, *i.e.*, by the Secretary of State; and that officer is made removable from his post in the same way and on the same grounds as a Judge of the Federal Court. This is but proper, as the duties of the Auditor-General are of a kind that require this office to be made as completely free from political influence or Party manoeuvrings as could possibly be arranged. It follows, therefore, that the conditions of service of this officer must be such as to afford him the required independence and immunity from political influence. The provisions, therefore, of Section 166 (2), (3) and (4) are as correct in principle as they seem irreproachable in form. The only regret of an Indian commentator on such provisions is that Indians, perfectly suitable and qualified for this most important, though perhaps the least advertised, post, will have practically no chance of securing that appointment, and serving their country through it in every way the Auditor-General can.

The Auditor-General, being debarred, by Sub-section (2) of that section, from any further office under the Crown in India after he has ceased to hold the office of the Auditor-General, will be free from the insidious temptation that seems to beset a number of the higher officers of the Government in India. On their retirement, most of them obtain high paid posts with Indian States, or private corporations, on the tacit understanding that their knowledge and influence of the working of the Indian Government would enable them to obtain all desired, and at times not too legitimate, advantages for their new employers. Such a practice for a person in a post like that of the Auditor-General would be highly reprehensible, even if the understanding referred to above were not even breathed in his case with any prospective employer. The salary, etc., of the Auditor-General is rightly charged on the revenues of the Federation, and as such non-votable; while the salaries, etc., of his office and staff are to be paid out of those revenues, and may be open to Legislative vote.

Reserve Bank

The Governor and Deputy Governor of the Reserve Bank of India are appointed by the Governor-General *in his discretion*, and, so are fixed also their salaries, allowances and other terms of office. The same rule applies to the appointment of an officiating Governor or Deputy Governor of the Bank. The Reserve Bank, like the Railways, is supposed to be best managed if its staff, etc., are kept outside political influence and party manoeuvrings. In practice, however, political influence and party manoeuvring are supposed to be dangerous in these departments, only when they are alleged to be exercised by parties not sympathetic to the British steel frame in India. Otherwise it is difficult to understand or justify the appointment and withdrawal of the present Premier of the Punjab from the Deputy Governorship of the Reserve Bank.

(9) Inspecting and Co-ordinating Offices

A considerable amount of the Federal Government's powers of interference in, or supervision over, public administration in the Provinces and the States comprised in the Federation, will be carried out through the Federal Inspecting Officers. The Federal Inspectors will see to it that the rules of administration, or the laws made by the Central Legislature, on subjects within their jurisdiction, are duly carried out. These officers will be among those Civil officers, who may not form part of the regular Civil Service; but who will nevertheless be appointed, paid, promoted, pensioned under rules described in the preceding pages. The standard of efficiency in the public administration generally will depend, in a large measure, upon these Inspecting Officers. Their recruitment, therefore, must be a task of considerable responsibility and consequence in the well-being of the country collectively. The Governor-General will act, in such matters, on the advice of the Federal Ministers, subject to the express provisions of the law in regard to the protection and discipline of these Officers.

(10) Judicial Service

We shall describe, in so far as such description remains to be given, the Judicial Service under the

Federation in the Chapter devoted to the Federal Judiciary.

Summary

Taken collectively, the powers and functions of the Governor-General, in regard to the protection and safeguard of the Superior Services, mostly manned still by non-Indians, invest him with an effective and practically an absolute command of the administrative machinery. These powers extend, not only to the Federal Services proper, but also, as we have seen in the volume on Provincial Autonomy, to those members of these Services serving in the Provinces. Many of the appointments, their pay and conditions of service, pensions and allowances, are either to be determined by him, or by the Secretary of State above him; or guaranteed by the Constitution itself. With rare exceptions, the Governor-General is empowered in all these matters relating to the superior Services, to act **in his discretion,**—*i.e.*, without reference to the Ministers. The bulk of the salaries, allowances, pensions, etc., are *charged upon the revenues of the Federation, i.e.*, utterly outside the vote or discussion of the Indian Legislature. By this arrangement, the Governor-General is not only made the most important single cog in the administrative system of India; his Ministers' power and importance, their authority and influence, are diminished *pro tanto*. The powers of appeal and redress left to the Governor-General, or the Secretary of State; the right to afford compensation on stated contingencies to the individual officers fancying themselves aggrieved; and the fundamental principle running right through the entire legislation that no change or amendment in the system can be made, which would render the position of any given public servant less advantageous than it was before that proposal was made, make the Services Citadel as impregnable as could possibly be devised. No economy, retrenchment, or reform in the Services is possible, so long as this system is enforced rigorously upon us. Even the Indian members of these Services would be unamenable to suggestions of any relaxation in these their enormous and abnormal privileges, their insupportable salaries and allowances, so long as an outside guaranteeing authority remains in the land backed by all the material force the British Government commands in India,—unless the impulse of patriotism, the perception of the real, long-term interests of the country and its people, and the resolute stand taken by the Provincial and Federal Ministers and Legislatures work a miracle.

CHAPTER VIII

THE FEDERAL LEGISLATURE

The institution and functioning of the Federal Legislature is supposed to embody the essence of Responsible Government introduced under the new Constitution in India. This Legislature is different from the hitherto existing Indian Central Legislature, not only because it is a Legislature competent to make laws for the whole of British India and such of the Indian States as have acceded to the Federation; but also because, for the first time in the history of the Indian Constitution, the Legislature is empowered to hold Ministers Responsible to it for the working of the Government. How far this Responsibility is real; and to what extent it can or will serve the interests of political freedom, social reconstruction, and economic well-being in this country will be summed up at the end of this Chapter.

Plan of the Chapter

We shall consider in this Chapter:—

(i) The composition of the Federal Legislature, including therein:—

(a) The Bicameral form of the Legislature; relations of the two Houses; respective powers of the two Chambers; object and purpose of a Bicameral legislature, how far achieved in the Federation of India;

(b) The process of election of the Members; Franchise of Voters; Qualifications and

Disqualifications of candidates; Direct *vs.* Indirect Election;

(ii) Powers of the Federal Legislature;—in

(a) Law-making; formulation of national policy;

(b) Supervision and control of administration;

(c) Finance;

(d) Division of subjects,—Federal and Provincial;

(e) Residuary, overriding, and Emergency Powers.

(iii) The Legislature at work; Rules of Procedure; Officers of the Chambers; Privileges,—collectively of the House, and individually of Members; Payment of Members; Interpellations; Resolutions on Policy; other Motions affecting administration as well as policy; Joint Sessions of the two Chambers; Voting of Supplies; enactment of Financial Legislation.

(iv) Legislature and the Governor-General;

(v) Legislature and the Ministry;

(vi) Legislature and the Country.

The Legislature of the new Indian Government is to be instituted under Section 18 of the Government of India Act, 1935.

General

18.—(1) There shall be a Federal Legislature which shall consist of His Majesty, represented by the Governor-General, and two Chambers, to be known respectively as the Council of State and the House of Assembly (in this Act referred to as "the Federal Assembly").

(2) The Council of State shall consist of one hundred and fifty-six representatives of British India and not more than one hundred and four representatives of the Indian

States, and the Federal Assembly shall consist of two hundred and fifty representatives of British India and not more than one hundred and twenty-five representatives of the Indian States.

(3) The said representatives shall be chosen in accordance with the provisions in that behalf contained in the First Schedule to this Act.

(4) The Council of State shall be a permanent body not subject to dissolution, but as near as may be one-third of the members thereof shall retire in every third year in accordance with the provisions in that behalf contained in the said First Schedule.

(5) Every Federal Assembly, unless sooner dissolved, shall continue for five years from the date appointed for their first meeting and no longer, and the expiration of the said period of five years shall operate as a dissolution of the Assembly.

The Legislative Assembly, its Summoning and Dissolution

The Federal Legislature consists of two Chambers, called, the Council of State, and the Federal Assembly. The former is a permanent body, whose members retire one-third every 3 years, as laid down in Schedule I to this Act, quoted in Appendix I to this Chapter. The Assembly ordinarily has a life of 5 years from the date of its first meeting; but may be sooner dissolved by the Governor-General acting in his discretion.* There is no power, under the new Constitution, for an extension of the life of the Assembly beyond the statutory period of 5 years.†

Conventions have yet to be formed as to the circumstances and conditions under which the

*cp., Section 19 (2).

†cp., Section 18 (5). It is difficult to appreciate the **raison d'etre** of this provision. But, perhaps, in circumstances in which the Governor-General might come to feel the continuation of an existing Federal Assembly in office to be preferable to holding fresh elections even after 5 [illegible] h[illegible]apsed since the last general election, he can rely on the Sovereign British Parliament to amend this section, and strengthen his hands as desired. As it stands, this provision is likely to be mistaken for a step in a liberal direction, strongly out of keeping with the general tenour of the Act.

Federal Assembly may be dissolved before the statutory maximum of 5 years has expired. Generally speaking, dissolution should take place whenever a Ministry in office has ceased to command the confidence of a majority of the House at any given moment, on any substantial issue of national policy or finance; and yet is of opinion that an appeal to the country would restore the majority in the Assembly having confidence in the Ministry. There must, of course, be available no alternative Ministry, with which the Governor-General can carry on without a dissolution. The circumstances and conditions under which the Governor-General would dissolve the Assembly, literally *in his discretion, i.e.*, without any reference to the Ministry, are difficult to forecast; but the remark may be ventured that, in any dispute between the Governor-General and the Ministry,—which still has a majority having confidence in it in the Assembly; or which, if the Assembly is dissolved on an issue on which it is likely to be returned with the same or increased majority,—the Governor-General would rather rely on his extraordinary powers than challenge conclusions with the Ministers or the Electors. Accordingly, dissolution of the Assembly, exclusively *in the discretion* of the Governor-General, would be an exceptional, rather than a usual device.*

Note has been made, in the volume on Provincial Autonomy, of the fact that, under the terms of the new Constitution, the King-Emperor is associated more

*In the express wording of the Act, there is no right left to the Federal Ministry collectively, or to the Prime Minister individually, to demand a dissolution before the Assembly's term of office expires; and the Governor-General is in no way bound to agree to such a request, even if made. Summoning, prorogation, and dissolution remain exclusively in the discretion of the Executive Chief of the Government. It will all be a matter for Constitutional Conventions to regulate, when they are at last formed.

definitely with the Indian Legislature than was the case under the Act of 1919 and earlier. So far as the Federal Legislature is concerned, this association of the King directly with the Federal Legislature might be ascribed to the admission, in a common system of Indian Government, of the Indian States. But that reason would not explain the similar wording of Section 60, under which the King is made part of the Provincial Legislatures also. It is an imitation of the British Imperial practice, which associates the "King's most Excellent Majesty" in every Act of Parliament. Whether this association would be of advantage to India remains to be seen.

The Council of State

The Council of State is to consist of 156 representatives of British Indian Provinces, of whom 150 will be elected directly by a given electorate; and not more than 104 representatives of the Federated States, as laid down in Schedule I to this section. The remaining 6 are to be nominated by the Governor-General. In an aggregate body of 260, a maximum of 104 seats given to the Indian States seems to be out of all proportion to the population or wealth of the Indian States. The disproportion becomes all the more glaring when one recalls the fact that these representatives of the Federated Indian States will all be nominees of the Princes individually, or collectively as laid down in the Schedule. These, therefore, cannot be regarded as **representatives** in any proper sense of the term.

Direct and Indirect Election to the Federal Legislature

I (b): Elections to the Legislature

It is one of the strangest anomalies of the new Constitution that, whereas the Lower House, or the

Assembly, is to consist largely of members elected by **indirect** election from the Provincial Assemblies, the Upper House, or the Council of State, is to consist of directly elected members. In some other Federations, the Upper House is made to represent the component States of the Federation, each having equal representatives,— so that the peoples of these units can be said to be represented in the Upper Chamber of the Federal Legislature only indirectly. The Lower House is made to be truly a House of Representatives of the people, elected by direct Franchise of the peoples irrespective of State boundaries within the Federation. In India, on the contrary, it is the Lower House which is made, *pro rata,* representative of the Federating units,—at least so far as the British Provinces are concerned; while it is the Upper House which is, if there is any body truly representative of the people of the country, —representative of the people of India.*

Council of State,—How Far Representative

The claim of the Council of State to be representative of the people of India, however, rests on very slender foundations. The Franchise is exceedingly high, being a compound of high income tax payment, or the holding of some prescribed status, office, or title. Not more than perhaps 150,000 people at most would be entitled to vote at such elections throughout British India. Against this, the Provincial Electorates number, in the aggregate, some 36 million voters; while the adult population of British India alone would not be less than 140 millions. About 1 in a 100 adults is a voter; while each member of the Council would represent 1,000 voters on an average or

*cp., Appendix II to this Chapter.

100,000 adult people. The Council being a permanent, non-dissoluble body, its title to be always reflecting the popular opinion is questionable. Public opinion may well be assumed to be changing considerably in a space of 9 years, during which the entire membership of the Council may be said to have undergone the process of a new election. An elective body being made permanent, like the British House of Lords consisting of hereditary legislators, is itself incongruous. Add to this incongruity its initially non-representative character, and there will be no difficulty in holding that the Council of State can scarcely claim to be a representative institution.

The proportion of the representatives of the Federated States,—or, rather, of the Federated Princes,—is also much larger in the Council of State (40% of the maximum strength) than in the Assembly, where it is 33 and 1|3% of the total strength. The Representatives from the federating Princes can scarcely be called representatives, even in the sense that the representatives from the Provinces could be called representatives of the people. The States are, in point of population, about a third as important as British India,—or less, 271.5 millions against 81.3 millions in the States. Even if we take off the 14.667 million people of Burma the proportion would be 256.85 to 81.3 or over 3 to 1. In point of wealth the disproportion is much greater, British India being infinitely more wealthy. In point of the Revenues derived by the Federation the British Indian contribution will be, all told, over 90%, while the States might be said to contribute 10% or less, only if we reckon a part of the customs, salt and other indirect taxes as being paid by the States' peoples,—who are not to be represented in the Federal Legislature at all. In point of political consciousness and intellectual advance, there can be no comparison, British India being incalculably superior in the aggregate to the Indian States collectively. Nevertheless, disproportionate weightage is given to the States,—or rather the Princes,—joining the Federation in the Federal Legislature—most likely because British Imperialism must pay this price, at the expense of British India, to secure the adhesion of those reactionary elements in India which they conceive to be the best guarantee for the maintenance of British domination and of the British vested interests in India. It is not the only irony in the situation that this is alleged to have been necessary in order to concede "responsibility at the Centre" in the new Constitution of India.

I (b) Strength and Composition of the Council and the Assembly

The subjoined Tables give the number of representatives from each Province to the Council of State and to the Federal Assembly, as well as the scheme of rotation prescribed for the members of the Council of State.* Speaking generally, the number assigned to each Province is made proportionate to its population, wealth, and the hitherto accepted place in the scheme of Indian policy.

*See Chapter II, for the Table of Representatives of the Indian States, ante p. 105 et seq.

THE TABLE OF SEATS

The Council of State

Representatives of British India.

(i) *Allocation of seats.*

1. Province or Community	2. Total Seats	3. General Seats	4. Seats for Scheduled Castes.	5. Sikh seats	6. Muhammadan seats.	7. Women seats
Madras. ...	20	14	1	—	4	1
Bombay ...	16	10	1	—	4	1
Bengal ...	20	8	1	—	10	1
United Provinces ...	20	11	1	—	7	1
Punjab ...	16	3	—	4	8	1
Bihar ...	16	10	1	—	4	1
Central Provinces and Berar ...	8	6	1	—	1	—
Assam ...	5	3	—	—	2	—
North-West... Fr. Province	5	1	—	—	4	—
Orissa ...	5	4	—	—	1	—
Sind ...	5	2	—	—	3	—
British Baluchistan	1	—	—	—	1	—
Delhi ...	1	1	—	—	—	—
Ajmer-Merwara	1	1	—	—	—	—
Coorg ...	1	1	—	—	—	—
Anglo-Indians	1	—	—	—	—	—
Europeans ...	7	—	—	—	—	—
Indian Christians ...	2	—	—	—	—	—
Totals ...	150	75			49	

The Federal Assembly

Representatives of British India

1. Province.	2. Total Seats.	3. Total of General Seats	4. General Seats reserved for Scheduled Castes.	5. Sikh Seats.	6. Muhammadan Seats.	7. Anglo-Indian Seats.	8. European Seats.	9. Indian Christian Seats.	10. Seats for representatives of Commerce and Industry	11. Landholders Seats.	12. Seats for representatives of labour	13. Women Seats.
Madras	37	19	4	—	8	1	1	2	2	1	1	2
Bombay	30	18	2	—	6	1	1	1	3	1	2	2
Bengal	37	10	3	—	17	1	1	1	3	1	2	1
United Provinces ...	37	19	3	—	12	1	1	1	—	1	1	1
Punjab	30	6	1	6	14	—	1	1	—	1	—	1
Bihar	30	16	2	—	9	—	1	1	—	1	1	1
Central Provinces and ... Berar	15	9	2	—	3	—	—	—	—	1	1	1
Assam	10	4	1	—	3	—	1	1	—	—	1	—
North-West Frontier ... Province	5	1	—	—	4	—	—	—	—	—	—	—
Orissa	5	4	1	—	1	—	—	—	—	—	—	—
Sind	5	1	—	—	3	—	1	—	—	—	—	—
British Baluchistan ...	1	—	—	—	1	—	—	—	—	—	—	—
Delhi	2	1	—	—	1	—	—		—	—	—	—
Ajmer-Merwara	1	1	—	—	—	—	—	—	—	—	—	—
Coorg	1	1	—	—	—	—	—	—	—	—	—	—
Non-Provincial Seats	4	—	—	—	—	—	—	—	3	—	1	—
Totals ...	250	105	19	6	82	4	8	8	11	7	10	9

Qualifications of Candidates and Voters

Of the qualifications required of any one standing as a Candidate to a seat in either Chamber of the Federal Legislature and as representative of British India, the most important are that:*

(a) he, or she, must be a British subject, or the Ruler or subject of an Indian State which has acceded to the Federation;

(b) is at least 30 years of age, if he (or she) proposes to stand for the Council of State, or 25 years of age if he (or she) proposes to stand for the Federal Assembly;

(c) and possesses such other qualifications, if any, as may be prescribed.

The Ruler or subject of an Indian State which has not acceded to the Federation is not disqualified under the provision of (a) above, if he (or she) is eligible to a seat in the Provincial Assembly.

Members elected in the first instance are entitled, on the expiry of their term of office, to offer themselves for re-election. Those elected to fill casual vacancies are to hold office for the balance of the original term. The total seats are divided into: (i) General seats, made up of representatives of Hindus, and such other Minorities as have not been accorded separate representation through constituencies of their own; (ii) seats reserved for the scheduled Castes; (iii) Sikhs, (iv) Muhammadans; (v) women. There are, in addition, seats for the Anglo-Indian, the European and the Indian Christian Communities, which may be filled by Electoral College of each of these Communities consisting of the members of these communities in the Provincial Legislative Council, or the Assembly, as the case may be.

---

*cp., Appendix II to this Chapter.

Every Governor's Province and every Chief Commissioner's Province must be divided into territorial constituencies to fill (a) General Seats; (b) Muhammadan seats; and (c) Sikh seats, if any. To each of these territorial constituencies a given number of seats may be assigned for election to the Council of State.

Voters in the Sikh and Muslim Constituencies for election to the Council of State must be themselves, respectively, Sikhs or Muslims; and no one included in the electoral roll for either of these classes of constituencies is entitled to vote for a General seat. Anglo-Indians, Europeans, and Indian Christians are similarly disqualified from voting for General seats.

Representatives in the Council of State of British Baluchistan are specifically excluded from the foregoing rules, and may be chosen in any manner that may be prescribed.

Representatives of the Scheduled Castes in any Province must be chosen by representatives of the said castes in the Provincial Legislature; and the same rule applies to the women representatives.

Every candidate for a seat in the Council of State from a territorial constituency must be qualified to vote within that constituency. Anglo-Indians, Europeans, or Indian Christians, offering themselves as candidates for their respective seats in the Council of State, must possess such qualifications as may be prescribed in their case, though, apparently, they need not themselves be members of the Electoral College electing them.

Practically the same rules apply for election to the Federal Assembly, except that, in that case, the constituencies are made up of the Provincial Representatives of each community in the Provincial Legislative Assembly. In the N.W.F. Province and for backward areas or tribes, the holders of these seats in the Provincial Assembly concerned are to be treated as holders of general seats, and the election takes place according to the principle of **Proportional Representation by means of the single transferable vote.**

Representatives of the Scheduled Castes to the Federal Assembly are to be chosen by an electorate consisting of the successful candidates at primary elections to the Local Assembly. This Primary Electorate must elect 4 persons as candidates for each seat reserved for that community; and one of these is to be elected in respect of each seat reserved for that community to the Assembly. No one except these candidates shall be entitled to stand for such election to the Federal Assembly from the Scheduled Castes.

Women representatives in the Federal Assembly are to be chosen by an Electoral College in each Province consisting of the women members of the Provincial Assembly. Of the 9 women's seats, 2 at least must be Muslims, and 1 at least an Indian Christian.

Substantially the same rule applies for election to the seats in the Federal Assembly reserved for the Anglo-Indian, European and Indian Christian Communities, provided that voting in the Electoral College of the Indian Christian Community shall be on the principle of **Proportional Representation by means of the single transferred vote.**

Four non-provincial seats are reserved in the Federal Assembly for representatives of Commerce and Industry, and one for that of Labour. In addition, there are 8 representatives of Commerce and Industry and 9 of Labour allotted to the Provinces, as per table given **ante** p. 288. Seven seats are similarly allotted to Landholders and distributed in the different Provinces as set out in the Table referred to above.

The British Indian Representatives in the Federal Assembly will thus be divided, as between communities, as follows:—

General seats (including 19 for Scheduled Castes).	105
Sikh seats	6
Muhammadan seats	82
Anglo-Indian seats	4
European seats	8
Indian Christian seats	8
Commerce and Industry seats	11
Landholders seats	7
Labour seats	10
Women seats	9
Total ..	250

This secures, in British Indian Representatives, 33 per cent. of the total seats at least to the Mussulmans. And, if we add 2 women, 3 landholders, 3 Labour and 2 Commerce and Industry seats, as likely to be Mussulman seats, there will be an aggregate representation of the Mussulmans of 37 per cent. Europeans, Anglo-Indians and Indian Christians will, between them, secure at least 22 seats (20 ordinary seats, and 2 at least in the Commerce and Industry section), or 9 per cent. of the total, against a population not amounting to 1½ per cent. The majority community of the Hindus, including Scheduled Castes, Jains, Buddhists, and Parsis, is left with the so-called General seats aggregating 125 or 130 at most, or from 50 per cent to 52 per cent of the total British Indian seats. This is, of course, apart from the nominees of the Federated Princes.

As between the Provinces, the seats are distributed:—

Madras	37 or	15%
Bombay	30 „	12%
Bengal	37 „	15%
United Provinces	37 „	15%
Punjab	30 „	12%
Bihar	30 „	12%
Central Provinces	15 „	6%

British Baluchistan (1), Delhi (2), Ajmer-Merwara (1), Coorg (1) and Non-Provincial seats (4) make up the total of 250.

Assam	10 „	4%
N.W.F. Provinces	5 „	2%
Orissa	5 „	2%
Sind	5 „	2%

Direct vs. Indirect Elections

No considerable space need be devoted to the discussion of the relative merits of Direct vs. Indirect Election to such a body as the Chambers of the Federal Legislature in India; nor to the basis of Franchise and elections. The only ground on which Indirect Election to the Lower House could be defended is that of the immense areas and population of each electoral unit, if representatives to the Federal Lower House were to be chosen by direct election. There is force in that argument; but it can be carried to excess. In the Provincial Assembly elections, constituencies numbering over 100,000 voters are by no means exceptional, at least in the General Constituencies. Had the Franchise for the Federal Assembly been the same, the Federal constituency would be about 3 times as large. This will not be impossible to manage, especially as literacy and political consciousness spread among the Voters, and as more and more use is made of mechanical devices to collect voters, record votes, count them and declare the result. The existing difficulties are due largely to the ignorance and unfamiliarity of the Electorate as a whole with these forms of modern popular government; but they apply just as much whether the constituency is of 1,00,000 or 3,00,000. The method adopted in this Constitution, of indirect election through Provincial Assemblies, and by means of a single Transferred Vote on the basis of Proportional Representation, may reflect the balance of political opinion in the country; it will never reflect the real political opinion of the country collectively. The existence of provincial blocks for electoral purposes will, moreover, serve to emphasise provincial differences in interests or viewpoint, and not the national solidarity, which it is the desire of every Indian to promote. The elective element, such as it is, in both Houses, is likely to be swamped,—or at least considerably neutralised, by the presence of the Federated Princes' nominees in such huge blocks, constituting 1|3rd of the Assembly, and 2|5ths of the Council of State;—so that, what seems to have been granted by one hand is more than taken away by the other. The Federal Legislature, therefore, collectively, or in either Chamber, is so constituted as not to be able always to reflect truly the prevailing Indian public opinion on the political issues agitating the public mind, especially where it is in opposition to the vested interests, or British Imperialism.

Communal Electorates

We have already commented, in the volume on Provincial Autonomy, upon the undesirable consequences,—from the standpoint of national solidarity,—of the existence of so many separate Communal and class electorates in the Indian Legislature; and so no more need be said on that subject in this place. This is, of course, not to say that considerable Minority communities,—like the Mussulmans of India,—should not seek to obtain their fair share in the representative institutions of the country. But, if the same objective can be achieved through Joint Electorates of the communities concerned, by such devices as a guaranteed number of minimum reserved seats; or proportional representation, the national unity would never be impeded; and the common welfare of the country at large doubly assured because of the absence of bitterness that is engendered in such separate electorates and special treatment.

If the Franchise is widened to make every adult citizen a voter, irrespective of any of the numerous and complicated qualifications now disfiguring Schedule I to the Act of 1935, no community need fear its representation falling below its legitimate share, especially if some form of Proportional Representation is adopted. Besides, what is reasonable, even innocuous, and duly safeguarded, for such large Minorities scattered throughout the country as the Mussulmans, becomes an unmitigated obstacle and altogether undesirable, when extended to such microscopic Minorities as the Europeans, Anglo-Indians and Indian Christians; and that, too, with such disproportionate weightage in seats as has already been shown in the case of these 3 communities named.

Even without the artificial emphasis which these separate electorates undoubtedly lend to the Communal sentiment, India has, it must be confessed, Communal divisions among its peoples. But whereas the Indian statesman, anxious to achieve and cement the national solidarity, seeks to minimise communal sentiment ever when it cannot be altogether avoided, the framers of the new Constitution have extended the vicious principle of separate Communal Electorates in every direction they could possibly think of, regardless of the unquestionably evil tendencies of that principle of the evolution and perfection of national solidarity in this country.

Bicameral Legislature: Conflict between the two Chambers

The institution of a Bicameral Legislature for the Federation is calculated to complicate needlessly the governmental machinery. The Second Chamber, or the Council of State, is, it must be admitted, not such an absolute innovation in the Central Government of the country, as it is in the Provinces. But even at the Centre, it is not more than 16 years old, dating, as it does, only from the Government of India Act, 1919. The reasons which led Lord Morley, in 1909, to reject the proposal for a Second Chamber in the Central Legislature were as operative in 1919 as in 1909, and in 1935. But while the old Democrat Morley would not hear of setting up this obsolete relic of British Feudalism in India, his successor Montagu could not avoid looking upon the Council of State as a desirable and necessary bulwark against the very mild dose of the popular element introduced in the Central Legislature of those days (1919). The framers of the Act of 1935, in their turn, found, in the proposed institution of the Federation of all India, a Second Chamber, or the Council of State, in the Federal Legislature altogether indispensable for the due representation and proper safeguard of all communities and interests, and above all of British Imperialism. The Council of State in the Indian Federation is, of course, not a representative of the component units of the Federation, in the sense in which the Senate in the United States is of the different States. Its powers and functions, moreover, are, as will be seen more fully below, such that its possible claim to be the special guardian of Minorities, or the particular safeguard for national interests which would otherwise be helpless in the unheeding march of Democracy, is wholly illusory. It has coordinate powers in all matters of Legislation,—except in regard to Finance Bills, which can only be introduced in the Assembly; and in regard to the voting of supplies, the grants for which can be moved only in the Lower Chamber.* There is no right to insist upon a Joint Sessions of the two Chambers to settle, by a majority of votes at such a joint sitting, differences on matters of legislation between the two Houses. If and when the Governor-General is pleased to call a Joint Session,† the Upper House has no special power to make its viewpoint prevail. In all matters in which there is a disagreement, between the two Chambers, the view of the Lower House would ultimately prevail, if the British model of constitutional practice is followed in this regard, even though the Upper House is directly elected, and the Lower House only a pale shadow of the Provincial Assemblies in their aggregate. The only power the Council of State has is to delay, not to negative, the decision of the Lower House. With no other rights or functions belonging to it than what ordinarily appertains to a Legislative Chamber,—*i.e.*, without the Judicial powers of the House of Lords in Britain, or the title to be peculiarly the representative of the Communes, or the Rural districts which the Senate can claim in France,—the Indian Federal Council of State would have no reserve of indirect power or influence to make its view prevail, even for the time being. Finally, the Constitution of the Council is so reactionary and ossified, that any hope of a progressive policy from the Council, any chance of a truly popular sympathy, must be ruled out; while the

*cp., Sections 34 (2) and 37.

†See ante p. 188 and p. 320 also Section 31.

objects usually sought to be achieved through a Second Chamber in a Federal or unitary Legislature are equally impossible to accomplish through the Indian Council of State.

(a) Powers of the Federal Legislature

Let us next consider the powers of the Federal Legislature. We might study that subject under the following subheads:—

(a) Legislative Powers;

(b) Formulation of general National Policy;

(c) Finance;

(d) Supervision and control of the adminstration; enforcement of Ministerial Responsibility;

(e) Residuary, overriding, and emergency powers.

(a) Legislative Powers

The Legislative powers of the Federal Legislature are defined by Sections 99 to 110. Of these, Section 99 lays down the general Legislative Powers, Section 100, the particular subjects (contained in the Lists given in Schedule VII to this Act) on which the Federal Legislature may legislate exclusively, concurrently or in super-session, as it were, of the Provincial Legislature; Section 101 excludes the power of the Federal Legislature to legislate for a Federated State

> "otherwise than in accordance with the Instrument of Accession of that State and any limitations contained therein."

Section 102 gives power to the Federal Legislation to legislate even for the Provinces in an Emergency,

> "whereby the security of India is threatened, whether by war or internal disturbance".

Section 103 lays down the power of the Federal Legislature to legislate for two or more Provinces by mutual consent even on Provincial subjects; while Section 104 defines the Residuary Powers of legislation vested in the Federal Legislature, as empowered by notification of the Governor-General issued in his discretion. Section 105 authorises the Federal Legislature to provide by Act for the maintenance of discipline in the Indian Naval Forces; Section 106 gives power, with the previous consent of the Governor of the Province, or of the Ruler of the State affected, to legislate for giving effect to international agreements. Provision is made, in Section 107, for the settlement of conflict between Federal and Provincial Legislation, while certain restrictions and conditions for introducing Bills in the Federal (and Provincial) Legislature are laid down in Section 108. These requirements of the previous sanction of the Governor-General (and of the Governor in certain cases, and of recommendation in others, are matters of procedure only, says Section 109; while the final Section in that Chapter contains certain savings.

Having considered, in the volume on Provincial Autonomy, the general nature of these provisions and their effects, it is unnecessary to devote any great space to that subject in this Chapter. Points of special interest in connection with the Federal Legislature particularly may, however, be noticed with advantage. Under Section 99—

99.—(1) Subject to the provisions of this Act, the Federal Legislature may make laws for the whole or any part of British India or for any Federated State, and a Provincial Legislature may make laws for the Province or for any part thereof.

(2) Without prejudice to the generality of the powers conferred by the preceding subsection, no Federal law shall, on the ground that it would have extra territorial operation, be deemed to be invalid in so far as it applies—

(a) to British subjects and servants of the Crown in any part of India; or

(b) to British subjects who are domiciled in any part of India wherever they may be; or

(c) to, or to persons on, ships or aircraft registered in British India or any Federated State wherever they may be; or

(d) in the case of a law with respect to a matter accepted in the Instrument of Accession of a Federated State as a matter with respect to which the Federal Legislature may make laws for that State, to subjects of that State wherever they may be; or

(e) in the case of a law for the regulation or discipline of any naval, military, or air force raised in British India, to members of, and persons attached to, employed with or following, that force, wherever they may be.

The Federal Legislature has plenary powers to legislate for the whole of India, including the Federated States, on the subjects which are reserved for that Legislature so far as the States are concerned. But such laws will have to be in accordance with the terms and conditions of the Instruments of Accession of particular Federated States. To the extent that the Princes federating have agreed that the Federal Legislature may make laws for their territories and their peoples, the local sovereignty of those Princes must be taken to have been surrendered to the Federation. The Federal Executive would have automatic power to enforce the Federal laws even within the territories of the Federated Princes,—subject, of course, to the limitations and stipulations of their Instruments of

Accession. Under the provisions of Section 107 (3),* if on any of the agreed subjects of Federation, a local law of a Federated State conflicts with a Federal law on the same subject, the Federal law must prevail, and the State law be a thing of nought. Even within the State, and as regards the subjects of the State, on matters which have been accepted by the Ruler as those on which the Federal Legislature may make laws, that body can do so to the exclusion, or at least to the supersession, of the local Legislature.

The terms of Section 100 do nothing to detract from the wide generality of this provision. The theory, however, of the division of powers between the Federal and the Provincial Legislature is a complete clear-cut separation or distribution of powers, with very little ground overlapping, as shown in the Concurrent List. The Federal Legislature has exclusive authority to legislate on subjects in the so-called Federal List in Schedule VII. Under certain conditions, it may also legislate on subjects in the Provincial List in the same Schedule. No Provincial Legislature, however, has power to legislate on any subject included in the Federal List proper, though in the common or Concurrent List of subjects, both the Legislatures are entitled to legislate. There is only one condition imposed by Section 107 (1): that whenever a Provincial Law conflicts with a Federal Law, on a subject on which the Federal Legislature is entitled to make laws, the latter shall prevail, and the former be void in so far as it is repugnant to the Federal law. In the

*Says that Section:—

"If any provision of a law of a Federated State is repugnant to Federal law which extends to that State, the Federal Law, whether passed before or after the law of the State, shall prevail, and the law of the State shall, to the extent of the repugnancy, be void."

Concurrent List of subjects, however, if a Provincial law is in any respect incompatible with, or repugnant to, an earlier Federal law on the same subject; and if that Provincial law

> "having been reserved for the consideration of the Governor-General, or for the signification of His Majesty's pleasure, has received the assent of the Governor-General or of His Majesty,"

then that Provincial law shall prevail in that particular Province, without prejudice to the right of the Federal Legislature to enact further legislation on the same subject.* Any Bill to make such further provision by Federal law, which would be repugnant to a Provincial law, duly reserved and assented to by the authorities mentioned above, must, however, receive "the previous sanction of the Governor-General in his discretion" before being introduced or moved in either Chamber of the Federal Legislature.†

> 100.—(1) Notwithstanding anything in the two next succeeding subsections, the Federal Legislature has, and a Provincial Legislature has not, power to make laws with respect to any of the matters enumerated in List I in the Seventh Schedule to this Act (hereinafter called the "Federal Legislative List").
>
> (2) Notwithstanding anything in the next succeeding subsection, the Federal Legislature, and, subject to the preceding subsection, a Provincial Legislature also, have power to make laws with respect to any of the matters enumerated in List III in the said Schedule (hereinafter called the "Concurrent Legislative List").
>
> (3) Subject to the two preceding subsections, the Provincial Legislature has, and the Federal Legislature has not, power to make laws for a Province or any part thereof with respect to any of the matters enumerated in List II in the said Schedule (hereinafter called the "Provincial Legislative List").

*cp. Section 107 (2).

†Section 100.

(b) Formulation of National Policy

The influence of the Federal Legislature on the formulation of national policy has nowhere been provided for by express terms of the Constitution; but may be presumed to be deduced from

(a) the Responsibility of Ministers;

(b) control over the Federal Finances, especially voting of grants and passing financial legislation;

(c) such other rights of Interpellations to the Ministers, Resolutions of Policy, and miscellaneous Motions like a Motion for the Adjournment of the House to discuss a definite matter of urgent public importance, whereby not only the sentiment of the House could be recorded on given questions of national policy; but also the Ministry collectively can be censured or displaced.

Ministerial Responsibility to the Federal Legislature

The Responsibility of the Ministers to the Legislature is a matter exclusively of constitutional convention. It has little authority in the express terms of the Act of 1935 to justify the maintenance of that doctrine as the keystone of the new Constitution. The Governor-General is bound to act on the advice of his Ministers, except in matters which are left to his sole discretion, or those in which he is required by the law to use his individual judgment.* But there is no provision of the Constitution, which makes Ministers expressly responsible to the Legislature for their actions and policies.

This makes the Ministers not only the nominees of the Governor-General; but dependent upon him for their salaries as well,—until the Federal Legislature by Act determines their salaries. This is the one and

*cp., Section 9 (1).

only important contact of the Ministers with the Legislature. But, even here, the power given to the Legislature over the Ministers is indirect only. The Governor-General appoints them, summons them to office, assigns them their work, and regulates their relations with their departments, subordinates, and himself.* He is instructed, no doubt, by the King-Emperor to appoint as First Minister the person who seems to him to be supported by a majority in the Legislature; but that is a matter for the sole discretion of the Governor-General. The Legislature, or the Assembly, has no direct means to indicate to His Excellency that a majority of its members support his choice, or not. There is a practice in France, for example, for each new Ministry to demand a Vote of Confidence from the *Chambre des Deputes;* and such Votes may make and unmake Ministries from time to time, whether specifically provoked, or coming up accidentally. In Britain, direct votes of no confidence in the Ministers are rare, the last noteworthy instance being that moved by Mr. Asquith in 1924 against the first Labour Government, which being carried, the Government resigned. Usually it is sufficient if a Government in office suffers an irretrievable defeat in the Commons on a major issue of policy, when they must resign.

It remains to be seen whether in India, also, such Constitutional Conventions develop, not only to enable the Governor-General to see who has, and who has not, the support of a majority in the Assembly; but also to enable the Legislature to take a more direct initiative in the choice of the Federal Ministers. As, however, the letter of the Constitution stands the Governor-General, **acting in his discretion**, is the sole

*cp. Section 17 and ante p. 239.

authority for the appointment, summoning, and dismissal of the Ministers. There is, besides, nothing in the Constitution to oblige him to dismiss those Ministers, or any of them, who have lost the confidence of a majority in the Legislature.* Even the principle of Collective Ministerial Responsibility depends upon an Article in the Governor-General's Instructions. It has no place in the letter of the Constitution as it stands. In fact, Section 10 (4) might well be interpreted to mean that the Constitution does not contemplate collective responsibility; or at least does not insist upon it, since it forbids any Court,—and, presumably, therefore, also the Legislature, by implication or analogy,—to enquire into the question what advice was tendered to the Governor-General by any given Minister. The rationale of such an interpretation of the Constitution could be found easily in the Instruction that the Ministry should contain representatives of the Federated States, and of important Minorities,—who may not always be found to hold the same political sentiments as the representatives of the Majority in the Legislature. Collective Responsibility among Ministers without an identity of political sentiment is an absurdity. Hence, if these two requirements of the Governor-General's Instructions seem to conflict, obviously the more reasonable interpretation of the Constitution would be to discard the convention of Joint Responsibility. If the Governor-

*We have used the term "Confidence of the Legislature" or "of the Assembly" indiscriminately in these observations. But Article VIII of the Draft Instructions to the Governor-General speaks of the Legislature only, and not of the Assembly. The importance of the Lower House is assumed by us in these observations following the British Constitutional conventions, without sufficient warrant for the same in the relevant Indian Constitutional documents. Needless to add there is no Instruction about the dismissal of Ministers, and the principles on which that act of the Governor-General is to take place. It is a matter literally to the sole discretion of the Governor-General, who may, however, evolve his own conventions for the purpose.

General does not dismiss a Minister or Ministry, and the latter does not resign if a majority in the Legislature is adverse, there is no provision in the Constitution which would compel the Governor-General to dismiss his Ministers, or the latter to resign. This is of particular significance in the Federal Government, where the composition of even the Assembly is such that, with a little adroit wire-pulling a temporary lack of majority for Ministers favoured by the Governor-General could be easily rectified.

The Ministers' connection with the Legislature is found in Section 10 (2), which lays down that a Minister who fails to find a seat in either Chamber of the Federal Legislature "for any period of consecutive six months" must vacate office at the expiration of that period. This is, however, possible to circumvent, if the Governor-General is so minded, by securing the nomination of the individual concerned in either Chamber through one of the obedient Federated Princes, or, in the Upper House, directly by the Governor-General himself. The presence, moreover, of a Minister in a Chamber of the Legislature, is no guarantee that his Responsibility to that body would be more directly enforced; or that it would be a living reality and not a constitutional fiction.

The only means whereby the Legislature can enforce responsibility upon the Ministers is through its power to vote their salaries. Sub-section (3) of Section 10 allows this power to the Federal Legislature; Observe, however, that this power can be used only by a solemn Act of the Legislature, and not by a mere annual vote. Besides, during the term of a Minister in office, his salary cannot be varied (to his prejudice?)

even by an Act of the Legislature. Section 33 (3) (c) includes, among the items "charged on the revenues of the Federation",—*i.e.*, not subject to the Vote of the Legislature,—

> "the salaries and allowances of Ministers, of Counsellors, of the Financial Adviser, of the Advocate-General, of Chief Commissioners, and of the Staff of the Financial Adviser".

One can understand the non-votable character of the salaries of the Counsellors, the Financial Adviser, the Advocate-General and the Chief Commissioners, as also of the staff of the Financial Adviser.* But to include the salaries and allowances of the Federal Ministers in the same category, especially after it has been provided by law that the salary of a Minister cannot be varied during his term of office, seems wholly against the spirit of constitutional usage accepted everywhere where this kind of democratic government is in vogue. If the Federal Legislature, therefore, desires to bring home to the Ministers their responsibility, such as it is, to the chosen representatives of the people, it has no alternative, but to resort to a straight vote of no-confidence; and if that is not attended to,—which it very well might not be,—proceed to amend the law regulating Ministerial salaries, knowing that the Ministers for the time being cannot be affected by any revision downwards of their salaries; and, further, that the law,

---

*cp. particularly the terms of Section 15 (3), which leaves it to the discretion of the Governor-General (see sub-section (4) of the same Section) to determine the numbers of the staff and their conditions of service in the office of the Financial Adviser. Section 247 (4) charges on the revenues of the Federation the salaries and allowances of all persons appointed to a Civil Service or to a Civil Post by the Secretary of State; and the staff of the Counsellors would be similarly treated, being appointed by the Secretary of State, under Section 244 (2), until Parliament otherwise enacts. It is, therefore, difficult to appreciate the special reason which necessitates the particular mention of the staff of the Financial Adviser appointed by the Governor-General,—unless it be that all the financial functions of the Governor-General, in which the Financial Adviser is to advise him, are not within the sole discretion of the Governor-General.

even if passed by the Legislature, may not be assented to by the Governor-General. It cannot be emphasised too much that the Legislature has no say in the choice or removal of the Federal Ministers, who are selected for their office, and removed from it, by the Governor-General **in his discretion.** Hence the introduction of an element of Ministerial Responsibility,—collective or individual,—is a very shadowy illusive advance in the direction of a working democracy in this country.

Since the Legislature's control over the Ministers is thus rudimentary; since they have no voice, directly at least, in determining the personnel of the Federal Cabinet; and much less in their removal from office; since even the financial reins are in the Legislature's hands only limply; and since all conventions regarding the relations of the Ministry with the Legislature have yet to grow,—if they grow at all; and then one cannot say on what lines they would grow,—the rôle of the Legislature in shaping or formulating the national policy is of the slenderest degree.

There, are no doubt, provisions of the Constitution, which warrant the belief that Rules would be made to permit the Legislature to ask Questions to the Ministers, and thereby indirectly criticise the conduct of Government; to move specific Resolutions on general questions of policy, indicating the popular opinion on given subjects of national concern. But even assuming,—which is by no means justified by the terms of the Act,—that the Resolutions on questions of Policy accepted by the Legislature will hereafter be binding upon the Ministry and the Governor-General, at least on those subjects on which the Governor-General is bound to discharge his functions on the advice of his Ministers,—it would rest with the Government, and more correctly, with the Governor-General, how effect is given to such Resolutions of policy. Except in so far as the line of policy desired by the country is embodied in an Act of the Legislature, duly passed it is impossible to say if the Legislature would really have any say at all, strictly speaking, in the formulation, moulding, or even indicating the National Policy on grave issues of national importance.

Motions for Adjournment on specific matters of urgent public importance, are only a negative help in forming the national policy. Usually they are utilised in censuring the Government,—at least under the present regime,—for acts or events for which the Government could be held responsible. For any positive indication, Adjournment Motions are really of no avail. We may, therefore, conclude, that the rôle of Legislature in forming National Policy would be of the slightest importance in practice, until at least conventions are formed and honoured which accord to the Legislature a rôle that the letter of the Constitution does not give it.

The actual terms of the Section permitting Interpellations, Resolutions, and other Motions of the kind just noted, are worth considering on its own merits.

Procedure Generally

38.—(1) Each Chamber of the Federal Legislature may make rules for regulating, subject to the provisions of this Act, their procedure and the conduct of their business:

Provided that as regards each Chamber the Governor-General shall **in his discretion**, after consultation with the President or the Speaker, as the case may be, make rules—

(a) for regulating the procedure of, and the conduct of business in, the Chamber in relation to any matter which affects the discharge of his functions in so far as he is by or under this Act required to act in his discretion or to exercise his individual judgment.

(b) for securing the timely completion of financial business;

(c) for prohibiting the discussion of, or the asking of questions on, any matter connected with any Indian State, other than a matter with respect to which the Federal Legislature has power to make laws for that State, unless the Governor-General in his discretion is satisfied that the matter affects Federal interests or affects a British subject, and has given his consent to the matter being discussed or the question being asked;

(d) for prohibiting, save with the consent of the Governor-General in his discretion,—

(i) the discussion of, or the asking of questions on, any matter connected with relations between His Majesty or the Governor-General and any foreign State or Prince; or

(ii) the discussion, except in relation to estimates of expenditure, of, or the asking of questions on, any matter connected with the tribal areas or the administration of any excluded area; or

(iii) the discussion of, or the asking of questions on, any action taken in his discretion by the Governor-General in relation to the affairs of a Province; or

(iv) the discussion of, or the asking of questions on, the personal conduct of the Ruler of any Indian State, or of a member of the ruling family thereof;

and, if and in so far as any rule so made by the Governor-General is inconsistent with any rule made by a Chamber, the rule made by the Governor-General shall prevail.

(2) The Governor-General, after consultation with the President of the Council of State and the Speaker of the Legislative Assembly, may make rules as to the procedure with respect to joint sittings of, and communications between, the two Chambers.

The said rules shall make such provision for the purposes specified in the proviso to the preceding subsection as the Governor-General in his discretion may think fit.

(3) Until rules are made under this section, the rules of procedure and standing orders in force immediately before the establishment of the Federation with respect to the Indian Legislature shall have effect in relation to the Federal Legislature subject to such modifications and adaptations as may be made therein by the Governor-General in his discretion.

(4) At a joint sitting of the two Chambers the President of the Council of State, or in his absence such person as may be determined by rules of procedure made under this section shall preside.

If these are to be taken as recognised and effective constitutional means of enforcing Ministerial Responsibility, and for enabling the Legislature to take a real part in formulating national policy; we must point out that:—

(a) The power to make its own rules of procedure and the conduct of business, by either Chamber of the Legislature, is negative rather than positive. The section does not say,—and no other section says,—what particular business the Chamber would be entitled to transact besides law-making and voting supplies. We have seen how these two items are narrowly circumscribed, carefully restricted, and minutely conditioned. In the absence of positive authority laying down the business open to the House to transact, the power to influence national policy is, to say the least, rudimentary.

(b) In regard to those functions which the Governor-General is to discharge in his discretion, or in regard to which he is to exercise his individual judgment, even the rule-making power is taken away from the Houses of Legislature. The Governor-General makes those rules in his discretion; the obligation to consult the Presidents of both the Houses is only a formal courtesy shown to those dignitaries, without any real share being assigned to them to make those rules more liberal than they would be if the Governor-General promulgated them on his own authority, as he is entitled to make them **in his discretion.**

(c) The obligation on the Governor-General that rules must be made to secure a timely completion of the financial business every year is another hindrance in the way of an effective discussion of public questions. The old British principle of "ventilation of grievances before the voting of Supplies" has been observed, in a manner of speaking, in the existing Indian Legislative Assembly's rules, in that there is neither any time limit, nor any particular rules of relevancy, as regards matters the Members can bring up for discussion in their speeches on the various stages of the Finance Bill. There is a real danger that even this insignificant room for ventilation of public grievances and indirectly influencing public policy, will disappear when the Governor-General makes these rules, and prescribes the Budget time-table through those Rules.

(d) The provisions of sub-section (1) of this section, and the subdivisions of clauses (c) and (d) of the same, bring out the negative nature of this power of the Legislature, since a number of subjects are barred from discussion or even Interpellation, except with the consent of the Governor-General. On the face of them, these exclusions may not seem unreasonable or unprecedented; but they indicate the underlying spirit of restricting and conditioning the powers,—such as they might be,—of the Legislature as narrowly and minutely as could be conceived. Hence the apprehension that, in the face of such limitations, the Legislature cannot possibly have any real influence on the national policy.

(c) Financial Powers of the Federal Legislature

Law-making and general administrative powers being thus limited, the only remaining source of real power and authority might be sought in the region of finance. The Federal Assembly is granted* certain powers of control and voting the Federal supplies. But the effective value of these powers is considerably reduced by:—

(a) The presence of a Special Responsibility on the Governor-General, under Section 12 (1) (b), for the maintenance of the Financial stability and credit of the Federal Government. This is to be a real responsibility, particularly as considerable amounts of unproductive, unwelcome, and external expenditure have been charged upon the Federal Revenues.

(b) The Governor-General being aided, in matters of finance, by an independent Financial Adviser, who will be rather a check on his Ministers, than their help in widening or maintaining intact the powers of the Legislature.

(c) In matters of finance, the Governor-General's rule making powers, to enable financial business in the Legislature to be completed in time. These will also act as an additional restriction on this Power of the Purse supposed to be vested in the Federal Legislature.

(d) The existence of considerable and expensive departments of Government, which are wholly removed from the control of the Legislature or the Ministers responsible to it. The expenses of these departments are estimated and defrayed by the Governor-General in his discretion, that is to say without any reference to the Ministers, or to the Legislature,—except that these amounts may be included in the annual financial statement presented to the Legislature.†

---

*cp., Sections 34 (2) and 37.

†cp., Chapter XI below on Federal Finance.

(e) Under Section 33 (3), the exclusion of specified items of expenditure from a vote of the Legislature, *viz.*:—

(1) The salary and allowances of the Governor-General and other expenditure relating to his office for which provision is required to be made by Order-in-Council;

(2) Debt charges for which the Federation is liable including interest, sinking fund charges and redemption charges, other expenses relating to the raising of loans and the service and redemption of debt;

(3) Salaries and allowances of Ministers, of Counsellors, of the Financial Adviser, of the Advocate-General, of Chief Commissioners, and of the staff of the Financial Adviser;

(4) The salaries, allowances and pensions payable or in respect of Judges of the Federal Court, and the pensions payable to or in respect of Judges of any High Court;

(5) Expenditure for the purpose of the discharge by the Governor-General of his functions with respect to defence and ecclesiastical affairs, his functions with respect to external affairs in so far as he is by or under this Act required in exercise thereof to act in his discretion, his functions in or in relation to tribal areas, and his functions in relation to the administration of any territory in the direction or control of which he is under this Act required to act in his discretion; provided that the sum so charged in any year in respect of expenditure on ecclesiastical affairs shall not exceed 42 lakhs of rupees, exclusive of Pension charges;

(6) the sums payable to His Majesty under this Act out of the revenues of the Federation in

respect of the expenses incurred in discharging the functions of the Crown in relation to the Indian States;

(7) Any grant connected with the administration of excluded areas in any Province;

(8) Any sum required, to satisfy any judgment, decree or award of a Court, or arbitral tribunal;

(9) Any other expenditure declared by this or any other Act to be charged upon the revenues of the Federation.

The aggregate of these amounts, in the normal Federal Budget now envisaged, would be considered in the Chapter dealing with Federal Finance. But there can be no doubt, that, thanks to these items being excluded from the vote of the Federal Assembly, the actual region in which the Assembly vote will have any effect is less than ¼ of the total Federal expenditure, if even so much.

Within this amount open to the vote of the Federal Legislature, the powers of the Governor-General under section 35 take away practically all the power of the Legislature in voting supplies, thanks to his right to issue a schedule of authorised expenditure. He may, include therein any grant that may have been refused or reduced by the Assembly, if it appears to him necessary for the effective discharge of his special responsibility. This section and the one preceding define the power of the Asssembly and of the Council of State in regard to the Financial Grants; as such, they are well worth quoting in full:—

"34—(1) So much of the estimates of expenditure as relates to expenditure charged upon the revenues of the Federation shall not be submitted to the vote of the Legislature, but nothing in this subsection shall be construed as

preventing the discussion in either Chamber of the Legislature of any of those estimates other than estimates relating to expenditure referred to in paragraph (a) or paragraph (f) of subsection (3) of the last preceding section.

(2) So much of the said estimates as relates to other expenditure shall be submitted in the form of demands for grants to the Federal Assembly and thereafter to the Council of State, **and either Chamber shall have power to assent or to refuse to assent to any** demand, or to assent to any demand subject to a reduction of the amount specified therein: Provided that, where the Assembly have refused to assent to any demand, that demand shall not be submitted to the Council of State, unless the Governor-General so directs and where the Assembly have assented to a demand subject to a reduction of the amount specified therein, a demand for the reduced amount only shall be submitted to the Council of State, unless the Governor-General otherwise directs; and where, in either of the said cases, such a direction is given the demand submitted to the Council of State shall be for such amount, not being a greater amount than that originally demanded, as may be specified in the direction.

(3) If the Chambers differ with respect to any demand the Governor-General shall summon the two Chambers to meet in a joint sitting for the purpose of deliberating and voting on the demand as to which they disagree, and the decision of the majority of the members of both Chambers present and voting shall be deemed to be the decision of the two Chambers.

(4) No demand for a grant shall be made except on the recommendation of the Governor-General".

Section 35.—(1) The Governor-General shall authenticate by his signature a schedule specifying—

(a) the grants made by the Chambers under the last preceding section;

(b) the several sums required to meet the expenditure charged on the revenues of the Federation, but not exceeding, in the case of any sum, the sum shown in the statement previously laid before the Legislature:

Provided that, if the Chambers have not assented to any demand for a grant, or have assented subject to a reduction of the amount specified therein, the Governor-General may, if in his opinion the refusal or reduction would affect the due discharge of any of his special responsibilities, include in the schedule such additional amount, if any, not exceeding the amount of the rejected demand or the reduction, as the case may be, as appears to him necessary in order to enable him to discharge that responsibility.

(2) The schedule so authenticated shall be laid before both Chambers, **but shall not be open to discussion or vote therein.**

(3) Subject to the provisions of the next succeeding section, no expenditure from the revenues of the Federation shall be deemed to be duly authorised unless it is specified in the Schedule so authenticated."

Stages in Budget Procedure in the Federal Legislature

The four sections, 33-36, lay down the stages of the Budget procedure in the Legislature as a whole, and define also the powers of either Chamber, as well as of the Governor-General, in regard to national finance.*

The first stage commences with the submission of an annual Financial Statement to *both the Chambers.* There is neither priority nor pre-eminence accorded to the Lower House in this behalf, which is a significant feature of the new Constitution. This statement must distinguish between expenditure *charged upon the Federal Revenues*, and therefore nonvotable by and that open to a vote of the Legislature. It must also distinguish between Capital and Revenue expenditure proper; and finally, it must distinguish between the sums directed by the Governor-General to be included because he considers them to be indispensable for the due discharge of his special responsibilities; and those sums without any such direction.† Even at this

*We are not concerned, in this study of the Constitution, with the regulations governing the preparation of the Annual Financial Statement or Budget in the various Executive Departments of Government. It is, however, a most interesting and important process in the administration of the country, and has a close bearing upon its efficiency. The student interested in such matters is referred to the **Sixty Years of Indian Finance** by the present writer.

†cp. Sections 33 (1) and (2).

first stage of the Budget, the Legislature is made aware of what sums they cannot vote; and what, if voted upon differently from that shown in the Statement, may necessitate the Governor-General utilising his special powers to restore such sums as he had originally directed them to be included.

The second stage commences with a general discussion of the Financial Statement as a whole. Under Section 34 (1), only 2 of the 9 times charged upon the Federal Revenues are excluded from a general discussion in the Legislature,—*viz.*, the salaries and allowances of the Governor-General, and the sums paid to the Representative of the Crown in its relations with the Indian States. A review of the administration in general; a criticism of the policy pursued by the Government in any department; and a discussion even of the items which are not open to a vote of the Legislature for being granted, may take place during this stage. Rules of procedure made by the Governor-General *in his discretion*, to see that the financial business is completed in time, may come into operation at this stage. They may curtail the right of the Legislature to review the national policy to ventilate the grievances of the people, and to make suggestions even on the excluded or reserved departments, on the ground of the larger membership in the Federal Legislature. This discussion is ineffective, not only because no vote need be taken upon it on any specific issue; but also because the very latitude of discussion may occasion repetition, irrelevance and mere verbosity. It is, however, necessary for the ordinary member to tell his constituents what part *he* is playing; and as such, in a democratic government, cannot be dispensed with.

The third stage would commence with the submission of **demands for grants** on particular heads. These demands are first to be submitted to the Assembly, or the Lower House. After that body has voted upon each of these demands, as many of them as have been passed, or upto the reduced amount upto which a demand has been passed by the Assembly, may be placed before the Council of State. *Both Chambers have equal rights in voting grants which are open to their vote.* Thus the Assembly has a slight priority in the submission of each grant. If a grant is refused by the Assembly, it cannot be placed before the Upper House at all, unless the Governor-General specially directs that the amount originally asked for, or less, should be submitted for vote by the Council of State. In the case of a reduced grant, only the reduced amount can be asked for from the Council of State, unless otherwise directed specially in that behalf by the Governor-General. The intervention of the Governor-General at this stage is unprecedented, unnecessary, and likely to produce of needless irritation, which might well have been avoided, in view of the fact that the ultimate authority is left with him in any case.

It must be noted that no grant can be asked for except on a recommendation from the Governor-General in that behalf.* This is supposed to serve the interests of economy which are believed to be endangered in a democratic regime. In fact, in our Constitution, and under Indian conditions, it serves to emphasise the overriding powers of the Governor-General, even in financial matters, which are supposed

*cp., Section 34 (2).

to be the keystone of Responsible Government. There is, indeed, the British precedent to warrant this particular provision of the Constitution; but there is no comparison between the powers and authority of Parliament and of the Ministers of the Crown in Britain, and their prototypes in India under the new Constitution.

If the Chambers disagree as to any grant, the Governor-General is required by law to call a **joint sessions** of the two Chambers. Joint sessions were, though permitted under the Act of 1919, never tried. Under the new Constitution they threaten, thanks to such provisions, to be an annual epidemic. For, in such a case the Governor-General has no option, nor discretion. The collective vote of the two Chambers sitting together being regarded as the final vote on any demand, it can be readily understood what indirect influence is accorded to the Governor-General in controlling the financial policy and administration of this country under the new Constitution. The composition of the two Chambers, sitting together is such,—as we have already seen,—that the will of the Governor-General will have 3 chances out of every 4 to prevail in such joint sessions.* There is no precedent for such compulsory joint sittings of the two Chambers of a Federal Legislature in matters of finance, in which, under the general constitutional usage all over the British Commonwealth, the Lower House is supreme.

*In a full sessions of the two Chambers, 230 members would be drawn from the States, who would, of course, be always available to do the Governor-General's bidding. Of the remaining 355, if the Governor-General can secure 65 votes from all the Landlords, Communalists, Commercial magnates, Anglo-Indians, Europeans, Indian Christians, and non-provincial members, which number 38 in the Lower House without counting 82 Mussulmans, 10 Labour, 9 Women, 6 Sikhs and 10 depressed classes, and at least 10 in the Upper House, the Governor-Genral can always snap his fingers at the Assembly every time it differs from him on a financial issue.

In so far as this device succeeds in enabling the Governor-General to avoid the exercise of the still more extraordinary and overriding power reserved to him by the Constitution, it will only emphasise the difference of viewpoint between the Governor-General and his Minister, or the Lower House; and make the Upper House more clearly the mouthpiece of the Governor-General.

The next stage deals with the procedure when all demands have been voted upon, whether singly by each Chamber, or in joint sittings. The verdict of the Legislature, even in the very limited field left open to it, is not final, whether each Chamber has singly considered the several demands for grants, or in joint sessions. While authenticating the schedule of Authorised Expenditure, the Governor-General is entitled, under the proviso to Section 35 (1), to restore a grant refused by the Chambers, or to restore a grant in its original amount if the same had been refused by a Vote of the Chambers,

> "if in his opinion the refusal or reduction would affect the due discharge of any of his special responsibilities".

This is a very elastic excuse, and might be used to neutralise any vote of the Legislature, if the Governor-General feels so advised, the more so as this authenticated schedule of authorised expenditure is, under sub-section (2) of Section 35, not open to any vote by the Chambers to whom it is submitted as piece of information only.

As the same rule applies to Supplementary Expenditure* not provided for in the Annual Financial

*cp., Section 36.

Statement, any amount of expenditure can in effect be incurred and defrayed by the executive without the authority or vote of the Legislature.

The last stage of the Financial procedure might be said to be comprised in any Financial Legislation which becomes necessary as the result of the year's budgeting. This is provided for under Section 37, which defines Financial Legislation, and restricts its introduction only to the Assembly in the first instance, and that, too, subject to the recommendation of the Governor-General, as an indispensable condition precedent for its introduction.* This is the only distinctive privilege of the Federal Assembly, or the Lower House of Legislature in matters of finance,—if it can be called a privilege at all. In all other matters, of voting the supplies, or considering the Financial Statement, or discussing any item therein as a matter of national policy, the powers of the two Chambers are identical.

Summing up the financial powers of the Legislature, we cannot but recognise that the field of finance open to the Legislature is strictly limited. Even in the limited field, every attempt is made to drown or neutralise the voice of the chosen representatives of people in the Lower House. At every stage in the course of the annual Budget through the Federal Legislature, the Governor-General is given powers of intervention, suggestion, and dictation. The last word rests with the Governor-General, and his word shall prevail, even after the combined vote of the two Chambers of the National Legislature has decided a case against the suggestion of the Governor-General. As finance is the keystone of the arch of Responsible

*cp., Section 37.

Government, these restrictions on the authority and powers of the Federal Legislature in matters of finance tell their own tale of suspicion and distruct of the Indian politician, of a grim resolve of the British Imperialist elements to keep India, subject and an undiminished field for their exploitation.

(d) Supervision and Control of the Administration

The powers of the Federal Legislature in respect of the general supervision and control of the Legislature have already been discussed, indirectly at least, while considering the question of Ministerial responsibility. There is little more to be added, except that, such powers as there are left to the Legislature in this behalf by the Constitution can be exercised only indirectly. Questions on specific issues of administration, or popular grievances with the work of administrative department; Resolutions on matters of general policy; Motions for adjournment or inquiry,—these are the commonest forms of supervising and controlling the Administration.

Committees of the House

The routine work of the Assembly would, to a great degree, be conducted by Committees, which are not mentioned in the Constitution, but which will nonetheless be set up. These Committees are usually of an advisory or investigating character; and have no powers of initiative. They are generally appointed in relation to questions in which no great imperialist interest is at stake.

There are *Standing Committees*, under the existing Constitution, on Finance, Railways, and Public Accounts, which are almost certain to be repeated in the new Constitution. These may not be doing any specially constructive or initiative work; but they serve as controlling or checking agents on behalf of the Assembly, and will be more increasingly useful under the new regime. Advisory Committees, like those in the Department of Commerce; or administrative committees, like the so-called Kitchen or Library Committees, may also wear the label of Standing Committees. The new Legislature might have to set up many more of such committees, *e.g.*, for the accommodation and conveyance of members during sessions time; a Press Committee, or even a Committee of Privileges if so considered desirable. Select Committees on particular measures, or *ad hoc* Committees, may also be set up to do the detailed, uninteresting, but most important and useful, work of the Legislature, to which the executive Government, or a part of it, is supposed to be responsible.

Committees may not be of much service in the more spectacular aspects of these democratic institutions; and they might not be of much use in shaping fundamental policy, or laying down basic principles of Government. But they are utterly indispensable for the detailed work of supervision and control of the Administration. Not infrequently do they carry out great pieces of constructive legislation, or public economy. Investigation of a complicated social problem, prior to legislation, may be, and frequently is, carried out by such Legislative Committees, the value of whose service can never be exaggerated. In the days of full responsible Government, they would be excellent means of liaison between the Ministry and the public in educating them in a proper perception of the real achievements of a given Ministry. But this has yet to be; and all that we can say at the moment is that the device is too good, too common, and too serviceable, particularly when the Legislature is composed of fairly large numbers, to be neglected or abandoned under the new regime.

Of the extraordinary features of the Legislature at work, it is impossible to say anything at present, while these bodies have yet to be established. But, given the Federal Constitution, and certain excluded Departments, it is not unlikely that some standing machinery may be instituted to make the Legislature keep in touch with these Departments, at least from their financial side; and, secondly, to avoid overlapping or conflict with the Provincial Governments or Legislatures. A Committee of Federal Defence; another on Federal, State and interprovincial relations to keep watch on these matters, and report to the Legislature from time to time, so as to smoothen administration, and bring the national policy more and more into line with the wishes of the people, may also come to be regular features of the Federal Legislature.

(d) Residuary, Overriding and Emergency Powers of the Federal Legislature

The Residuary, Overriding, and Emergency powers of the Federal Legislature are confined only to the making of laws. In each case, they are subject to the special permission of the Governor-General. The Constitutional provisions in this regard are to be found in Sections 102, 103, 104 and 107.

Residual Powers.

The residual powers of the Federal Legislature are provided for in Section 104:

104.—(1) The Governor-General may by public notification empower either the Federal Legislature or a Provincial Legislature to enact a law with respect to any matter not enumerated in any of the Lists in the Seventh Schedule to this Act including a law imposing a tax not mentioned in any such list, and the executive authority of the Federation or of the Province, as the case may be, shall extend to the administration of any law so made, unless the Governor-General otherwise directs.

(2) In the discharge of his functions under this section the Governor-General shall act in his discretion.

Though, in the theory of the Constitution Act, there is a clean division of subjects for legislation between the Federal and the Provincial Legislatures; and though, further, there is a concurrent List for legislation on which, under given conditions, both the Provincial and the Federal Legislatures can legislate, this provision is inserted to guard against new developments and unforeseen subjects for legislation, which the march of human progress and science might give birth to. On any subject, which is not definitely classed in any of the three Lists given in Schedule VII to the Act, the Federal Legislature is entitled to legislate provided the Governor-General empowers, by public notification issued **in his discretion** that Legislature to do so. He may, however, similarly empower even a Provincial Legislature to legislate on any such unclassed topic. It is, therefore, not strictly accurate to say that the Federal Legislature is alone the repository of the undistributed, residual, powers. The real,—the one and only—repository of such residual power is the Governor-General acting in his discretion; and the authority to the Legislature, Federal or Provincial, is only an empty husk.

Federal Legislation for Two or More Provinces

The power of the Federal Legislature to legislate for two or more Provinces on a Provincial matter for legislation is regulated by Section 103. This power is exercisable only if the Provinces concerned agree to have a common legislation by the Federal Legislature. The willingness of the Provinces concerned to have such a common central legislation must be evidenced by formal resolutions passed to that effect by all the Chambers of the Provincial Legislatures affected. And even so, after such Federal Legislation has been enacted, the right of the Provinces affected to repeal or amend such legislation by their own local legislation is absolutely reserved.

Federal Legislation supersedes in Cases of Conflict

We have already noticed Section 107, which allows the Federal Legislation a sort of pre-eminence in the event of a conflict between the Provincial Legislation and the Federal Legislation, on subjects on which both were equally competent to pass laws; and so need not repeat what has already been said.

Emergency Powers

The most considerable of these is the power to legislate for all India in an emergency. This is provided for by Section 102, which says:—

102.—(1) Notwithstanding anything in the preceding sections of this chapter, the Federal Legislature shall, if the Governor-General has in his discretion declared by Proclamation (in this Act referred to as a "Proclamation of Emergency") that a grave emergency exists whereby the security of India is threatened, whether by war or internal disturbance, have power to make laws for a Province or any part thereof with respect to any of the matters enumerated in the Provincial Legislative List:

Provided that no Bill or amendment for the purposes aforesaid shall be introduced or moved without the previous sanction of the Governor-General in his discretion, and the Governor-General shall not give his sanction unless it appears to him that the provision proposed to be made is a proper provision in view of the nature of the emergency.

(2) Nothing in this section shall restrict the power of a Provincial Legislature to make any law which under this Act it has power to make, but if any provision of a Provincial law is repugnant to any provision of a Federal law which the Federal Legislature has under this section power to make, the Federal law, whether passed before or after the Provincial law, shall prevail, and the Provincial law shall to the extent of the repugnancy, but so long only as the Federal law continues to have effect, be void.

(3) A Proclamation of Emergency—

(a) may be revoked by a subsequent Proclamation;

(b) shall be communicated forthwith to the Secretary of State and shall be laid by him before each House of Parliament; and

(c) shall cease to operate at the expiration of six months, unless before the expiration of that period it has been approved by Resolutions of both Houses of Parliament.

(4) A law made by the Federal Legislature which that Legislature would not but for the issue of a Proclamation of Emergency have been competent to make shall cease to have effect on the expiration of a period of six months after the Proclamation has ceased to operate, except as respects things done or omitted to be done before the expiration of the said period.

A Proclamation of National Emergency, under this section, due to internal disturbance or a foreign war, is in marked contrast with a similar Proclamation issued by the Governor-General in his discretion, under Section 45. While in issuing a Proclamation under Section 45, the Governor-General has merely to satisfy himself

"that a situation has arisen in which the Government of the Federation cannot be carried on in accordance with the provisions of this Act", and therefore may be due to a purely political impasse, or irreconcilable difference between his Ministers and the Legislature, or between the Ministers and the Legislature on the one hand, and the Governor-General with his extraordinary powers on the other; a Proclamation under Section 102 can be issued only if the Governor-General declares

> "that a grave national emergency exists whereby the security of India is threatened, whether by war or internal disturbance".

On no other ground can a National Emergency of the type here contemplated be declared; and, without a declaration of such an emergency, there can be no occasion for the use of such special powers as this section vests in the Federal Legislature.

Secondly, whereas for the coming into effect of Section 102, so far as the law-making powers of the Federal Legislature are concerned, the Governor-General's previous sanction or permission for the introduction of any bill or amendment of an existing law on the subject must be obtained, there is no need of any such previous permission, sanction, or approval from any superior authority for such measures as the Governor-General takes in virtue of a Proclamation under Section 45. This clearly establishes the Governor-General as a superior, controlling, even overriding authority over the Legislature; while he himself acknowledges no such superior, or check,—not even the Secretary of State, or the British Parliament. All his deeds under the Proclamation under Section 45 are, so to say, approved in advance by his superiors, whatever they may be. He is, of course, in no way responsible to the Indian Legislature for anything done under that Proclamation in respect of a purely Constitutional impasse. To appreciate fully the enormity of this difference let us give one illustration of what could or may have to be done in each of these two cases. To meet a merely political emergency,—like the one we had in the Provinces between April and July 1937,—the Governor-General can, by Proclamation under Section 45, suspend the entire Federal Legislature, and arrogate to himself all its law-making and financial powers. For doing so, he is in no way responsible to the Indian Legislature, and is exculpated in advance for any responsibility he may owe to Parliament. On the other hand, in a real national emergency, threatening the very existence of this country, *e.g.*, an invasion from Russia and Japan simultaneously, which may necessitate the conscription of our entire man power, and the commandeering of all private wealth and property to cope with, even though the Governor-General has issued a Proclamation, and recognised the immense gravity of the situation, the Federal Legislature would still have its hands not completely free; and, under contingencies that are not utterly inconceivable, the Governor-General may veto its measures, duly passed, even though he had himself sanctioned their introduction in the first place.

Needless to add, that even though the Governor-General has previously sanctioned the introduction of a Legislative measure in the Legislature, to deal with a grave national emergency threatening the very existence of the country, he is not bound to assent to any law that may be passed, even after such previous approval of that measure. Section 109 is very clear on this point. Wherever in any instance the previous sanction of the Governor-General is necessary under the provisions of the Constitution for the introduction of any Bill or amendment in the Federal Legislature, and such sanction has been given by the Governor-General *in his discretion,*

> "the giving of the sanction or recommendation shall not be construed as precluding him from exercising subsequently in regard to the Bill in question any powers conferred upon him by this Act with respect to the withholding of assent to, or the reservation of, Bills".*

The previous sanction is, in effect and in essence, only a procedural formality. This is made still more clear by subsection (2) of Section 109, which recognises Federal and Provincial legislation to be valid, even though the required previous sanction was not obtained, if assent to that legislation was finally given by the same authority or one higher than the one whose previous sanction was needed, *i.e.*, by the Governor-General or the King, in the case of Provincial Legislation needing previous sanction of the Governor, and by the Governor-General himself or the King, in the case of Federal Legislation.

Thirdly, the Governor-General is precluded from giving his previous sanction to any legislative measure to be introduced in the Federal Legislature, in the case of a grave national emergency,

> "unless it appears to him that the provision proposed to be made is a proper provision in view of the nature of the emergency".

No corresponding safeguard is included in Section 45.

Fourthly whereas the state of grave national emergency, endangering the very existence of the country,

*Section 109 (1).

only allows the Federal Legislature to make laws for a Province even on subjects primarily within the scope of the Provincial Legislature, the Proclamation under Section 45, even though designed to meet a merely political deadlock, allows the Governor-General:

(i) to extend his discretionary functions, *i.e.*, those in which he need not refer to his Ministers at all, to any extent he specifies in the Proclamation;

(ii) to assume all or any of the powers vested by the Constitution in any Federal institution,—except the Federal Court;

(iii) make, by the same document, any consequential and incidental provisions which he considers necessary or desirable to give effect to the objects of the Proclamation. (A Constitutionalist would shudder to contemplate what may be included in this wide sweeping authority vested in the Governor-General);

(iv) to suspend the entire Constitution in so far as it relates to any Federal authority, except the Federal Court.

None of these vast powers, or any semblance of them, is given to the Federal Legislature to legislate in a grave national emergency imperilling the very life of the nation. The Governor-General's power and authority, by the Proclamation under Section 45, may extend even to the Indian States in the Federation; but the Federal Legislature's power to make laws under Section 102 can only extend to British India. While the Governor-General, under a Proclamation issued under Section 45, can arrogate to himself even law-making powers, suspending the entire Federal Legislature, the latter under Section 102 has no room in the executive powers and authority of the Governor-General; much less can it in any way suspend or supersede the Governor-General as the chief executive in the Federation.

The duration of the Emergency legislation,—and even the Proclamation of Emergency under Section 102, is limited to a much shorter period than the duration of the state of suspended Constitution by Proclamation under Section 45; for there is nothing in Section 102 to correspond to the *proviso* in Section 45 (3):—

> "Provided that, if and so often as a resolution approving the continuance in force of such a Proclamation is passed by both Houses of Parliament, the Proclamation shall, unless revoked, continue in force for a further period of twelve months from the date on which under this subsection it would otherwise have ceased to operate".

The maximum period of such operation of a regime of Proclamation is three years at any one time, after which Parliament may amend the entire Constitution. The same applies to the Governor's Proclamation under Section 93.

III. LEGISLATURE AT WORK

We shall next consider the Federal Legislature at work.

This subject may be subdivided into the following heads:—

(i) Assembling of the Legislature, including summons, oath by Members, etc., Disqualifications of Members.

(ii) Election of officers of each Chamber,—*i.e.*, Speaker of the Assembly, President of the Council of State, deputies for both these officers, etc., position of the presiding officers, their importance in the scheme of the Constitution; Secretariat of the Legislature;

(iii) Privileges,—collectively of the House, individually of Members;

(iv) Payment of Members;

(v) Kinds of work before the Legislature: (a) Bills, their several stages through the Legislature; (b) Resolutions on questions of policy; (c) Interpellations; (d) Other Motions. Procedure in general; (e) Financial business;

(vi) Joint Sessions of the two Chambers.

(i) Meeting of the Legislative Chambers

As already observed elsewhere, it is the right of the Governor-General to summon the Legislature to work, to prorogue the Chambers, and to dissolve the Legislative Assembly.* The Council of State cannot be dissolved, as it is a permanent body. The only imperative obligation on the Governor-General in this connection is the provision of Section 19 (1), which requires that

> "The Chambers of the Federal Legislature shall be summoned to meet once at least in every year, and twelve months shall not intervene between their last sitting in one session and the date appointed for their first sitting in the next session".

Within these limitations, the Governor-General has **absolute discretion** to summon the Chambers to work. The form of the summons to individual members has not much constitutional importance; and the usual method is by announcement in the Press, supplementing the individual summons.

*cp., Section 19.

Before the Members can proceed to work, they must take an oath, or make an affirmation, in the prescribed form.* The only constitutional points of interest connected with this formality are:—

(a) There are three forms of Oaths: for British Indians, for the subjects or nominees, and for the Rulers, of the Indian States becoming Members of the Legislature. The first makes the member promise—

> "to be faithful and bear true allegiance to His Majesty the King-Emperor of India, His heirs and successors, and that I will faithfully discharge the duty upon which I am about to enter".

There is here no reservation of any prior allegiance, even to the Indian nation, or the Indian people;† and no reference to the capacity as member of the Legislature,—thereby making a reservation, which is of vital significance in regard to the two other forms prescribed for nominees of the Indian Princes, or one of that Order becoming a member of the Federal Legislature.

The second form, appropriate for the Ruler of a State becoming a member of the Legislature, makes pointed reference to the oath being taken only in the capacity of a Legislator. Such a person swears

> "to be faithful and bear true allegiance in my capacity as member of this House"—whatever that may be: "to His Majesty the King-Emperor of India, His heirs and successors".

The oath makes no reservation regarding any duty owed by such a person to his own State, and the people thereof,—thereby indicating that there is no distinction, in the view of this Constitution, between the person of a Ruling Prince and his State.

---

*See Schedule IV (Sections 24, 67, 200 and 220) for the form of the Oath.

†See however the oath taken by the Congress Members of the Provincial Legislatures at the National Convention at Delhi in March 1937.

The oath being sworn, or affirmation made, to bear allegiance to the King, Emperor of India, his heirs and successors, will, presumably, commit the swearer to the same allegiance even to a republican ruler succeeding in Britain to the office of the King to-day. The Princes may not intend it; but the implication of the Oath seems inevitable in the sense just quoted.

The third form relates to the nominee or subject of an Indian Prince. In this case, an express saving is permitted in regard to "the faith and allegiance" owed to the Ruler nominating, his heirs and successors. Specific reference is also made to the oath being taken only in the capacity of the Legislator.

(b) There is no objection to an affirmation being substituted for an Oath; and so no constitutional issues are likely to arise on grounds such as are associated with the name of Charles Bradlaugh in British Constitutional History.

By Section 24, this Oath is to be taken, or affirmation made, before a member takes his seat. Its solemnity is vouched for by the fact that it must be administered by the Governor-General, or by some person appointed by him, usually the presiding officer of the Chamber.

Disqualifications for Membership, for Sitting and Voting, in the Federal Legislature

There are several types of disqualifications for membership of the Federal Legislature, of either Chamber, and for sitting and voting. Appropriate penalties are provided for the violation of these provisions.

(i) Under Section 25, no person can be a member, at the same time, of both the Chambers of the Federal Legislature. Power is given to the Governor-General to exercise his individual judgment in making rules to provide for the vacation of his seat by a person elected to both the Chambers in one of them.

(ii) Under Section 68 (2), no person can be a member, at the same time, of the Federal as well as of a Provincial Legislature. The Governor of the Province affected is empowerd to make rules, exercising his individual judgment, to require that the seat in the Provincial Legislature shall be vacated by such a pluralist Legislator, unless he has previously resigned in writing his seat in the Federal Legislature.

(iii) His seat in the Federal Legislature must be vacated if the member concerned is affected by any of the Disqualifications mentioned in Section 26 (1); or by resigning it in writing duly signed; or by continued absence for 60 days from the meetings of the Chamber, without counting any period during which a Chamber may be prorogued, or adjourned for more than 4 consecutive days.

(iv) Six different types of disqualifications are mentioned in Section 26 (1), *viz.*:—

(a) Holding of an office of profit under the Crown in India, unless the same has been declared by an Act of the Federal Legislature not to be disqualifying under this section. By subsection (4) of the same section, being a Minister of the Federation, or of a Province, and, while serving a State, being a member of one of the Services of the Crown in India, are not among the disqualification under this section;*

(b) being of unsound mind, and certified as such by a competent tribunal;

*But this may not cover the case of Parliamentary Secretaries to the Ministers. These must be regarded as holding an office of profit, and may as such be disqualified until Federal Legislation removes the disqualification.

(c) being an undischarged bankrupt or insolvent;

(d) having been convicted, or found guilty, of a corrupt or illegal practice under the elections law, or Order-in-Council in such behalf, which entails disqualification for membership of the Legislature, unless such period has elapsed as was specified in that behalf in the Order or Act, eliminating the disqualification;

(e) being convicted of any offence and sentenced to transportation or imprisonment for not less than 2 years, unless a period of 5 years, —or such other period as the Governor-General acting in his discretion may allow,—has elapsed;

(f) failure to lodge an Election-Expense-Return as required by law or Order-in-Council, if the person in question has been nominated as a candidate for the Federal or Provincial Legislature, unless 5 years have elapsed since the date appointed for lodging the return, or the Governor-General has removed the disqualification.

A person serving a sentence of transportation or of imprisonment for a criminal offence cannot even be a proper candidate to be chosen for either Chamber.

A person who by conviction, or conviction and sentence, becomes disqualified, does not automatically vacate his seat, if, at the time of the disqualification applying, he or she was already a member of the Legislature. Three months are allowed, presumably for appeal against the conviction or petition for revision of sentence. Pending the disposal of such appeal, or petition, the seat remains occupied. The member, however, in such a predicament, is not allowed to take the seat, or vote in the Chamber.*

*cp., Section 26 (3).

Penalty of Sitting, or Voting, When Disqualified

Says Section 27:—

27. If a person sits or votes as a member of either Chamber when he is not qualified or is disqualified for membership thereof, or when he is prohibited from so doing by the provisions of subsection (3) of the last preceding section, he shall be liable in respect of each day on which he so sits or votes to a penalty of five hundred rupees to be recovered as a debt due to the Federation.

(ii) Officers of the Chambers

Section 22 allows each Chamber of the Federal Legislature to choose a presiding officer, and his deputy. Such an officer for the Council of State is called the President, while the deputy is called the Deputy President. In the Assembly, the corresponding officers are styled the Speaker and the Deputy Speaker. Each time that either of these offices becomes vacant, the Council is to elect to the vacancy. The office of President or Deputy-President is vacated by

(a) ceasing to be member of the Council;

(b) resignation of the office in writing, duly signed, and addressed to the Governor-General;

(c) removal from office by a vote of the Council, provided that no such vote can be moved unless at least 14 days notice has been given of this intention to move such a resolution in the Council.

If the office of the President is vacant, the duties of that office are discharged by the Deputy-President; and, if his office is vacant, by such person as the Governor-General may appoint for the purpose. During the temporary absence of the President, the duties of his office are to be performed by the Deputy; and if he too is absent at the same time, by such person as the rules of procedure may provide; or if no such person is present, such other person as may be determined by the Council. The new Council of State would thus have the nominal power to elect its presiding officers, but the power is considerably circumscribed by the provisions of the Constitution.* The President and Deputy President are to be paid such salaries as may be fixed by an Act of the Federal Legislature. Until provision is so made by Act of the Legislature, these emoluments are to be determined by the Governor-General.

Substantially the same provisions apply to the presiding officer and his deputy in the Federal Assembly. The Speaker need not vacate his office when the Assembly is dissolved, until immediately before the first meeting of the new Assembly. The office is automatically vacated if he loses his seat at an election, or becomes disqualified to sit in the House.

The Constitution is silent regarding the Secretary to either Chamber. Presumably, however, these may be appointed by the House concerned, and from among non-members of the Chamber. The matter will be provided for by Rules of Procedure, in all probability. The Secretary has considerable duties in the routine of the House; but not much importance in the Constitutional machinery.

---

*cp., Section 22 (1), (2) (3) and (4). The Lord Chancellor being ex-officio President of the House of Lords, it may be said the British Upper Chamber has no right to elect its own Chairman. But the Lords may in debate completely ignore the Chancellor, who, if not a Peer, cannot even be a member of their Chamb The Chancellor's disciplinary powers also are in no way comparabl to those of the Speaker of the House of Commons.

The office of the presiding officer is of considerable importance, even in the ordinary course of routine business before the Legislature. Points of order, with far reaching constitutional consequences implied in the decision given, constantly arise. Decision has to be given almost immediately on each as it arises. Matters of privilege of the Members, or of the House collectively, and also of its dignity, arise equally suddenly. Even the possibility of sharp conflict with the Governor-General under the new Constitution, and with the other Chamber, on Constitutional issues of the utmost complexity and importance, cannot be ruled out as unlikely or even rare. The personality of the Speaker or the President tells at once in such contingencies and the decisions given may have far flung consequences. That is why all parties consider these posts as of key importance. These officers are expected to have no partisan sentiment, even though they may have been, before election, Party candidates; to conduct the proceedings *suaviter in modo, fortiter in re*; to maintain the dignity, discipline, and decorum in the House, and its prestige outside. The larger membership, and the more active traditions of work in the Lower House ordinarily make the office of the Assembly Speaker far more important than that of the Council President, who, however, will preside at joint sessions of the two Chambers.*

(iii) Privileges: Collective and Individual

The only positive, statutory privilege accorded to the members of the Legislature, by Section 28, is "freedom of speech in the Legislature". This is subject to the provisions of the Act, and to the Rules of Proce-

*cp., Section 38 (4).

dure and Standing Orders of each Chamber. The most important consequence of this freedom of speech in the Legislature is that:—

> "No member of the Legislature shall be liable to any proceedings in any court in respect of anything said or any vote given by him in the Legislature or any committee thereof, and no person shall be so liable in respect of the publication by or under the authority of either Chamber of the Legislature of any report, paper, votes, or proceedings."*

Other privileges may be conferred upon the Chamber or Chambers collectively by Act of the Federal Legislature; or upon individual members. But the Constitution categorically forbids the Legislature to confer upon themselves, or either Chamber, or upon any Committee thereof, the status of a Court, and the right to inflict punishment.† Even disciplinary powers, except the right to remove or exclude persons infringing the rules or standing orders of the House, are denied to the Legislature or either Chamber thereof. Hence, even on its members, officers, or outsiders, it has no punitive authority, though they might be guilty of the grossest disrespect to the House. The power to remove or exclude persons, who behave disorderly,—no reference is contained in the section referred to to disrespectful behaviour on the part of members, or visitors, like Ministers from the other Chamber, even if they behave disrespectfully,—is not eough to maintain the dignity and prestige of the Legislature to the degree consistent with its exalted position in the life of the nation. Even Section 28 (4) permitting provision to be made for the punishment, on conviction before a proper Tribunal, of persons who refuse to give

*Section 28 (1).

†cp., Section 28 (3). This would impede the Legislature considerably whenever it wants to conduct an enquiry in any administrative matters.

evidence, or produce documents, before a Committee of enquiry into a public question appointed by a Chamber of the Legislature, is not enough as an aid for making a thorough enquiry, not only because the power to punish does not flow directly from the authority of the Chamber itself to judge of the offence; but also because considerable exceptions are allowed.* This must reduce substantially the authority of the Legislature. Needless to add, there is nothing like the offence known as contempt of Parliament (or of court in India) so far as the Legislatures are concerned.

It is unnecessary to speculate upon other privileges, which the Legislature by an Act can confer upon themselves. The privilege, known as the Power of the Purse, and forming the keystone of the British system of Parliamentary Government, is, as already seen, of the most rudimentary in India, if it can be said to exist at all. The right of the British Parliament to receive Mass Petitions from the people may have its shadowy reflection in this country. But, inasmuch as the power of the Legislature over the Executive Government of the country is restricted, conditioned, or illusory, the right, even if it exists, is of very insignificant concern.

Who May Speak in the Legislature

Who may speak in the Legislature, and avail themselves of the privilege, known as the freedom of speech for anything said in the Legislature? The presiding officers,—the Speaker of the Lower House, particularly, —have the fewest occasions to speak ordinarily, except in so far as it is necessary to conduct the proceedings of the House, to give rulings, to announce the result of any vote or election, to convey the messages from the Governor-General, and the like. The Speaker and the President have ordinarily no vote in the divisions taking place in the Chamber.* He is not supposed to take any part in the routine proceedings or debates in the House, except in so far as it may be necessary to maintain order, and decide points of order raised in the course of the debates. The Governor-General has the right to send messages, and also to address the Chambers in person; and he can, for that purpose, order the attendance of the members in either House he chooses.† Though formally a part of the Legislature, he cannot, however, take part in any proceedings within either Chamber. The conventions regarding the Governor-General's address to the Legislature, its form, contents and frequency, have not yet been settled. In the new Constitution, it would, therefore, be difficult to say what line this particular feature of the written Constitution will develop upon.

Ministers, whether they are members of a given Chamber or not, are entitled to address either Chamber, and take part in the debates, but not vote in the Chamber of which they are not members. According to Section 21:

> 21. Every Minister, every Counsellor and the Advocate-General shall have the right to speak in, and otherwise to take part in the proceedings of, either Chamber, any joint sitting of the Chambers, and any committee of the Legislature of which he may be named a member, but shall not by virtue of this section be entitled to vote.

It is interesting to note that while the Counsellors who are advisers only to the Governor-General in the

*Section 23 (1), para. 2: "The President or Speaker or person acting as such shall not vote in the first instance, but shall have and exercise a casting vote in the case of an equality of votes."

†cp., Section 20 (1).

excluded departments, are entitled specifically under this section to speak in the Legislature, the Financial Adviser, who is an adviser as much to the Governor-General, as, in effect, to the Ministry, is not mentioned by name. He cannot be regarded as being included in the term Minister, or Counsellor. Unless he is specifically nominated to the Council of State as an Ordinary Member of that body, and is not disqualified for that purpose as holding an office of profit under the Crown,* he might not have the right to address the Legislature at all, or explain the advice he may have given to the Governor-General, or to his Government.

Of the other non-members ordinarily found in the Chamber, none except the Secretary has the slightest right of speech. That right is confined to making announcements, or reading out formal notices, which may be allowed him under the Rules of Procedure or Standing Orders of the House.

On the whole the Chapter of the Privileges of the Legislature in India has none of the Constitutional interest or significance, none of the historical romance, that has gathered round the corresponding subject in Britain. There is nowadays no question of the Member's obsolete privilege of freedom from arrest or judicial process. But the question is not altogether free from doubt, if the rights or privileges of the Legislature are not violated when members duly elected are prevented by executive action, or detention without trial, from attending to their duties in the House. It is permissible to hold that the Federal Legislature can

*cp., Section 26 (1). But can the Federal Legisature by its Act modify Section 16 of this Act, and declare the office of the Advocate-General not to be an office of profit under Section 26 (1)? Schedule II concerns only the authority of Parliament to amend this Act.

correct and finally settle this doubt by making exemption from such detention a privilege of members by Act of the Federal Legislature.

(iv) Payment of Members

The British model of utterly honorary public service has been followed in this country, so far as the Legislators are concerned, even after the British Parliament had itself discarded its centuries old practice, in 1911. In practice, however, public service of this kind in India has not been quite an unqualified burden. All reasonable, out-of-pocket expenses according to a fairly liberal scale, for travelling from a member's residence to the place where the Legislature holds sittings, and the daily allowance by way of hotel expenses, are allowed, under certain none too strict regulations. Members are not unknown, either nowadays or in the past, who have made considerable savings out of these handsome allowances. But, theoretically, these are only expenses actually incurred. The time and energy devoted by the member, and the sacrifice of his private business involved in his presence away from his own place of business, receive no monetary compensation from Government.* In the volume on Provincial Autonomy, we have considered at greater length the whole question of paid vs. gratuitous public service of this kind, from the standpoint of public interest and individual integrity; and so need not repeat ourselves here

*Any Legislator, who would do his duty honestly, even on a limited number of subjects in which he would specialise, would find a twelve hours working day, including attendance throughout its sittings in the House, none too liberal an allowance for his work. But even legislators are human; and more of them are often found chatting in the lobbies or in the refreshment rooms than attending to their duties in the House. It is to be hoped in the new order of things, a more rigorous standard of public duty would be observed by these beings.

on the main theme. Suffice it to add that, corresponding to Section 72 in the case of the Provincial Legislators, there is Section 29 in the case of the Federal Legislature, which says:—

29. Members of either Chamber shall be entitled to receive such salaries and allowances as may from time to time be determined by Act of the Federal Legislature and, until provision in that respect is so made, allowances at such rates and upon such conditions as were immediately before the date of the establishment of the Federation applicable in the case of members of the Legislative Assembly of the Indian Legislature.

This speaks for itself, even if we had not added comments on the purport of Section 72 in the case of the Provincial Legislators. The only general remark we need add here is, that given the present atmosphere, there seems to be no hope of economy in this direction, whether they follow the existing practice of out-of-pocket allowance, or introduce the system of paid Parliamentary Service in India.

(v) Kinds and Course of Business in the Legislature

Let us next consider the kinds of business normally coming before either Chamber of the Legislature. With the single exception of Financial legislation which can originate only in the Assembly, and precedence in the submission of grants for expenditure, **both the Chambers of the Federal Legislature have identical rights and powers** in dealing with the normal business coming before the Legislature. Accordingly, the outline description of one would serve to illustrate the nature and course of business in both.

There are five types, normally speaking, of business before a Chamber of an Indian Legislature:—

(a) Interpellations; with Supplementary Questions;

(b) Resolutions on matters of public policy;

(c) Motions for Adjournment, and other specific motions allowed by the Rules of Procedure or the Standing Orders;

(d) Bills, or proposals for legislation,—which may be divided into ordinary Bills, and

(e) Financial Bills.

(a) Interpellations and Supplementary Questions

Rules of Procedure and Standing Orders govern the conditions of previous notice in each case. As in the case of the Finance Bills, they also designate the persons, if any, who alone can move certain types of Bills, Resolutions, etc. Questions, for instance, under the existing rules of the Indian Legislative Assembly, have to be notified at least 10 clear days before the day on which they are expected to be answered.* On the day they are answered, there are certain rules about the number that can be answered, the days on which Questions regarding particular Departments may be answered, starred and unstarred Questions, Supplementary Questions, Short Notice Questions, etc. Usually, an hour is set apart every day for answering Questions. They serve the very useful purpose, not only of directing the searchlight of public opinion on particular aspects of Adiminstration, but also, incidentally, advertising the active share taken by the Member putting such Questions in attending to the interests of his constituents, and carrying out the mandate given to him. Questions require considerable alertness; and Supplementary Questions require

*According to the latest amendments of the Standing Orders, no member can ask more than 5 Questions on any one day: and the days are fixed by the Speaker on which alone Questions relating to particular Departments may be answered. Short notice Questions require a much shorter notice.

still greater study and skill to ask without rudeness, and be answered to some purpose. Only one member in the existing Indian Assembly could really be called a master hand at asking Questions, and adding supplementaries of great information and forensic skill. If even half a dozen such stalwarts are found in the new Federal Assembly, the Governor-General, his Counsellors, and even the Ministers would have their work cut out for them. It is one of the drawbacks of a great popular Party holding Ministerial appointments that such healthy and useful criticism of their administration as is reflected in the Questions would tend to disappear because of the weakness of the Opposition.

(b) Resolutions

Next after Interpellations, occasion for distinguishing himself is provided for the private member by Resolutions on public questions and national problems of policy. In the new Constitution, it is not unlikely that this privilege is more or less monopolised by the Ministry, in which case the private member will have no chance. These, too, have to be notified a given number of days in advance. Usually particular days are set apart in each sessions for moving what are called non-official Resolutions. For choosing the resolutions to be moved on days so set apart in advance, there are elaborate rules of balloting, etc. Rules, also prescribe the time limit on speeches; and, as these are usually matters of national policy, on which the Legislature makes recommendations to the Governor-General, members are usually keen rather to get a vote of the House, than to air their knowledge, insight, or originality. In the existing Constitution, these Resolutions had no other value than that of mere recommendations to the Governor-General. The latter was in no way bound to follow the policy suggested in a Resolution passed by either Chamber. There are scores of cases on record in which the clearly expressed wishes of the Legislature, in the form of such Resolutions, have met with no response whatsoever from the Bureaucratic Government. Whether the same tradition will be continued, or whether Resolutions will be allowed to be more mandatory in form, when a system of Responsible Ministry comes into being, remains to be seen. The matter is not free from doubt, inasmuch as the Governor-General has, even in the new Constitution, a wide margin of discretion, which may not only affect *ab initio* the Rules governing Resolutions, but which may render particular Resolutions of the Legislature, or of either Chamber, inoperative; and truncate the others so that the essence of the policy suggested is more than sacrificed. The responsible Ministry may, possibly, have to answer to the House for such a fate meted out to its Resolutions; but there are innumerable ways in which official excuses can whittle away the stark indifference shown by the Governor-General towards the wishes of the Legislature so solemnly, formally, expressed.

(c) Other Motions

We have already commented on the nature, purpose, and fate of the Motions for Adjournment in another section of this Chapter; and so need not devote any further space to that matter.

(d) Bills

Of proposals for legislation, Bills are the most considerable. Usually there are three or four stages in the life of a Bill through the Legislature. The motion for, "leave to introduce the Bill", corresponds to the First Reading, when hardly any discussion of its basic principle, or particular details, takes place. Leave is generally granted without much difficulty, as it does not commit the House to anything. At times, this stage has been dispensed with by a mere publication of a Bill in the Gazette; but that nowadays rarely happens.

At the Second Reading stage, reached on the Motion to take the Bill into consideration, general discussion of the principle takes place. If the Motion is rejected, the Bill is killed for all practical purposes. A number of other Motions may also be made, such as referring the Bill to a Select Committee; or circulating it for opinion; or considering it in the (Committee of the) whole House. Except in regard to Finance Bills, or controversial legislation of first class national importance, this last course will not ordinarily be followed.

Only after the principle of a Bill has been accepted, can it be referred to a Select Committee. Bills referred to Select Committees are thrashed out in detail by the Committee; but the final report of the Committee, when taken into consideration by the Chamber, may be considerably modified by the House. Bills circulated for opinion are usually politely shelved, unless Government are interesting in expediting the Legislation. The third stage usually commences when Bills are taken into consideration by the House in detail. They may then be amended in the course of the discussion in any respect, short of negativing the basic principle of the Bill.

If in the course of the discussion the Bill, or at any stage after the Introduction, the Chambers are prorogued, the Bill in question is not *ipso facto* killed. Nor will a Bill, introduced and pending in the Council of State, would lapse if the Assembly is dissolved in the meantime, without that Chamber having considered or passed the Bill. A Bill introduced in the Assembly, and pending at any given stage; or which, having been passed by the Assembly through all its stages, is pending in the Council of State, will be deemed to have lapsed, if the Assembly is dissolved in the meantime, subject to there being no Joint Sessions of the two Houses called to consider such a Bill, within 6 months of its passage by one of the Houses.* No Bill is deemed to have passed both Chambers of the Legislature, which has not been agreed to by both Houses in identical terms.†

In the so-called Third Reading Stage of the Bill, only a Motion for its complete rejection is in order, to permit funeral orations by the Party defeated in the course of the general and detailed discussion of the principle and provisions of the Bill. No amendments are allowed to any specific provision at that stage of the Bill.

Throughout the various stages of a Bill in the Legislature, there is under the existing system no time limit on the speeches in support or opposition to any given provision, or to the general principle, except that under the Rules of Procedure to be made in that behalf, Financial legislation must be completed within

*cp., Section 30.
†Ibid (2).

a given time.* Under the new Constitution many if not all of these rules or conventions of procedure may be repeated.

When a Bill has passed through all the prescribed stages in the Chamber in which it was first introduced, it is sent up to the other House, where it has to go through practically the same stages of discussion and dissection, amendment and adoption. Usually, however, the Lower House being the more important Chamber, all the more considerable legislative proposals originate in that body; and the fate there meted out to the measure would generally be repeated in the Upper Chamber without much further discussion. In the new Constitution, however, this stage of things may not remain, especially in regard to measures supposed to affect Indian States, or which have a strong minority to oppose it even in the Assembly. When the Chamber which originated a Bill has passed it, and the other Chamber rejects it; or does not agree to the Bill in the identical form in which it has left the originating Chamber; or more than 6 months have elapsed since the date of the introduction of that Bill in the other Chamber without its coming up for the Assent of the Governor-General.

> "the Governor-General may, unless the Bill has lapsed by reason of a dissolution of the Assembly, notify to the Chambers, by message if they are sitting or by public notification if they are not sitting, his intention to summon them to meet in a joint sitting for the purpose of deliberating and voting on the Bill."†

Under an express proviso added to this section, the Governor-General is empowered to summon a joint

*cp., Section 38 (1) (b and c).
†cp., Section 31 (1).

sessions, even before 6 months, in the case of a Finance Bill, or a Bill that affects any of his discretionary functions, or those in which he is required to exercise his individual judgment. This makes the procedure of a joint sitting a much more regular point in the programme than has been the case under the existing constitution,* and may quite possible affect the fundamental importance and position of the Assembly, as the direct representative of the people of India.

(e) Finance Bills

Financial Bills have to follow practically the same procedure, except that, they originate only in the Assembly, and the intermediate period of 6 months will not be necessary for summoning a joint sitting of the two Houses for putting an end to the differences, if any, between the Houses.

(vi) Joint Sittings

The procedure at Joint Sitting is outlined in Section 31 (4):—

31—(4) If at the joint sitting of the two Chambers the Bill, with such amendments, if any, as are agreed to in joint sitting, is passed by a majority of the total number of members of both Chambers present and voting it shall be deemed for the purposes of this Act to have been passed by both Chambers: Provided that at a joint sitting—

(a) if the Bill, having been passed by one Chamber, has not been passed by the other Chamber with amendments and returned to the Chamber in which it originated, no amendment shall be proposed to the Bill other than such amendments (if any) as are made necessary by the delay in the passage of the Bill;

*cp., Section 31 (5), which provides: "A joint sitting may be held under this section and a Bill passed thereat notwithstanding that a dissolution of the Assembly has intervened since the Governor-General notified his intention to summon the Chambers to meet therein."

(b) if the Bill has been so passed and returned, only such amendments as aforesaid shall be proposed to the Bill, and such other amendments as are relevant to the matters with respect to which the Chambers have not agreed, and the decision of the person presiding as to the amendments which are admissible under this subsection shall be final.

This, it need hardly be added, is a means, not to avoid the differences between the two Chambers; nor even to provide for negotiations and amicable settlement of these differences. It is only an arbitrary manner of settling them,—which will in no way add to the harmony between the Chambers.

Assent or Veto

When Bills have passed through all the stages in both Houses of the Legislature, they do not *ipso facto* become laws. The Governor-General must assent to them before they can have the force of law.

We have spoken elsewhere of the various forms of the final authority vested in the executive chief in regard to legislation, *viz*., assenting to, withholding assent from, or reserving bills for the significance of the pleasure of superior authorities, including therein specific disallowance of a measure passed by the Indian Legislature, as well as a silent veto,— and so need say no more on that head in this place.

The Private Member

It may be mentioned here that, in the new Constitution more even than in the existing one, the ordinary Private Member has very little scope for personal distinction or initiative in matters legislative, or even in laying down lines of public policy. With the growth of strong, disciplined Parties and with the increase in the number of members, what little scope was left under the existing Constitution to Private Members will disappear. Moreover, while in the existing Constitution, practically all elected members tended to make common cause against the Government, under the new Constitution, with its theoretically Responsible Government made up of Ministers chosen from among the Members of the Legislature, important legislative business, as well as matters of policy would be more and more monopolised by the Government. The Private Member,—except perhaps when the Opposition is strong and powerful,—would have little scope but to register his vote for his Party every time that a Division Bell intimates the need for such service. The Parties guaranteeing election will virtually free the member from that sense of direct personal responsibility to his constituents, which spurred individual members under the existing Constitution to make special efforts for personal initiative or distinction,—for which under the new Constitution there would be no great scope.

III. The Legislature and the Ministry

Of the remaining subheads of this Chapter, we have already discussed at some length the subject of the Legislature and the Governor-General:* The relations of the Legislature and the Ministry, are difficult to forecast, while the Federal Legislature has yet to come into being. This much, however, is clear: The Federal Ministry will be even more composite and heterogenous than that in the Provinces. It is possible that no single Party might obtain an absolute majority, at least in the initial period, in the Federal Legislature collectively, even though in the Federal Assembly,

*Chapter VI, ante p. 221.

there might be a single Party in absolute majority, over all other groups or Parties put together. But even that seems a very, very remote possibility. The Cabinet being composed of elements, representing not only the dominant Party, but also particular Minorities and the Federated States, as far as practicable, it will have affiliations with a number of groups, which may not all remain equally loyal or cohesive for the life of the Assembly. There may develop, under the peculiar conditions created or emphasised by this Constitution, that multifarious Group system in the National Legislature, which is such an outstanding characteristic of the French political system. With these groups, the personnel of the Ministry may go on frequently shifting; and the loyalties of the larger portion of the Assembly would change with it. A Ministry in such a delicately balanced position may quite possibly find the Legislature more exacting and critical than would consort with harmonious relations. The only permanent elements might be the Governor-General's non-responsible Counsellors for the reserved or excluded Departments, and, perhaps, the representatives of the Federated States. From the standpoint of a working democracy, this consummation, if it occurs, is not altogether desirable; but there seems to be no possibility of altogether avoiding it, at least in the first years of the new regime. For the rest the reader must be referred to the chapter on Ministry.

The Legislature and the People

The same must be said, on the whole, regarding the relations between the Federal Legislature and the Indian people. The more popular Chamber, the Assembly, would be only indirectly elected. It would be a reflection of all the communities, interests and classes, which may not have the same urge to cementing the national solidarity as a directly elected House of Representatives of the People might show. The Upper House, paradoxically, is an elected body. But the electorate is extremely narrow, and mainly reactionary. Its voice will, therefore, in all probability, never be in harmony with the popular voice, and so not of the weight and importance which attach to a really popular expression. Besides, the Council of State is a permanent, non-dissoluble institution; its members have a tenure of 9 years; and though a third of them might retire every three years, their contact with the real public sentiment is apt to be obsolete, disjointed, unreal. Methods of keeping the electorate in direct touch with the doings of the Assembly, or of the Council of State, may be devised hereafter, more efficient and expeditious than is the case so far.

One of the handicaps, however, to a close and constant popular contact with the Federal Legislature would be the rule of the Constitution that "all proceedings in the Federal Legislature shall be conducted in English."* Though the same section has a proviso permitting, by special rules of procedure, members insufficiently acquainted with the English language to express themselves in another language, the fact remains that so long as the proceedings of the Legislature are to be mainly in a foreign language, the mass of the people unacquainted with that language cannot take a close and steady interest in the proceedings of the national Legislature.

*Section 39.

The Legislature and The Press

The principal agency for keeping up contact between the public and the Legislature would be, of course, the Press. Except providing a Press gallery, the Indian Legislature has hitherto done little towards keeping up a living contact with the masses. India is unfortunate in having no National News Agency of its own, though, in recent years, the deficiency has been attempted to be remedied by such ventures as the United Press of India. These are, however, still in their infancy; and the fact of their well-known popular sympathy bar them from any substantial aid or material sympathy from the powers that be. Official patronage for the dissemination of such matter, as the proceedings of the Legislature, the plans of the Ministry, etc., is still reserved mainly for non-Indian News Agencies. It may be questioned if the powerful vested interest already established in this field will ever surrender the advantages enjoyed by them, simply in order that Indian enterprise or Nationalist News Agencies may grow, and flourish. Party propaganda would, of course, make up the deficit; but obviously Partisan statements or propagandist publicity suffers from a severe though intangible handicap. Exigencies of maintaining Party discipline, or the inmost fondness of Party bosses for unquestioned authority, may lead to a stifling of discussion in the Press, which might then be only a first step towards Fascist dictatorship. Already there are omens of such a development in some of the most influential political circles in India. And unless the love for civil liberties is somewhat deeper than the irresistible allure such ideas have always offered in the abstract to individuals of ardent imagination, there is appreciable risk of the new regime in India offering stone when the people have been crying for bread.

The ordinary newspaper has a limited circulation and resources, is usually handicapped very badly for finance as well as in respect of writers; and has very little organisation of its own to procure, judge, sift, or disseminate information. Reporting in India is scarcely born; and the institution of the Special Correspondent is a luxury open only to the select few. Foreign connection is rudimentary, and the domination of one or more capitalists often fatal to the independence as well as the integrity of the Press. Nevertheless, such as it is, it is doing considerable service in the cause of national awakening, and spreading political consciousness. For doing political education of the masses, the daily press is perhaps not so well suited as the periodical; but even that is in its infancy. The radio and the cinema, as efficient weapons of political education, have yet to be appreciated. Taking it all in all, the new India will have to evolve its own press, or methods of propaganda, if the task of a thorough political awakening among the masses, leading to an unbending resolve to win our birthright at any cost, is to be carried out satisfactorily.

CHAPTER IX

SECRETARY OF STATE FOR INDIA

The doctrine of the British Parliament as Trustee of the Indian people, responsible for the welfare and good government of India, is still maintained. The medium and vehicle for the enforcement of that responsibility, and the carrying out of that Trust, continues to be the Secretary of State for India. With the institution, however, of a measure of Responsibility to the elected representatives of the Indian people in the Provincial Legislatures, and also in the Federal Legislature when Federation becomes at last established, the necessity of retaining the full measure of control and authority in a member of the British Cabinet disappears,—at least in the theory of the new regime. In practice, of course, as we have already seen in part, the Secretary of State for India retains vast powers of the same essential type as those vested in him under the Government of India Acts right down to 1919. But the letter of the law has modified considerably the legal powers of the Secretary of State over the Provincial and the Federal administration, in part at any rate. The machinery, also, described under the system in force before the Act of 1935, is brought fully into operation, as the Council of India,—with the corporate entity called, the Secretary of State for India in Council,—has been altered and renamed; and the routine functions entrusted to that entity modified in accordance with the Constitutional changes.*

Though the outward form and designation may have been altered, the substance of power and authority vested in the Secretary of State remain unaffected by the Act of 1935. To appreciate more accurately the significance of this constitutional camouflage, it is necessary to recall the powers that the Secretary of State, single or in Council, had under the system in vogue before the Act of 1935 altered it. Briefly stated, the powers of the Secretary of State are summarised in Section 2 of the Government of India Act, 1919, sub-section (2) of which lays down:—

> "In particular, the Secretary of State may, subject to the provisions of this Act or rules made thereunder, superintend, direct and control all acts, operations and concerns which relate to the Government or Revenues of India, and all grants of salaries, gratuities and allowances, and all other payments and charges, out of or on the revenues of India".

Besides this general power and authority, Sections 2-19 of that Act, and those relating to the Property, Contracts, financial and other liabilities, the right to sue and be sued, gave the Secretary of State in Council power

(a) to dispose of real or personal estate vested in the Crown;

*Says the Joint Select Committee who scrutinised the Government of India Bill, 1935,

"We cannot doubt that under a system of responsible government in India the Secretary of State-in-Council could not continue on the present basis. It will no longer be necessary, with the transfer of responsibility for finance to Indian Ministers, that there should continue to be a body in the United Kingdom with a statutory control over the decisions of the Secretary of State in financial matters, nor ought the authority of the Secretary of State to extend to estimates submitted to an Indian Legislature on the advice of Indian Ministers. But in our opinion it is still desirable that the Secretary of State should have a small body of Advisers to whom he may turn for advice on financial or service matters and on matters which concern the Political Department."

(b) to raise money by way of mortgage, and make, vary or discharge contracts;

(c) to have the proceedings in any suit, to which the Government or any official in India or elsewhere was a party conducted in his corporate name;

(d) to raise loans in England for the Government of India;

(e) to conduct, through the Council of India, business in the United Kingdom in relation to the Government of India, and the correspondence with India.*

Matters which by law had to be decided by the Secretary of State in Council were usually disposed of by a simple majority of votes. But the Secretary of State was entitled to overrule the majority of his Council, except as regards

(i) grants or appropriations of any part of the Indian revenues;

(ii) sale or disposal of real or personal estate and the raising of money thereon by mortgage or otherwise;

(iii) making contracts including Instruments of Contract of civil offices in India;

(iv) application to the Government of India and any Local Government of authority to perform on behalf of the Secretary of State-in-Council of any of the obligations in (ii) and (iii) above;

(v) passing of any orders affecting the salaries of members of the Governor-General's Council;

*It is in connection with this power that the device arose of a Secret Committee of the Council, which conducted certain kinds of correspondance, —mainly on political matters,—which was not laid before the whole Council. Secret and Urgent Orders were issued through this Committee, in which the Secretary of State had always a decisive voice. Questions of War or Peace, relations with Indian States, and treatment of Political Agitation, might be handled by or through this Committee.

(vi) making rules to regulate various matters connected with the Indian Public Services.

Opinion in India is not identical regarding the effective value of these powers vested in the Secretary of State-in-Council, singly or as a Corporation, with that in Britain, from the standpoint of the immediate interests of India. Speaking historically, it must be admitted that these powers were introduced as check upon the insatiate desire for expansion in the local Indian Bureaucracy, rather than with the set purpose of making the Secretary of State dominant in the actual administration of India.

Under the Act of 1935, there is nothing exactly corresponding to the authority called the Secretary-of-State-in-Council;* or even the Secretary of State only, as that authority was under the system existing till then. The Constitution, powers, and functions of the Secretary of State for India under the new Constitution are scattered over a number of Sections and Chapters. Many of them are only indirect or of implied powers; being clothed in legal terminology by some paraphrase, such as "His Majesty in Council, or "Orders in Councils". Let us consider the institution as it can be found in the specific provisions of the several sections, and the powers and functions as directly entrusted to that officer, or derived from the unavoidable implication of certain provisions of the Constitution.

The Secretary of State and His Advisers

Sections 278-284 provide for the institution of the Secretary of State to exercise such of the powers of

---

*Says Section 278 (8). "The Council of India as existing immediately before the commencement of Part III of this Act shall be dissolved."

But under the next following sub-section a person who was a member of the India Council immediately before its dissolution may be re-appointed as Adviser for any period less than 5 years.

supervision, direction and control that remain still vested in that officer, and other powers required for the proper exercise of duties and functions still required to be discharged on behalf of the Indian Government in Britain. Section 278 requires that there should be not less than 3 nor more than 6 persons, according as the Secretary of State may determine from time to time, to advise him "on any matter relating to India, on which he may desire their advice"* One half of these Advisers at least must be persons who had held office for at least ten years under the Crown in India, and had not retired from those official duties more than two years before the date of their appointment as Adviser.† This guarantees the preponderance of the Service element in the Advisers of the Secretary of State, who may be said to take the place of the Council of India existing until the Act of 1935 came into force. Though numerically reduced, these Advisers of the Secretary of State will, essentially speaking, be in no way different from the India Councillors whom they have replaced. The Service elements are notoriously unsympathetic to the Nationalist aspirations of India. And though the scope of their activity is considerably reduced by the new Constitution,—as will be seen more fully below,—the dominance of the Secretary of State in regard to the privileges of all the Superior and Organised Services is assured by this provision.

The tenure of office of these Advisers is reduced to 5 years, and the opportunity for reappointment is abolished.‡ The appointment, however, may be termi-

*Cp. Section 278 (1).

†Cp. 278 (2).

‡Cp. Section 278 (3).

nated earlier than 5 years, either by resignation in writing tendered to the Secretary of State, or by the Adviser becoming unfit for the office owing to some bodily or mental informity. In the last mentioned contingency, the Secretary of State is empowered by order to remove such an Adviser from his post.* Inasmuch as a majority of these Advisers would, presumably, be persons with a full term of service in India, the chances of such infirmities developing are by no means utterly unthinkable. The provision seems, therefore, a move in the right direction in contrast with the corresponding provision in the Act of 1919, which made the term of appointment capable of extension. The Councillors were more independent of the Secretary of State than the Advisers henceforward to be appointed. But that, by itself, will not make the Advisers necessarily subservient to the Secretary of State.

The disability imposed upon the old India Councillors regarding a seat in either House of Parliament† is maintained in regard to the new Advisers of the Secretary of State. Their powers and functions, however, are entirely dependent upon the discretion of the Secretary of State,—except in regard to Service matters. Says Section 278 (6):—

> "Except as otherwise expressly provided in this Act it shall be in the discretion of the Secretary of State whether or not he consults with his Adivsers on any matter, and, if so, whether he consults with them collectively or with one or more of them individually, and whether or not he acts in accordance with any advice given to him by them."

*No corresponding provision was to be found in the Act of 1919; nor is the provision of Section 3 (7),—which made the old India Councillors irremovable from their office, except by the King on an address by both Houses of Parliament.

†cp., Section 4 of the Act of 1919.

This marks the Advisers out sharply from the old Councillors, who were entrusted with certain statutory duties, in which the Secretary of State could not act except with their advice, or with a majority voting with him.* The reason is perfectly clear: Whereas the old India Council was intended not only to inform and advise, but also to be a check and a restraint upon a Secretary of State who may be influenced by British Party considerations, the new Advisers have no such functions entrusted to them. The Secretary of State is not bound even to make rules for the conduct of business which he himself decides to submit to his Advisers. Nor is there any need for him to be consistent or systematic in submitting any given class of business for the advice of these his statutory counsellors. A subject upon which he seeks their advice on one occasion may not be consulted about at all on another occasion; a matter on which on one occasion he seeks the advice of all Advisers may on another occasion be discussed with only one Adviser, or not discussed at all. In every respect the choice, or discretion, rests with the Secretary of State,—except, of course, as regards some Service matters, property, and contracts, which will be mentioned a little more in detail hereafter.

What then is the purpose of having these Advisers at all, and paying them so highly as laid down in Section 278 (5)†—except to squeeze as much out of India as could possibly be managed? The payments, it is true, are to be made "out of moneys provided

*cp., above p. 363.

†They are to be paid £ 1350 each p.a. out of the monies provided by Parliament, as against the £ 1200 p.a. paid to the old India Counsellors. An Overseas, or "subsistence" allowance to those domiciled in India at the date of their appointment of £ 600 p.a. remains the same as under the old Act.

by Parliament". But the provisions of Section 280 are not only ambiguous; they are misleading. Says that:

> 280.—(1) As from the commencement of Part III of this Act the salary of the Secretary of State and the expenses of his department, including the salaries and remuneration of the staff thereof, shall be paid out of moneys provided by Parliament.
>
> (2) Subject to the provisions of the next succeeding section with respect to the transfer of certain existing officers and servants, the Secretary of State may appoint such officers and servants as he, subject to the consent of the Treasury as to numbers, may think fit and there shall be paid to persons so appointed such salaries or remuneration as the Treasury may from time to time determine.
>
> (3) There shall be charged on and paid out of the revenues of the Federation into the Exchequer such periodical or other sums as may from time to time be agreed between the Governor-General and the Treasury in respect of so much of the expenses of the department of the Secretary of State as is attributable to the performance on behalf of the Federation of such functions as it may be agreed between the Secretary of State and the Governor-General that that department should so perform.

Arrangement will have to be made for fixing a sum which the Federal Government will have to pay to the British Exchequer for the remuneration for those services which the India Office, in addition to the High Commissioner, is supposed to discharge on behalf of India.* At the present moment that sum is in the neighbourhood of £150,000 per annum. But many of the functions which the India Office had to discharge, even after the institution of an India High Commissioner, would now disappear, or be at least considerably reduced. Hence, it is a matter for consideration what sum, if any, should be paid to the

*Under the Budget Estimates for 1937-38 the total cost of the India Office and the High Commissioner's Office to the Indian Exchequer is Rs. 40.75 lakhs, of which 17.42 is voted and 23.33 non-voted. Rs. 13.6 lakhs is stated, in the Detailed Estimates and Demands for Grants to be contribution on this account to H.M.'s Treasury.

Secretary of State for discharging functions, which either are no more, or which could well be entrusted to the High Commissioner, or the Trade Commissioner, or a branch of the Reserve Bank of India in Britain.

Assuming that the charges of the India Office, the Secretary of State and the Advisers to the Secretary of State,—together with such Parliamentary assistance as that officer might need,—are correctly a British charge, exclusively, it is difficult to see what functions could now be left with the Secretary of State which would demand such special remuneration from India. The grant of "Subsistence",—or, as it is known in India, Overseas,—Allowance to those Advisers, who, at the time of their appointment, were domiciled in India, is only an excuse for the much larger sum demanded from India on account of the Overseas Allowance to the British members of the Steel Frame. The entire institution of the Advisers is therefore, mischievous, wasteful, unnecessary, and ought to be accordingly abolished.*

All existing accounts in the name of the Secretary of State in Council are to be transferred to the name of the Secretary of State. But any order or instrument with reference to that stock or money, executed before the dissolution of the Council, either by the Secretary of State or any one else duly authorised for the purpose, would make a proper discharge for the Bank.† Similarly, all persons on the permanent establishment

*cp., Section 278 (7), which permits, even in cases where, under the Constitution the Secretary of State is enjoined to obtain the concurrence of his Advisers, the requirement of the law is supposed to be satisfied if the matter is disposed of at a meeting where at least half the number of Advisers were present, or where no objection had been raised by any Adviser after due notice of a proposed course of action, and opportunity for raising objection, if any had been provided.

†cp., Section 279.

of the Secretary of State in Council, immediately before the coming into effect of Part III of the Act, are transferred to the establishment of the Secretary of State as reconstituted. All their rights to pension, etc., are carefully preserved.* The personnel thus transferred is specifically protected against any treatment less favourable than they were entitled to expect while they were on the staff of the Secretary of State in Council. The same treatment is secured, by Section 281 (4), even to the non-permanent staff employed by the Secretary of State in Council. Provision is made, by Section 282, for a *pro rata* charge upon the revenues of the Federation for such of the superannuation charge, as an Order in Council might consider to be due to service before the date of such transfer.† Any payments thus authorised to be made out of the Federal Revenues, would be charged upon those revenues, and as such non-votable by the Federal Legislature.‡

Under the Act of 1935, the powers of the Secretary of State are mainly concerned with

(a) The supervision, direction and control of the Governor-General, and of the Provincial Governors through the Governor-General, in so far as these officers are entrusted with powers and functions to be exercised in their discretion, or in which the exercise of their individual judgment is enjoined. This would comprise also the so-called excluded Departments of State;

(b) Recruitment, and protection of certain Services, and Posts;

(c) Issue of Orders-in-Council, or any act by His Majesty-in-Council,—an indirect power derived

*cp., Section 281.

†cp., Section 282 (1).

‡cp., Section 282 (3).

from the general principles of the British Constitution. This may include the exercise of the King's Statutory power, in respect of the Indian Constitution, to assent to, to withhold Assent, or to disallow Indian Legislation;

(d) Powers of the Crown in regard to Indian States, not coming within the provisions of the Federal Government's authority;

(e) Financial powers, with regard to borrowing in Britain on account of the Federal or Provincial Government; payment of certain pensions, interest, etc., on behalf of the Indian Government in Britain;

(f) Contracts and other Liabilities;

(h) Audit of Accounts,—or Auditor-General's Department;

(i) Emergency Powers, and those in regard to inter-provincial disputes in regard to water supplies; Trade Convention, etc.

(a) Powers of Supervision, Direction and Control

As regards the first group of powers, the most important, considerable, and general power is contained in Section 14 relating to the Governor-General, and Section 54 relating to the Governors.

Section 14 read:

*14.—(1) In so far as the Governor-General is by or under this Act required to act in his discretion or to exercise his individual judgment, **he shall be under the general**

*It is interesting to note that, in the Original Bill, there was only one clause in this section: and that the reference to the Instrument of Instructions was brought in directly by making his subordination to the Secretary of State specifically subject to the Instructions issued to him.

(2) The sub-section as it now stands gives the Instructions a wholly secondary place. The same is repeated in Section 54. The limitation on the controlling and directing power of the Secretary of State, imposed by this sub-section is a triumph of those vested interests and minorities, which have won themselves the privilege of being regarded as the Special Responsibility of the executive head which the Instructions require these officers particularly to protect.

control of, and comply with such particular directions, if any, as may from time to time be given to him by the Secretary of India, but the validity of anything done by the Governor-General shall not be called in question on the ground that it was done otherwise than in accordance with the provisions of this section.

(2) Before giving any directions under this section, the Secretary of State shall satisfy himself that nothing in the directions requires the Governor-General to act in any manner inconsistent with any Instrument of Instructions issued to him by His Majesty.

Practically the same language is adopted in Section 54, except that the controlling officer in this case is the Governor-General, and not the Secretary of State. Inasmuch, however, as, in all such matters, the Governor-General himself is under the controlling authority of the Secretary of State, the ultimate control of the British Minister, even over Provincial affairs, is thus assured, though in a somewhat roundabout manner. Had the Governor-General's directive or supervisory powers been made exercisable on the advice of the Federal Ministers, there might be something to be said for such a procedure, such a reserve of authority in the National Government. But Section 54 (1) distinctly says:

54.—(1) In so far as the Governor of a Province is by or under this Act required to act in his discretion or to exercise his individual judgment, he shall be under the general control of, and comply with such particular directions, if any, as may from time to time be given to him by the Governor-General **in his discretion**, but the validity of anything done by a Governor shall not be called in question on the ground that it was done otherwise than in accordance with the provisions of this section.

(2) Before giving any directions under this section, the Governor-General shall satisfy himself that nothing in the directions requires the Governor to act in any manner inconsistent with any Instrument of Instructions issued to the Governor by His Majesty.

As the Governor-General acts, in this matter of supervising, directing, or controlling the Provincial

Governors entirely in his discretion; and as in all matters left to his **discretion**, or in which he is to exercise his **individual judgment**, he is himself under the direction and control of the Secretary of State, it is obvious that the ultimate authority of the Secretary of State over the Provinces is as strong as over the Governor-General, and Federal Government. The saving in regard to the Instrument of Instructions,—itself issued under Section 13 to the Governor-General, and Section 53 to the Governors,—is no real reservation in favour of the Instruction. For the Secretary of State, or the Governor-General is merely required by the sections quoted to " satisfy himself " that nothing in the directions he issues requires the Governor-General (or the Governor, as the case may be) to act in contravention of those Instructions. As to who shall be the judge, whether anything was in contravention of any such Instruction, nothing is said in the Act. Its terms leave the matter wholly within the discretion of the officer concerned, whose authority thus becomes practically paramount, and supersedes the Instructions for all practical purposes.

As to the subjects, or departments, comprised within this section, so far as the Governor-General is concerned, all the Reserved Departments of the Federal Government,—*e.g.*, Defence, External Relations, Government of Tribal or Excluded areas, and Ecclesiastical affairs,—are obviously under the controlling and directing authority of the Secretary of State. The expenses of these Departments, and the financial reaction of the same on the national Budget, are likewise brought under the controlling power of the Secretary of State. Dealings with the Indian Princes outside the Federation; questions of Paramountcy even with the

States who have federated; supervision over Provincial Governors; appointment, dismissal, distribution of work amongst the Federal Ministers, and certain extraordinary powers in regard to the Federal Legislature,—are all matters within the discretion of the Governor-General. And in these he would be* under the authority of the Secretary of State. Similarly, in the discharge of his so-called "Special Responsibilities", he is likewise subordinated to the Secretary of State. *Mutatis mutandis*, the same applies to the Provincial Governors, *vis-a-vis* the Governor-General, as regards matters left to their discretion, or those in which they are to exercise their individual judgment.†

Recalling the discussion, both in this volume and in the one devoted to a study of the Provincial Government, as regards the wide scope of these extraordinary powers of the Governor-General, and of the Provincial Governors, we cannot but realise that this margin of controlling or directive powers left to the Secretary of State will make of that officer a real, controlling, and even dictating force, in the most vital concerns of the Government of India. The belief, therefore, that the ultimate authority and control of the British Imperial Government has been relaxed under the new Constitution, or because of a transfer of power and responsibility to the chosen Ministers of the Indian people, is a figment of the imagination, rather than a reality of the situation.

In all Indian legislation, power is reserved to the King to disallow Acts duly passed by the Provincial or

---

*cp., ante, Ch. VI for a list of the Goveronr-General's Discretionary powers, and those in which he is to exercise his individual judgment.

†See for a list of these matters, **Provincial Autonomy**, Chapter III.

the Federal Governments.* If that power is ever exercised in practice, the Secretary of State would be the ordinary Constitutional Adviser of the British King in such matters. It is not merely a theoretical power reserved to the British King, and his constitutional adviser in Britain. In view of the stringent provisions in regard to the problem of commercial or financial discrimination against British interests in India; in view also of the serious possibility of the Indian requirements for intensive industrial and commercial development of the country coming into sharp conflict against the vested interests of these aliens in India, the powers reserved for disallowing Indian Legislation in this behalf may be of great practical help to the British interests. We may, accordingly, be certain the British Imperialist advisers of the Sovereign will not hesitate to advise active use of these powers, every time the vested interests of British capital, or of British members of the Indian Public Services, are alleged to be threatened.

Similarly, in all extraordinary legislative powers given to the Governors, or the Governor-General, regarding the passing of Ordinances, or the enactment of executive legislation,—styled Governor's Acts, or the Governor-General's Acts,—the Secretary of State has reserved powers to extend, repeal, or modify such extraordinary legislation, through the right to be informed of the same, and the duty to place the same before Parliament.†

Finally, the right to suspend the entire Constitution,—except the Federal Court, or the Provincial High

*cp., Sections 32 and 75 of the Government of India Act, 1935. Also ante, Ch. VIII, and Provincial Autonomy, Ch. VI.

†cp. Sections 43-4 and Sections 89-90 of the Government of India Act, 1935.

Courts,—vested in the Governor-General or the Governors,—is to be exercised subject to the general control of the Secretary of State.* The entire exercise of this power being *in the discretion* of the Governor-General, —and of the Governor,—these officers come, under the terms of Section 14 and 54, under the general control of the Secretary of State.

For this particular power, Section 45 (3) specifically provides:—

> "A Proclamation issued under this section—
>
> (a) shall be communicated forthwith to the Secretary of State and shall be laid by him before each House of Parliament;
>
> (b) unless it is a Proclamation revoking a previous Proclamation, shall cease to operate at the expiration of six months.
>
> Provided that, if and so often as a resolution approving the continuance in force of such a Proclamation is passed by both Houses of Parliament, the Proclamation shall, unless revoked, continue in force for a further period of twelve months from the date on which under this subsection it would otherwise have ceased to operate."

Section 93 (3) is in identical terms so far as a similar Proclamation relating to a Province is concerned. Parliament thus gets a right to watch over the suspended Constitution; and if it is so minded it may continue this non-constitutional regime in a Province, or over the entire Continent of India, for a further period of twelve months by a simple Resolution of both Houses of Parliament.

This supreme right of Parliament to make, suspend, and abrogate the Indian Constitution will really be exercised at the instance of the Secretary of State,

*cp., Sections 45 and 93, for the Federation and the Provinces respectively.

though theoretically the entire British Imperial Government would be responsible for such an action in India. So far as the Federation is concerned, this extraordinary power may affect even the Federated States, for at least two years, during which they may be governed,—so far as federal subjects are concerned,—under a regime of Proclamation suspending the Constitution. And even thereafter, there is nothing to guarantee that if, under the terms of Section 45 (4), Parliament deems fit to legislate for a new and radically different Constitution, the Federated States, or any of them, would necessarily be allowed to leave the Federation *ipso facto* the altered Constitution.

In the Provinces the Proclamation regime can continue for 3 years at most. But no provision is made, corresponding to that in Section 45 (4) for the Federation, for a new Constitution, even if in a Province the non-Constitutional regime of government by Proclamation has lasted for three years.* Responsible Government in the Provinces is claimed to be the greatest contribution for a constitutional advance under the Act of 1935. Yet, the entire Constitution is not only placed at the discretion of the Governor; no arrangement is made for the substitution of a more constitutional regime for one of frank autocracy of the Governor under the Proclamation,—not even such as is made for the Federation under Section 45 (4). The Secretary of

*Under Section 93 (3) it is distinctly stated:—

"No such Proclamation shall in any case remain in force for more than three years." By Section 93 (4) any law made by a Governor, under the power given to him by the Proclamation, "shall, subject to the terms thereof, continue to have effect until two years have elapsed from the date on which the Proclamation ceases to have effect." It is an interesting speculation as to what would happen to any particular Province where the Constitution remains suspended for more than 3 years under Section 93? Would Parliament legislate, and provide a separate Constitution on a different basis for such a Province? If so, that would be the reaction of such a suspension on other Provinces, and on the Federal Constitution?

State can, under such a system, continue to be the dictator of the Provincial Government through the Governor-General, where the Constitution is suspended for an indefinite length of time, if Parliament does not provide for an alternative constitution even after three years have elapsed; and the Proclamation itself has ceased to operate. There is nothing to prevent a new series of Proclamation regime being started, after a nominal Constitutional interval, in which the supreme Executive Authority is unable to co-operate with the leaders of the people's representatives; and which has, therefore, to be suspended on the same grounds, and by the same Proclamation, as led to the initial suspension of the Constitution.

Excluded Areas

The Secretary of State remains the supreme authority in regard to all those areas which have been specifically excluded from the regime of Constitutional Government. It is the Secretary of State who, under Section 91, prepares the draft of an Order in Council, which declares certain areas in India to be wholly or partially excluded from the benefits of Constitutional Government; it is the Secretary of State, who submits this Draft to Parliament, which has neither the time nor the knowledge to examine critically, and alter for the better, such a Draft; it is really the Secretary of State who rules these areas through the Governor. or the Governor-General, acting in his discretion. Says Section 92:—

92.—(1) The Executive Authority of a Province extends to excluded and partially excluded areas therein, but, notwithstanding anything in this Act, no Act of the Federal Legislature or of the Provincial Legislature shall apply to an excluded area or a partially excluded area, unless the Governor by public notification so directs, and the Governor in giving such a direction with respect to any

Act may direct that the Act shall in its application to the area, or to any specified part thereof, have effect subject to such exceptions or modifications as he thinks fit.

(2) The Governor may make Regulations for the peace and good government of any area in a Province which is for the time being an excluded area, or a partially excluded area, and any Regulations so made may repeal or amend any Act of the Federal Legislature or of the Provincial Legislature, or any existing Indian Law, which is for the time being applicable to the area in question.

Regulations made under this sub-section shall be submitted forthwith to the Governor-General and until assented to by him in his discretion shall have no effect, and the provisions of this Part of this Act with respect to the power of His Majesty to disallow Acts shall apply in relation to any such Regulations assented to by the Governor-General as they apply in relation to Acts of a Provincial Legislature assented to by him.

(3) The Governor shall, as respects any area in a Province which is for the time being an excluded area exercise his functions in his discretion.

Large blocks of territory, and equally large chunks of population, have been excluded, under the Order in Council, issued under Section 91, wholly or partially, from the normal, constitutional regime. The general argument in support of this extraordinary treatment is that the population in these excluded regions is backward; and that, therefore, they would not be able to avail themselves of the mechanism of Constitutional Government established by the Act of 1935. But such an agreement has no justification in fact, for the simple reason that, by a proper grouping of the Constitution, coupled, where necessary, with the device of a special reservation of seats for the representatives of these classes,* this sort of exclusion of such areas and population could well have been avoided.

*In principle, the device of such reserved seats for special classes seems as objectionable as the separate Communal Representation. But, if Parliament had really intended to relax the doctrine of British Trusteeship for India, in the slightest degree, this device could well have been adopted to avoid making such needless breaches in the stronghold of Provincial Autonomy.

National Emergency

The same powers, practically, of supervision and control are vested in the Secretary of State, under Section 102, concerning a National Emergency, in which the very existence of the country is threatened by internal disorder or a war. As already noted in another Chapter,* the Federal Legislature is entitled, under this Section (102) to act in such an emergency But the Governor-General is vested with discretionary powers to permit any action by the Federal Legislature; and the Secretary of State is entitled to have communicated to him a Proclamation issued under this Section for submission to Parliament, which has the same right of extending the Proclamation regime by resolution, as under Section 45, and 93.

Disputes re: Watersupplies between Federated Units

The powers under Section 131 for the settlement of disputes between two or more Federated Units,—States or Provinces, regarding the use of common watersupplies, are indirect. The supreme appellate power, as it were, is exercised by His Majesty in Council; and the Secretary of State is the obvious constitutional adviser of the British King in all such matters.†

FINANCIAL POWERS

Though powers of borrowing on account of India have been taken away from the Secretary of State by Section 161, during the Transition Period, the Secretary of State has been given special authority to raise sterling loans under Section 315, if the necessary authority for the purpose is granted already by an East India

*Chapter VIII, ante p. 279.

†cp., Section 131.

Loans Act of Parliament; and provided that at a meeting of the Secretary of State and his Advisers, the borrowing is approved by a majority.* By Section 157, the Secretary of State is entitled to be kept in funds by the Federal as well as the Provincial Governments, in respect of all liabilities on account of India to be met in Britain, as also in regard to the Pensions payable by the Secretary of State on account of the Indian or Provincial Governments.

Audit of Indian Accounts

The appointment of an Auditor-General, for the proper audit of Indian Accounts is provided for under Section 166, empowering His Majesty to make that appointment. This means, in practice, the Secretary of State, who also, under the disguise of the same Sovereign authority, would determine the conditions of service for the Auditor-General. His duties and functions would be prescribed to the Auditor-General by an Order in Council, in the first instance; and by an Act of the Federal Legislature subsequently, provided that no Bill can be introduced in the Federal Legislature for the purpose without the previous sanction of the Governor-General in his discretion. Those only who can appreciate the immense (though invisible) rôle played by an efficient Auditor-General in the national economy can understand the effective power retained by the Secretary of State, or the British Imperial Government, to dominate India's national economy; to prevent any orientation of

*cp., Section 315 (2). By Section 314, the control of the Secretary of State over the Government of India during the transition period is specifically provided for. But that officer is required, under Section 314 (2), to have the concurrence of a majority of his Advisers in any matter touching a grant or appropriation from the revenues of India in order to give directions to the Governor-General-in-Council on such matters. During the transition period the number of his Advisers is to be not less than 8, nor more than 12, Section 314 (3).

it which could in the least suggest a risk to the vested interests for which Britain constitutes herself a Trustee.*

Contracts, etc.

By Section 175 (4) personal liability of the Secretary of State in respect of any contract or assurance made or executed is avoided; and instead the Federal and the Provincial Governments are made liable in their corporate capacity.

Inasmuch as the Judges of the Federal Court as well as of the Provincial High Courts are appointed by His Majesty, under the Royal Sign Manual, the Secretary of State will have considerable indirect influence in the choice of the highest judiciary in India, their conditions of service, etc.†

Protection of Public Services

The most considerable function, however, of the Secretary of State is in connection with the protection of the Public Servants, particularly those recruited by himself. A number of sections provide for the varying aspects of this extraordinary power of the Secretary of State.

The entire department of India's National Defence being in the sole discretion of the Governor-General, the Secretary of State has practically unlimited authority in settling the numbers and prescribing the pay,

*Section 168 gives authority to the Auditor General to determine the form in which the accounts of the Federation are to be kept. He may also lay down the principles or methods according to which Provincial accounts may be kept. This power is exercisable subject to the approval of the Governor-General.

†cp., Section 176. Under Section 178 (3) deduction is forbidden from any payment of Principal or Interest on Sterling Loans raised by the Secretary of State under any existing or future Indian, Federal, or Provincial Legislation. The same immunity is granted by Section 315 (4) for Sterling Loans contracted in the transition period.

pensions, allowances and other conditions of the Defence Services.* Even though the actual orders may be made by the Governor-General in his discretion, the Secretary of State has the final right of approval and sanction of the rules and regulations made; and, in so far as the Indian Defence Forces are still virtually an integral part of the Imperial Defence organisation, this right of approval or sanction has the utmost significance.

In the Civil Services, he makes the initial appointments to the Indian Civil Service, the civil branch of the Indian Medical Service, and the Indian Police Service, pending other arrangements made by a Parliamentary Statute.† Similarly, to all the civil posts or services, instituted to aid the Governor-General in the discharge of his functions which he is to exercise in his discretion, it is the Secretary of State who would make the first appointments and determine the respective strength of such services.‡ He also makes rules regarding the number and character of the civil posts, which are to be reserved for persons appointed by him to a civil Service under the Crown in India.§ Under Section 247, the conditions of service of all such officers appointed in the first place by the Secretary of State, —as regards their pay, leave and pensions, and medical attendance,—are prescribed by the Secretary of State under rules made for that purpose. For all other matters rules made by the Governor-General as

*Section 235 provides that the Secretary of State may from time to time, with the concurrence of a majority of his Advisers, specify what rules, regulations and orders affecting the conditions of service of His Maje y's Forces in India shall be made only with his previous approval.

† cp. Section 244 (1).

cp., Section 24 (2)and (3). Also Irrigation Engineers under Section 245.

cp., Section 246.

regards posts under the Federation, and by the Governors as regards posts in the Provinces,—in cases where the Secretary of State has not made the necessary Rules, —would provide Rights of appeal and complaint are reserved from these officers to the Secretary of State (Section 248); while Section 249 secures adequate compensation being paid, at the instance of the Secretary of State, if the conditions of service of any officer appointed by him are adversely affected by anything done under this Act. The powers of the Secretary of State in these matters are to be exercised with the concurrence of a majority of his Advisers.*

Powers of the Representative of the Crown in Relation to Indian States

The constitutional position regarding relations with Indian States outside the Federation,—and even with those who have federated, in so far as what are called Paramountcy powers are concerned,—is by no means clear. The fundamental maxim of the British Constitutional Law, *viz.*, that the King can only act on the advice of a Minister, if applied, would bring these concerns also within the orbit of the Secretary of State. Sections 285-7, dealing with "Crown and the Indian States", specifically exclude those relations,—except in so far as the Instrument of Accession authorises the application of any provision of this Act,—from the scope of this Constitution.† That means the only adviser of the King,—and, therefore, the only control over the representative of the Crown,—in its dealings with the Indian States outside the Federal Constitution, is the Secretary of State. The Governor-General, like-

*Section 261.

†cp., Section 285.

wise, acts "in his discretion"* in meeting the expenses of the representative of the Crown in its relations with Indian States. By Section 33 (3) (f):—

> "The sums payable to His Majesty under this Act out of the revenues of the Federation in respect of the expenses incurred in discharging the functions of the Crown in its relations with Indian States."

are included among the expenditure charged upon the revenues of the Federation, *i.e.*, non-votable by the Federal Legislature. Several sums may be payable to the Indian States under Sections 147-9 particularly to the Federating States, or some of them; and these must be made good to the Viceroy by the Governor-General out of the Federal Revenues, acting in his discretion, *i.e.*, without reference to his Ministers; and therefore responsible only to the Secretary of State. Similarly, expenses of the armed forces in the Indian States, or for due discharge of the Crown's obligations in respect of these States, must

> "be deemed to be expenses of His Majesty incurred in discharging the said functions of the Crown."

Considerable indirect, or imperceptible, influence would also be exercised by the Secretary of State in the nomination of the Federated States' representatives in the Federal Legislature, which, however, would be extra-constitutional activity; and as such need not be emphasised here.

Miscellaneous Powers of the Secretary of State

Of the miscellaneous powers of the Secretary of State, the most considerable may be found in his right to grant leave, under the Instrument of Instructions, to the Governor, or the Governor-General during the

*cp., Section 286 (2).

term of office of these officers. Section 309 provides for the issue and responsibility for Orders in Council,—the Secretary of State being the Minister responsible for the Order, whether issued while Parliament is in sessions, and, therefore, upon an address of both Houses that the Order as submitted be issued; or in periods when Parliament is prorogued.*

On a general review of all these varied and substantial powers, the Secretary of State still stands out unmistakably as the most dominant authority in the Indian Constitution. His powers may not be so imposing in appearance as those of the Governor-General or the Provincial Governors. But these are merely his creatures, obedient to every nod from the jupiter of Whitehall, amenable to every hint from this juggler of Charles Street. His powers extend not merely to matters of fundamental policy; to the protection of British vested interests; to the safeguarding of Britain's imperialist domination. They comprise even matters of routine administration, the more important doings of the Indian Legislature, and even the appointments, payment or superannuation of certain officers in the various Indian Services or Governments. He has, in fact, all the power and authority in the governance of India, with little or none of its responsibility.

*Section 294, dealing with extra-territorial or Foreign Jurisdiction on behalf of India is of too technical a juristic nature to be commented upon in this work.

CHAPTER X

FEDERAL JUDICIARY

Part IX of the Act of 1935, sections 200-231, both inclusive, deal with the Judicature in India. We have already dealt, in the Volume on "Provincial Autonomy," with the Provincial section of the Judicial Administration in India. The most important,—in the sense of the most voluminous,—judicial work of the country is done in the Provincial High Courts, and Courts subordinate to those institutions. For the Federation, however, Judicial provision of some sort is indispensable, not only because there is a great likelihood, under the new Constitution, of considerable litigation of a Constitutional type; but also because of the need to co-ordinate the entire judicial system of the country.

Hence, for the Federation, there is to be a Federal Court* consisting of a Chief Justice of India, and such other puisne Judges, not exceeding six, as the King may from time to time direct. The number of Federal Judges may be increased by an address from the Federal Legislature to the Governor-General praying His Majesty to increase the number of those Judges.† Judges of the Federal Court are appointed by Royal Sign Manual, and hold office during good behaviour, or until they attain the age of 65, when they would be provided with a most handsome Pension if they

*Cp., Section 200.

†The Chief Justice of India was appointed, along with 2 Puisne Judges, for the Federal Court, in the Autumn of 1936. The Order-in-Council, fixing their pay, pension or gratuity allowances is on a most lavish scale imaginable. The Legal Profession thus continues to command the prize posts in the Government of the country, and more than maintains the common ground for criticism describing that Profession as parasitical.

have put in a requisite service. Apart from resignation in writing addressed to the Governor-General, Federal Court Judges cannot be removed from their office, except by His Majesty by warrant under the Royal Sign Manual.

> "on the ground of misbehaviour or of infirmity of mind or body, if the Judicial Committee of the Privy Council, on reference being made to them by His Majesty, report that the Judge ought on any such ground to be removed.*

That Judges should be beyond the buffets of political partisanship in Democracies would be almost axiomatic. But the old aphorism of Bacon, that Judges are lions, but lions under the Throne, has, in India, something more than a merely historical value to show off the obsequious nature of one of the greatest thinkers of Britain.

In this country, if the people's will is ever to take the place of the Royal authority as sovereign power, Judges, as well as any other officials, ought to be made responsible, in the ultimate analysis, to the popular will. More than in other countries, the problem is complicated in India because of the hold upon the country, its resources and its people, of a foreign exploiting, often un-understanding, and unsympathetic Bureaucracy. If the Judges are to be truly independent, and above the gusts of Party sentiment, they ought to be no more the minions of the Bureaucracy in power than of the changing Ministers created by the varying favour of Democracy. The appointment of the highest Judicial officers in the hands of the British King,—*i.e.*, in the hands of the Secretary of State,—and, through him, of the alien Indian Bureaucracy,—

*cp. Section 200 (2) (b).

is in itself an objectionable feature of the Constitution. So long as the Judges owe their allegiance, primarily and obviously, to an outside authority, unconsciously biassed in favour of the existing order, they cannot but,—quite unconsciously, perhaps,—lean in favour with the class or the power that gives them their place, and their importance in the scheme of life. In the United States, the complete separation between the Judiciary, the Executive, and the Legislature, has always caused Constitutional difficulties, which in India, by this arrangement, are likely to be tenfold more bitter, because of the suspicion of non-Indian or anti-Indian sympathies in the powers that be who really appoint Judges as well as all high officials of State in India. Class differences, and a class-conscious mentality, are rapidly growing in India; and Judges cannot be exceptions to this characteristic of our ago, so long as they are human. Hence the supposed attribute of impartiality induced or encouraged by this method of appointing Judges to the highest tribunal in India would fail to accomplish the object in view; while there is at least an equal danger of its promoting something quite the reverse.

Apart from the power of appointment, the power of removal from office has also to be considered. In Britain, the Judges are, in effect, appointed practically for life by the Ministry of the day. But in the event of any misbehaviour, the removal is decreed by an address from both Houses of Parliament to the King, —the nominally appointing authority. That there has never been a case in which a Judge of the Supreme Court of Judicature has had to be removed from office in this manner only proves the soundness of the doctrine which reserves the ultimate authority, in case of need, in the hands of the real Sovereign of the land. In India, the Judges of the Federal Court are appointed for a term of 12 (?) years ending with the 65th year of the incumbent, and not for life "during good behaviour" as in England.* This is a method of squeezing the country by such inflated salaries, pensions, and allowance, which cannot but react injuriously upon the aggregate national economy. Had the right to remove the Judges of the Federal or a Provincial High Court been left, with any reservations deemed necessary, in the hands of the local authorities,—*e.g.*, by means of an address of the Federal or Provincial Legislature (as the case may be),—for such action by the Governor as representing the King, the requirement of keeping the supreme judicial officers outside the vortex of Party Politics would have been met, side by side with securing the ultimate authority in the hands of those people who pay for these services.

Under Section 201:—

201:—The Judges of the Federal Court shall be entitled to such salaries and allowances, including allowances for expenses in respect of equipment and travelling upon appointment, and to such rights in respect of leave and pensions, as may from time to time be fixed by His Majesty in Council:

Provided that neither the salary of a judge nor his rights in respect of leave of absence or pension shall be varied to his disadvantage after his appointment.

*The reason may, perhaps, be found in the desire to earn a Pension,—a handsome allowance to such officers. The maximum Pension of a Grade I Judge is £ 1800 p.a.; the salary allowed is Rs. 72,000 per annum to the Chief Justice of the High Court at Calcutta, Rs. 60,000 p.a., to the other Chief Justices. (Nagpur only Rs. 50,000), and Rs. 48,000 p.a., to the Judges of the High Courts at Bombay, Madras, Calcutta, Allahabad, Patna and Lahore. The Chief Justice of India is to be paid Rs. 84.000 p.a. and the Puisne Judges of the Federal Court Rs. 72,000 p.a. (?) Cp. Schedule 2, Order-in-Council, dated March 18, and published in the Gazette of India, April 1, 1937, p. 37 et seq.

By Section 33 (3) (d), the salaries, allowances and pensions of the Federal Court Judges are charged on the revenues of the Federation,—which means they are not to be voted in the annual Budget by the Federal Legislature. This corresponds to the British practice of placing these estimates on what are known as the Consolidated Fund Charges, which do not fall within the annual vote of Parliament, as the Supply Services do. But, what is for Parliament no more than a self-denying Ordinance, detracting in no way from the unquestioned and absolute Sovereignty of Parliament, becomes in this country an indisputable evidence of the distrust of the Indian people and their representatives in the Legislature, an index of the control reserved to Parliament, or guarantees exacted for good behaviour, as it were, of the Indian Legislature, on behalf of the Public Services.

The qualifications for appointment as Judge of the Federal Court are such that a foreign element must necessarily predominate. According to Section 200 (3).

200 (3):—A person shall not be qualified for appointment as a judge of the Federal Court unless he—

(a) has been for at least five years a judge of a High Court in British India or in a Federated State; or

(b) is a barrister of England or Northern Ireland of at least ten years standing, or a member of the Faculty of Advocates in Scotland of at least ten years standing; or

(c) has been for at least ten years a pleader of a High Court in British India or in a Federated State or of two or more such Courts in succession.

In computing for the purposes of this sub-section the standing of a barrister or a member of the Faculty of Advocates, or the period during which a person has been a pleader, any period during which a person has held judicial office after he became a barrister, a member of the Faculty of Advocates or a pleader, as the case may be, shall be included.

(4) Every person appointed to be a judge of the Federal Court shall, before he enters upon his office, make and subscribe before the Governor-General or some person appointed by him an oath according to the form set out in that behalf in the Fourth Schedule to this Act.

This is welcome departure from that provision in Section 220 (3) which includes a Civilian element in the Judges of the Provincial High Court. For in the section just quoted, the Federal Court can have only professional lawyers as Judges, unless those promoted from a Provincial High Court are included even though they originally belonged to the Indian Civil Service with judicial experience. But in so far as equal rights to Indian lawyers born and trained in this country alone are concerned, this provision is no more liberal than the existing arrangement.

Temporary vacancies in the office of the Chief Justice of India, owing either to the absence from India of that official, or to some disability which incapacitates him for a while from discharging his duties, are filled by the Governor-General acting in his discretion* from among the other Judges of the Federal Court.

Jurisdiction of the Federal Court

The Jurisdiction of the Federal Court appears to be both Original and Appellate. The Court is also

*Cp., Section 202. There is no mention in this section, of a similar vacancy in the office of the other Judges of the Federal Court. Looking to the wording of Section 200 (2), it would seem that every substantive appointment to the office of a Federal Judge is made by the King; but there is no provision for officiating or acting Judges, Temporary or Additional Judges of the Federal Court, as there is in regard to Provincial High Courts under Section 222 (2) and (3).

authorized to advise the Governor-General on any point he may refer to them, under Section 213. We shall notice more particularly hereafter the intent and bearing of this section on the Constitution,—especially in comparison with the corresponding practice in the United States or in the United Kingdom itself. Under Section 204 of the Act, the Original Jurisdiction of the Court is confined to any dispute between any two or more of the parties in the Federation, *i.e.*, the Federation, any of the Provinces, or any of the Federated States, "if and in so far as the dispute involves any question (whether of law or fact) on which the existence or extent of a legal right depends.

This is, however, not confined only to Constitutional issues between the parties mentioned; but may involve any legal right. It is also not identical with a mere interpretation of the Constitution authoritatively, as the Supreme Court does in the United States, or as the Privy Council does for any British Dominion or Colony. The judgment of the Federal Court is to be purely a declaratory judgment in the exercise of its Original Jurisdiction; but even so, it can declare the existence or extent of a legal right, without making that right necessarily a constitutional right.

So far as a Federated State, or States, are a party to such a dispute before the Federal Court, the section clearly provides:—

Provided that the said jurisdiction shall not extend to—

(a) a dispute to which a State is a party, unless the dispute—

(i) concerns the interpretation of this Act or of an Order-in-Council made thereunder, or the extent of the legislative or executive authority vested in the Federation by virtue of the Instrument of Accession of that State; or

(ii) arises under an agreement made under Part VI of this Act in relation to the administration in that State of a law of the Federal Legislature, or otherwise concerns some matter with respect to which the Federal Legislature has power to make laws for that State; or

(iii) arises under an agreement made after the establishment of the Federation, with the approval of His Majesty's Representative for the exercise of the functions of the Crown in its relations with Indian States, between that State and the Federation or a Province, being an agreement which expressly provides that the said jurisdiction shall extend to such a dispute;

(b) a dispute arising under any agreement which expressly provides that the said jurisdiction shall not extend to such a dispute.

This distinction between the Original Jurisdiction of the Federal Court in respect of the Federated States, and in respect of the Provinces, arises out of the different status and conditions attending the inclusion in, or accession to, the Federation of the two classes of units. Presumably, in the case of the States, the Federal Court would have no jurisdiction in:—

(a) any interpretation of a question of law or fact on which a legal right depends, even though the question may arise as between the State concerned and the Federation, or one of the Provinces.

(b) any dispute which is specifically excluded by agreement from the Jurisdiction of the Federal Court, even though it may involve questions of interpreting the Constitution.

In regard to the Federal Court's jurisdiction for the interpretation of the Constitution, the jurisdiction can apparently only arise if and when a dispute occurs between the Federation and one of the Federating units, or between any two or more of such units.* Interpretation of the Constitution by a simple reference from a Provincial, State, or the Federal Government is not provided for, even though under Section 213:—

> 213.—(1) If at any time it appears to the Governor-General that a question of law has arisen, or is likely to arise, which is of such a nature and of such public importance that it is expedient to obtain the opinion of the Federal Court upon it, he may in his discretion refer the question to that court for consideration, and the court may, after such hearing as they think fit, report to the Governor-General thereon.
>
> (2) No report shall be made under this section save in accordance with an opinion delivered in open court with the concurrence of a majority of the judges present at the hearing of the case, but nothing in this sub-section shall be deemed to prevent a judge who does not concur from delivering a dissenting opinion.†

As already pointed out in the appropriate place, the Constitution, such as it is, is bound to cause infinite litigation, because of a wide region of doubtful provision, or overlapping authority. The absence of any authority finally to interpret the Constitution authoritatively, in the absence of any specific dispute arising, or even in the absence of any reference by the Governor-General, is likely to make the Constitution clumsy to work, and expensive. It is also very likely to lead to needless impasse between authorities, which

*The practice in this respect seems indentical with that in the United States, where the Supreme Court can not intervene except to try a specific case; and then give a decision which would interpret the Constitution.

†It is interesting to note that nothing is said in this section, or any where else in the Act, regarding the fate of the Report made under this section by the Federal Court to the Governor-General. Is the Governor-General bound to give effect to this opinion? Under Section 212, the law declared by the Federal Court is binding on all other Courts in British India, and, in respect of interpreting the Constitution, etc., upon the Courts in the Federated States; but it says not a word about the binding character of the opinion given by the Federal Court upon the Governor-General, even though he himself had made the reference.

honestly conceive their constitutional powers differently from one another.

Interpretation of the Constitution

The primary interpreter of the Constitution in India seems to be the Provincial High Courts.* Section 205, defining the Appellate Jurisdiction of the Federal Court, permits appeals to it

> "from any judgment, decree or final order of a High Court in British India, if the High Court certifies that the case involves a substantial question of law as to the interpretation of this Act or any Order-in-Council made thereunder, and it shall be the duty of every High Court in British India to consider in every case whether or not any such question is involved, and of its own motion to give or to withhold a certificate accordingly."

The right of appeal is given, under 205 (2) in all cases where such a certificate is given by the High Court which originally tried the case. The ground for appeal may be that the question of law involved as to the interpretation of the Act, as stated in the certificate, was wrongly decided. Parties concerned are also entitled to appeal to the Federal Court on any ground on which they could have appealed, before the advent of this Constitution, to the Privy Council without special leave. "No direct appeal shall lie to His Majesty in Council either with or without special leave." But appeal may be made to the Federal Court, with the leave of that Court, on any other ground. This provides a very wide margin for appeal; and so does not in any way minimise the rather objectionable feature of litigation in India,—too many appeals.

The appellate Jurisdiction of the Federal Court is extended to Civil cases from any Provincial Court,

*cp. Section 223. Under the existing jurisdiction the Chartered and other High Courts are entitled to discuss constitutional issues in the form of specific cases coming before them; and that jurisdiction remains.

if the point at issue involves, both in the first instance and on appeal,

(a) a sum of money not less than Rs. 50,000, or such other sum not less than Rs. 15,000|- as may be prescribed by the Act of the Federal Legislature granting such appellate jurisdiction in Civil Suits;

(b) property of the like value;

(c) any case in which the Federal Court gives special leave for appeal.

This extension of appellate jurisdiction can only be made by the Federal Legislature by a solemn enactment; and if granted, provision may also be made, by the same or another Act of the Federal Legislature, to abolish appeals in such cases to the Privy Council as heretofore, either with or without special leave. There is, it may be noted, no provision in all these sections of corresponding appeals to the Federal Court in Criminal Cases, which, presumably, remain as under the existing constitution of the High Courts.

None of these provisions for appellate jurisdiction in Civil matters apply to the High Courts in any of the Federated States. But the right of appeal to the Federal Court from a High Court in a Federated State is provided for under Section 207, in cases involving questions concerning the interpretation of the Constitution Act, or of an Order in-Council made thereunder, or the extent of legislative or executive authority vested in the Federation by virtue of the Instrument of Accession of the particular State. In cases, also, which concern the interpretation of administrative agreements made under Part VI of the Act.* Appeals

*Cp. Section 125 for such agreements.

to the Federal Court under this section are to be in the form of a case stated for the opinion of the Federal Court by the State High Court; and authority is vested, by sub-section (2) of this section, in the Federal Court to demand that a case be so stated for its opinion. An opinion given on such cases is as binding as an ordinary judgment on appeal, which is given effect to by the High Court from which the case was originally appealed against.*

This Original and Appellate Jurisdiction, as well as the general authority and prestige of the Court, are assured and safeguarded by Section 210. All authorities, civil and judicial, throughout the Federation, are required to act in aid of the Federal Court. The Court is empowered to call any witness, and require the production of any document needed in evidence. It can also punish any disrespect to its orders, summons, etc., as contempt of Court, like any High Court. All its orders regarding costs in any proceedings before it are made enforceable practically throughout the Federation as the orders of the highest tribunal within any unit through such tribunals.

Federal Court not a Supreme Court

In spite, however, of this wide Original and Appellate Jurisdiction, the Federal Court of India is not the

*209.—(1) The Federal Court shall, where it allows an appeal, remit the case to the court from which the appeal was brought with a declaration as to the judgment, decree or order which is to be substituted for the judgment, decree or order appealed against and the court from which the appeal was brought shall give effect to the decision of the Federal Court.

(2) Where the Federal Court upon any appeal makes any order as to the costs of the proceedings in the Federal Court, it shall, as soon as the amount of the costs to be paid is ascertained, transmit its order for the payment of that sum to the court from which the appeal was brought and that court shall give effect to the order.

(3) The Federal Court may, subject to such terms or conditions as it may think fit to impose, order a stay of execution in any case under appeal to the Court, pending the hearing of the appeal, and execution shall be stayed accordingly.

same thing as the Supreme Court in the United States. It is not the final appellate authority,—the last authoritative judicial interpreter of the Constitution, or the ultimate declarer of the civil law of the land. That power is vested still in the Privy Council by Section 208. In all Constitutional cases,—*i.e.*, in cases in which the Federal Court has given judgment in the exercise of its original jurisdiction in the interpretation of the Constitution, the Instrument of Accession of any Federated State under this Act, or the interpretation of an agreement under Section 125, with a Federated State,—the appeal can be made *without leave* of the Federal Court; and in all other cases, by leave of the Federal Court, or of the Privy Council. The hope of any uniformity of the common law in India through the interpretation of a single Tribunal in appeal, is thus doomed to disappointment, until such time as a supreme Court of Justice is instituted in India, with the highest, final, appellate powers, and without any possibility of an appeal against its decisions in the cases in which it has original or appellate jurisdiction. The law declared by the Privy Council,—and, in cases unappealed against, by the Federal Court,—is the final exposition of the Constitutional law of India, as also of the ordinary law in so far as British India is concerned. As such, it is binding, until amended by the appropriate Legislature, on all Courts in British India, and, as regards constitutional matters, in all Federated States.

Power to make Rules

The Federal Court is empowerd, by Section 214, to make rules, with the approval of the Governor-General in his discretion, to regulate:—

> "generally the practice and procedure of the Court, including rules as to the persons practising before the Court, as to the time within which appeals to the Court are to be entered, as to the costs of and incidental to, any proceedings in the Court, and as to the fees to be charged in respect of proceedings therein, and in particular may make rules providing for the summary determination of any appeal which appears to the court to be frivolous or vexatious or brought for the purpose of delay."*

These rules of procedure etc., also have to fix the minimum number of Judges that can constitute a proper Tribunal; but no Court can consist of less than three judges.† If the Federal Legislature enacts legislation extending the appellate jurisdiction of this Court, the Rules of the Court made under this section must provide for a special division of the Court to decide those cases which would have normally come before the Court even if its appellate jurisdiction had not been enlarged by Act of the Federal Legislature.‡ Much of the administrative powers and functions would be left to the Chief Justice of India, *e.g.*, what judges are to constitute a given Division of the Court, and what cases are to go before given Judges,—unless the Rules prescribe otherwise.§ Judgments of the Court must be delivered in open Court, and must be of a majority of the Judges present at the hearing of the case, though the right is expressly reserved of individual Judges, if they differ from the Majority, to record their dissent.

If these powers are not enough, the Federal Legislature may, under Section 215, enact legislation

---

*Cp. Section 214 (1).

†Cp. Section 214 (2).

‡Ibid., Proviso.

§Cp. Section 214 (3).

conferring such further supplemental powers upon the Federal Court, not inconsistent with the powers and functions assigned under the Constitution Act,

> "as may appear to be necessary or desirable for the purpose of enabling the Court more effectively to exercise the jurisdiction conferred upon it by or under this Act."

Needless to add that the Federal Court is a Court of Record, and that it would ordinarily sit at the Federal Capital, Delhi. Section 203, however, permits of its sitting at any other place or places, if the Chief Justice of India so appoints with the approval of the Governor-General. This possibility of the Federal Court of India becoming an itinerant institution does not seem calculated to add either to its effectiveness or economy in administration. Its expenses, however, are charged, under Section 216, upon the Federal revenues, and as such are exempt from Public discussion.*

Peculiarities of Judicial Administration in India

Though the preceding outline of the organisation of the Judicial administration in the proposed Federation of India may have noted, in the appropriate places, the several peculiarities of that system, let us sum up these special features in a single place at this stage. The Judicial system in India, as every other aspect of the country's governmental machine, is subordinate to the supreme authority located outside the country. The highest appellate Tribunal, and the most authoritative exponent of the Constitutional as well as the common law of the land, is not in India. The fact

*Sub-Section (2) of Section 216 is not calculated to make any economy in this regard, apart from the fact that it seems inconsistent with the spirit of sub-section (1).

that an outside body, whose members or a majority of them must necessarily be unfamiliar with our customs, and often unsympathetic to our ideals and aspirations, is empowered to lay down the final law binding on all the citizens, authorities and tribunals in this country, is bound to militate, not only against the correct, sympathetic, and satisfactory interpretation and application of our juristic ideas and ideals; it is likely to thwart, unconsciously perhaps, our ambitions in the political or constitutional field, which depend in no small measure upon a sympathetic outlook of the highest Courts of Justice for their fructification. Those who know the history of the growth of constitutional freedom in England cannot but be aware of the supreme importance a sympathetic judiciary has, not only in guarding and enforcing popular liberties against encroachments of autocratic rulers, but also in protecting the community against the vagaries of the political atmosphere. They will, also, readily understand the hardship and handicap this absence of the final appellate power and authority in the Indian judicial system for deciding all questions of common or constitutional law. But, whether the British politician still distrusts the Judiciary in India, or treats it as incompetent in the inmost recesses of his heart, or desires to reserve the fat profits to the legal profession of this monopoly of ultimate appellate powers for his own countrymen, the fact remains that, in spite of all persuasions to the contrary, Parliament has refused to accompany this dose of constitutional advance in India with the gift of the supreme judicial authority for Indian cases to the highest tribunal in India.

The real interpretation of the Constitution, also, is left with an outside authority, even though those who suffer from a defective or objectionable interpretation or application of constitutional powers would be Indians. The Federal Court has, as already noticed, certain limited powers in the interpretation of the Constitution. But these can only be used to determine the existence of a legal right, or to interpret an Instrument of Accession, or an agreement signed thereunder. It can only apply to cases of disputes between members of the Federation, or between the Federation and any unit composing it. The constitutional rights of the individual citizens, or constitutional problems,—such as the one which occurred at the very outset of the system of Provincial Autonomy, when the majority party in some of the leading Provinces refused to undertake Ministerial responsibility unless certain assurances were given by the Governor,—cannot be pronounced upon finally and authoritatively, unless and until a specific case arises, within the terms of Section 204, between the parties therein described. The Governor-General may, no doubt, under the power given to him by Section 213, invite the opinion of the Federal Court upon any question of law actually before the country, or which is likely to arise, and which is of such a nature and of such public importance, that he considers it expedient to obtain the opinion of the Court upon it. But the Governor-General acts, in this matter, *in his discretion i.e.*, no one can make him use this power to solve peacefully and amicably such a problem as agitated the whole of India when the system of Provincial Autonomy was first introduced. The fact that the Governor-General never lifted his finger all through that historic impasse, in this direction, is sufficient evidence to conclude that this will not be one of the normal ways in which constitutional issues of such importance could and would be judicially settled. The Act does not lay an obligation upon the Governor-General; nor is the wording of the section referred to such as to make it imperative upon the Court necessarily to make a report to the Governor-General giving the highest available judicial solution to the problem.* Ordinary citizens in this country are either too indifferent to such matters, or too unfamiliar with the mysteries of Constitutional law, or too unconcerned in the actual problem, personally to move the machinery of Justice to redress such wrongs, or solve such issues. There is, therefore, no means of interpreting finally, authoritatively, and sympathetically, the constitutional law of India in India; and, consequently, there is no machinery to allay needless public apprehensions on this vital national concern.

The lack will be felt all the more because there are, under the Constitution, no specific Fundamental Rights of citizenship, which could be relied upon, in the ultimate analysis, to safeguard civil liberty. True, there are no such specifically defined Rights of the Citizens, guaranteed by the Constitution, even in Great Britain. But the traditions of constitutionalism, of the rule of law, universally prevailing there; and the

*During the Constitutional impasse at the commencement of Provincial Autonomy, the entire Federal Court was not constituted. But the Chief Justice of India and two other Federal Court Judges had already been appointed; and had the Governor-General desired to solve the tangle in this manner, he could have availed himself of the provision contained in Section 213 just as much as they might have had recourse to Section 310, and obtained an Order-in-Council,—recording or embodying a judgment of the Privy Council,—so as to satisfy the very modest demand of the Congress, and allay apprehensions which had been aroused in the public mind as to the nature and use of the Extraordinary Powers of the Provincial Governors.

identity in race of the governors with the governed in that country, automatically avoid such constitutional complications, and psychological misunderstandings, which are unfortunately inevitable under Indian conditions. Given the communal discord and the habits of autocratic rule ingrained in the entrenched bureaucracy, it is more important in India than any where else, that certain common rights of the Citizens should be declared to be sacrosanct and guaranteed by the Constitution, even as the privileges of the Services, the claims of the creditors, and the demands of the Minorities have been guaranteed and safeguarded by specific provisions of the Constitution.

Says the report of the Joint Select Committee of Parliament, which examined this Constitution in its Bill form, apropos of the proposal of the British India Delegation to introduce in the Constitution Act a declaration of the Fundamental Rights of Citizenship:—*

> "The Statutory Commission observe with reference to this subject: 'We are aware that such provisions have been inserted in many Constitutions, notably in those of the European States formed after the War.' Experience, however, has not shown them to be of any great practical value. Abstract declarations are useless, unless there exist the will and the means to make them effective."

And this they deem sufficient answer to those who demanded a specific inclusion of a categoric declaration of the Fundamental Rights of Citizenship! Further comment is superfluous.

Because there is no specific declaration and guarantee of the fundamental rights of Citizenship in India,—and because such a clear enunciation is

*Cp. Report Joint Select Committee para. 366.

particularly necessary in the proposed new members of the Federation,—the Indian States, where hitherto Civil Liberties are conspicuous by their complete absence,—the problem of maintaining the Civil Liberties of the Indian people, and keeping up the progressive ideals of Government, becomes all the more difficult in this country. The Federal Court, constituted as it is, and with the powers and functions it is entrusted with, cannot reasonably be expected to aid the ordinary citizen in this regard. The other High Courts are equally powerless to protect that which does not exist. The Bureaucracy has, of late particularly, been conspicuous by its disregard of the liberties of the Indian people. Government by Ordinance, which was the order of the day between 1930-1934, amply testifies to the alarm that they have taken, and the fear complex that seems to have overwhelmed the reason of the *de facto* rulers of India. In the times to come, this alarm, and this fear complex are not likely to abate. Hence it is all the more necessary to have, in the Constitution Act proper, some clear enunciation of the Fundamental Rights of Citizenship under the new regime. Once declared, the will to maintain these rights and the power to make them effective will be forthcoming of their own accord.

Because there are no specifically declared Rights of the Citizens, the presence in the highest Judiciary of India of a large element of non-Indian lawyers, and administrative officers, makes the administration of Justice in India fundamentally different from that in the other Dominions or in the United Kingdom. All throughout the British Commonwealth of Nations, the tradition is observed of elevating to the highest judicial posts only those who have distinguished themselves as practising advocates. To that extent the Continental model of appointing to judicial offices only trained jurists in preference to advocates; or experienced judicial officers, is both different and perhaps unsuitable. But India is unique, even among the British countries, in having (i) non-Indians in considerable proportions in the highest Judiciary; and (ii) in having senior Civil Servants on the Bench of the High Courts, and perhaps also of the Federal Court. Not only these might lack a proper appreciation of the people's customs and ideals, and so fail to render real justice; they might even be,—and, under existing conditions, there is grave risk of their actually being, —unsympathetic and hostile to the aspirations of the people towards fuller civil liberties and greater national freedom. Cases may arise involving directly or indirectly, such issues; and on those occasions, the presence on the Bench of such non-Indians, or Civilians, might conceivably result in a serious miscarriage of justice, and a needless thwarting of the people's ideals. Indianisation of the highest Judiciary,—and its recruitment from among trained, experienced jurists, even in preference to practising advocates, is a desideratum for reform in the judicial administration of India which is bound to come into the forefront, as public consciousness awakens.

CHAPTER XI

FEDERAL FINANCE

Let us now consider the financial aspects of the new Constitution. Though dealing mainly with the constitutional side, as Finance is an important clog in the smooth working of the Constitution, it would not be possible always to avoid the *financial* aspect proper in the discussion that follows.

Part of the constitutional aspect has already been considered in the volume on **Provincial Autonomy**, and so, we shall avoid going over the same ground in this work as far as possible.*

We shall attempt in this chapter:

(1) a general review of the resources of the Federal Government, as provided for in the several clauses of the Act of 1935, and the Instruments of Accession with the several Federated States, as also under such arrangements as have been made by Orders-in-Council, like that recommended by Sir Otto Niemeyer.

(2) review of the obligations or items of expenditure, imposed upon the Federal Government by the Constitution, and the various Orders of Instruments thereunder.

(3) the constitutional aspect of borrowing, including the treatment of the existing

*A proper, logical, comprehensive consideration of the financial aspects of the entire Constitution would be better achieved if the entire Constitution was studied in one work. For reasons explained in the Preface to **Provincial Autonomy**, circumstances have necessitated a separate treatment of the financial aspects of the Federal and the Provincial Governments. A certain amount of repetition or overlapping would be, therefore, inevitable. Whereever possible, however, reference will be made in foot-notes to the volume on **Provincial Autonomy** (Second Edition), with a view to avoid such repetition..

debt and allied obligations, (*e.g.*, in respect of certain Service Funds.)

(4) A summary of the financial position, its critique, and appreciations of the future trend in matters financial.

No single chapter of the Constitution gives in one place all the financial provisions of the Constitution. Part VII of the Act of 1935 is described by the Act as relating to "Finance, Property, Contracts and Suits." But it does not give all the relevant provisions. Sections of the Act, however, which, directly or indirectly, affect the financial administration of the country, are also to be found scattered in those other parts of the Act which deal with the power of the Governor-General and procedure of the Legislature; the rights and duties of the Public Services; Judicial Department; and the Defence organization.

Financial obligations arising out of the several Reserve Departments, such as that of Defence, External Affairs, Ecclesiastical matters, Excluded Areas and tribal districts, together with the amounts payable under the Constitution to the Representative of the Crown in its relation with the Indian States, federated or not, will also involve a considerbale financial strain on the Constitution. The entire Chapter, again, relating to the Indian Railways, comprising Sections 181-199, has profound financial bearing upon the Constitution. Similarly, the provisions in regard to the Secretary of State, his Advisers and department, (Part XI Sections 278 to 284) as well as Section 302 relating to the High Commissioner for India; and 304 and 305 relating to the Acting Governors-General and the Secretarial staff of the same, have financial implications, which have a considerable significance upon the working of the Constitution. Lastly, though Burma and Aden have been separated from India, the separation of Burma particularly has an immense financial reaction upon the Constitution and administration of India, which can only be glanced at in the survey that follows.

I. FEDERAL RESOURCES OF REVENUE

Broadly speaking, the Act of 1935 seeks to make a clear division of resources between the Federal Government, and those of the component units. So far as the Federating States are concerned, their financial obligations will depend, in a large measure, upon the terms of the individual Instrument of Accession of each State. To the extent that the provisions of the Act prescribe these obligations to contribute to Federal resources, they are outlined and critically considered below more particularly. As regards the British Provinces, the division of resources and obligations is more thoroughly attempted in Schedule VII, which, primarily, is intended to provide Lists of Federal, Provincial, and Concurrent subjects for legislation; but which necessarily contain items that serve as excellent subjects for taxation or revenue levied and collected upon the authority of the Federal or Provincial Legislation as the case may be.

I

1. Customs Duties, including export duties.

2. Excise Duties on tobacco and other goods manufactured or produced in India except—

(a) Alcoholic liquors for human consumption;

(b) Opium, Indian hemp and other narcotic drugs and narcotics; non-narcotic drugs;

(c) Medicinal and toilet preparations containing alcohol, or any substance included in sub-paragraph (b) of this entry.

3. Corporation Tax.

4. Salt.

5. State lotteries.

6. Taxes on income other than agricultural income.

7. Taxes on the capital value of the assets, exclusive of agricultural land, of individuals and companies; taxes on the capital of companies.

8. Duties in respect of succession to property other than agricultural land.

9. The rates of stamp duty in respect of bills of exchange, cheques, promissory notes, bills of lading, letters of credit, policies of insurance, proxies and receipts.

10. Terminal taxes on goods or passengers carried by railway or air; taxes on railway fares and freights.

11. Fees in respect of any of the matters in this list, but not including fees taken in any court.

Provincial Government

II

1. Land revenue, including the assessment and collection of revenue, the maintenance of land records, survey for revenue purposes and records of rights.

2. Excise Duties on the following goods manufactured or produced in the Province, and countervailing duties at the same or lower rates on similar goods manufactured or produced in India—

(a) Alcoholic liquors for human consumption;

(b) Opium, Indian hemp and other narcotic drugs and narcotics; non-narcotic drugs;

(c) Medicinal and toilet preparations containing alcohol, or any substance included in sub-paragraph (b) of this entry.

3. Taxes on agricultural income.

4. Taxes on lands and buildings, hearths and windows.

5. Duties in respect of succession to agricultural land.

6. Taxes on mineral rights, subject to any limitations imposed by any Federal Legislature relating to mineral development.

7. Capitation taxes.

8. Taxes on professions, trades, callings and employments.

9. Taxes on animals and boats.

10. Taxes on the sale of goods and on advertisements.

11. Cesses on the entry of goods into a local area for consumption, use or sale therein.

12. Taxes on luxuries, including taxes on entertainments, amusements, betting and gambling.

13. The rates of stamp duty in respect of documents other than those specified in the provisions of List I with regard to rates of stamp duty.

14. Dues on passengers and goods carried on inland waterways.

15. Tolls.

16. Fees in respect of any of the matters in this list, but not including fees taken in any court.

Considering these Lists* in the aggregate, it is impossible not to notice the fact that while all the progressive or elastic and productive sources of revenue are reserved for the Federal Government, all the inelastic and obviously burdensome items are assigned to the Provinces. The only relief to the Provinces—such as it is—is to be found in the terms of Section 138 relating to the division of the Income Tax Proceeds, after a time, between the Units and Federation; and of Section 142, under which certain subsidies are to be paid by the Federal Government to certain Provinces. Both these subjects have been investigated into, and the necessary aid to the Provinces thereunder has been recommended by Sir Otto Niemeyer, whose report has been considered in some detail already in the volume on **Provincial Autonomy** under the new Constitution to which reference may be made.

The provisions of Section 137, requiring uniform taxation, and centralised collection of such items as

(i) Succession duties to property other than Agricultural Land;

(ii) Stamp duties mentioned in the Federal Legislative List;

(iii) Terminal taxes on goods or passengers carried by railway or air; and

(iv) Taxes on railway fares and freight

***In the concurrent Legislative List, there are a number of items, which might be utilised for taxation, though it is not clear that the law-making power will also include the power to pass legislation taxing such acts as marriage and divorce (Item VI), wills, intestacy and succession, save as regards agricultural lands (Item VII), or transfer of property and other agricultural lands, (Item VIII) by means of stamp duties or registration fees.**

may afford financial aid to the Provinces in the future. But the fact that they are to be imposed and collected by the Federal Government, for distribution of the net proceeds* among the component units, will not permit the Province to vary the rates, and graduate the burden to the differing abilities of their citizens. This will render Provincial revenue from these sources utterly inelastic, and unsuitable for any ambitious project of social reconstruction or economic development in the Province. Besides, the section reserves to the Federal Government the right to impose a surcharge on all these items of revenue for their own exclusive use. This means that the property, wealth, and business acumen of every Province is, in the ultimate analysis, open to the Federal Government for its own particular, and, generally, unproductive purposes, without any corresponding obligation to contribute directly or substantially towards the economic development of the Provinces. Section 140, holding out a remote, unlikely hope of the Federal Government some day distributing among the component units part of the proceeds of the Salt Duty, Federal Excise and Export Duties,—if an Act of the Federal Legislature authorises it to do so,—is misleading in the very hope it engenders. Viewing the position as it is to-day, there appears no chance of the Federal Government ever having such a superabundance of funds as will admit of this generosity to the Provinces and the Federated States. The only exception to this appreciation of that section may be found in sub-section (2) of that section, which requires one-half or more of the net proceeds of the jute export

*cp., Section 144.

duties to be distributed among the jute-growing provinces. Sir Otto Niemeyer has recommended that 5|8ths of such proceeds should be made over to those Provinces. It must be admitted that the Provinces of Bengal, Bihar, and Assam have derived substantial aid to their resources from this concession. But, even so, the case of the jute-growing Provinces for the entire proceeds of this export duty should not be lost sight of altogether. Besides, those who endorse the principle underlying that provision in the U. S. A. Constitution, which forbids the Federation to levy any such duty on the product of a State, cannot altogether deny the justice of the claim made on this account by the jute-growing Provinces.

It must also be remembered that, though the list of revenue resources made available to the Provinces under the Act may seem imposing, many of the Provincial items are really made over to the local bodies like Municipalities and District Boards. Section 143 (2) expressly permits these sources of revenue to remain at the disposal of the bodies which now enjoy them, until the Federal (or Provincial?) Legislature may otherwise direct. Even Section 141 is no real protection or safeguard to the Provincial Governments in face of an extravagant or impecunious Federal Government, as is most likely to be the case. For though without the prior sanction of the Governor-General, given in his discretion, no Bill or amendment can be introduced in the Federal Legislature affecting any of the taxes or duties in which Provinces may be interested, or by which they may be affected, (*e.g.*, those succession, stamp or terminal duties on passengers, fares or freight, which are levied by the Federal Government for distribution among the units, or which impose surcharges on them, or on the Income Tax), that would not necessarily or for ever prevent such proposals being mooted in or passed by the Federal Legislature.

The Governor-General is enjoined, it is true, not to give his prior sanction to any Bill or amendment in the Federal Legislature,

> "unless he is satisfied that all practicable economies and all practicable measures for otherwise increasing the proceeds of Federal taxation,...... would not result in the balancing of Federal receipts and expenditure on revenue account.*

But even that injunction will not always enable him,—even if he is so inclined,—to be an effective protector and guardian of Provincial interests. The reason is quite clear. His primary and Special Responsibility, imposed by Section 12, is to see to the financial stability and credit of India as a whole. Given the present state of the Central finances; and given the nature of the burdens imposed upon the Federation, it is impossible to see how the Governor-General will ever be able to protect or safeguard the interests of the Provinces in this behalf, consistently with his own primary responsibility in that regard. Even when their resources expand, or exceed there obligations, a democratic Federal Government of India may be trusted to discover new and useful channels for additional Federal expenditure, so that no accession to Provincial resources is feasible.

The real position of the Revenues and Expenditure of the Federal Government of India may be appreciated

*Cp. Section 141 (2).

from the Budget Estimates for the Government of India in 1937-38.* They provided for a total net revenue, on the then (*i.e.*, the 1st of March 1937) existing basis of taxation, of 79.99 crores; and an aggregate net expenditure of 83.41 crores. This meant a deficit of 3.42 crores. This the Finance Minister proposed to meet partly from the existing revenue reserve (Rs. 184 lakhs), and partly from additional taxation.† But this does not present a complete picture, even though the Niemeyer recommendations in regard to aid to the Provinces had been adopted and acted upon in part, and though settlement with Burma had also been arrived at. The Instruments of Accession with the various States have yet to be executed; and they might affect materially important items of revenue as well as expenditure. Future improvements in revenue are difficult to forecast at the present moment, while room for retrenchment in expenditure is exceedingly limited, if it exists at all, given the meticulously protected position of the services and other vested interests.

The main factors which affected the Central finances, in the Budget for 1937-38, and would continue to affect them even after the Federation comes into existence, may be summarised, in the language of the Finance Member, as follows:—

> ‡" But apart from the changes of form, there are two major changes of scope which affect the estimates for 1937-38. I refer, of course, to the separation of Burma and to the Niemeyer

---

*See Table appended.

†The sugar excise was increased from Rs. 2|- per cwt., and estimated to yield Rs. 115 lakhs: and the silver duty was raised from annas 2 to 3 per oz. yielding Rs. 50 lakhs

‡Vide Budget Speech of the Finance Member, 1937-38, Para. 12.

Award, including in this term all the other alterations consequent upon the introduction of Provincial Autonomy. The effects of these changes run through practically every head of the Budget..
From Table I of the Financial Secretary's Memorandum it will be seen that the general effect of the Separation of Burma **is a net reduction of Revenue of Rs. 138 lakhs,** and a net increase of Expenditure of Rs. 92 lakhs—these figures taking no account of a betterment of Rs. 13 lakhs in the net balance of the P. & T. Department. **The net cost of separation is therefore Rs. 233 lakhs.** At this stage I should explain that on the Revenue side we have taken credit for the receipt, under the Amery Award, of

(i) Rs. 2,29 lakhs in respect of the debt and other liabilities taken over by Burma, and

(ii) Rs. 94 lakhs in respect of Burma's liability for pensions in course of payment on the 31st March 1937.

Apart from these the net loss on account of separation would be Rs. 5,56 lakhs. Needless to say all these figures are of a provisional character. There are many uncertain factors to be taken into account, particularly under the heads Customs and Taxes of Income; and, moreover, the final material for the calculation of the annuities payable by Burma will not be available until some time after the 31st March.

* * * *

As regards Provincial Autonomy, **the net results are a reduction of Rs. 51 lakhs in Revenue combined with an increase of Rs. 1,34 lakhs in Expenditure,** *i.e.*, a total cost to the Centre of Rs. 1,85 lakhs.

The sum of these two figures, *viz.*, Rs. 418 lakhs represent the extra burden on our budget (*i.e.*, additional to that assumed in earlier years) arising from the constitutional changes due on 1st April next. The charges assumed in earlier years including the devolution of 50 per cent. of the Jute Duty, and the subventions to the N.W.F.P., Sind and Orissa, amount to more than as much again."

* * * *

Later on, the same authority observes:

*" Have we in the disappointment of the year 1936-37 any reason for doubting the soundness of the conclusions of the Niemeyer Report in regard to the ability of the Centre to bear the cost of the successive stages by which the new Constitution is being introduced? A year ago I prophesised that with the help of a Revenue Fund of Rs. 2 crores, we could see our way through 1937-38, and that thereafter the normal growth of revenue would provide step by step for the liabilities which would come upon us from year to year. Our Reserve Fund has turned out to be somewhat less than we expected, and Revenue has shown a distinct falling off. Contrary to our hopes, therefore, we are between Rs. 1¾ crores short of a balance in 1937-38; and unless we assume a growth of revenue during the year greater than we have any right on past experience to expect, this should connote a deficit in 1938-39 too of something like the same amount. Are our calculations then all wrong and, are we pursuing a chimaera in judging that we can finance the new Constitution? I do not think so.

* * * *

On the whole I do not think that I shall be indulging in unjustifiable optimism if I say, as a result of considering the various factors at work, that there is no reason why the Niemeyer prognostications should not be realised in the long run, and that even in the nearer future his programme can be fulfilled with the help of no more than a very

*Vide. Budget Speech of the Finance Member, 1937-38, Para. 25.

modest addition to our resources, which I should estimate to be roughly from Rs. 1½ to Rs. 1¾ crores by which we are short of a balance this year. Of course, I am always pre-supposing the absence of internal disorder or external strife. How are we to find this extra amount?"

Considering only British India, then, the revenue position under the new Constitution is satisfactory neither to the Provinces, nor to the Centre. The former are crippled by want of funds and deprived, at the very start, of any hope to develop any of their available resources which may have been kept undeveloped all this while; or undertake any projects of social reconstruction or economic betterment of their people which may be long overdue.* The latter, already sunk to the neck by the intolerable burdens of unproductive expenditure, are unable to say whether, in spite of reserving all productive and elastic resources for themselves, they would really be able to make both ends meet in the new regime. In the passages cited above from the Budget speech, no account is taken of the very probable increase in Federal expenditure simply because of the institution of the Federation. This may amount, on the existing scale of such expenditure, from Rs. ¾ crore to 1½ crores per annum. But of this we shall treat elsewhere.

Federated States and Federal Revenues

Let us now consider the financial position, as outlined in the Constitution Act, from the point of view of the States intending to federate. The provisions of the Constitution introduce certain novel features, or make new arrangements, which need to be carefully studied by every intending member of the Federation.

*See Chapter VII Provincial Autonomy (2nd Edition) pp. 309-363.

Broadly speaking, there is a discrimination in favour of the Provinces,

(i) In regard to the subventions from Federal Revenues to what are called Deficit Provinces, *viz.*, Sind, Orissa, Assam, North-West Frontier Province, Bihar, and Bengal, aggregating over Rs. 4.5 crores.

(ii) In regard to the remission of debts due from them, included, of course, in the foregoing; but, nevertheless, in the manner of this concession, as well as in its extent, it is a material point worth noting by itself. The States in debt or deficit will get no such consideration.

(iii) In the distribution of certain resources, like the taxes on jute export or income, etc. The Provinces will obtain, when the scheme recommended by Sir Otto Niemeyer matures, an advantage in which the States will not participate to the same extent as the Provinces. Nor will relief in regard to Succession Duties, Stamp Duties, Terminal taxes on goods and passengers by rail or air, under Section 137, help the States. They will only make themselves liable to the surcharges for Federal purposes under these heads in the bargain, even if we discount altogether the undesirable re-action of introducing some of these taxes in States where they do not exist at all. The experience of the Australian Commonwealth, in regard to the distribution of the surplus by the Commonwealth among the member States, is very discouraging; and there is every reason to fear it may be repeated in India.

(iv) Some additional liabilities are imposed upon the Federated States, which the latter are not in law or ethics bound to assume; and which, once assumed, will have to be maintained by contributions from the States as also from the

Provinces, the benefit, however, not being shared equally.

(v) A new viewpoint is adopted of the liabilities on the Federal Revenues, which would make the gross obligations of the Federation upon the new members thereof, *i.e.*, the States, much more heavy and considerable than appear at first sight.

Altered Angle of Vision

Take the last first. The definition of Federal Revenues, as given in Section 136, runs:—

> " Subject to the following provisions of this Chapter with respect to the assignment of the whole or part of the net proceeds of certain taxes and duties to Provinces and Federated States, and subject to the provisions of this Act with respect to the Federal Railway Authority, the expression " Revenues of the Federation " includes all revenues and public monies raised or received by the Federation, and the expression " Revenues of the Province " includes all revenues and public monies raised or received by a Province."

It is noteworthy that:

(a) There is no mention in this definition, of the revenues of a Federated State, or even of Federated States collectively. It is difficult to imagine the purpose behind this omission, unless it be that, while for the purpose of charging the Provinces with all the liabilities of the Federation only those resources are to be required, or brought into operation, which are or can be included in the above definition, wide as it is,—for the corresponding purpose in regard to the States no limit is imposed by law.

(b) The omission cannot but be regarded as significant. Perhaps it is also intentional. For the States have, in fact, been mentioned in the earlier part of the section, where it speaks of a

> future distribution of proceeds of certain taxation among the States as well as the Provinces; and they have been quite clearly omitted in the portion of the section giving the actual definition of Federal and Provincial revenues.

The definition of Federal Revenues is, it must be admitted, wide enough, in all conscience. It will include both the ordinary, recurrent revenue,—in the shape of proceeds of taxes, duties, rates and fares on transport services, postage dues, fees for other services rendered by the State;—as also monies "raised or received" by way of Loans, Bonds, Deposits, Treasury Bills, or any other form of raising the wind (*e.g.*, Contributions ordered from units). The inclusion of such non-recurrent forms of receipt under the ordinary revenues is open to the most serious objection, on constitutional as well as financial grounds. In the first place, it confounds in one and the same category two essentially different classes of public resources,—tax-yield, and proceeds of borrowing or the like. By this confusion into one category of two different categories, efficiency in financial administration will be gravely jeopardised.* This, in its turn, would endanger India's public credit. For, once the administering authority is freed from the obligation to observe the generic distinction between current, normal revenues derived from taxation, etc., and the non-recurrent resources derived from public borrowing or windfalls, there will be inevitable and unconscious laxity, which cannot but militate against the continued correctness, economy, and efficiency of financial administration, and therefore of the national credit.

*Cp. Section 33 (2) for an obvious inconsistency with this Section 136.

This apprehension is strengthened by the provisions of Section 150, defining the charges on the Federal Purse. As this subject, however, is discussed at some length in the volume on **Provincial Autonomy,** we need not repeat those arguments here.

Under the several provisions of the Constitution Act, the States would have to contribute to the Federal Purse, directly or indirectly, in a variety of ways. Let us enumerate the sections of the Act which affect the States in this behalf.

The Federation will raise its revenues from:

(a) Ordinary taxation, **to which the States will be expected to contribute in normal times:**

(i) Customs Duties (Items No. 19 and 44 of the Federal Subjects).

(ii) Export Duties (Items No. 19 and 44 of the Federal Subjects).

(iii) Excise Duties on commodities other than alcohol, opium, Indian hemp, narcotic and non-narcotic drugs, whether intended for human consumption or for use in medicinal and toilette preparations (Item No. 45).

(iv) Salt (Item No. 47).

(v) Corporation Tax (Item No. 46) after 10 years.

(b) Ordinary Taxation **to which the States will NOT be expected to contribute in normal times.**

(vi) Taxes on Income, other than agricultural (Item 54) and surcharge on Income Tax.*

(vii) Property Taxes, *i.e.,* Taxes on capital value of individual's assets, or of companies, (other than agricultural land) (Item 55).

---

*Cp. Section 137 (3).

(c) Extraordinary revenue, **to which the States will be expected to contribute in times of financial stringency,** which is chronic in all democracies, more particularly in Federations, and still more particularly in India, *viz.*,

(viii) Surcharges on Income-Tax.*

(d) Extraordinary sources of revenue **to which States will not be expected to contribute even in times of financial stringency.**

(ix) Surcharges on Succession Duties (Item No. 56) Section 137.

(x) Surcharges on Terminal Taxes on goods or passengers carried by rail or air, and on taxes on railway freights and fares.

(xi) Surcharges on Stamp Duties in respect of Bills of Exchange, Cheques, Promissory Notes, Bills of Lading, Letters of Credit, Policies of Insurance, Proxies and Receipts; (Item No. 57, Section 137).

(e) Sources of revenue not derived from taxation, to which the States, or their people, have to contribute, directly or indirectly, *viz.*:—

(xii) Fees in respect of matters included in the Federal List.

(xiii) Profits (if any) on the working of the Postal services, including Postal Savings Banks.

(xiv) Profits (if any) on the operation of Federal Railways.

(xv) Profits (if any) from Mint and Currency operations.

(xvi) Profits (if any) from any other Federal enterprise; *e.g.*, Reserve Bank.

(xvii) Direct contributions to Paramount Power, from Federated or non-Federated States, under Treaties, etc.

---

*cp. Section 138 (3).

In addition to the taxes and sources of revenue thus listed under Section 104:—

> " (1) The Governor-General may by public notification empower either the Federal Legislature or a Provincial Legislature to enact a law with respect to any matter not enumerated in any of the Lists in the Seventh Schedule to this Act, including a law imposing a tax not mentioned in any such List, and the executive authority of the Federation or of the Province, as the case may be, shall extend to the administration of any law so made, unless the Governor-General otherwise directs.
>
> (2) In the discharge of his functions under this section the Governor-General shall act in his discretion."*

Taken in the terms in which it is couched, this extra-Schedule authority for taxation by the Federal (or Provincial) Government may involve the Federated States in heavy burdens. This is the more so, as the Governor-General is entitled, under this Section, *to act in his discretion, i.e.*, without consulting his Federal Ministers, if he so think proper. If the States have expressly kept themselves out of this, they may be a little better protected; but it is exceedingly doubtful if they would be allowed to keep out of this. The entire scheme of Federal Finance, as evidenced by the chapters and sections of the Act dealing with that branch of the administration, seems to contemplate uniform burdens, from which no federated unit will be allowed to claim exemption, unless the same has been expressly and legally provided for.

---

*It is not absolutely clear: but it seems likely that the States not being on the Sea-coast, or not having ports of their own, might be forced to contribute even to the Provincial Purse, by such duties as those levied by the Port authorities at Bomba or Calcutta on passengers and their luggage. Even such items of tax tion as, for instance, a duty on raw cot on grown in the Bombay Presid cy, or exported through the ports of tha Province, may have to be bor by the States affected. There is no pr vision in the constitution to pr ent such imposts by Provinces. Section 297 will not avail, since it y applies to provincial attempts to res rict movements of goods, or to ttempts at discriminatory treatment as bet een members of a common Federation. Nor will States be exempt from contributing indirectly to any new industry conducted as Government monopoly from which handsome profits may be derived.

All taxes, forming the normal or abnormal sources of Federal revenue, will be imposed and collected by the Federal Government; and some of even those which are not normally federal revenue. The States may contract themselves out by the special provision in the sections concerned, *e.g.*, (Sections 138 and 139); or by the operation of an agreement under Section 125, in consideration of paying a lump sum in respect of such tax receipts collectable in their jurisdiction, and payable to the Federal Government. But, until they do so, they will be liable to a most vexatious exercise of Federal authority within their jurisdiction, and so impair their internal autonomy which no State can sincerely welcome.

Apart, however, from the political aspect of these provisions, the financial aspect proper is disquieting enough, to the States as much as to British India. The Federal Government will keep for itself exclusively Customs, including Export Duties, Imperial Excises, Salt, Corporation Tax, and Income Tax,—a stated proportion,—Taxes on the capital value of non-agricultural assets of individuals or companies, and a surcharge, during financial emergencies, on Income Tax. This may involve many States, who to-day levy Customs or Excise Duties of their own, into surrendering those sources of their revenue to the Federation. The consideration for this surrender is difficult to perceive. Sections 147 and 149 do, indeed, provide for certain refunds or remissions of State dues, or commuted payments for the surrender of "privileges and immunities." But the language of those sections is anything but expressive; and their working would avoid complication and misunderstanding—only by a miracle.

Refunds to States Customs

There are several considerations of constitutional law or usage worth remembering in these two Sections 147 and 149. The set-off, etc., is allowed in consideration of the remission of cash contributions payable by the Federating States in respect of paramountcy payments, or other dues from the States to Suzerain. Apart from the remission of such payment, the term "**privilege or immunity**" is singularly inept, if it is to apply to such inherent rights of local sovereignty as the Maritime and even inland Customs duties levied by the States, or the issue of their own currency, metallic or paper. Where such rights have been surrendered by specific agreement, the States cannot, of course, at this time, raise afresh these matters as immunities, rights, or privileges, for the sacrifice of which in federating, they ought to be compensated in some form, *e.g.*, by remission of cash contributions due from them. But, where these are ancient and still surviving rights of local sovereignty, and where they have been exercised as such from time immemorial, it seems a violent departure from existing practice to treat them as on a par with the rights and privileges or immunities enumerated in Section 147 (6).

The Government of India have managed, by a long series of treaties with the inland States, to abolish, over the greater portion of the land, internal Customs Duties, which in effect amounted to Transit Duties. Now, on the eve of the Federation, their threat to those Maritime States, who, having their own sea-ports, are entitled to and do levy their own Customs duties, either on the British Tariff Schedule, or, in rare cases, at their own rates, to re-introduce against them these obsolete transit duties in the form of a Customs cordon is a frank violation of the spirit if not the letter of the treaties still subsisting. Their offer to compensate individual States by a cash subsidy for the sacrifice of this their ancient right is itself an admission that the pressure they exert on the States concerned to join the Federation and sacrifice this revenue needs some substantial justification, or some presentable camouflage. Even if the States do not find this offer sufficient bribe to surrender their ancient right, they are not all in a position successfully and profitably to defy the Government of India. But that does not make the case of the British Government of India any more just or reasonable; and if the States concerned do eventually surrender, it will be no proof that they admit themselves to have been in the wrong.*

It must be admitted, of course, that the demand of the Maritime States to keep the whole of the Customs revenue collected at their ports for themselves is not absolutely just. Even when there is no suspicion of unfair or illegal practices to swell the State's revenue from this source, a good proportion of this revenue, it must be admitted, is derived from people other than those of the State concerned. On the former, this impost is a burden, which, in justice as well as reason, ought to go to the common purse,—that of the Federal Government of India. But, essentially sound and unassailable as this theoretic position is, it is nevertheless impossible to apply it rigorously in India without causing greater injustice. The Indian Federation is not the ideal union of all equal and autonomous communities. There is neither free consent nor equal benefit

*cp. however Articles XIV and XV of the Instrument of Instructions to the Governor-General.

expected of this association. Besides, Treaties, however obsolete, have a sanctity, which the British Government of India at least ought to be the last to question, even indirectly,—seeing how adamantine they have shown themselves in protecting and safeguarding the much less sacred rights of the Public Servants and British capitalists in this country. Finally, the States so situated can claim this particular source of their ancient revenue as being no more than a proper utilisation of a gift of nature to them. In the case of many a British Indian port, its present importance is due to acts of man rather than gifts of nature, *e.g.*, the layout and termination of railway lines. These have succeeded in taking away a great portion of the trade the States ports formerly enjoyed. It is only recently that they have begun to counteract in some slight measure the effect of these manmade attractions to trade. The claim of the States, therefore, to retain for themselves the whole of the Customs duties collected at their ports, is impossible effectively to resist on grounds of international advice, or even of National economics, let alone political justice or sanctity of treaties.

A general measure, like the present Act, will scarcely be a suitable means to abrogate those rights, even if the acceding States interested in such rights themselves waive them, and agree to accept some *Quid pro Quo* for such waiver. Room is left, no doubt, in the concluding lines of Section 147 (6), which would safeguard such rights of the States, and yet permit them to be compensated for the whole or partial surrender of such rights on entry into the Federation. But satisfactory arrangement under such clumsy, complicated provisions is extremely difficult to make; and that is why the greatest difficulty is being even now experienced in respect of the Customs rights of the "Maritime States."

States and Excise

Similarly, also, the field for Federal Excise was deemed to be considerably restricted, both by the Percy Committee, and in the Memorandum of the Government of India. The recent introduction of a countervailing excise on steel, sugar, etc., opens up infinite possibilites of such indirect taxation of State subjects for Federal purposes. The States will not be able to claim exemption from such Federal Excises on industrial output in their own territories, either under Section 147, or under Section 155. Even the industries conducted as collective State enterprise in any State may not, in all likelihood, escape Federal Taxation by way of surcharge on the Income Taxes, Corporation Tax (when it becomes applicable to the States), or Excise, should the particular production be liable to Federal Excise.

The revenue position, then, of the Federation as well as of the units,—whether States or Provinces,—is anything but satisfactory, as revealed in the Constitution. Existing resources are either inadequate for the purpose of everybody concerned; or are possible to replenish at a normal and economic cost, which no one who has the welfare of the Indian people at heart can contemplate without a shudder.

II—FEDERAL EXPENDITURE

Let us now turn to the expenditure side of the Federal Finance. The definition of Public Expenditure, as given by Section 150, has already been commented upon in the volume on **Provincial Autonomy,** and so, need not be repeated here.

The Constitutional provisions in respect of Expenditure are to be found, among others, in the following sections:—

Section 11—excluding certain Departments of State, *e.g.*, Defence, External Affairs, Ecclesiastical Affairs, and Tribal areas. Expenditure in regard to these is outside the control of the Legislature, though the Instructions of the Governor-General require him to keep his Ministers in touch with the expenditure on Defence by holding joint consultations between his Counsellors in the Excluded Departments and Ministers. Various other sections, dealing with these departments, including salaries, pensions, etc., of the officers and staff under the same are made expressly charged on the Revenue of the Federation, and as such, non-votable by the Federal Legislature, and so non-controllable.

Section 12 (1) (b)—imposing a Special Responsibility on the Governor-General to safeguard the financial stability and credit of the Federal Government. Under this he can arrogate to himself practically dictatorial power, over Federal finances.

Sections 33-36—prescribing the financial procedure in regard to expenditure of the Federal Government. Under these, certain items of expenditure cannot be voted upon by the Federal Legislature; and authorise expenditure upto a certain extent even on those departments in which the Legislature is entitled to vote the grants. The device of Supplementary Estimates is also to be found in these sections, tending to weaken still further the control of the Federal Legislature upon the expenditure of the State in India.

Section 150—defining Federal Expenditure and its purposes.

Sections 200-230 and Sections 240-253. These relate to the Courts, their establishments and expenditure by way of salaries, pensions, allowances of Judges, pensions, gratuities, decrees and awards against the Government or any official of the same. Other administrative expenditure in connection with the Courts of Justice in India, as also in regard to other services to which appointments are made by the Secretary of State or the Governor-General in his discretion, are also placed outside the control of the Legislative Vote.

Liability in respect of (i) the Public Debt, and other obligations of the Federal Government, including

(ii) payments, to the representative of the Crown in its relations with the Indian States,—Section 285-7;

(iii) contributions to the States under the terms of Sections 147-149,

(iv) subventions to the Provinces under the terms of Sections 137-142,

are also outside the vote of the Federal Legislature. No possible relief is to be thought of under any of these non-productive heads of public expenditure.*

Scale of Federal Expenditure

The financial aspect of these provisions may be translated into figures as follows:—

Items which are to-day non-voted, and which will be "charged upon the revenues" of the Federation under the new Constitution, according to the Budget estimates of 1937-38 of the Government of India:

	(In lakhs of Rs.)
Staff, Household and Allowances of Governor-General	15.54
Public Service Commission	4.95

*The distribution of the proceeds of certain taxes, duties, etc., e.g., those under section 137 or 139 levied by the Federal Government on account of federated units; or the refund of a share of income tax (Section 138) or of the Jute Export Duty (140), are not included in the above as these are not Federal Expenditure proper.

Ecclesiastical Department ..	..	27.82
Tribal Areas ..	..	192.05
External Affairs ..	..	52.24
Baluchistan ..	..	64.94
	Total ..	357.54
Add: Payments to Representative of the Crown		105.55
Interest on Debt (nonvoted amount)	..	1323.65
Defence Expenditure (net) ..	..	4462.00
Pensions ..	..	286.00
Grants in aid to Provinces ..	..	316.00
	Total ..	6850.74

This is out of a total expenditure of about 80 crores or 86% roughly of the total. It does not, of course, tell the whole tale, since it takes no note of that portion of the interest, etc., payment, for which the Federal Government would be responsible, and which would be charged on the Federal Revenues, but is supposed to be received from the Railways, Post Office, Provincial Governments, etc. Nor does it include such Pensions as those on account of Civil Administration Charges. The grants to the States under Sections 147-149, if the Federation is achieved as planned, have been estimated to add another crore to this class of expenditure; while the expenses of the Federal Court, the Advocate-General, the Counsellors, Financial Adviser and their staff, would likewise add considerable amounts to such non-votable expenditure.

Defence Expenditure

There is every reason to fear a steady expansion in these items. Thus the charges of Defence must grow inevitably in the near future,* even after allow-

*The debate in the Indian Legislative Assembly, on September 5, 1937, on a non-official resolution to reduce defence expenditure, brought forth a clear warning from the Army Secretary that the expenditure may very soon have to be increased.

ance has been made for the tardy and scanty refund made to India by the British War Office towards the cost of the disproportionately heavy army maintained by India on British Imperialist account; and even after allowance has been made for the relief due to the separation of Burma, who would now provide for her own defence. The purpose, officially recognised, of maintaining such a heavy Defence provision, is said to be to protect India against aggression from without, and, secondly, against disorder or anarchy from within. The natural defences of India, and the characteristics or equipment of her immediate neighbours, are scarcely taken into account in framing and maintaining this expenditure, thanks mainly to the demands of British Imperialist ambitions. Not only is there the inevitable tendency for increasing costs in this department free from the salutary control of the Legislature, because of constant innovations and advances in the art and equipment for warfare; but the demands of British Imperialist diplomacy involve India in an incessantly shifting morass of international relations, in which she must maintain an utterly disproportionate military preparedness. Were this of any material benefit to India directly, there might be something to be said for keeping out the Defence Budget of the Legislative vote. As it is, the States and Provinces will alike feel it an unmitigated burden, unrelieved by any counter gains to the parties who shoulder it. For the States, the burden is all the more indefensible, some of them at least maintain their own Defence forces, however obsolete their equipment, and however inefficient their direction. Notwithstanding Treaty obligations for the States' Defence, these additional burdens will have to be shouldered by the States as the price of the privilege to join the Federation.

Debt Charges

As for the expenditure on account of the so-called Public Debt of India, the legal, constitutional position has been examined in detail by a Select Committee of the Indian National Congress in 1931, to whose Report attention may well be directed in this connection. The only remark we need add, from this standpoint, is that in the years that have followed, the legal, or moral, or even economic justification has in no way improved.

Confining our attention only to the financial aspect, we find the provision for reductions of the existing debt, or its avoidance in the future, is dangerously low in the present Budget. Material developments, or improvements in the Social Services in the country, have been deferred so long, that all possible haste will have to be made by the Federal Government to part with a respectable proportion of such items of revenue, as, though levied and collected by the Federal Government, are intended for distribution, wholly or partially, among the units composing the Federation. Almost every Province has an immense leeway to make up in education and public health, industrial development and agrarian reconstruction. And all that would need money, even after the Congress limit of official salaries has been enforced all round. True economy, for the benefit of the people, while limiting the maximum salaries, must guarantee a living wage to the lowest grade of public servants. If the Congress thus re-grades salaries upward as well as downward, it may be doubted if any very great saving will be made by such regrading. The States are notoriously backward in what might be called the moral and material progress of the people under their charge. If, in spite of such considerations, they still join the Federation, and cripple still further their financial resources,—none too strong,—they will be jeopardising, not only their own local Sovereignty, but also their chances of material progress within their jurisdiction,—which alone could justify their continued existence as independent units, such as they are:

Non-Voted Expenditure

Section 33 classifies among "the expenditure charged upon the revenues of Federation", and, therefore, non-votable by the Federal Legislature:

(i) Salaries and Expenses of the Governor-General and his office;

(ii) Debt, Sinking Fund, Redemption, and Loans charges or service of the Debt;

(iii) Salaries and allowances of Ministers, Counsellors, Financial Adviser, Advocate-General, Chief Commissioners, and staff of the Financial Adviser;

(iv) Salaries, Allowances and Pensions of Federal Court Judges, and Pensions of other High Court Judges;

(v) Expenditure in connection with Defence, Foreign Affairs, Ecclesiastical Affairs, Tribal areas and other special responsibilities of the Governor-General;

(vi) Grants or the payments to the States;

(vii) Grants for purpose of the administration of excluded areas;

(viii) Judgment decrees or other awards of courts;

(ix) any other expenditure required by this or any act of the Federal Legislature to be so charged.

All this, put together, may amount to more than 4|5ths of the total recurring revenues of the Federation.*

The Legislature would have no right to vote on any and all of those items.†

Authenticated Schedule of Expenditure

The procedure relating to an authenticated schedule of expenditure, as defined in Section 35, is quite capable of vesting absolute and overriding power in the Governor-General in such matters of finance. The possibility of submitting Supplementary Estimates, and an authenticated schedule of the same, as contemplated in Section 36, only adds to this absolutism. If the terms of these Sections were carefully scrutinised, it would seem that, under the new dispensation, India would have little more than a shadow of financial autonomy.

To meet these extraordinary obligations being imposed upon the Members of the Federation,—States and Provinces included,—resources are proposed to be added to the Federal fisc which have hitherto not been part of the all-India sources of revenue. The Federated States are not bound, in ethics or under treaty obligations, to shoulder any portion of the pre-Federation Debt. Nor need they assume the corresponding Pensions charges of the Government of India, which the present Constitution seeks to impose upon them. If

*See ante p. 434. Appendix II of the Financial Secretary's Memorandum gives the following distribution (1937-38):—

Voted:	Rs.	90.12 crores
Non-Voted	„	106.88 „
Total	„	197.00 „

But this includes the Gross Charges of the Railways and Postal Services which amount to 80 crores, and which, under the new Act, will, so far as Railways are concerned, be outside the Legislative control definitely.

†cp., Section 34 (1).

the States accept without reserve that item in the Federal List of subjects, as given in Schedule VII to the Government of India Act, 1935, they would make themselves liable for burdens against which they receive no benefits whatsoever. This debt was never incurred for the benefit of any of the States, nor with their consent. A considerable portion of it was even used to aid in their further subjugation, where absolute annexation was not adopted.

Financial Equilibrium before Federation

The show that is being made of the Central Budget balancing before any of the States consent to Federate will not deceive anybody, since

(1) the presence of a continued deficit on account of the Railways.*

(2) the shrinkage in the important item of the Customs Revenue;

(3) the addition of still more liabilities in respect of the grants to be made to certain of the Provinces, aggregating some 4½ crores of Rupees

---

*In the Budget for 1937-38, the Railways are estimated to show a small net surplus; but the main causes which made for the long continued deficit in this department are even now not ended; and so one is entitled to assume, as Sir Otto Niemeyer throughout his Report apprehended, this to be a very doubtful source of surplus revenue. The Experts' Railway Enquiry Committee of 1937 have thrown a cold douche on any hope of obtaining aid from this source hereafter. The accumulated deficit on Railways account between 1930 and 1937, aggregating some 62 odd crores, has been written off. This means that to that extent the burden of debt on the general tax-payer has been increased. Any expectation of even a future contingent relief to the general revenues when the Railway again made a surplus, is finally negatived.

In their own interests, it would be best for the States intending to federate, to suggest and insist that before they accede, the Federal Budget be split up into two,—say, for a period of 20 years at the most.—one containing all the items which do not concern the Federated States, because these represent charges incurred before the States became part of the Federation; and because in respect of these they had received no benefit; and the other containing all items of really common concern. The States, we need hardly add, would be well advised to restrict federal obligations only to the latter. The suggestion may be said to be impracticable but there is good precedent for it in the Act itself. (e.g., Section 138).

per annum from the commencement of the new regime;

(4) the loss, also, in respect of the disappearance of the Central Revenues derived from Burma, estimated at 2.38 crores of net reduction of revenue;

(5) the additional charges in respect of the new Constitution itself, about 1 crore per annum;

(6) the remission of contribution from the States, and the refund of some portion of revenues to certain States in respect of ceded districts, etc., another ½ crore or more, and

(7) the dangerously low provision in respect of the reduction of avoidance of debt,

make a gap of some 12 crores per annum, which makes it impossible for the Central, or Federal Budget really to balance, even with a very much reduced provision for reduction or avoidance of Debt in the near future.*

Financial jugglery might make two sides seemingly equal; but in reality there is no evidence of such equilibrium being possible when the Federation is established; much less would it be maintained for long thereafter.

Under such circumstances, the Government of India's present Budget cannot be assumed to be balancing,—whatever might be said of the Provincial finances being placed on an even keel, especially after the Niemeyer Report.†

*Economics on account of the Debt charges due to the conversion of the higher interest bearing Debt into a lower interest bearing obligation has made for some immediate saving, which, however, in the long run would mean no real relief to the Indian tax-payer, since the conversion terms are far too liberal.

†The Conference of the Provincial Financial Ministers, in the 1st week of June 1937, in Bombay, was, however, unanimous in bewailing the financial lot of the Provinces, under the new dispensation. It is more than doubtful if any of the grandiose schemes for provincial developments of the new ministries in the Provinces would anywhere be possible to accomplish, simply for lack of funds, under the prevailing canons of national economy.

III—BORROWING POWERS OF THE FEDERATION

The borrowing powers of the Federation are regulated by Chapter II of Part VII of the Act of 1935. Under Section 161, the powers of the Secretary of State to borrow in England on the security of the revenues of India are abolished,—except in so far as any such borrowing is necessitated during the transition period pending the establishment of the Federation. These powers are to be exercised, when the Federation has been proclaimd, by the Federal Government under Section 162:—

> "162. Subject to the provisions of Part XIII of this Act with respect to borrowing in sterling, the executive authority of the Federation extends to borrowing upon the security of the revenues of the Federation within such limits as may from time to time be fixed by Act of the Federal Legislature and to the giving of guarantees within such limits, if any, as may be so fixed."

The authority of the Federal Legislature in this respect is, however, subject to the overriding powers of the Governor-General, on whom a special responsibility is imposed by Section 12 (1) (b) for the maintenance of the financial stability and the credit of India.* Borrowing, moreover, is an executive act, in which the influence of the Governor-General, and the counsel of his Financial Adviser, would necesarily preponderate, because of the several discretionary and extraordinary powers vested in him by the Constitution. The purpose of borrowing, its terms and conditions of interest, repayment etc., even if prescribed by legislation in any given instance, would be materially influenced by this executive head of the Government. Any Loan which is intended to nationalise large-scale

*Cp. Article X of the Instructions to the Governor-General, (p. 214) who must make it his duty to see that a borrowing or budgetary policy is not followed which would seriously prejudice the credit of India.

productive enterprise, or start it afresh, may quite possibly be vetoed by the Governor-General, particularly if it has a tendency to expropriate capitalist British vested interests.* How far borrowing will help the responsible Federal Government, if and when it comes inot being, in face of the enormous first mortgage created by the Act in respect of the British Imperialist vested interests and the existing Debt of the Government of India,†—to realise its plans for economic development and social reconstruction in the country, is not so much a Constitutional as a Financial question. Accordingly we need not dwell here at length upon it.

We may, however, notice the constitutional difference in treatment, in this matter of borrowing, between the British Provinces and the Indian States. Both are free to raise Loans in the public market, or borrow from the Federal Government.‡ But whereas, under Section 163, the Federal Government have some sort of a control over the Provincial borrowing, not only in regard to those loans which the Federal Government themselves make to the Provinces, but also in regard to loans sought to be raised in open market by a Provincial Government outside India, no such control or supervision is insisted upon as regards borrowing by a Federal State either in the open market, or from the Federal Government. Whereas Section 163 relating to Provincial Governments' borrowing insists upon prior consent of the Federal Government for raising loans outside India; and imposes certain conditions under certain circumstances for borrowing in India, Section 164, relating to

*cp. Section 299.
†cp. Section 157 and Sections 302 to 313.
‡cp. Sections 163 and 164.

borrowing by the Federal States is very liberal in comparison.

> "164. The Federation may, subject to such conditions, if any, as it may think fit to impose, make loans to, or, so long as any limits fixed under the last but one preceding section are not exceeded, give guarantees in respect of loans raised by, any Federated State".

Whether this liberal treatment will help the States is a different question. Many of the States are already considerably indebted to the Government of India,—the aggregate running into over 50 crores. In more than one case that Government has been forced, either to write off particular amounts of the debt, or take very drastic steps to effect recovery. With the possible exception of not more than a dozen leading states, financial administration in these relics of medieval India is by no means conspicuous for its soundness or economy. Occasions for financial waste and extravagance are much more numerous; the possibilities for economy and retrenchment limited; and the mechanism for adequate and efficient check upon spending practically unknown in the States. The Rulers are more parasites than protectors; their Ministers and advisers more skilled in sycophancy than in financial acumen or administrative integrity; and the secret, invisible exploitation, to which the States are subjected by the minious or mandatories of the Paramount powers, so intense, incessant and exacting, that any scope for sound budgeting or healthy finance must be altogether discounted in a vast majority of these ancient haunts of vice and waste. The States, as already noted, have a long leeway to make up in the economic development of their territories. This concession in the matter of borrowing may, therefore, seem, at first sight, to be a substantial inducement to make up for the arrears. In view, however, of the immense burdens of the Federal regime; and in view of the known laxity of financial administration in the States, it is more than doubtful if this provision will aid them in the task before them.

IV—AUDIT

In the Federation, the Provinces, as well as the States, the only guarantee,—if the phrase may rightly be used,—for a sound, economical financial regime under the Constitution is to be found in the provisions regarding the appointment of an Auditor-General for India, as also for the Provinces if so desired. Under Section 166:—

"166—(1) There shall be an Auditor-General of India, who shall be appointed by His Majesty and shall only be removed from office in like manner and on like grounds as a judge of the Federal Court.

(2) The conditions of service of the Auditor-General shall be such as may be prescribed by His Majesty in Council, and he shall not be eligible for further office under the Crown in India after he has ceased to hold his office:

Provided that neither the salary of an Auditor-General nor his rights in respect of leave of absence, pension or age of retirement shall be varied to his disadvantage after his appointment.

(3) The Auditor-General shall perform such duties and exercise such powers in relation to the accounts of the Federation and of the Provinces as may be prescribed by, or by rules made under, an Order of His Majesty in Council, or by any subsequent Act of the Federal Legislature varying or extending such an Order:

Provided that no Bill or amendment for the purpose aforesaid shall be introduced or moved without the previous sanction of the Governor-General in his discretion.

(4) The Salary, allowances and pension payable to or in respect of an Auditor-General shall be charged on the revenues of the Federation, and the salaries, allowances and pensions payable to or in respect of members of his staff shall be paid out of those revenues."

The appointment of the Auditor-General of India by the King may be justified on the ground of securing the completest possible independence for that officer, and an absolute security of tenure, to enable him to do his work fearlessly and efficiently. However sound in intention or in working, this arrangement would necessarily detract from the supreme authority of the Indian Government, and of the Indian Legislature to appreciate the bearings of sound financial administration on the success of the new democracy.

The work of the Auditor-General of India may, however, serve to keep open the eyes of the representatives of the people as regards the financial administration of their country. Under Section 168, he is entitled to give directions to the accounting staff in India as regards the methods and principles of keeping accounts both for the Federation, and for the Provinces wherever so permitted. And though, under Section 169, the Auditor-General reports only to the Governor-General of India as regards the accounts of the Federation,—and not to the Federal Parliament of India directly,—the Governor-General is required, by the same section to submit the same to the Legislature.* Whether the mass of the Legislators will fully understand the mysteries of the accounts laid before them in the Auditor-General's Report, or appreciate and adopt the lessons of financial economy contained therein, remains to be seen.

V—SUMMARY

On a general review of the Constitutional aspect of Federal Finance, it appears that:—

*The same practice is ordained upon the Governor of a Province as regards the accounts of the Province.

(1) Revenue resources are unevenly distributed between the Federation and the units. They are utterly inadequate for the Provinces at any rate to undertake any serious project of economic development or social reform. The system is neither simple nor productive. The new items of revenue contemplated in the Constitution might prove burdensome, and cause complications.

(2) Much of the Expenditure is outside the control of the representatives of the States and Provinces in the Federal Legislature. Almost all the Federal Expenditure is unproductive and burdensome, due mainly to the Imperialist or exploitive fountain-springs of the new Constitution. The charging of some of these burdens upon the new members of the State in India, is open to question on ethical, historical, as well as economic grounds.

(3) Borrowing powers, though liberal in conception, are unlikely to be of any real help in the task of Provincial, State, or National development, or social reconstruction, in view of the rigid mortgage imposed by the Act on account of the existing Debt.

(4) Redistribution of the National wealth, by means of a proper system of taxation, or appropriate lay out of the public expenditure, is all but unthinkable in view of the heaviness and rigidity of the burdens imposed.

(5) Accounting and Audit provisions of the Act may help to induce a degree of soundness and economy in the financial administration,—if those who have the right to review the accounts and benefit by the lessons of the review are able to do so.

STATEMENT OF THE REVENUE OF THE CENTRAL GOVERNMENT.

(In Thousands of Rupees.)

	HEADS OF REVENUE	Budget Estimate 1937-38
	PRINCIPAL HEADS OF REVENUE	
I.	Customs	42,60,50
II.	Central Excise Duties	7,16.00
III.	Corporation Tax	1,44,94
IV.	Taxes on Income other than Corporation Tax	12.85.06
V.	Salt	8.25,00
VI.	Opium	49,52
VII.	Land Revenue	18.53
VIII.	Provincial Excise	21,12
IX.	Stamps	36.05
X.	Forest	14.62
XI.	Registration	91
XII.	Receipts under Motor Vehicles Taxation Acts	2,81
	Total ...	73,75,06
	IRRIGATION, ETC.	
XVII	Works for which Capital accounts are ... kept—Gross Receipts	4,80
	DEDUCT—Working Expenses ..	3,84
	Net Receipts.	96
XVIII.	Works for which no Capital accounts ... are kept	5
	Total ...	1,01

STATEMENT OF THE EXPENDITURE CHARGED TO REVENUE OF THE CENTRAL GOVERNMENT

(In Thousands of Rupees)

	HEADS OF EXPENDITURE	Budget Estimate 1937-38
	DIRECT DEMANDS ON THE REVENUE	
1.	Customs	1,19,12
2.	Central Excise Duties	8,55
3.	Corporation Tax	5,80
4.	Taxes on Income other than Corporation Tax...	69,40
5.	Salt	1,06,72
6.	Opium	25,37
8.	Provincial Excise	4.38
7.	Land Revenue	6,00
9.	Stamps	16,18
10.	Forest	20,88
11.	Registration	9
12.	Charges on account of Motor Vehicles Taxation Acts	2,05
	Total ...	3,83,89
	CAPITAL OUTLAY ON SALT WORKS CHARGED TO REVENUE	
5A.	Capital outlay on Salt Works	36
	REVENUE ACCOUNT OF IRRIGATION, ETC. WORKS	
17.	Interest on Works for which Capital accounts are kept	7,44
18.	Other Revenue Expenditure	3.91
	Total ...	11,35

POSTS AND TELEGRAPHS		
XIX.	Posts and Telegraphs	
	Gross Receipts	11,15,93
	DEDUCT—Working Expenses ...	10,38,95
	Net Receipts.	**76,98**
DEBT SERVICE		
XX.	Interest	71,35
CIVIL ADMINISTRATION		
XXI.	Administration of Justice	1,39
XXII.	Jails and Convict Settlements	2,10
XXIII.	Police	25
XXIV.	Ports and Pilotage	21,27
XXV.	Lighthouses and Lightships	8,55
XXVI.	Education	1,50
XXVII.	Medical	1,85
XXVIII.	Public Health	2,96
XXIX.	Agriculture	2,47
XXX.	Veterinary	5,98
XXXI.	Cooperative Credit	
XXXII.	Industries...	19
XXXIII.	Aviation	1,24
XXXIV.	Broadcasting	5,50
XXXV.	Indian Stores Department	17,75
XXXVI.	Miscellaneous Departments	16,73
	Total ...	**91,73**
CURRENCY AND MINT		
XXXVII.	Currency	66,80
XXXVIII.	Mint	39,69
	Total ...	1,06,49
CIVIL WORKS ETC.		
XXXIX.	Civil Works	34,71
MISCELLANEOUS		
XLII.	Payments from Indian States	69,77
XLIV.	Receipts in aid of superannuation ...	7,49
	Carried Over ...	

CAPITAL ACCOUNT OF IRRIGATION, ETC. WORKS CHARGED TO REVENUE		
19.	Construction of Irrigation, etc., Works Financed from Ordinary Revenues	
POSTS AND TELEGRAPHS REVENUE ACCOUNT		
20.	Posts and Telegraphs Interest on Debt ...	72,75
POSTS AND TELEGRAPHS CAPITAL ACCOUNT CHARGED TO REVENUE		
21.	Capital outlay and Telegraphs	7,05
DEBT SERVICES		
22.	Interest on Debt other Obligations	45,94,10
	DEDUCT—Interest transferred to—	
	Railways	28,17,90
	Irrigation	7,44
	Posts and Telegraphs	78,28
	Other Commercial Departments	6,88
	Provincial Loans Fund	
	Provincial Governments	5,52,57
	Commuted Value of Pensions	23,86
	Total Transfers ...	34,81,88
	Net ...	**11,12,22**
23.	Appropriation for Reduction or Avoidance of Debt	3,00,00
	Total ...	**14,12,22**
CIVIL ADMINISTRATION		
25.	General Administration	1,72,78
26.	Audit	1,01,35
27.	Administration of Justice	7,80
28.	Jails and Convict Settlements	23,10
29.	Police	30,07
30.	Ports and Pilotage	28,70
31.	Lighthouses and Lightships	8,55
32.	Ecclesiastical	27,82
33.	Payments to Crown Representative	1,04,88
34.	Tribal Areas	1,92,05
35.	External Affairs	52,24
36.	Scientific Departments	72,01
	Carried Over ...	

STATEMENT OF THE REVENUE OF THE CENTRAL GOVERNMENT—CONCLD.

(In Thousands of Rupees.)

HEADS OF REVENUE	Budget Estimate 1937-38
Brought Forward	
XLV. Stationery and Printing	25,84
XLVI. Miscellaneous	38,91
Total ...	1,41,51
DEFENCE SERVICES	
XLVII. Defence Receipts —Effective ...	4,80,79
XLVIII. Non-Effective	41,81
Total ...	5,22,10
CONTRIBUTIONS AND MISCELLANEOUS ADJUSTMENTS BETWEEN CENTRAL AND PROVINCIAL GOVERNMENT	
L. Miscellaneous Adjustments between Central and Provincial Governments	
EXTRAORDINARY ITEM	
LI. Extraordinary Receipts	3,23,11
LII. Transfers from Revenue Reserve Fund	1,84,09
Total ...	5,07,20
RAILWAY REVENUES AS PER RAILWAY BUDGET	30,13,74

STATEMENT OF THE EXPENDITURE CHARGED TO REVENUE OF THE CENTRAL GOVERNMENT—CONT.

(In thousands of Rupees.)

HEADS OF EXPENDITURE	Budgete Estimat 1937-38
Brought Forward	
37. Education	24,11
38 Medical	22,10
39. Public Health	22,00
40. Agriculture	58,28
41. Veterinary	10,61
42. Cooperative Credit	58
43. Industries	9,14
44. Aviation	25,04
45. Broadcasting	15,35
46. Indian Store Department	23,51
47. Miscellaneous Departments	16,82
Total ...	10,42,79
CURRENCY AND MINT	
48. Currency	14,77
49. Mint	19,28
Total ...	34,37
CIVIL WORKS ETC.	
50. Civil Works	2,87,23
MISCELLANEOUS	
54. A Famine Relief	46
55. Superannuation Allowances and Pensions ...	2,79,77
56. Stationery and Printing	41,98
57. Miscellaneous	54,55
Total ...	3,76,76

STATEMENT OF THE REVENUE OF THE CENTRAL GOVERNMENT—CONCLD.

(In Thousands of Rupees.)

HEADS OF REVENUE	Budget Estimate 1937-38
REVENUE TOTAL ...	**1,19,41,88**

STATEMENT OF THE EXPENDITURE CHARGED TO REVENUE OF THE CENTRAL GOVERNMENT—CONT.

(In Thousands of Rupees.)

HEADS OF EXPENDITURE	Budget Estimate 1937-38
MISCELLANEOUS CAPITAL OUTLAY CHARGED TO REVENUE	
55. A Commutation of pensions financed from Oridnary Revenues	6,38
DEFENCE SERVICES	
58. Defence Service—Effective	42,84,27
59. Defence Services—Non-Effective	8,41,90
60. Transfers to Defence Reserve Fund ...	1,42,25
Total ...	**49,83,92**
CONTRIBUTIONS AND MISCELLANEOUS ADJUSTMENT BETWEEN CENTRAL AND PROVINCIAL GOVERNMENTS	
61. Grants-in-aid to Provincial Governments ...	3,14,27
62. Miscellaneous Adjustments Between the Central and Provincial Governments	1,63
Total ...	**3,15,90**
EXTRAORDINARY ITEMS	
63. Extraordinary charges	1,19
64. Transfers to Revenue Reserve Fund ...	
Total ...	**1,19**
RAILWAY EXPENDITURE AS PER RAILWAY BUDGET	29,98,92
TOTAL EXPENDITURE CHARGED TO REVENUE	**1,19,34,71**

CHAPTER XII

THE DEFENCE OF INDIA

The question of India's National Defence has been touched upon in the preceding chapters more than once, *e.g.*, while discussing the powers of the Governor-General, or of the Federal Legislature. But these discussions have been more in the nature of passing references, than as part of a specific and comprehensive examination of the Constitutional provisions in regard to our National Defence.* This chapter is, therefore, devoted to a comprehensive consideration of the Constitutional aspect of the Defence of organisation of India as a nation.

Sections of the Constitution Act (1935) relating to the organisation and provisions for the Defence of the country are scattered throughout the Act of 1935. They

*"It was natural that the authors of the Report, writing in the crisis of the spring of 1918, after mentioning with admiration the services rendered to the common cause by Indian arms, and expressing satisfaction at the increased recognition which was being given to such services, should have contented themselves with noting the urgency and importance of the Army questions which would emerge after peace had been attained. But this does not alter the fact that the constitutional future envisaged by Mr. Montagu's declaration of 20th August, 1917, and the new scheme elaborated in the Report and embodied in the Act of 1919, inherently involved a tremendous question which is not, we think, formulated or indeed referred to in the Report, *viz.*, what, in view of the resolve that British India should advance to the goal of self-government within the Empire, is the nature of the arrangements which must be contemplated and in due course reached for her external defence and her internal security? We feel strongly that it would be a great disservice both to Britain and to India for this question now to be shirked, or for a method of treatment to be adopted which is confined to the search for temporary expedients wrapped up in soothing generalities, which only serve to foment suspicions of the bona fides of British policy on the one hand, and to divert attention from the ultimate and fundamental difficulties which Indian politicians themselves will have to face on the other. The best service we can render in this regard is to set out, plainly and fearlessly, for the consideration both of the British Parliament and of the political leaders of India, the special features of India's military problem which must be provided for before Army administration can be a function of a self-governing India."

Report of the Indian Statutory Commission, Volume I Survey.—Paragraph 112.

have to be correlated to enable the student to see the question in its proper perspective. The principal provisions are:

Section 4, relating to the appointment of the Commander-in-Chief;

Section 11, excluding the Department of Defence from the scope of Ministerial responsibility, and placing it under the exclusive discretion of the Governor-General;

Those parts of Sections 33 and 34, which require expenditure in connection with the Department of Defence to be **charged upon the revenues of the Federation**, and, as such, non-votable by the Federal Legislature;

Section 100, and Items 1 and 2 in the Federal Legislative List in Schedule VII, permitting the Federal Legislature to legislate for the raising of troops in all branches of the Defence organisation and the Naval, Military and Air Force Works;

Sections 232 to 239, concerning the Defence Services, including such matters as the recruitment of troops, appointment or commissioning of officers, their pay, allowances, etc.;

Sections 285 to 287, relating to the obligations of the Crown with reference to the Indian States.

In addition, there are such Sections as 150, defining the purposes on which the revenues of the Federation may be expended,—and which may thus include contribution for the use of Indian Defence Personnel in Britain's Imperialist Wars; Section 145 for certain payments to be made to the Representative of the Crown in its relations with the Indian States; Section

127 for the acquisition of land for Federal purposes including defence, etc.

Constitutional Problems of Indian National Defence

The main Constitutional Problems in regard to the Defence of India may be summed up as follows:—

(i) The purpose for which the Defence Organisation is maintained;

(ii) Civilian Control of the Defence Organisation;

(iii) Indianisation of the personnel in superior ranks;

(iv) Conscription for National Defence;

(v) The problem of relative cost, though that is not, strictly speaking, a purely Constitutional problem. In the Federation of India, however, the problem of sharing the burdens of the Federal subjects equitably among the different members of the Federation,—States as well as Provinces,—will needs be a Constitutional issue.

(vi) The problem, moreover, of building up industries in India, which, directly or indirectly, provide the munitions and equipment for the forces of National Defence, may also wear a constitutional aspect. Especially would that be so, if those Armament or Munitions Industries are established and operated as Federal Enterprise. These may need land, capital, buildings and machinery; which may lead, in emergencies, to commandeering private resources. They may also involve compulsory acquisition of contributory industries. All these would bear intimately on the Constitution.

We would glance at these problems briefly in the pages that follow.

I. Purpose of Defence Organisation

It may be said at the outset that nowhere does the Constitution Act specifically state the exact purpose of maintaining such a huge organisation in the name of the Defence of the Country as the Government of India have been maintaining. Under Section 100, the Federal Legislature is entitled to pass laws regarding

> "His Majesty's naval, military and air forces borne on the Indian establishment, and any other armed force raised in India by the Crown."

Such legislation, when duly enacted by the Federal Legislature, may define the purpose of maintaining such forces. For the moment, however, the Constitution Act of 1935 does not give any indication of any purpose for which the whole vast organisation is maintained. Unless we consider the maintenance of the Defence provision as part of the Sovereign's prerogative, which is not affected by this Act, it would be difficult to find any constitutional authority to maintain this immense organisation at all.*

The generally accepted purpose of maintaining any Department of Defence at all in India may be said to be three-fold:

(1) The Defence of the country against any aggression outside its frontiers.

(2) The maintenance of civil order and the established regime.

(3) The contribution which such provision may permit the Indian Government to make towards the defence of the British Empire as

*This purpose may be gleaned, such as it is, from the various Royal Commissions, etc., which have investigated the problem of organising the Defence of India, its personnel and its cost from time to time, as also from the official pronouncements upon the findings or recommendations of such Commissions, made from time to time, by the highest authority in India or in the British Parliament.

a whole, or towards the cost of Britain's Imperialist wars.*

This third is not expressly stated in so many words, but is nevertheless quite an important ingredient for prescribing the size as well as the equipment of our Defence organisation.

(1) Protection against External Aggression

In the first purpose mentioned above, the whole country, Provinces as well as the States, may be said to be equally interested. The States, however, maintain at their own cost armed forces, of a sort and upto a prescribed strength, themselves. But these forces are regarded as not equal to the exigencies of modern warfare with a first class European or Europeanised power. The Defence provision, therefore, in such States Budgets as maintain it, may be regarded as so much needless expenditure, justified, if at all, on traditional grounds of the Ruler's prestige, rather than any ground of the objective benefit, or military value of such forces. Some of the States, are, by specific engagements with the British Government, entitled to armed protection from the paramount power against

*"External defence, on the other hand, may be viewed in a double aspect; it may be regarded not solely as the concern of India (though India would be the first to suffer, if its frontiers were not adequately guarded), but as affecting the integrity of the whole Empire and as bound up with general Imperial policy." Report of the Indian Statutory Commission, I, Survey p. 106. Para. 126.

See also Para 178, Joint Parliamentary Committee's Report on the Government of India Bill "There have been many occasio which the Government of India have found themselves able t spare conting .. for operations overseas in which considerations of Ind n defence have not been involved; and we may presume that such o asions will recur. There appears to be some misconception in India on this point, which it would be desirable to remove. It is not the case that because a Government can in particular circumstances afford a temporary reduction of this kind in its standing forces, the size of these forces is thereby proved excessive: or, conversely, that if it is not excessive troops cannot be spared for service elsewhere. These standing forces are in the nature of an insurance against perils which may not always be insistent but which nevertheless be provided for."

Further comment on this is superfluous.

aggression from without or disturbance from within. Nevertheless, the Rulers of these States would not listen to any suggestion for doing away with these forces. And even if they wanted to, it is more than doubtful if the British Imperialist Government would suffer them to do so without some *quid pro quo*. Their contribution to the common need of India's defence must, naturally, be affected by these considerations, even if they become part and parcel of the Federal Organisation.

(2) Maintenance of Internal Security

The question as to what are the probable dangers to India as a whole of aggression from her neighbours, against which she must guard, is more a political than a constitutional question. But in this case, also, all parts of the country as a whole are equally interested. British Provinces are alleged to have within them forces of internal disorder, tendencies to anarchy, or conflicts of communities, which are supposed to be kept in check by the presence of military forces, that may be employed in the ultimate resort to quell such disorders. How far this is a real danger, and how far it is magnified by Imperialist reasons by the powers-that-be, is a matter not of direct constitutional importance, and as such need not be discussed here. So far as the States are concerned, almost every one of them is guaranteed a peaceful administration and immunity from aggression from without by the paramount power, *viz.*, the British Government. Hence, on occasions when the internal security of any State is endangered, or the legitimate rights of any Ruler are imperilled, the State or the Ruler concerned may well claim the aid of the strong arm of the British Government, to maintain this position or authority. But for this purpose, the present proportions of India's defence forces cannot but seem excessive.

(3) Contribution to Imperial Defence

As for the third purpose mentioned above, the powers-that-be have never specifically denied the existence of some such ground, which necessitates India maintaining a provision for Defence far in excess of her own immediate requirements. Exactly how much of our Defence organisation and expenditure is really due to reasons or considerations of the Empire Defence is, of course, difficult to say. But the fact may be mentioned that, after years of claiming, and against a very large amount of claims, the British Government have, at last, accepted the award of an Arbitral Tribunal, whereby they would make an annual contribution of about £ 1,500,000 towards the cost of the army, etc., in India. This is sufficient indication that a certain proportion of the expenditure on India's Defence is, undoubtedly, for Imperial reasons.

It has been the contention of Indian authorities,—including in the past several members of the Government of India themselves,—ever since the Roberts Report of 1879,—that India should not be made to bear any portion of the cost, either of the actual hostilities, or of the normal provision needed for Britain's Imperialist wars for the Defence of the Empire. If the Defence organisation and equipment of India were determined and regulated exclusively by considerations of India's own requirements, much of the present cost and strength of the Defence Forces maintained in India would have to be considerably reduced. Several items of the so-called War Office Charges on account of training, transport, pay, etc., of the British troops maintained in India would be discontinued; and even the British garrison forces in India dispensed with.

Because this last purpose plays such an important part, all the constitutional questions relating to the organisation of Defence in India have to be correlated with the corresponding requirements of the United Kingdom. That is one reason why the Departments of Defence as well as External Affairs have been kept completely outside the competence of the Responsible Federal Ministers. Again, the position of the Indian High Command has been so ordained as to function in subordinate co-operation with the British War Office, and the Imperial Defence Organisation. The conventions governing the appointment of the Commander-in-Chief,—who is alternately an officer of the army in India, and then from the British Army,—fairly evidence the necessary co-operation between these two organisations, which contribute jointly to the Defence of the Empire.

II. Civilian Control of the Defence Organisation

The relations, again, of the Commander-in-Chief with the supreme civil authority in India, *viz.*, the Governor-General, are another indication of this ulterior purpose for which such a Defence organisation is maintained in India. The very fact that even in peace time a separate Commander-in-Chief is provided for by the Constitution, in stead of the Governor-General, as representative of the King-Emperor, being the ex-officio Commander-in-Chief, is evidence of the phenomenon.* The Commander-in-Chief is appointed by the King-Emperor by Warrant under the Royal Sign Manual (Section 4). His salary, allowances and conditions of service are such as the King-in-Council directs.† These directions need not provide for any definite subordination of the Commander-in-Chief to the supreme civil authority in India. The historic episode between two strong personalities,—Lords Curzon and Kitchner,—a generation ago, only serves to illustrate a somewhat amorphous position still occupied by the Commander-in-Chief in relation to the Governor-General.

It is worth noting that while under the Government of India Act, 1935, the two offices of the Viceroy and the Governor-General are possible to combine under one and the same officer (cp. Section 3), there is no power to combine the two offices of the Governor-General and the Commander-in-Chief, as is the case in all Dominions. The explanation of this distinction and separation of the two high offices is to be found, not only in the desire to exploit as much as possible the resources of India; but also in order

*Says the Report of the Joint Select Committee of Parliament, para 172, "The White Paper proposes that the Governor-General shall himself direct and control the administration of the Departments of Defence, External Affairs, and Ecclesiastical Affairs; these matters will, therefore, remain outside the Ministerial sphere, and the Governor-General's responsibility with respect to them will be to the Secretary of State and thus ultimately to Parliament."

†cp. Section 232. The Commander-in-Chief is, it is true, not to be a member of the Federal Government as he used to be of the Government of India under the Act of 1919. But that, if anything, would make the position more complicated and likely to lead to want of harmony. It may be added that both section 37 and 39 of the Act of 1919 will remain in force during the transition period before the Federation is established.

The position may be made more definite by the terms of the Warrant of appointment and the Order-in-Council relating to the pay, etc., of the Commander-in-Chief (Section 232) after the Federation of India has been proclaimed and established. But for the present the absolute constitutional supremacy of the civil authority over the military is by no means assured. In the Dominions the Governor-General is ex-officio ever, is outside the vote of the Legislature.

to give special emphasis to the military hold of the British over India. Time and again it has been pointed out, by critics not always unsympathetic to the British dominion in India, that the accompaniment in India of armed force on all solemn occasions, like the Coronation Durbar, with ceremonial which is essentially civil or religious in Britain herself, is a needless and undesirable emphasis on the basis of force in the governance of India. But the military spectacle has never been abandoned, despite the political impropriety of its presence on such occasions of essentially civic ceremony. And because the reliance on military force, in the last analysis, as the ultimate prop of British power in India, is not merely a nightmare of too ardent Nationalist imagination, the Constitution itself provides this prominence to an office and an element, which in England itself is abandoned; and which in the Dominions is merged in the chief executive office.

It is interesting to contrast the constitutional position of the Governor-General under the Act of 1935 with that under the Act of 1919. Says Section 33 of that Act:—

> "Subject to the provisions of this Act and rules made thereunder, the superintendence direction and control of the civil and military government of India is vested in the Governor-General-in-Council, who is required to pay due obedience to all such orders as he may receive from the Secretary of State."

Contrast this language with the provisions of Section 3 of the Act of 1935, or with that of Sections 7, 8, 9, 11, 12, 13 and 14 of the Act of 1935. True, the institution of Provincial Autonomy does require a certain relaxation of the powers of superintendence, direction and control vested under the old Act in the Governor-General. The advent of the Federation, when it happens, would also involve some modification of the existing position. But, making every allowance for these considerations, one fails to understand the necessity of withdrawing from the supreme authority of the Governor-General the Department of Defence, as this contrast suggests.

The Constitutional question in regard to the position of the military arm is not free from ambiguity. In the Dominions, they have, since the last European War, demanded and maintained the independent existence of the local Armies and Navies, with their own independent command. The land forces, were, from the beginning, under the Dominion Ministries; the Naval Forces have since 1911 been more and more under local control. The Dominion problems of providing for local defence, by conscription, etc., have been also solved, so as to vest the complete control and supreme authority in the Dominion Parliaments and in the Dominion Governments, in such matters. In times of War, wherein the whole Empire is engaged, the conflicting requirements of Dominion Autonomy,—Sovereignty,—and the need for co-ordinated action between all the forces of the Empire collectively, would be met by the equally permissible alternative of Dominion Armies and Navies acting independently, or working in concert with the Empire Forces under British command, the Dominion's share in shaping the policy and the strategy being secured by participation in some sort of a War Cabinet.*

*Says Prof. Keith (op. cit. p. 428):—"In the event of any Dominion desiring to use its forces overseas in an Empire War, the legislature of the Dominion can make the amplest provision for their control, and even in

(*Continued on page 462*)

The supreme authority for the Defence of India is, however, the Governor-General, acting in this discretion, and without any right to the Ministers to be at all consulted in such matters.*

The Commander-in-Chief of His Majesty's armed forces in India was a member of the Government of India under all the Constitution Acts relating to the governance of India upto 1935. The Act of 1935 retains the office of the Commander-in-Chief; but his place in the Governor-General's Council would be taken by a Defence Counsellor.

No doubt, the civil authority is held to be ultimately supreme. Perhaps the sad experience of the Mesopotamin Campaign of 1915-16 still reinforces this idea. But, so far as India is concerned, the absolute subordination of the Governor-General, the supreme executive authority in this country, to the Secretary of State for India, and through him to the British Government, leads one necessarily to conjecture that the ultimate authority for the Defence of India, for correlating its command and controlling its

---

(*Continued from page 461*)

the War period of 1914-18 before the Statute of Westminster, the powers of the Dominion Parliaments added to the Army Act availed to remove any possibililty of the lack of legal authority. The Dominion may either in such a case retain control of its own forces, or co-operate more completely by placing them, as during the War, under the British Commander-in-Chief, while sharing through some form of War Cabinet for the Empire with the British Government the supreme control of their employment.'' It may be added that the Statute of Westminster, passed in 1931, has assured Dominion independence in these respects far more effectively than was the case in 1914: though, even now, the question is not free from doubt whether the Dominions can declare War or Peace on their own, apart from, or in opposition to, the British Imperial Government. See Op. Cit. 69 et seq.

*Cp. Section 11.

general strategy, vests, not so much in the Government of India, as in the powers-that-be at Whitehall.*

In this connection, it may be pointed out that there are several Articles in the Instructions to the Governor-General, which particularly emphasise this peculiar constitutional position of the Department of Defence. Says Articles XVII:—

> "And seeing that the Defence of India must to an increasing extent be the concern of the Indian people, it is Our will in especial that Our Governor-General should have regard to this Instruction in his administration of the Department of Defence, (*i.e.*, practice of joint consultation between himself, his Counsellors and his Ministers); and notably that he shall bear in mind the desirability of ascertaining the views of his Ministers when he shall have occasion to consider matters relating to the general policy of appointing Indian Officers to Our Indian Forces, or the employment of Indian Forces on Service outside India."

The final decision on all questions relating to Defence remains, of course, with the Governor-General **in his discretion.** But the practice of joint consultation with the Ministers; and particularly the importance assigned to financial considerations necessarily involve the Ministers,—though they have no legal responsibility for such decisions. How far this may modify the

*The Report of the Statutory Commission, presided over by Sir John Simon, made a curious suggestion (Vol. I para 126) of creating a Dominion Army in India mainly for internal purposes; and advocated a division of responsibility for the Defence of India, which is summarised as foll ws by the Government of India in their despatch on the Commission's ecommendations dated 20th September 1930; "The essence of their prop sal, as we understand it, is a mutual agreement between Great Britain and India that, for the time being, the Defence of India should be regarded as an Imperial concern carried on in co-operation with, but outsid the Civil Administration of, the country. By similar agreement, a fixed total sum would be made available from Indian revenues for defence expenditure, subject to revision at suitable intervals." Needless to add that the Indian authorities threw out the suggestions of the Royal Commission.

viewpoint of the non-responsible militarists in the Federal Cabinet, and make them appreciate the viewpoint of the responsible Indian Ministers, remains to be seen.*

The ascendency, however, of the Commander-in-Chief is secured by the very next Articles of Instructions.

> "Further it is Our will and pleasure that in the administration of the Department of Defence Our Governor-General shall obtain the views of Our Commander-in-Chief in any matter which will affect the discharge of the latter's duties and shall transmit his opinion to Our Secretary of State whenever the Commander-in-Chief may so request on any occasion when Our Governor-General communicates with our Secretary of State upon them."

By this means the Commander-in-Chief can always outmanoeuvre the Federal Government of India, in any instance in which the Imperial British interests are in conflict with the Indian National interests.

III. Indianisation of the Personnel

The problem of nationalising the Defence organisation of India, commonly confused with that of Indianisation of the Defence services, consists not merely in replacing the British personnel by the Indian. That a real and complete self-government for India is not possible without a complete control by the responsible Indian authorities over the country's Defence organisation is admitted on all hands. But many difficulties of a detail or technical character are adduced to stave off the handing over of the supreme control over India's

---

*By Article XIX of the Instructions the Federal Finance Department is to be kept in close touch with the expenditure on defence, which, however, is outside the vote of the Legislature.

National Defence to Indian Ministers responsible to the Indian Federal Legislature. A correct view of these difficulties would be possible if we analyse the problem of nationalising the defence organisation of India in its constituent parts.

Properly viewed, the problem consists of three parts:

(1) Indianisation of command and policy in regard to the constitution and function of the Defence organisation of this country. That is to say, the equipment, use and control of all the armed forces of India should be motived by considerations exclusively of India's own needs and by no other consideration.

(2) replacement of the British officers now commanding practically the entire Defence system of India by Indian officers, subject to the latter being suitably trained, experienced, or efficient for the purpose.

(3) Complete Indianisation of the troops, so that the present element of the British army proper stationed in India, whether as Imperialist garrison or for guaranteeing peace and tranquillity of the country, should be dispensed with.

As regards the first of these, not only should the appointment of all the highest officers, from the Commander-in-Chief downwards, rest with the Indian Government; but the entire High Command of the Army, the Air Force, and the Navy, whatever its personnel, should be made clearly subordinate to the Federal Government of India. The Constitution of 1935 is silent on this subject. But its basic principles seem to imply that this desideratum, as part and parcel of the constitutional progress of India, is not to be immediately achieved. Under the Act of 1935, all appointments to positions of command are in the hands or under the control of the Secretary of State.* As for the routine administration, the Department of Defence is reserved in the sole discretion of the Governor-General. Under Section 14, he is under the authority of the Secretary of State; and so there is no possibility of an Indian national viewpoint being brought to bear upon the day to day affairs of the Department.

The cognate Department of External Affairs must also be brought under the supreme control of the responsible Federal Ministry. For, unless and until the foreign policy and international relations of India are conducted on strictly national considerations of India, the mere control over the Department of Defence will not suffice. All aspects of the policy affecting the defence of a country need to be correlated; and India is no exception to the rule.

As regards (2), the experiment made since 1917-18 of appointing certain officers with the Viceroy's Commission has not proved a success, mainly because of the lower status assigned to such Indian officers. Indian

---

*Cp. Sections 4, 232-234. The Defence Sub-Committee of the Round Table Conference recommended the institution of an Indian Sandhurst (including an Indian Woolwich for naval training, and an Indian Cranwell for airial training) to train Indian officers for all branches of the Defence services. Though an institution of this type at least for training up army officers has been set up, the number of cadets trained and appointed as officers in the Indian army is so small that there seems little hope of all officers in the Indian army being Indians on this side of the present century. As against the reported need of 130 to 160 officers in the Army every year, we barely have still a dozen Indians appointed to the lowest ranks of officers in the Indian army: and every one of the officers so appointed will take at least 20 years before they can rise to be Colonels in the ordinary course of promotion.

officers holding the King's commission, and, therefore, equal in status with the British officers, have been few in number. Even the so-called Eight Units Indianisation Scheme is progressing so slowly, that not before 1946 at the earliest could Indian officers reach the position of command even in a single battalion or regiment. Even when it is achieved, it will fall far short of indianising completely the superior ranks of the Indian Army.* The argument drawn from the difficulties of finding suitable material, adequate training and experience in the officers needed for posts of command have been urged in explanation of the very slow progress of this scheme. The steps taken to remove this difficulty do not indicate any very noticeable enthusiasm on the part of those responsible for this kind of slow trend towards Indianisation in the higher ranks. The Skeen Committee had actually recommended a much faster rate of Indianisation; but the powers-that-be have practicably abandoned the recommendations of that Committee. The New Constitution leaves it utterly vague and indefinite as to when, if ever, positions of command and authority in the Indian Defence Organisation will come into the hands of Indian officers.

As regards (3), argument of cost,—which is far more heavy, proportionately speaking, in regard to British troops stationed in India than for the corresponding Indian troops—has been adduced time and again to prove the impossibility of maintaining such an ele-

---

*While the Military Requirements Committee of 1922 had considered it possible to Indianise completly the officers in the Indian Army in 10 years, the Skeen Committee had considered 28 years sufficient for the purpose But the latest policy of the Indian Government, especially as embodied in the Act 1935, does not hold out any hope of Indianisation even in the rest of this century.

ment in the Defence Organisation of India.* There seems no indication, however, in the present Constitution, which could lead one to hope that, whether for reasons of cost, political sagacity, or constitutional proprietory, this element of British troops and officers will be dispensed with at an early date. The continued maintenance of British Troops in India, taken in conjunction with the principle that the margin of safety needed by the British vested interests in India require a proportion of 1:2 between European and Indian elements, render all suggestions for economy abortive.

The question of establishing industries needed for the equipment of modern Armies, Navies and Air Forces, may similarly be regarded as forming part of the larger issue of national development; and accordingly, we may content ourselves here by simply observing that, in so far as constitutional power is lacking in the Indian authorities to take steps in this direction, any ambitions entertained by nationalist India in this direction are doomed to be disappointed.

IV. Conscription for National Defence in India

The problem of putting forth the maximum effort the country is capable of, in its hour of direst need, is complicated, from a constitutional standpoint, by the advent of the States in the Indian Federation. In all Dominions, the obligation on every ablebodied adult citizen to bear arms in the Defence of the country is undoubted; and the Dominion Legislature has every power to legislate on such a subject. British Imperial-

*According to information supplied in the Indian Legislature, man for man a British soldier is between three and four times as costly to the Indian tax-payer as the Indian soldier. Cp. **Sixty Years of Indian Finance**, Part II, Ch. II.

ism has, however, its own reasons not to encourage such ideals in this country. Without necessarily being a jingoist, one may nevertheless appreciate the need for a proper, economical, and efficient national organisation, equal to any emergency, in this country. But even if, for its own needs, the Imperial Government were ready to concede to India the right to arm every citizen in National Defence, it is doubtful if the States becoming members of the Federation would consent to such powers of legislation over their peoples also being vested in the Federal Legislature. Even as regards the Arms Act, forbidding Indians to bear arms, it may be questioned if the Federal Legislature would be suffered easily to repeal it even if it is competent to pass such legislation. Here also, accordingly, the New Indian Constitution is far less of an instrument of self-government for the people of India than is enjoyed by the Dominions.

CHAPTER XIII

MISCELLANEOUS

There are certain provisions of the Constitution Act of 1935, which it is impossible to classify under any of the conventional divisions of a Constitution. Thus, Chapter III of Part VI of the Act of 1935, containing provisions with respect to discrimination etc., Sections 111 to 121, both inclusive; or Chapter III of Part VII relating to property, contracts, liabilities and suits, Sections 172 to 180; or Part VIII, relating to the Federal Railway Authority, Sections 181 to 199, are impossible to be classified under any of the ordinary heads, under which a national Constitution may be studied. Provisions with regard to the Reserve Bank, which is designed also to play an integral part in the Constitution, are not contained in the Act of 1935. We need not, therefore, discuss that mechanism, which controls a most important key position in the governance of India. We shall briefly outline some of these, partly because they are integral parts of the Indian Constitution, and partly as emphasising certain features in the governance of India, which constitute grave political problems that the future of India will have to face.

I Anti-Discrimination Clauses

Taking first, the Provisions in regard to the so-called Discrimination by legislation or executive action in India against British interests in India, it may be premised that the spirit of the entire chapter is to maintain sacrosanct the vested interests of British capital, and so facilitate the continued exploitation in this country. Any desire that the Indian nationalist may have, however, legitimate it be, to neutralise at least the advantage which generations of connection and association have procured these British vested interests in India, in their competition with the nascent Indian enterprise in the same field, cannot be achieved so long as these interests hold the field, and so long as this Constitution remains unchanged.

These alien interests are established in the most productive branches of industry and commerce; in the most paying grades of the public service. Their toll, therefore, upon the national wealth of India is necessarily higher in proportion. The rôle of a national government in our days in aiding the local industry and enterprise pitted in unfair competition against the foreigners; and in encouraging local talent in all branches of the nation's life, is too well recognised to require any elaborate advocacy in support of it by Nationalist India. In all progressive modern communities, wherever nationalist consciousness has grown, legislation has been increasingly passed in recent years to reserve the corresponding field of economic activity or opportunity to the nationals of one's own country; and executive action has more than kept pace with this aim of the national legislature. India is stirred by their example. She is becoming more and more aware of the opportunities for remedying, in part of least, the impoverishment of the people, due to this connection with the British Imperialism and the Capitalist exploitation resulting therefrom. Had she the power, she would not fail, progressively and intensively, to develop her own industry and enterprise, and so retain in the country for the benefit of her own people the advantages resulting from such development.

The provisions of Chapter III, Part V, are, therefore, intended to make the protection, safeguard and defence of the existing vested interests of British capital and British professional men working in India to be as comprehensive, rigid, universal, and permanent, as possible. It is not a matter to be left to the discretion of the Chief Executive; nor to be entrusted to the administrator of British blood in India. The progress of nationalist sentiment may render it impossible for these authorities, unbacked by statutory sanction, to safeguard adequately these precious interests. And the memory of treatment accorded to India in the height of British power are so strong that a guilty conscience itself has compelled the British Parliament to lay positive prohibition upon the Federal or Provincial authorities to disturb or endanger these interests in any way.

(a) Freedom of Movement for British Nationals

The very first section (111), therefore, provides that British subjects, domiciled in the United Kingdom, shall be exempt from any Federal or Provincial Law, which imposes a restriction on the right of entry of Europeans in India. The same applies if it creates any disability, liability, restriction, or condition in regard to travel, residence, acquisition, holding, or disposal of property, or of public offices, or carrying on any trade or business or profession, by reference to the place of birth, race, descent, language, religion, domicile, residence, of any such British national in India.

It may be noted that the Federal or the Provincial Legislature is not prohibited from passing any law restricting immigration into India of foreigners, or imposing any disability or conditions upon their movement and activities in this country. In so far as such restrictions are imposed against the Germans or the Japanese, the French or the Italians, Indian Legislature would be utterly free to do so. Perhaps the British authorities in India would even secretly welcome them, as leaving the field of competition more completely at their mercy. Even Dominion subjects are not included in the privilege of this section. It simply exempts the European British subjects domiciled in Britain from the operation of any such law being passed. It is permissible to hope that, in the event of reprisals becoming necessary against any of the Dominions, imposing discriminatory treatment against Indians within their jurisdiction, there will be no difficulty for the Federal Government of India to retaliate.

It must be added that the Section makes a show of reason and reciprocity of treatment between the United Kingdom and Federation of India by adding a proviso:

> "Provided that no person shall by virtue of this sub-section be entitled to exemption from any such restriction, condition, liability or disability as aforesaid if and so long as British subjects domiciled in British India are by or under the law of the United Kingdom subject in the United Kingdom to a like restriction, condition, liability, or disability imposed in regard to the same subject matter by reference to the same principle of distinction."

This, however, does not apply to execute discrimination against Indians in Britain, as the Governor-General or the Governors are enjoined by their instructions, and in virtue of specific responsibility laid upon them, to see that no such administrative discrimbination takes place against Britishers in India. Much less can this prevent the private individual discrimination that takes place against Indian students or businessmen in Britain who are anxious to learn British technique in business or industry.

From the operation of this section, quarantine regulations even against Britishers are necessarily excluded. Individual British citizens, also, regarded as undesirables, are excluded from the operation of this section. This is to say, it is permissible, under section 111 (2), for India to pass regulations excluding undesirable individuals, or to deport them, from British India. Even if no law is passed on that behalf, under sub-section 3 of Section 111, it is permissible for the Governor-General or the Governor of a Province, by public notification, to suspend the operation of sub-section (1). He need only certify that, in order to prevent a grave menace to the peace and tranquility of any part of India or of a Province, or, in order to combact crimes of violence in India to overthrow the Government, the operation of sub-section (1) of Section 111, exempting the British European subjects from any Indian Legislation imposing restrictions upon the right of entry or movement within this country, should be suspended. Needless to add, the functions of the chief executive will be exercised in this connection **in his sole discretion** without any reference to the responsible ministers.

(b) Discrimination against Companies

The principle of no discrimination is enunciated generally by Section 112 (1), as regards individuals and companies. Any law, which seeks to discriminate against British subjects of the United Kingdom or Burma, or companies incorporated in the United Kingdom or Burma, before or after the passing of this Act, would be invalid, in so far as it contravenes the provisions of Section 112. What exactly would constitute such a law, is not very clearly defined. Under sub-section 2 of Section 112, however it is laid down that, if the effect of any law is such that British subjects of the United Kingdom or Burma would become liable to greater taxation than that to which they would be liable if domiciled in British India or incorporated under the laws of British India, then that law would be invalid.

So far as Companies are concerned, Section 113 precludes the Federal or Provincial Legislation from any discrimination against companies incorporated in the United Kingdom before or after passing of this Act. Any attempt to introduce such discrimination, indirectly, *e.g.*, by prescribing that directors or shareholders upto a given proportion at least must be natives or residents of India is doomed to failure. For this section categorically lays down that Companies incorporated in the United Kingdom, before or after the passing of this Act, will automatically be deemed to fulfill all such requirements of language, religion, domicile, residence, etc. This means that the Federal or Provincial Legislature cannot pass laws, which would, in effect, debar British subjects of the United Kingdom from carrying on any company, or holding any stock or interest, by requiring that a given proportion of this interest, capital, or control should be held by people born in India, or of Indian descent, or speaking any Indian language, or domiciled in any Indian Province or State.

The principle of reciprocity, of course, is maintained in regard to this legislation, so that no corresponding discrimination could be made by any law of the United Kingdom, in regard to companies incorporated by or under the laws of British India and carrying on business in the United Kingdom. It is one thing, however, to prohibit, by such provisions, the discrimination, and a totally another thing to assure that no discrimination shall, in actual practice, take place, owing to the prejudices or self-interest of the individuals concerned. In India, particularly, the powers that be being sympathetic to individuals or companies of British origin exploiting Indian resources and Indian business conditions, such provisions may succeed in preventing any kind of indirect advantage sought to be given by the Indian Ministers or Legislatures to corresponding enterprise of their own country-men. But, in England, no such guarantees are really forthcoming, despite the provisions of this law. There is the same general *proviso* in regard to reciprocity under this section as under Section 111 (1).

It must also be noted, that the section precludes any discrimination on the grounds mentioned therein. But it does not preclude direct encouragement, which it may be possible by legislation or administrative action to give to the local industry from being so afforded. By the Instrument of Instructions, however, the executive chief in the Provinces as well as the Federation is required to see to it that no such administrative discrimination takes place against British subjects working in India. The sub-section (2) allows the same exemption from or preferential treatment in respect of taxation to British Companies as is given to Indian Companies under any Federal or Provincial

Legislation, conditioned by any of the conditions mentioned in sub-section (1).

As regards companies incorporated in India, British subjects domiciled in the United Kingdom are deemed, under Section 114, automatically, to comply with such requirements of any Federal or Provincial laws, relating to place of birth, race, descent, language, religion, domicile, etc., as may be imposed for serving as members of the governing body of the company, or to be holders of its shares, etc., or to be its officers, servants, and agents. The principle of reciprocity contained in the *proviso* to Section 111 (1) is applied here also.

Practically, also, the provision of Section 113 (2) is repeated under sub-section (2) of Section 114, as regards preferential treatment or exemption from taxation, imposed by Federal or Provincial law.

(c) Discrimination re: Shipping and Air-craft

Provision has been made by Section 115 as regards ships and air-craft plying in Indian waters, or carrying on transport business in India. No ship registered in the United Kingdom can be subjected, under any Federal or Provincial law, to any discriminatory treatment affecting either the ship itself, or the captain, officers, crew, passengers or cargo, in contrast with corresponding ships registered in British India, on a basis of reciprocity with regard to Indian registered ships in the United Kingdom. The same provision applies as regards air-craft in India.

The effect of this prohibitionary legislation is that any attempt at recapturing the coastal or overseas carrying trade of India by ships owned or built in India, or manned by Indians, is doomed to failure. For no encouragement can be given by law to Indian enterprise of this kind against its most formidable competitor,—the British enterprise of the same kind working in India. British enterprise of this kind is not only well established, and has far-reaching business connections in India; it has evolved methods of retaining such business, in the shape of secret rebates, etc. which no new commercial competitor of Indian origin can hope to counteract without some sort of a State protection or encouragement.

(d) Subsidies & Bounties

The same may be said as regards any kind of direct encouragement to be given by Indian Government, Provincial or Federal, in the shape of subsides, etc. For, Section 116 (1) lays down that any company, incorporated in the United Kingdom, and carrying on business in India, shall be eligible for any grant, bounty or subsidy, etc., payable out of the revenues of India or of any Province, for the encouragement of any trade or industry, in the same manner as companies incorporated under British India may be eligible therefor. Neither the key industries nor any other business of national importance may be directly encouraged by means of bounties or subsidies out of India's own resources, which are not automatically extended to the corresponding enterprise of Britishers in India. In so far as India is backward in regard to many a key industry, or essential business; and in so far as in the corresponding industries and business British competition is already well-established, and, so more to be dreaded, no headway can be made by native Indian enterprise, unless an equal benefit is simultaneously extended to the most formidable rival of such Indian enterprise. Protection, or encouragement, of local industry by such direct methods is both more effective and economical, than by the indirect method of protective customs duties. For the latter bear upon the consumers, and so their real incidence is lost sight of; while the full burden of the former is always noticeable. In the past, whenever any Indian industry has demanded fiscal protection, the spokesmen of British interests have emphasised the claims of the consumers to deny or minimise such protection. But they had no such opposition to offer against this provision of direct burden upon the Indian tax-payer, the moment they themselves were made eligible to this benefit,—which, probably, they least need.

It may be added that this provision, however, is confined, by sub-section (2) of Section 116, to British companies, which are engaged in British India already, before any law, giving any special encouragement or assistance was passed. That is to say, a company, which was not engaged in British India at the time of passing of such legislation in any branch of trade or industry, proposed to be encouraged by direct grant, bounty, or subsidy, will not be eligible for such benefits. Indian legislation may require that such a company would be eligible for such encouragement, only if it is incorporated under the laws of British India, or even of a Federated State; that a certain proportion, not exceeding one-half, of the members of the governing body, are British subjects, domiciled in British India or Federated States; and that the company should provide such facilities, as may be prescribed under the law, for training British subjects, domiciled in India or Indian Federated States. By this provision, future competitors of non-Indian origin seem to be excluded. But, even there, sub-section (3) says that an established company, incorporated under the laws of the United Kingdom, must be deemed to be carrying on business in India, if it owns ships which habitually trade to and from ports in India.

Section 117 extends the principle of this provision to any "ordinance, order, bye-law, rule or regulation," which has the force of law, under any existing Indian, or Federal, or Provincial Legislation.

It is provisions like these which will force the pace for the nationalisation of all key industries and business. Once nationalised and conducted as Government enterprise, there can be no question of descrimination of this type.

(e) Trade Convention

After all these restrictions upon Indian Legislatures to enact any law which would introduce discriminatory treatment in respect of any special encouragement from the State to any particular trade or industry, or exemption from taxation or disability in settlement, and movement of British individuals within the Federation, Section 118, however, provides for the conclusion of a trade convention or agreement between the British Imperial Government and the Federal Government of India.* Under such convention, similarity of treatment would be assured to British subjects, domiciled in the United Kingdom, as also to companies incorporated by or under the laws of British

* 118.—If after the establishment of the Federation a convention is made between His Majesty's Government in the United Kingdom and the Federal Government whereby similarly of treatment is assured in the United Kingdom to British subjects domiciled in British India and to companies incorporated by or under the laws of British India in British India to British subjects domiciled in the United Kingdom and to companies incorporated by or under the laws of the United Kingdom respectively, in respect of the matters, or any of the matters, with regard

(*Continued on page 481*)

India. Conversely, the same treatment would be accorded in British India to British subjects and companies of the United Kingdom. If such an agreement is made, and the necessary legislation passed to give effect to the legislation, the King-in-Council may declare that the purposes of Sections 111 to 117 are covered by that Convention. Britain herself desires to reserve her freedom of negotiations; and that opinion is commonly shared also in the Dominions. Each of the Dominions, India, as well as the United Kingdom, have, moreover, particular customers, with whom they would specially desire to have special arrangements. Accordingly, this plan of bilateral agreements seems to be generally accepted in preference to an all-round agreement for Imperial Preference.

(f) Professional and Technical Qualifications

Apart from these general provisions, in regard to prohibiting discrimination against British subjects of the United Kingdom, in respect of taxation, settlement, movement, holding of property, etc., special provision is made for professional and technical work and qualifications to protect British technicians and professional men working in India. By Section 119 (1), the Governor-General's sanction, in his discretion, is necessary, before any bill could be introduced in either chamber of the Federal Legislature, which prescribes (or em-

(*Continued from page 80*)

to which provision is made in the preceding sections of this chapter, His Majesty may if he is satisfied that all necessary legislation has been enacted both in the United Kingdom and in India for the purpose of giving effect to the convention, by Order-in-Council declare that the purposes of those sections are to such extent as may be specified in the Order sufficiently fulfilled by that convention and legislation, and while any such Order is in force, the operation of those sections shall to that extent be suspended.

An Order in Council under this section shall cease to have effect if and when the convention to which it relates expires or is terminated by either party thereto."

powers any other body to prescribe) the professional and technical qualifications necessary in British India to carry on any given profession. The Governor-General is enjoined by sub-section (2) of this section, not to give this sanction, if in his opinion the effect of the proposed legislation would be to impose a disability, liability, restriction, or condition upon any one who was practising a given profession or business before the passing of such a law or continuing the same. The section, however, allows the ground of public interest, it seems, to create such a bar by legislation; but it is next to impossible to say what public interest would be so recognised by a British Governor-General. This rule also applies as regards holding any office in British India, and carrying on any trade or business.

Such Restrictions not in Indian States

Note, however, that this provision applies only to British India, and not to the whole of the Federation. This may be intended to provide relatively a free field in the Indian States. But, the Indian States cannot be presumed to have either so much independence, or so much strength, as to pay special attention and give direct encouragement to their own subjects, or to their British Indian brethren, in preference to Britishers or other non-Indians carrying on any business, profession, or trade within the State, or holding any office. If any of the States do not accede to the Federation for such purposes, then, a theoretical freedom would be reserved to such of them for this purpose. But, even so, the overwhelming might of the Supreme Government of India, however it is constituted, may make it practically impossible for any State, however powerful, to resort to any such discriminatory treatment, in favour either of its own citizens, or of British Indians.

The sub-section, it may also be added, is silent, as regards those who may come hereafter in the same field. Presumably, the Indian legislatures would not be bound to afford equal treatment, or be restrained from imposing any discriminatory treatment for the future upon non-Indian entrants into such professions, trades, or holding such office, in favour of native or permanently domiciled Indians.

All these restrictions, it may be added, proposed by any Federal or Provincial law, or regulations in this behalf, must be published at least four months before they are intended to be brought into effect, in such manner as the Governor-General or the Governor may direct. The purpose of such publication is that any party, feeling adversely affected by such provisions, may complain, if so deemed proper, to the Governor or Governor-General. Sub-section (3) of Section 119 empowers the Governor or the Governor-General, if, within two months of any such publication, complaint is received that any of the regulations would operate unfairly against any class of persons affected thereby, to disallow those regulations any time before they are declared to come into effect, if he is satisfied that the complaint is well-founded. The Governor-General, however, in this matter, is required to exercise his individual judgment. He must, therefore consult his Ministers. If, however, he considers the advice of the Ministers not just or appropriate in any given case, he would be entitled to disregard that advice.*

*This exercise of the Governor-General's individual judgment is extended by public notification to direct that the provision of this law may also apply to any existing law, as regards sub section (3) already mentioned.

(g) Medical Profession

The most important section of this Chapter, however, relates to medical qualifications. The General Medical Council of the United Kingdom has been very severe in the last ten years in dealing with Indian Medical qualifications; and there has, in consequence, been a current of resentment in Indian circles affected. A solution, in part at any rate, has been found by the Institution of an Indian Medical Council under the Act of 1934-35. This, however, cannot undo the privileged position accorded to the British officers serving in the Indian Medical service, or other medical practitioners holding British University Degrees, or quailfications registered in the United Kingdom. Section 120 requires that a British subject, domiciled in the United Kingdom or in India, who is entitled to practice or be registered in the United Kingdom as qualified medical practitioner, by virtue of the Diploma granted to him to that effect in the United Kingdom, shall not be excluded from practising medicine, surgery or mid-wifery in British India, by any of the existing Indian laws, or any legislation of the Federal or Provincial Legislature in the future, either in British India or in any other part thereof. Nor can such a person be debarred from being registered as qualified to practice medicine, etc., on any other ground, except that the diploma held by him does not furnish a sufficient guarantee of the requisite knowledge and skill for the practice of his profession. Even this last mentioned exclusion can only be made on the ground of a law to that effect being passed by the Federal or the Provincial Legislature. Such a law must provide that no proposal for excluding the holders of any particular diploma from practice or registration should become operative until twelve months have elapsed after notice thereof has been given to the Governor-General, the Universities, or any other body granting that diploma. The power of the Privy Council practically to annul such legislation is specifically reserved by Section 120 (1). That body, on appeal made to them, is entitled to decide that the diploma in question ought to be recognised, despite the Indian legislation, as furnishing the necessary and sufficient guarantee of knowledge and skill required. Such power to decide on the merits of technical qualifications, vested in the judicial committee of the Privy Council seems an usurpation of the legitimate authority of the Indian Legislatures. But as such usurpation or denial all round is the basic theory of this Constitution, and necessarily arises out of distrust or contempt for the Indian sense of justice and fair-dealing, no further comment is necessary on that point.

The application to the Privy Council mentioned above should be made by a University or other body in the United Kingdom, which grants the medical diploma. In the alternative, it may be made by a person holding such a diploma, and considering himself aggrieved by the proposal to exclude holders of such diploma from practice or registration in India. The Privy Council when any such complaint is received, must give to the authorities and the persons concerned, in India as well as in the United Kingdom, opportunities for tendering evidence or submitting representations in writing on either side of the case. When they have heard all these pleas, they may decide whether the diploma in question does or does not furnish the requisite guarantee of skill, etc. in the practice of medicines, etc. This decision of the Privy Council will have to be notified to the Governor-General, who must communicate to those authorities in India, or publish it, as he thinks proper for the purpose.*

Needless to add, the principle of reciprocity seems to be maintained in this section also, *i.e.*, in regard to discriminatory action in the United Kingdom for the practice of medicine, etc. by Indians holding medical diplomas or degrees of Indian Universities. The right of appeal to the Privy Council is also given to such Indian practitioners in England, in case their diploma is declared in the United Kingdom as not furnishing sufficient guarantee of knowledge, skill, and experience in the party concerned; and the same procedure is allowed for hearing the case and the disposal of it. No liability, disability, restriction or condition would be imposed, either in the United Kingdom or in British India, on the respective holders of medical diploma, practising in the other country, which it does not impose on the corresponding practitioners of that country's own diploma-holders.†

Critique of the Constitutional Provisions in regard to Discrimination

Taking all these provisions together, it is obvious that they arise out of the British doubt of the Indian Legislatures and Ministers of the future being either just or fair to the competing British interest in India; or secondly, out of a dread of India's active effort to promote local industry, enterprise, or talent, in the fields hitherto monopolised by Britishers in India. As many

*Sub-section (2) of Section 120.

†The powers of the Medical Council in India to suspend or debar any person from practice on the ground of misconduct, or to remove any persons from a register on that ground, are not affected by this provision.

of these fields are, however, of a most important strategic character in regard to the economic development of the country, the desire of Indians, when they attain effective power in their own country, to take all possible steps for securing by native enterprise or talent the possession of these fields,—and, thereby, retaining the wealth produced therein for use in the country itself,—is as natural as it is legitimate. The British desire, on the other hand, to prevent such legislation materialising, or to prevent effect being given to the spirit of such proposals by executive action, by means of a specific instruction given to the Governors or the Governor-General in that behalf, or even by imposing special responsibilites on such officers for this purpose, is equally understandable. So long as they can maintain effective command of the Indian fields of enterprise, which yield no small proportion of England's annual wealth, they would naturally prevent any counter effect being made. The provision in regard to the reciprocity is only a pretence. In the much stronger English field, competing Indian enterprise has not the ghost of a chance. Hence, the provision against any discrimination in the United Kingdom against Indians is, in reality, no more than an eye-wash for Indians. Not only is the Indian enterprise insignificant in the British market, but the secret discrimination actually being made by British industrialists or professional and technical people against the corresponding Indians working in the United Kingdom is impossible to prevent by law. Nor does there seem any desire to do so in the powers that be in the United Kingdom. Accordingly, these provisions which appear as unmitigated burdens upon the Indian public are calculated to provoke immediate and lively clash with the forces of Indian Nationalism in the Constitutional machinery hereafter.

II. Statutory Railway Authority

The Statutory Railway Authority is a new creation of this Act. It is intended to take railways out of the management of politicians, and place them under such an authority as would prevent any danger of needless waste or lack of economy. The Indian Railways, however, have not hitherto been conspicuous for any such economic management as to justify the implied charge against the Indian Legislature of the future controlling the finances of the railway. In fact, during the last few years, since some railways have come directly under the control and management of the State in India, intensive efforts at retrenchment and economy have not been wanting, during the period that the Railway Budget has been separated under a special convention or resolution of the Indian Legislative Assembly in that behalf. These Railways have made considerable profits even on a directly commercial basis. And though they suffered in the years of Depression, even more perhaps than other departments of Government, the record of railway management does not reveal any conclusive evidence to show that Indians are incapable of managing this great public enterprise. But the most dominant consideration seems to have been that considerable foreign capital is invested in the Indian Railways. And these creditors, presumably, lack that confidence, which Indian people were forced to place in Indian railways management in the years before 1920, when they were hopelessly losing concerns. It is, perhaps, to reassure the foreign bond-holders of the Indian railways that the institution of a special Federal Railway Authority is provided for in Part VIII and Schedule VIII of this Act.

The one real factor explaining the possible weakness in the management of railways, that has not been touched upon above, lies in the apprehension of a possible use of political pressure to staff and man this enterprise. It is assumed that, if the management of the railways is placed in charge of a Statutory Authority, independent of the political control from the Ministers or the Legislature, this danger would be avoided.* Rules and regulations, after and within the constitutional provision in this Act itself, relating to the employment in the Indian railway enterprise of the different communities in their stated proportions, are such that it is impossible to believe political influences would be completely removed from the staffs or personnel of the Indian railways.

Be the reasons what they may, the institution of a Statutory Railway Authority for the whole Federation is, henceforward, to be an integral part of the constitutional machinery of India.

Scope of Railway Authority

The executive authority of the Federal Government, in regard to the regulation and construction, as well as the maintenance and working of railways, is entrusted, by Section 181, to a Federal Railway Authority. The sphere of activity of this Authority extends to all Federal Railways, as well as all enter-

---

*cp. Section 242 (2) which manifests particular solicitude for the continued employment of the Anglo-Indian community in the Railways. "The specific class, character and numerical percentage of the posts hitherto held by members of that community, and the remuneration attaching to those posts" have to be duly regarded by the Railway Authority in making these appointments to superior as well as lower posts.

prise carried on as ancillary to the railways, or which may hereafter come to be so carried on.* The Authority is also entrusted with making subsidiary arrangements with other persons or organisations for carrying on any undertaking, deemed to be incidental to the railway enterprise collectively. This may include not only subsidiary or feeder motor services, but may also include such other industry or business enterprise, as the keeping and maintenance of hotels and restaurants, providing refreshments, workshops, iron-foundries, rubber plantations, forests, and any other material which may be necessary for the construction, maintenance, or operation of the railways.

Federal or Provincial Legislation is applicable to the Authority, only in so far as it is relevant to the working of the Authority. The relations between the Federal Railway Authority and the railways in any of the Federated States, as a matter of special agreement, are provided for separately under Part VI, Sections 121 to 128.

Government Supervision over Railways

The Federal Government is given powers of supervision, by sub-section (3) of Section 181, in regard to construction, equipment and operation of railways, with a view to secure safety both of passengers and the staff working in the railways. This power of supervision may include the power of holding inquiries in causes of accidents, etc., if the Federal Government so please. In such cases, it may order inquiries to be held by persons independent of the Railway Authority.

Employment on Railways

The regulation of employment in the Railways, particularly in Railway Service Class I and Class II is governed by Part X of the Act, Sections 240 to 250 in particular. As this subject has in general already been discussed, we need not go into details in this place, beyond remarking that the basic principle of guaranteed service, assured pay, promotion, pension, and other privileges applies here as rigorously as in any other department.

The Federal Railway Authority is a body corporate entitled to sue and be sued in its corporate capacity.

Constitution of the Railway Authority

The Constitution in detail of the Railway Authority is provided in Schedule VIII, which lays down that the Federal Railway Authority shall consist of seven members. The Governor-General is entitled to nominate not less than 3/7ths of the total number of members constituting the railway authority.* He acts in his discretion in regard to this function, as also in appointing one of the members to be president of the railway Authority. The qualifications required for a person to be appointed as a member of the railway authority are, that he must have experience in Commerce, Industry, Agriculture, Finance or Administration. If he has, within the last preceding twelve months, been a member of the Federal or any Provincial Legislature, or an officer under the Crown, or a railway official, he would not be qualified to be so appointed.†

Of the first members appointed to the Authority, three must be appointed for three years, subject to

*cp. Section 182 (1).

†cp. Schedule VIII Article 2. It is curious to note that under Article 7 of this schedule a person holding or interested in a contract under the Railway authority is not disqualified from membership but is only required to make a full disclosure of the facts, and refrain from taking part in the discussion or voting. This seems to be perverted logic, and at best obviously profiteering ethics characteristic of individualist society.

being re-eligible for the same office for a further period of three years, or at most five years. With this exception, all other members are appointed for five years, and are re-eligible to the office for another term not exceeding five years.* The Governor-General has the power, in the exercise of his individual judgment, to terminate the appointment of any member, if he is satisfied that the member in question is, for any reason, unable or unfit for continuing his duties.† In case of temporary vacancies, power is given to the Governor-General, in the exercise of his individual judgment, to make rules for appointing acting members in place of any temporarily unable to perform their duties.‡ These provisions may be amended by Federal Legislature under Section 182 (2); but no Bill or amendment for such a purpose can be introduced in the Legislature without the previous sanction of the Governor-General in his discretion.

The members of the Railway Authority are entitled to receive such salaries and allowances, as the Governor-General, exercising his individual judgment, determines.§ But, during the term of office of any member, his emoluments cannot be reduced.

All acts of the Authority and all questions before them must be decided by a majority of members present and voting at a meeting of the Authority.¶ The president has a second and casting vote, in the event of an equality of votes at any meeting. The Governor-General is entitled to depute any one or more persons

*cp. Schedule VIII Article 3.

†Ibid. Article 3.

‡Ibid Article 4.

§cp. Ibid. Article 5.

¶cp. Article 6 of the Schedule.

to attend any meeting of the Railway Authority, and such persons are entitled to speak there as his representatives, but they are not entitled to vote.*

Executive of the Railway Authority

For the discharge of its own business, the Authority is entitled, by Article 9 of the Schedule VIII, to make standing orders for the regulation of their proceedings and business, and to modify or revoke or alter any such order.

The executive of the Railway Authority is headed by a Chief Railway Commissioner,† who must be a person with experience in railway administration. He is appointed by the Governor-General, exercising his individual judgment, after consultation with the Authority. This Railway Commissioner is assisted in his work by a Financial Commissioner, who is also appointed by the Governor-General, presumably on the advice of his Ministers. All other executive officials or heads of departments are appointed by the Authority itself on the recommendation of the Chief Commissioner only.‡ The Chief Commissioner is not removeable from his office by the Authority, except with the approval of the Governor-General, exercising his individual judgment; while the Financial Commissioner cannot be removed from his office, except by the Governor-General himself, exercising his individual judgment.§ The Chief Commissioner and the Financial Commissioner are entitled to attend any meeting of the railway Authority; and the Financial Commissioner is entitled to demand that any

---

*cp. Schedule. Article 8.

†Ibid 11.

‡Ibid. 12.

§Ibid. Article 13.

matter which relates to or affects finance should be referred to the Authority.*

The Indian Railway Authority, by article 15 of Schedule VIII, is exempted from the Indian Income-tax or super-tax on any of its "income, profits or gains."† The logic of this provision is difficult to appreciate, particularly in view of the financial prospects of the Federation when it comes into being. This is a public utility corporation deriving its gains from a practical monopoly. Its profits or surplus of income over expenditure is really due to a tax upon the community; and, as such, there is no reason to exempt these gains from taxation. Assuming the net profits of the Railways, after meeting working expenses, to be Rs. 40 crores, the loss to the Federal revenues may be estimated at about Rs. 5 crores per annum.

All the monies of the railway Authority in India for immediate requirement must be banked in the Reserve Bank of India. The Authority must employ the Bank as their Agents for all transactions, including remittances, exchange and banking. The Bank undertakes the custody of such monies and deposits, as well as agency work on such terms and conditions, as they undertake the corresponding work on behalf of the Federal Government.‡

Working of the Railways

By Section 183, the railway Authority is required to act on "business principles" in the exercise of the functions assigned to them. This is an exceedingly ambiguous expression; and neither the Act nor the

*cp. Schedule VIII. Article 14.

†Ibid. Article 15.

‡Ibid. Article 16.

Schedule provides any definition of what is to be understood by "business principles." Perhaps they are to be interpreted in contrast with "charity", or again in opposition to the usual routine of administrative redtapism. In either case it needs to be more clearly explained. The only explanation the Act gives is: "business principles" are to be interpreted, so as to have "due regard to the interests of agriculture, industry, commerce, and the general public."* Particularly, the Authority is required to make proper provision for meeting out of their receipts on revenue account all expenditure, to which such receipts are applicable under this Act. The Central Government is entitled to give instructions on questions of policy to the railway Authority; and the latter are bound to observe such instructions in the exercise of their functions. If any dispute arises under this provision between the Federal Government and the Railway Authority, as to whether a question is or is not a question of policy, the decision of the Governor-General, **in his discretion**, is final.

All the powers given to the Governor-General to be exercised in his individual judgment, as also those in connection with his Special Responsibilities, are also to apply as regards matters entrusted to the Railway Authority. In other words, for all supervision, control or direction that the supreme Federal authority is to exercise over the Railways of India, the position is as if the executive authority of the Federal Government were vested in the Governor-General, and, as if the functions of the Railway Authority were the functions of the Ministers. The Governor-General may issue to these Authorities such directions as he

*cp. Section 183 (1).

deems necessary. With reference to any matter that appears to involve any of his special responsibilities, or wherein he is requried to act in his discretion, or to exercise his individual judgment, the Railway Authority must implicitly obey any directions so issued by the Governor-General (133).

Railways and the Federal Government

The relations between the Federal Government and the Railway Authority are to be guided and conducted by rules made for the purpose, after consultation with the Railway Authority, by the Governor-General, exercising his individual judgment.

> "The rules shall include provisions requiring the Authority to transmit to the Federal Government all such information with respect to their business as may be specified in the rules, or as the Governor-General may otherwise require to be so transmitted, and in particular provisions requiring the Authority and their chief executive officer to bring to the notice of the Governor-General any matter under consideration by the Authority or by that officer which involves, or appears to them or him likely to involve, any special responsibility of the Governor-General."*

As regards the acquisition or the sale of land, etc., needed on account of the working of the various railways, and for making contracts and working agreements, the Federal Government is entitled to make regulations. Except as provided for in these regulations, the Railway Authority is not to acquire or dispose of any land. Whenever land is to be acquired compulsorily for the railways, it must be by the Federal Government, and not directly by the Railway Authority. So also, contracts made by or on behalf of the Authority are to be enforced by or against the Authority itself; and not by or against the Federal

*cp. Section 184 (2).

Government,—except in the case of a contract supplementing one already in existence before the Authority comes into being.* The same rule applies to the making of working agreements with a State or any other corporation operating a railway in India.

Finance of the Railway Authority

The Railway Authority is enjoined to establish, maintain and control a fund, called the Railway Fund, under Section 186. All receipts by the Railway Authority, whether on capital or revenue account, must be credited to that Fund. All monies provided even from the Federal purse to enable the Railway Authority to carry on its functions must be likewise credited to the same account. Conversely, all expenditure of the Railway Authority must be defrayed out of that Fund. Separate Provident Funds may, however, be maintained by the Authority for the benefit of those who are or have been employed in connection with the Railways.

Under sub-section (2) of that section:—

"The receipts of the Authority on revenue account in any financial year shall be applied in

(a) defraying working expenses;

(b) meeting payments due under contracts or agreements to railway undertakings;

(c) paying pensions, and contributions to provident funds;

(d) repaying to the revenues of the Federation so much of any pensions and contributions to provident funds charged by this Act on those revenues as is attributable to service on railways in India;

(e) making due provision for maintenance, renewals, improvements and depreciation;

---

*cp. Section 185 (2).

(f) making to the revenues of the Federation any payments by way of interest which they are required by this part of this Act to make; and

(g) defraying other expenses properly chargeable against revenue in that year.

This order of priority, or preference, in payments of railway obligations throws a strange light upon the motive underlying this provision. While working expenses,—including wages, salaries, stores, etc.—are given pride of place, payment on account of interest comes last but one in the list. Provision by way of renewal, replacement, or depreciation takes precedence over Interest charges. Of course, the surplus open to division between the Federal Government and the Railway Authority would be available only after all these charges have been met. That the Railways have been, for the greater portion of their existence in India, a net drain upon the revenues of the country; and that, even to-day, on balance India has spent more on account of the railways than derived benefit from that source, does not seem at all to have influenced those who drew up this section.

Even the next following sub-section makes little amend for the omission, since it provides:—

> "186 (3) Any surpluses on revenue account shown in the accounts of the Authority shall be apportioned between the Federation and the Authority in accordance with a scheme to be prepared, and from time to time reviewed, by the Federal Government, or until such a scheme has been prepared, in accordance with the principles which immediately before the establishment of the Authority regulated the application of surpluses in railway accounts, and any sum apportioned to the Federation under this sub-section shall be transferred accordingly and shall form part of the revenues of the Federation."

Considering that, in the years of Depression alone, between 1930-36, the Railways lost some 62 crores on the balance; and that they have ceased to make any contribution to the national revenues for over 7 years, this is a very lenient and partial treatment accorded to the railways, which the record of that enterprise in India scarcely deserves. Interest charges on capital invested in the Railways by the Government of India are, under Section 187, to be made good by the Authority to the Federal Government, at rates to be agreed upon, or, in default of such agreement, as fixed by the Governor-General in his discretion. The phrase, however, used in the section, which speaks of the sum provided for capital purposes "out of the **revenues** of India or of the Federation," is open to considerable misrepresentation; since not all the sums spent on capital purposes in connection with the railways were provided "out of the revenues of India" or of the Federation. True, the definition of the revenues of the Federation, as given in Section 136, may include borrowed monies as much as monies taken out of the recurrent income. But that definition is extremely artificial, not to say misleading; and it did not apply under the Government of India Acts between 1858-1919. It is to be hoped this obvious ambiguity will not involve litigation, and consequent danger of heavy loss to the Indian tax-payer. The prospects of this somewhat obsolete enterprise in the years to come are sufficiently gloomy to justify the worst apprehensions.

Railway Rates Committee

Section 191 provides for a Railway Rates Committee to be appointed by the Governor-General—

> "to give advice to the Authority in connection with any dispute between persons using, or desiring to use, a railway and the Authority as to the rates or traffic

facilities which he may require the Authority to refer to the Committee."

This is different from the Railway Tribunal, which is mentioned in Section 193, and which is entitled to hear disputes between the Authority and any State in connection with mutual facilities needed for the efficient and economic operation of the railways.*

Critique of the Railway Authority

The other provisions of this Part of the Act are of a detail or consequential nature; and, accordingly, need not be discussed at length in this place.

The setting up and working of the Railway Authority is a new experiment, whose success cannot be judged at the present moment. Inasmuch, however, as it is obviously a creation of distrust of the democratic principle in government, or of the Indian politician come into power, its object as well as nature must meet with the strongest criticism. Not only it effectually and materially restricts the authority of the responsible Federal Ministry; it makes no provision by way of economy and retrenchment in the ordinary management of the railways by means of this new creation. Vast capital investment, already made on this account, will naturally dispose every critic of the Indian railway management to be more circumspect and restrained in his criticism than, perhaps, the facts of the case would absolutely warrant. But the division of subjects between the Federal and the Provincial Governments, and the absence of any incentive to economy in the Railway Authority, which would be naturally engendered by the necessity to pass its votes for expenditure through the Legislature, make the

*cp. Section 193 (1).

prospect more gloomy than one is disposed to contemplate. The cancellation of the recent debt due to the Indian Government by the railways, on account of current deficits in the Railway Budget in recent years, is an instance of solicitude and specially favoured treatment, which is hardly reciprocated in the constitution of this Authority, and is unlikely in the working of that body, when at last it is set going.

III. Property, Contracts, Liabilities and Suits

Chapter III of Part VII of the Act of 1935, relating to the above subjects, and embracing Sections 172-180, enunciate no new principle of Constitutional Law. Section 172 vests all lands and buildings, used for purposes of government, in His Majesty, and, through him, either in the Provincial or in the Federal Government. But that does not invest the King-Emperor with the ultimate ownership of all land in India, even as an incident of eminent domain. Constitutional authority, therefore, of the new Governments, in respect of levying a Land Revenue as a share of the produce due to the joint or ultimate owner, seems still to be lacking,—except, of course, in virtue of the rights of succession claimed by the British Government in India to the governments that went before them.

Lands and buildings vested in His Majesty for the purposes of His Majesty's Government in the United Kingdom, under Section 172 (1) (c), or used for governmental purposes, cannot be sold, or their purpose changed, without the consent of the Governor-General.*

The executive authority of the Federal or Provincial Government extends, subject to appropriate legis-

*cp. Section 172 (2).

lation, to the grant, sale, disposition or mortgage of property vesting in His Majesty for purposes of Federal or Provincial Government.* But—

> "any land or building used as an official residence of the Governor-General or a Governor shall not be sold, nor any change made in the purposes for which it is used, except with the concurrence, **in his discretion**, of the Governor-General or the Governor, as the case may be."†

All contracts in future made in the exercise of the executive authority of the Federation, or of a Province, are to be expressed as made by the Governor-General, or by the Governor, as the case may be. The contract so made shall be executed by such persons as the Governor-General, or the Governor, may direct. None of these, nor even the Secretary of State, are by Section 175 (4), to be personally liable in respect of such contracts. The Federation of India, and each Provincial Government, is entitled to sue and be sued in its own name, under Section 176. Special provision is made, by Sections 177 and 178, for the taking over of existing contracts of the Secretary of State-in-Council, as also as regards existing loans, guarantees and other financial obligations.

IV. Miscellaneous Provisions

Miscellaneous and general provisions contained in Part XII of the Act, Sections 285 to 311, have already been noticed in part, in their appropriate place, in the preceding pages. Sections 292-3 provided for the continuation of the existing Indian laws, and for their adaptation, wherever needed, to the altered condition under the new Constitution. A special Order-in-

*cp. Section 175 (1).

†Proviso to Section 175 (1)

Council was issued on the 1st of April, 1937, for the purposes mentioned in Section 293. Section 294 deals with the foreign jurisdiction of the Indian Government; but it is too technical to be discussed in this place.

Court of Revenue Appeal

A Court of Appeal in revenue matters is provided for by Section 296,—members of the Legislature being excluded from being appointed to such a body. In every Province the Governor is enjoined to constitute such a tribunal, and the members constituting the tribunal are to be paid such salaries and allowances as the Governor in his individual judgment may determine. These salaries and allowances are to be charged on the revenues of the Province concerned. It is, however, not clear what exactly will be the functions of this body, or its jurisdiction. Still less is it clear whether it would really help in easing the intolerable burden of the Land Revenue in the ryotwari Provinces.

Freedom of Internal Trade

Section 297 has a special significance. It forbids any Provincial Legislature or Government from taking any steps which would impede the free movements of goods from one province to another. Nor are they to be allowed to impose any tax, toll, cess or due, which would amount to discriminating treatment as between corresponding goods produced or manufactured in that Province, and those made elsewhere in the Federation. The wording, however, of the section makes it open to question if the principle of this section would apply to goods made in, or brought from, a Federated State into a Province.

Freedom of trade and movement within the Federation must be regarded as an essential ingredient in a common citizenship. But in so far as the Federating States are not definitely obliged to accord this treatment, the Federal system in India established by this Act cannot be said to be beyond criticism.

Equality of opportunity for service

Section 298 provides:—

"298 (1) No subject of His Majesty domiciled in India shall on the grounds only of religion, place of birth, descent, colour or any of them be ineligible for office under the Crown in India, or be prohibited on any such grounds from acquiring, holding or disposing of property or carrying on any occupation, trade, business or profession in British India.

(2) Nothing in this section shall affect the operation of any law which—

(a) prohibits, either absolutely or subject to exceptions, the sale or mortgage of agricultural land situate in any particular area, and owned by a person belonging to some class recognised by the law as being a class of persons engaged in or connected with agriculture in that area, to any person not belonging to any such class or

(b) recognises the existence of some right, privilege or disability attaching to members of a community by virtue of some personal law or custom having the force of law.

(3) Nothing in this section shall be construed as derogating from the special responsibility of the Governor-General or of a Governor for the safeguarding of the legitimate interests of minorities."

This section applies to the subjects of His Majesty domiciled in India. If it stood by itself, it would exclude from this privilege, or equality, those persons who are citizens of the Indian States, whether federated or otherwise. By Section 262, however, the Ruler or subjects of any Federated State are made automatically eligible to civil posts under the Crown in India; while power is given to the Governor-General to declare that the ruler or any subject of any Indian State, not federated, as well as the native of any tribal area, or of territory adjacent to India,—shall be eligible to hold any such office, provided that the office in question has been specified in the declaration. The same powers are given to Provincial Governors to make similar declarations with regard to specified civil posts being open to the ruler or subject of any specified Indian State, federated or not. The same applies to the Secretary of State in respect of posts to which he makes appointments. Subject to these exceptions,

> "No person who is not a British subject shall be eligible to hold any office under the Crown in India."*

Sex Bar in Public Service

While no disability is to be imposed upon any British or domiciled Indian subjects of His Majesty for holding any appointment under the Crown in India, the equality of sexes in this matter of holding posts in the service of the country is by no means as well guaranteed. Says Section 275:—

> "275. A person shall not be disqualified by sex for being appointed to any civil service, or civil post under, the Crown in India other than such a service or post as may be specified by any general or special order made—
>
> (a) by the Governor-General in the case of services and posts in connection with the affairs of the Federation;
>
> (b) by the Governor of a Province in the case of services and posts in connection with the affairs of the Province;
>
> (c) by the Secretary of State in relation to appointments made by him.

*cp. Section 262 (4).

The effect of this section is that women will be excluded from serving in any branch of the National Defence Organisation even of a noncombatant type, unless special legislation is passed by Parliament in that behalf. And even from given Civil Services or posts, they might be excluded, if a general or special order made by the appropriate executive authority debars them for such a purpose. As a matter of fact, under the rules for admission to the competitive examination for recruitment to the Indian Civil Service, only males seem to be entitled to compete,* while the power to nominate has so far never been exercised in favour of a woman for a post in the Indian Civil Service. This is, to say the least, retrograde in a Constitution which appears to be founded on the equality of all citizens of the same commonwealth. Women constitute the largest single minority in the country. But, it seems that for their protection not even the doctrine of Special Responsibility of the Governor-General or of the Governor in respect of safeguarding the legitimate rights of minorities would avail.

We have already commented upon Section 299 in regard to the compulsory acquisition of land or industrial enterprise, and so need not repeat our comments on that point here.

*See Rule 4 (2) which says: "A candidate must be a male."

CHAPTER XIV

A SUMMARY OF CONCLUSION AND RECOMMENDATIONS

In the previous chapters of this book the Government of India Act 1935, embodying the new Constitution for India, has been examined in some detail, and criticisms have been offered from the point of view of the Indian people's ideal of political evolution and progress. That ideal, it must be remembered, is based on the sovereignty of the people; and it refuses to recognise any limitations or reservations to this sovereignty.

But while we lay stress on the independence of India and the establishment of a free national State, we recognise fully that the world of to-day urgently demands an international order, and the fullest co-operation between nations, to solve the problems and end the conflicts that afflict mankind. Science and modern industry and trade and finance and transport and communications, in fact the whole basic texture of the world to-day, is international. Hence the problems we have to face are essentially international and require international solutions. To think or act in terms of a purely national State, largely cut off from the rest of the world and developing itself independently of it, is to ignore realities, and to refuse to take advantage of the many avenues of progress and advancement which modern conditions offer. A narrow autarchy does not fit in with these conditions and must inevitably lead to reaction and a throw-back.

Thus, though we stand for an independent national State, we are entirely opposed to a nationalism and a State ideal which are based on a hatred of other States, and a desire to dominate over other peoples. We have seen and see to-day how this limited and aggressive national outlook leads to a continuing state of international anarchy, developing from time to time into dreadful and devastating wars. International peace and the well-being of the world have become one and indivisible. That peace depends on a solution of the political and social problems of the world and the evolution of a world order. We believe that such a solution and order must inevitably be based on the principles of Socialism. But that is a larger question which we are not called upon to discuss here. We wish to emphasize here that our conception of an independent national State is in no way opposed to the development of this world order, and that we would be perfectly prepared to make sacrifices, and even to accept certain limitations and assume burdens, in common with others, in the interest of international co-operation.

But this co-operation must be real, effective, and between free units. The League of Nations, as constituted to-day, has demonstrated the futility of international co-operation on a wrong basis, and with the purpose of maintaining a *status quo*, unjust in itself and in the interest of a few dominating Powers. It has become an impotent instrument for maintaining peace and collective security, and is ignored and insulted at every turn. It cannot undertake the solution of any fundamental problem, because it has neither the power to do so nor the will to tackle the roots of that problem.

The so-called British Commonwealth of Nations is still less a nucleus of international co-operation, as it represents a dominating imperialist group, holding a large number of subject peoples in its power, and combating other imperialist groups and Powers. It will have to change beyond all recognition before it can serve as a basis for co-operation between free nations. India's association with this group is an enforced one, and it has worked, and is working, to the detriment of India. The people of India have, therefore, declared and emphasized their will to be dissociated with this group, and this has become a primary objective of the national movement. Any continuation of this association means a continuation, in some form or other, if not political then economic, of the domination of Britain over India, and the imposition of restrictions which prevent the people of India from developing on their own lines, and according to their own needs and desires. The independence of India, and the recognition of the sovereignty of the Indian people, are thus the essential pre-requisites for the consideration of the problem of India's future constitution.

When we examine the new Constitution critically in the light of our political objective and ideals, we find that the foundations laid there cannot serve even as a basis for raising the structure of a free India. The provincial part of this constitution is full of imperfections and restrictions, but the Federal part has nothing whatever to do even with the conception of a free India. It can only be considered as a barrier which has to be removed in its entirety before we can go ahead in any direction. We shall thus have to build anew on entirely new foundations. The National

Congress has demanded that the constitution for a free India must be drawn up by a Constituent Assembly, elected on the basis of adult suffrage, and this seems to us the only feasible and democratic method of procedure.

What will be the nature of this new Constitution? It is difficult in the changing and dynamic world of to-day to prophesy about the future. Old established notions, which were taken for granted but yesterday, have no sanctity to-day. Ideas are at war, not only on the ideological plane, but often enough on the field of battle itself, where argument and debate are drowned in the clash of arms. New hopes and desires of social equality fill the peoples of the world, while at the same time Fascism has raised its ugly head, and suppresses and pours contempt on the democratic process. Political democracy, which seemed so obvious and inevitable a generation ago, is weak and ailing, simultaneously attacked on two fronts, and deserted by many of its former adherents. On the one hand, political democracy is considered insufficient to solve the problems that confront us and resolve the conflicts of interests of classes or of nations, and an economic democracy is advocated. On the other hand, the very principle of democracy is attacked, and dictatorships and authoritarian methods of government find favour with many. Even the friends of democracy feel that some variations are necessary in the old nineteenth century methods and approach, for to-day our problems grow more and more complicated and technical, and difficult of detailed consideration by parliaments. Experts and special committees are taking an ever growing part in public affairs, and parliaments, even in the democratic countries, confine themselves to laying down general principles and policies. The State is being forced by stress of circumstances, even where capitalism prevails, to socialise public utilities and advance in the direction of socialisation.

In Spain we have had a disturbing example of a democratic State being attacked by vested interests, aided by foreign Powers, when these interests realised that the democratic process might endanger them. The issue there still hangs in the balance, but the lesson is clear that privileged classes and interests do not always submit to the democratic process when this threatens to weaken their special position. When votes are lacking recourse is had to arms, even the arms of the foreigner against one's own people.

In Russia there has been a swing towards political democracy, so far as the constitution is concerned. But this has not apparently made much difference to the methods of government, which are still largely authoritarian, though they are based on the consultation and participation of millions of people.

These, and like questions, trouble the minds of thinking people all over the world. They may trouble India's mind too later, far more than they are doing to-day. For the present, politically minded India is of one mind in this matter; and it works for the establishment of a fully democratic national State. Democratic constitutions are fundamentally similar, and it would serve little purpose for us to discuss the details of such a constitution. We shall content ourselves therefore by referring to certain aspects only of a constitution for India.

Sovereignty of the Indian People

Such a constitution must be based on the recognition, in law and in fact, of the sovereignty of the people of India. No foreign Power or authority can thus frame this constitution for us, and it must be the self-expression of the Indian people. Nor can any alien authority be permitted to interfere in any way in the working of this constitution. We recognise, however, that an independent India will gladly co-operate with other nations in the international sphere; and, for this purpose, it will be prepared voluntarily to limit its sovereignty, to the extent that other nations limit theirs, in the establishment of an international order. No other limitations or restrictions can be accepted.

The Unity of India—States

The Unity of India must be maintained by the constitution. This unity, both geographical and cultural, is a patent fact of Indian history, and political and economic unity has also become essential for us. Having regard to the vastness and diversity of the country, as well as other factors, a federal system of government seems indicated. But this federation will have to be entirely different from the Federation proposed under the Government of India Act 1935, under which there is no uniformity; and an unnatural alliance is sought to be made between feudal and autocratic States and more or less democratic Provinces. A large measure of uniformity is essential, and we should try to aim at removing all distinctions between what is called British India to-day and Indian India or the States. It is possible that, owing to the backwardness of the States, they might not be able to come up to the standard of the Provinces for some time. A transitional period, not too long, may be necessary to allow them to approximate to this standard. But, at the very beginning, the objective of having uniformity should be recognised and acted upon to the fullest extent possible. A large measure of democracy must come to the people of the States before the Provinces can federate with them. The same terms of federation should apply to Provinces and States alike. This will mean the giving up by the rulers of their autocratic powers, and also, inevitably, a considerable modification of their treaties. We cannot accept these hundred year old treaties as valid to-day or unchangeable.

Thus the States will have to fall in line with the Provinces in regard to political institutions and principles and methods of government. The establishment of a Federation will also necessitate a new regrouping of the States, either among themselves or with the adjoining Provinces. Even under the present Act some combinations have been formed for the purposes of representation in the proposed Federation. The States vary in size too much, and most of them are too small to be treated as federating units. Transport and irrigation have also necessitated co-ordination in the past. This co-ordination will necessarily increase in all departments with the economic development of the country.

Provinces

The present division of Provinces was made for administrative reasons only to suit the convenience of British administrators, or because of historic reasons connected with the growth of the British Power. It has little to do with linguistic, cultural or economic considerations, and there is no reason why we should keep it unchanged. While most of the States are too small to be treated as federating units, many of the Provinces are too large to make suitable economic or administrative units. The composite presidencies of Bombay and Madras sprawl over Western and Southern and Eastern India, and contain within their areas diverse elements which might well form separate provincial units. Bengal and the United Provinces are unified areas, linguistically and culturally; but both of them are enormous and have a vast population. We should, therefore, endeavour to reconstitute our provinces on a rational and scientific basis.

This does not mean that we should ignore local sentiment in this matter; that sentiment cannot be set aside even for important considerations. Indeed, we feel that the wishes of the people concerned must be the dominant factor in coming to a decision, and the reconstitution should be such as to give a fuller chance of self-expression to the people concerned. We do not wish to encourage in any way the formation of provinces on communal lines. But we feel that it might be possible, in a scheme of redistribution, to give important groups and minorities territories within which they can feel that they have full opportunities of self-development, without which a creative life is hardly possible. We do not think this will increase communalism or separatist tendencies. The sentiment of nationality is growing, and, with the removal of minor causes of friction, communal feelings will decrease.

The Indian National Congress has accepted and acted upon the principle of linguistic division of provinces. That division usually coincides with cultural groupings and local sentiment, and should be made the basis of a future reconstitution. The presidencies of Bombay and Madras would easily split up, according to this, into Gujarati, Marathi, Canarese, Telugu, Tamil and Malayali areas. In the North there is the huge Hindustani speaking *bloc*, which is much too big for a single province. Even the United Provinces might well be divided up into two or more suitable administrative and economic units. Bengal also is too large to be treated as a single unit, and should be made into two or more provinces. The Punjab seems to suggest a division into three parts.

But we need not consider a detailed scheme of reconstruction of provinces. If the principles are accepted the actual lines of division will not offer any great difficulty. These principles are: the province should not be too small or too big. If it is too small, the burden of administration is too heavy, and the possibilities of economic development are limited. If it is too large, then it is unwieldy and efficient administration becomes difficult. Large provinces are also to be avoided as they might tend to increase provincialism and separation. A large number of relatively small provinces will encourage the growth of a feeling of nationality and the unity of India. One or two large provinces, joining in a federation with many small ones, will tend to dominate the others. We feel therefore that provinces should be more or less of a uniform size, though we do not expect this principle to be applied with any strictness. Other, and more important considerations, will have to be borne in mind; and these will interfere with its application. These other considerations are: linguistic and cultural, economic and local sentiment.

It may also be possible to give, even within the framework of a Province, a measure of autonomy to a cultural group or minority. This has been done, with satisfactory results in the U.S.S.R., where the federating units have autonomous areas for national minorities. How far this will be possible in India, it is difficult to say, but the idea might be explored further.

Fundamental Rights of Citizenship

It is of the essence of democracy that the community should have the right to change or vary its constitution, but it is usual to have some safeguards in regard to certain fundamental provisions of the constitution. These hindrances to rapid change give a greater permanence to these provisions; they check the executive authority and prevent it to some extent from abusing the great powers it possesses; they protect minority rights, and thus give a feeling of security to the minority groups. What these fundamental rights should be would largely depend on the nature of the State. In an individualist capitalist State they would differ from corresponding rights in a people organised on a socialist basis, for in these two forms of State organisation both the basic institutions and governing outlook differ from each other. But whatever may be the future social organisation of India, there are certain fundamental rights guaranteeing the freedom of the individual, which we would like to endure and to be incorporated in the constitution. These rights are: freedom of conscience and religion; free expression of opinion; free association and combination; protection of the culture and languages of minorities; equality of all citizens before the law, as well as for public service or trade or calling, irrespective of religion, caste or sex; and others of a like nature.

The National Congress, at its Karachi Session in 1931, adopted a resolution on Fundamental Rights, and considerable value is attached to the assurances contained in this resolution by the minorities and various groups in India. The national movement is thus committed to the incorporation of these rights in the constitution. We are convinced that the Indian constitution should contain a guarantee in regard to these fundamental rights for the assurance of all minority groups in the country. For this purpose, the Karachi resolution of the Congress, and the provisions of Western constitutions relating to civil liberties, might be taken as models.

It should be remembered that civil and individual liberty, often restricted and circumscribed in what is known as British India, is totally absent in nearly all the Indian States. A guarantee of this nature is thus especially required for the peoples of the States.

Federal Government

With the establishment of a Federation, the executive authority of the Federal Government will extend to the whole country, and will comprise all the departments of the State in India, except in so far as a number of subjects come within the scope of provincial autonomy. The chief executive authority may be vested in the Head or Chief of the State, who may be given an appropriate designation in keeping with our traditions. *Rashtrapati* has already become a well-known and popular word in India, and the Chief of the State might well be called *Rashtrapati*. But the name is immaterial; what we have to consider is the position of such a person in our constitutional structure and the power and authority he is to possess. Should he be just a figure-head like the President of the French Republic, or should he have the large powers which the President of the U.S.A. possesses? We feel that he should exercise his functions exclusively on the advice of his ministers. At the same time we would not like him to be just a figurehead. Under the exceptional and dynamic conditions prevailing in the world to-day, some measure of initiative should be given to our Chief. His position might be midway between the Presidents of the French Republic and the U.S.A. He must act as the constitutional Chief of a responsible government.

The Federal Executive would consist of the Council of Ministers, recruited from that party in the Federal Legislature which commands a majority of votes in the legislature. These ministers will be collectively responsible to the Federal Legislature, and their salaries will be voted every year.

Federal Legislature

The Federal Legislature should be bicameral. We are against the two chamber system in the Provinces, but we think that in the Federation two chambers are desirable. One of these chambers, which for the sake of simplicity might be referred to as the Lower House, should be elected directly by the people of India on a simple uniform franchise such as adult suffrage. The other chamber, or the Upper House should be elected by the federating units as well as by special interests. The Upper House should be the guardian of the rights and interests of the federating units as well as of minority and cultural groups, and of the Fundamental Rights laid down in the constitution. Its legislative powers need not be coeval with those of the Lower House, and its authority in regard to the voting of the Finance Bill or the Federal Budget should certainly be considerably less than that of the Lower Chamber. Its special function will be to revise the legislative proposals of the Lower House and to scrutinise them from all points of view.

The device of the Joint Sessions of the two Houses is not a very happy one and often causes estrangement. It should not be used as a matter of course in every case of conflict, but should be rarely adopted and only for certain well-defined purposes, such as the amendment of the constitution, reconstitution of a province, regrouping of the federated States, or in the event of a sudden emergency arising. Such Joint Sessions should only be held on the advice of the ministry in office.

Each Chamber must have the right to regulate its own procedure, appoint its own officers, enforce its own decisions, and to conduct investigations by committees.

The National Economic Council

It will be advisable to set up, in the federal machinery of government, a National Economic Council. This body will be set up by the Legislature and will be subordinate to it. Nevertheless it should have a measure of independence in its own special domain. A modern government has to face difficult economic problems and to undertake complicated tasks which require careful thought and expert guidance. The

Legislature is almost always overburdened with work, and cannot give sufficient time or thought to these problems. An assembly of politicians is usually not a suitable forum for a detailed consideration of such subjects. The broad lines of policy should of course be laid down by the Legislature, but the working out of this policy must be the concern of experts and those especially interested in it.

The National Economic Council will thus lighten the burden on the Legislature, and will speed up the economic development of the country. It will supervise the trading enterprises of the State, such as Railways, Post Offices, the Reserve Bank and the like; India's foreign trade and negotiation and conclusion of trade treaties; economic relations with foreign countries; the working of the currency and credit mechanism within the country; the care of the labour and peasant population; relations between employers and employees; the agrarian relief of indebtedness, etc. The Statutory Railway Board set up under the Act of 1935 would get absorbed in such an Economic Council. The constitution of the Reserve Bank may have to be radically revised, especially in regard to the bank's functions, in order to make it conform to the National Economic Council.

The National Economic Council could also be entrusted with the task of planning the economic life of the community under the general direction and supervision of the Federal Government. This task is a stupendous one, and it may be necessary to create a special Planning Commission for the purpose. This Economic Council will have to include representatives of the federating units, and also representatives of special interests, such as Chambers of Commerce or Industry, Agriculture, Trade Unions of industrial workers, Peasant organisations, professional and technical associations, and scientific experts.

Provincial Government

In the Provinces there should be only one chamber representing the people of the Province directly on a basis of adult franchise. It would be desirable to encourage functional representation and to prefer this, wherever possible, to territorial representation. As there will be no second or revising chamber, provision should be made for a direct Referendum to the provincial electorates on certain specified matters of fundamental policy affecting the organisation of the province as a unit, or other subjects which are vital to the life of the province. If the method of Referendum is adopted, the constitution will have to provide for the minimum majority necessary to carry out a fundamental change of policy.

It will perhaps be unnecessary and uneconomical to begin with to have an Economic Council in the Province corresponding to the Federal Economic Council. It is desirable to avoid needless additions to the wheels of government machinery. But with the speedy development of our economic life and large scale planning, a provincial counterpart to the National Economic Council may become necessary. This Provincial Economic Council, when it comes into being, should co-operate and co-ordinate its activities with the Federal Council.

The Provincial Cabinet will be, we need hardly add, fully responsible to the Legislature.

Relations between the Centre and the Federating Units

However carefully the functions of government are divided by the Constitution between the Central Federal Government and the various constituent units of the Federation, there must remain a good deal of common ground in regard to which the authority of the Federal and Provincial Governments may overlap. There may also be an undistributed field of residual powers and functions which cannot be foreseen at the moment the constitution is framed. Life is ever changing and dynamic, more so in the present age than ever before. New problems are constantly arising owing to advances in science and technology, and because of other reasons. Even human habits and modes of life are undergoing rapid changes. Specific provisions must therefore be made in the Constitution to meet such contingencies.

We have already suggested that the Federal Upper House should be constituted the guardian of the rights of the federating units. This House should also have authority to deal with conflicts over the undistributed field of residual powers and functions. In the event of a dispute arising as to what constitutes undistributed and residual powers, the Supreme Court should be given the power to decide. It should be open to both the Federal and the Provincial Government to move the Supreme Court in a dispute of this kind.

Some of the provisions in the Act of 1935, regulating the relations of the Centre to the Provinces, might well be retained, with suitable changes. Section 102 of the Act authorising the Federal Legislature to legislate for a Province in an emergency; Section 103, empowering the Federal Legislature to legislate for two or more Provinces by mutual consent; and Section 104, disposing of the residual powers of legislation, are such provisions which it is desirable to retain.

The provisions of Sections 122 to 135 of the Act of 1935 offer a good model for the regulation of administrative relations between the Federation and the federating units. But the final authority in such cases should vest in the Supreme Court or the Federal Upper House.

Finance

In matters of finance, an effort should be made to have as complete a division of the resources and obligations as is possible under the circumstances. But, even so, an absolutely water-tight division cannot be achieved. Provisions like those contained in Sections 137, 138, 140, 142 and 144 of the Act of 1935 may be re-enacted in the new Constitution with suitable changes. Under present conditions, the provisions about borrowing in the Act of 1935 seem unobjectionable. But borrowing for directly productive purposes, or for taking over an already productive enterprise on the security of such enterprise, should be freely permitted.

Provincial Governments will have to explore the possibilities of new and additional sources of revenue. It is difficult to make concrete suggestions in this respect till further experience has been gained. The National Congress has already advocated the imposition of a graded tax on incomes from land, as well as death duties. An income tax on land should bring in a considerable revenue, especially in the permanently settled areas.

Judiciary

There should be a Supreme Court for India having the final appellate authority in all matters. The power to interpret the Constitution must also vest in this Court. Apart from this, the only original jurisdiction of the Supreme Court should be to try high-placed offenders charged with offences involving a violation of the Constitution. In such cases the Court should be debarred from accepting the plea of "Act of State" by way of justification.

The combination of judicial and executive functions should be forthwith abolished.

The salaries of judges, as of other high offices, will have to be considerably reduced from the present very high scale. But the independence of the judiciary may be guaranteed by their salaries, allowances, pensions, etc. being regarded as in the nature of Consolidated Fund Charges, which are not subjected annually to the vote of the Legislature at the time of the Budget.

Judges should be appointed during good behaviour. They may be removeable from office on proof of any default in their duties, or for bodily or mental disability or infirmity. When such action becomes necessary, the authority to move in the matter should be the Legislature of the Province or of the Federation, as the case may be. This legislature should present an address to the executive head requesting him to remove the judge from his office.

Judicial authority should be empowered and directed to maintain the Fundamental Rights and civil liberties guaranteed by the Constitution.

Organisation of Defence

The final test of the independence of a nation is the capacity to defend itself from external invasion or interference. If, therefore, India is to be independent, she must be in a position to repel foreign aggression, and to quell internal commotion through her own resources and without any outside help. She must, therefore, provide herself with armed forces sufficient for this purpose, as well as with well developed industries to supply the munitions and accessories of warfare. Warfare is becoming more and more mechanised. It is a well-known fact that no nation, which has not got a sufficiently developed industrial background, can hope to carry on a war effectively for any length of time. A non-industrial nation can thus hardly be called independent, as it is not in a position to defend itself for long against aggression.

The defence of India has, at the instance of the British Government and its officers in India, usually been considered from an entirely wrong angle. Most Indian politicians are too much occupied with the political and economic aspects of the Indian struggle for freedom, to consider the technicalities of defence. A certain mystery surrounds this, and Indians are told that they do not and cannot understand it. Fantastic threats are held out of possible invasions by foreign forces if the British retire, and we are told that our lives and property are only safe because of British protection. Our lack of trained officers, the inevitable result of long continued British policy in India, is made the excuse for continuing British officers in large numbers. A considerable British army remains permanently in India, and can only be looked upon as an army of occupation. The Arms Act has not only prevented the people from keeping arms or even knowing the use of them, but has also created a psychological background of weakness and want of self-reliance.

The problem of defence is usually considered from two points of view in India: Indianisation, and reduction of the heavy expenditure on the defence forces. Both are important, for an Indian army or navy or air force must be Indian and not foreign, and the present scale of expenditure is excessive and too great a burden on the State. But what is more important still is the policy underlying the defence organisation of the country. To-day the armed forces in India cannot be correctly called the defence forces of India. They are not primarily meant for the defence of India from foreign aggression, but rather for the defence of the British Empire in India and outside, as well as for holding the Indian people in check. The army, navy, and air force in India are thus organised and built up for a three-fold objective: to protect British Imperial interests in India from external invasion, and to take aggressive action beyond the frontiers of India in furtherance of those interests; to suppress internal activities and movements which may threaten these interests; and to provide a training ground for the British army. The interests of India and of the Indian people hardly come into the picture; and if occasionally they do so, it is only incidentally. Usually there is a conflict between the two, and inevitably British interests prevail. The Forward Policy in the North-West Frontier is an imperial policy, which is neither in the interests of India nor of the border tribes. Yet the tremendous burden of it falls on India; and our neighbours, with whom we wish to live in friendship and co-operation, are filled with hostility against us.

Indian troops have frequently been sent abroad in furtherance of British imperial interests; and India has been made an unwilling party to British wars. The National Congress has protested against this, and declared that India can be no party to such wars. As we write, Indian troops are being sent to Shanghai, where a Sino-Japanese war is raging. It is stated that these troops are being sent to portect Indian interests in China, but every body knows that there are hardly any Indian interests there. Besides, the troops are being sent without any previous reference to or approval of the representatives of the people, and indeed against their declared wishes. In view of the international situation, there is grave danger of India being entangled, as a kind of camp follower of Britain, in British wars for the furtherance of British imperialist interests.

We cannot, therefore, consider the organisation of our defence forces in terms of present policy. That policy will have to be fundamentally altered and based on dissociation from any imperialism, and on friendship with our neighbours. It will have to consider Indian interests only. A free India cannot tolerate foreign armies within its territories in any shape or form or for any purpose. Foreign officers can only remain for a transitional period as experts to train our men.

The department of Defence must be entirely a Federal concern, administered directly by the Federal Government. The Constitution should expressly provide that no other authority, whether a Provincial Government or State, should have any defence forces of its own. To maintain the principle of the supremacy of the civil over the military authority of the State, a member of the Federal Council of Ministers should be in charge of the department of Defence, and the Federal Ministry as a whole should be responsible for it to the Federal Legislature.

It will probably be desirable to have a Council of National Defence appointed by the Federal Government. This would correlate the various activities for defence, and would keep in touch with the national transport system.

The modern apparatus for defence and warfare is highly mechanised, and real strength in defence will depend far more on highly trained units and in proper air, naval and land equipment, than in large numbers of men under arms. Vast conscript armies are apt to become a burden in modern warfare, and to reduce the mobility and effectiveness of our forces. Mechanisation, and indeed every kind of warfare to-day, requires, as we have stated above, a highly developed basic industry.

The organisation for defence should, therefore, be based on a relatively small, but highly trained and mechanised, army, with an effective naval arm and a strong and well organised air force. We do not view conscription with favour, and we do not think that any necessity for it will arise, as there is a vast reservoir of man power in India and voluntary recruitment will serve our purpose. But unforeseen emergencies and crises might arise, and we think, therefore, that the Constitution should empower the Federal Government to provide for conscription for national defence, if a grave national emergency demands it.

In addition to the regular army, there should be a Militia which would be our second line of defence, and which would form a large reservoir for the regular army, navy, and air force.

We might mention here another matter which is not directly connected with Defence. Although we do not wish to encourage military conscription, we would welcome labour conscription of the entire citizenship of the country for building public works and performing social service for a fixed period. We think that this would have great value in disciplining our people, in teaching them co-operative habits, in improving the national physique and standards of health, and in raising the dignity of labour. This would also have some value in the general scheme of defence.

There is enough and more of fine material in India to build up a powerful defence organisation. The Indian soldier can compete with any other soldier. The only lack that we suffer from to-day is that of superior officers. We are convinced that the material for this is also good and easily available; and, as soon as we are in a position to do so, we shall take rapid steps to fill this gap. This does not mean just a carrying on, with perhaps greater speed, of what is called Indianisation. That word has a curious sound and strange implications. Almost, it would appear, that we were outsiders and aliens trying to encroach on another's property and preserve. It is not just an increasing Indianisation that we aim at, but the complete nationalisation of our defence forces. They will then be manned by our nationals subject to national control, filled with the national spirit, and meant for the advancement of the national interest. The change will thus be not not one of degree, but of kind.

The British Army of occupation in India will inevitably have to go from India, for its presence is incompatible with Indian freedom. Foreign officers will be required in India for some time as experts to train our people. But they must fit in with our scheme, and must be subject to the control of our federal department of Defence. The Arms Act will have to go.

The reduction in the present very heavy cost of the defence forces in India is a major item in the national programme. That reduction will come automatically with the removal of the British army from India, and the reduction of the British element in the Indian army. Our expenditure in other ways also, based on national standards, will be considerably less. Even when additional expense is involved in new undertakings, these enterprises and undertakings will have a social and an educational value for our people.

External Relations

India will have an absolutely free hand in conducting her foreign relations, in making treaties and alliances for trade or other purposes, and in declaring war or peace. All these foreign relations will be in charge of the Federal Government, which will appoint its diplomatic agents and representatives in other countries and to foreign governments, as well as to any international or supra-national organisations that might be formed. The general policy governing India's foreign policy will be to promote friendship with our neighbours and other countries, and world peace based on an equitable and progressive world order. Just as

India will not permit any aggression on her own territories or interests, she will deliberately avoid all aggression on others.

Conclusion

We have endeavoured in the above paragraphs to indicate what, in our opinion, the general character of a federal constitution for India should be. We have not discussed this constitution in any detail, but the broad outlines of the completed picture are visible. This constitution for India is vastly different from the present one, especially in its federal aspects; there is another back-ground, and the objective aimed at is entirely different. And yet the suggestions we have made are all capable of being acted upon, even under present conditions if the obstruction of vested interests in the way is once removed. We realise that this is a big if, but big things are happening in the world to-day, and India cannot remain static in a changing world. The social and economic problems that India has to solve are stupendous; she can only approach them with any hope of success with her hands and feet freed from the ropes of imperialist interests and feudal traditions. Complete political and economic freedom is essential for the solution of these problems.

The Constitution that has been suggested is essentially a democratic one. This is in keeping with the national demand for a free democratic State. We have indicated above, however, that we consider a reconstruction of the existing social system as essential for the well being of our people, and for the ending of the conflicts that oppress society to-day. The Constitution should, therefore, be so framed as to make such a change-over possible democratically, and to encourage the socialisation of society. There should be no restrictions in the Constitution on this change. Whether such a complete change-over is possible through the democratic process alone, it is difficult to say, in view of what is happening in the world to-day. But the attempt must be made.

JAWAHARLAL NEHRU

NARENDRA DEV

K. T. SHAH

INDEX

B

K